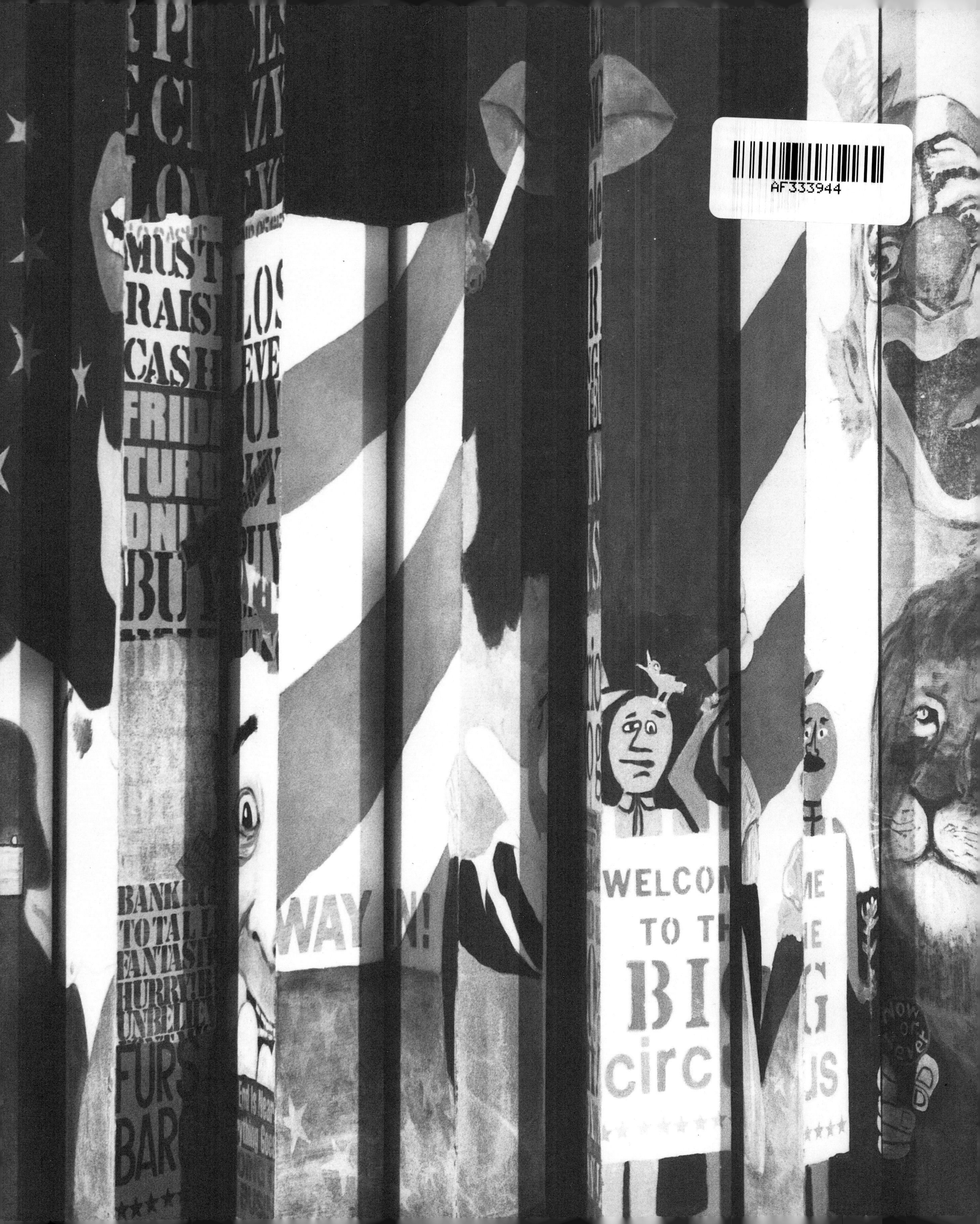
MUST
RAIS
CASH
FRID
TUR
ONL
BU
BANKR
TOTAL
FANTAS
HURRY
UNREL
FUR
BAR
LOS
EVE
UY
BUY
WAY IN!
WELCOM
TO T
BI
circ
ME
E
G
US
AF333944

BERNARD STERN

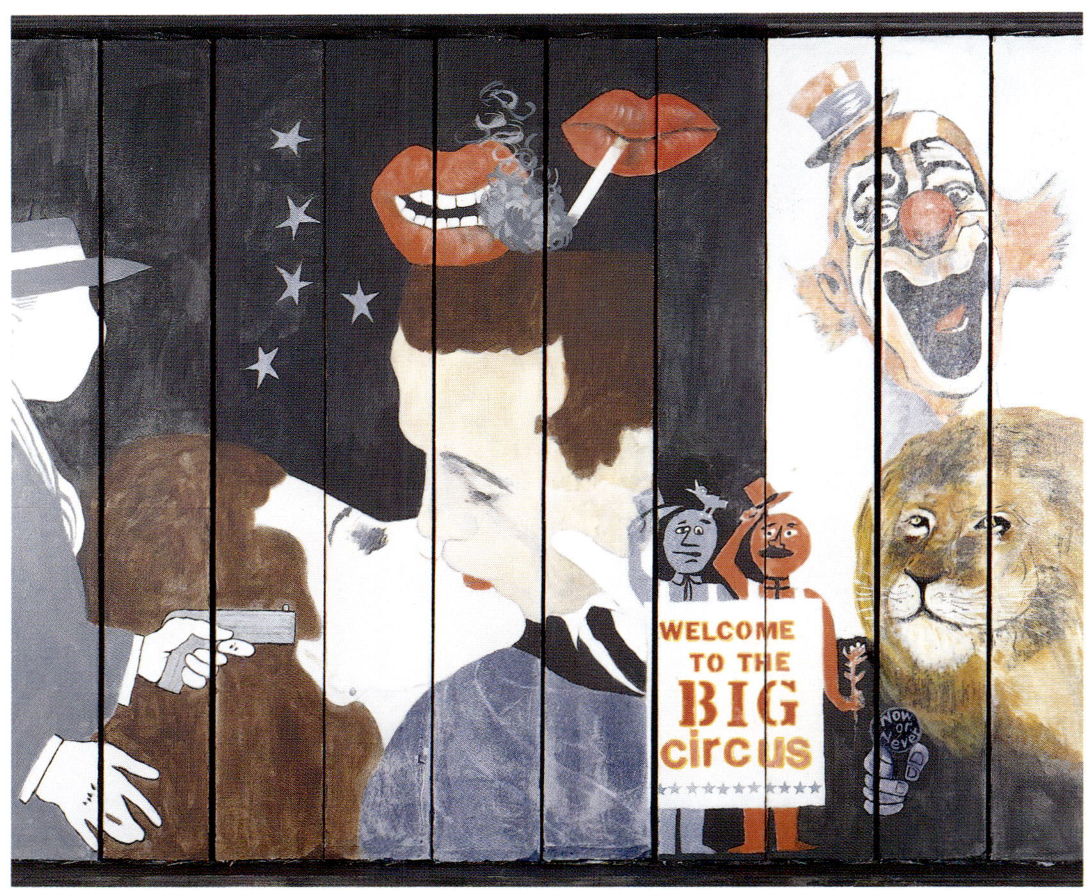

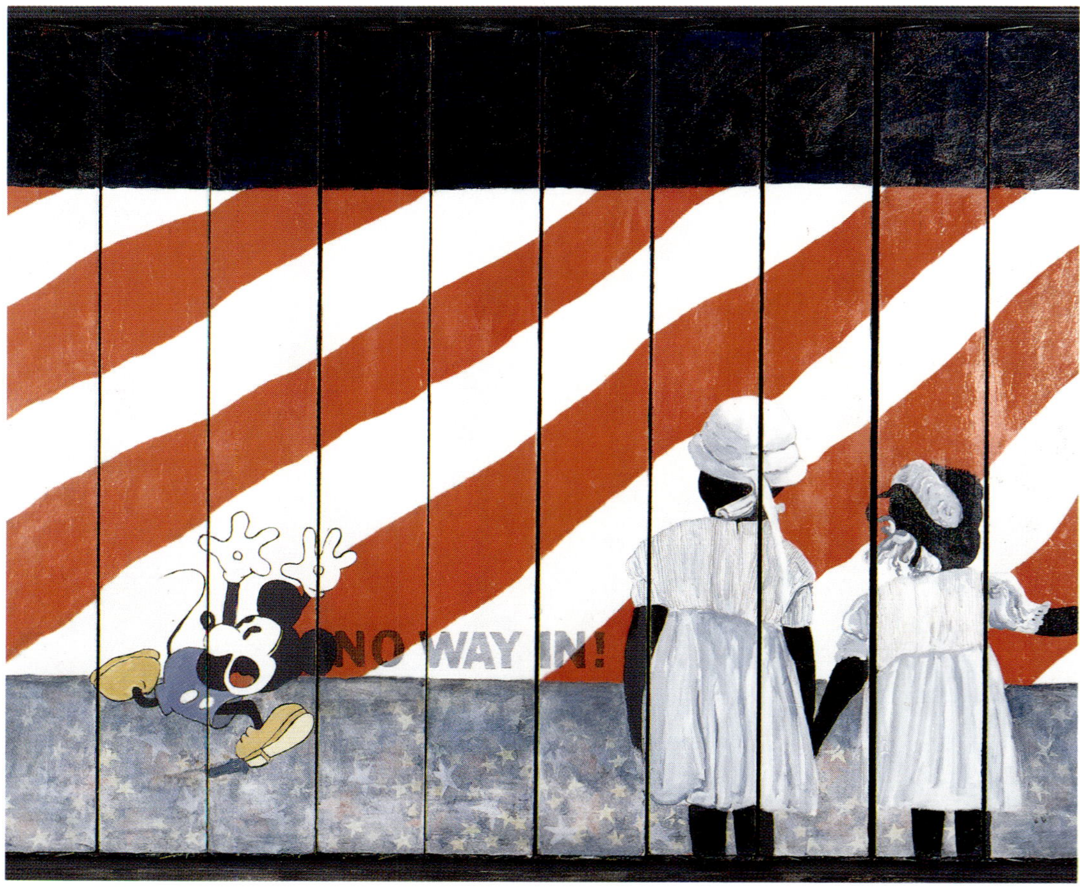

Welcome to the Big Circus, 1990, acrylic on canvas on wood, box frame 123x165cm and depth of frame 20cm
Three paintings, (two shown here), each on the face of three triangles, that pivot within a box frame
enabling the viewer to change and re-create the compositions

Pierre Restany

BERNARD STERN

ACADEMY EDITIONS / ST. MARTIN'S PRESS

ACKNOWLEDGEMENTS

We are grateful to Mickey Slingsby (London), Mark Stern (New York), Claudio Lehman (New York and Los Angeles) and Alain le Kim (Paris) for photography, and to Chantal de Gastines for translation.

Jacket front: *Défense d'Afficher*, 1989, acrylic on canvas, 183x183cm
End papers: *Welcome to the Big Circus*, 1990, acrylic on canvas on wood, box frame 123x165cm and depth of frame 20cm

Errata: p.11, final line: 'Art is funny! Whoopee!'; p.30, date: 1966; p.31, collection: Ruth Orenstein, Bad Homburg, West Germany; p.122: Private Collection, Frankfurt; p.154, painting: *Comedia dell'Arte*; p.162, top two watercolours: 1986.

Published in Great Britain in 1990 by
ACADEMY EDITIONS
an imprint of the Academy Group, 7 Holland Street, London W8 4NA

Published in the United States of America by
St. Martin's Press, 175 Fifth Avenue, New York, NY 10010
Library of Congress Catalog Card Number 90-052-977
ISBN 0-312-04923-4 (USA)

Printed and bound in Hong Kong

Contents

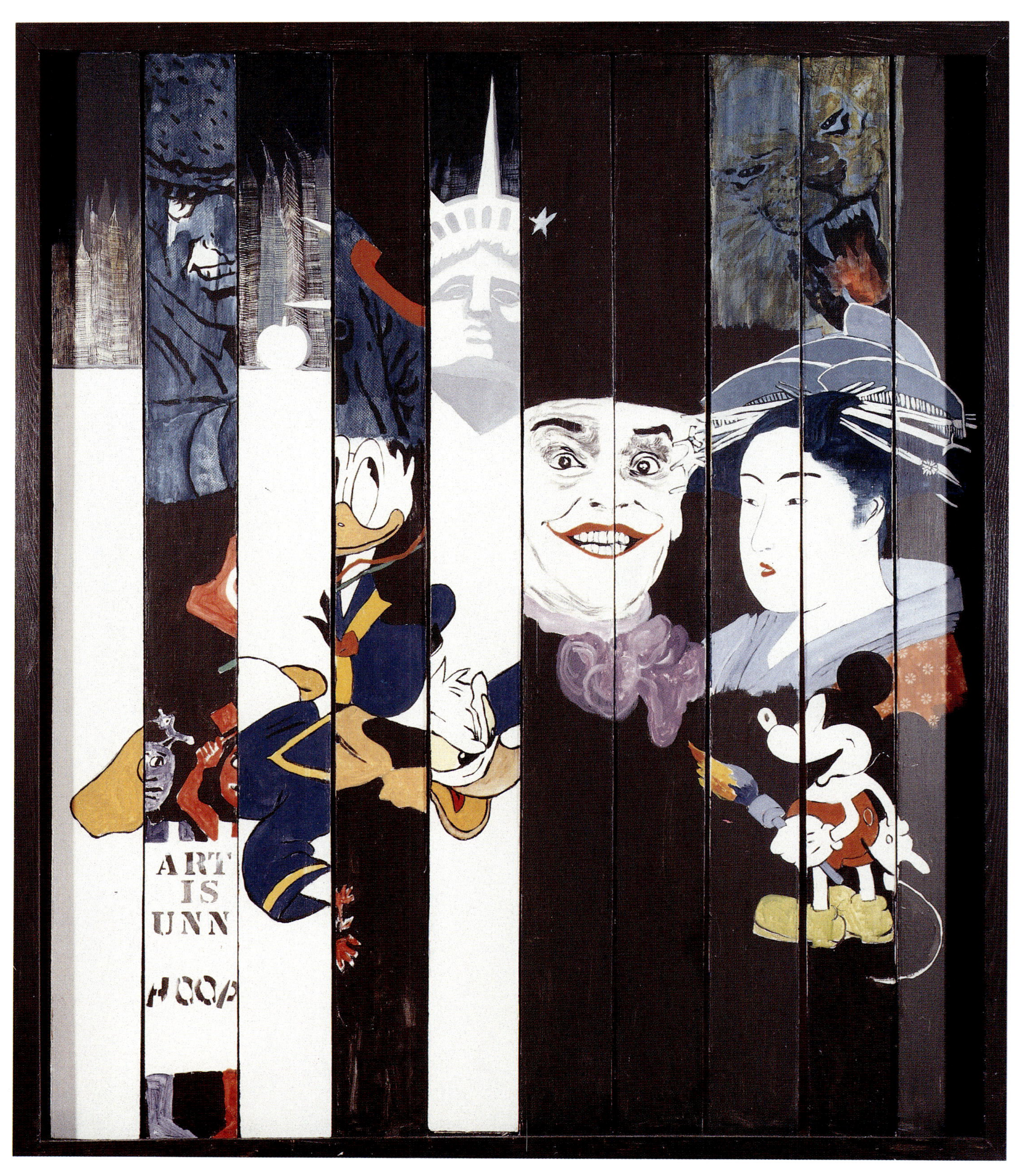

Many Happy Returns, 1989, acrylic on wood panels marouflaged with silk paper, 183x152cm and box frame 15cm, depth of frame 17.5cm

PIERRE RESTANY
BERNARD STERN:
PAINTING TO GO ON WRITING

Bernard Stern's work is lengthy, divided into periods and rich in changes of direction. It identifies itself totally with the existential projection of man, so much so that Edward Lucie-Smith was able to write in his preface to an exhibition which took place in New York in 1987: 'What most impresses me about the pictorial idiom which Bernard Stern has evolved is its flexibility – not only the fact that it reaches out beyond art, but the fact that it can deal with a very wide range of subject matter without losing pictorial identity'. This far-ranging pictorial identity has been much talked about by art critics. 'Bernard Stern paints the way a bird flies or the way a fish swims', says Max Wykes-Joyce.[1] J.P. Hodin goes further: '… It can be said that Stern's recent work is a challenge to the art systems offered today by the promoters of new "isms" … ',[2] and while Hodin was writing the above, in 1975, Louise Collis did not hesitate to state that, 'The career of Bernard Stern as a painter has just started.'[3]

This is music to my ears, since I am one of the promoters of the 'new isms which, according to Hodin, are more related to the pollution of nature than to communication between human beings'. The *Nouveaux Réalistes* movement which I created in Paris in 1960 is actually based on the meaning of the immense self-expressive potentiality of modern nature, our urban, industrial and mediatic nature.[4] And since I have caught on to Stern's work in the same way as one jumps on a train, I can say together with Louise Collis that his work is only at its beginning. I would date the beginning to 1989 and 1990 with the two kinetic series of pivoting and metamorphic compositions, *Many Happy Returns* and *Welcome to the Big Circus*. And I could easily convince Stern that I am justified in stating this, since all painters have the feeling that every new piece of work represents a new beginning. However, it would be wrong to get him to erase from his memory the enormous work of urban semiology and of X-raying the skin of walls, begun in 1978: a tide of signs whose cascading internal similarities and proliferating chains of self-similarities constitute the organic canvas and the molecular weave of the present fractalisations.

Deeper down there exists the memory's memory, all the iconic sedimentation of a life's experience inscribed in the eye – the eye of Stern, a timeless eye, the eye of a wise man, touched by the witness's mania. This memory's memory had to be registered without a framework by someone with the help of a mental camera. With the filmmaker Jean Antoine, our mutual friend, Stern has found the witness of witnessing. Jean Antoine relates how 'Forty years of work, the slow maturation of a trade and a technique, an almost systematic investigation of chosen specific interests: woman, family, clowns, presidents, fruits, trees and towns, all of this so that Bernard Stern can finally dare to undertake his first composition on graffiti.'[5]

Why did he wait so long, although the *Nouveaux Réalistes* had spread the practice of 'ungluing' posters and transferring whole strips of them onto the dados of galleries and living-rooms, when Hains and Villeglé in Paris, and Rotella in Rome had made us see the skin of the walls of our cities as if it were the daily museum-newspaper of our modernity? Bernard Stern was neither the precursor of graffiti art nor the first to use as a motif the semiotic reality of the New York urban landscape. To hold a dialogue with the walls is for the artist a very profound way of expressing the consciousness of being. It goes back to a global recollection which synthesises his difficult life in London in 1940, through the blitz and bomb alerts, when he was dying of hunger and had a job unloading fruit and vegetables at Covent Garden. The crates he used to handle were stamped with stencil marks; these distinctive letters will reappear massively in his painting in the early 80s.

This kind of globalising recollection easily adheres to personal legend and myths for internal use. One day, at dusk, while the sirens are wailing, he takes the time to stop in front of a leprous wall before stepping into the first available shelter, and reads the four letters of the word LOVE drawn in chalk. Stern will never forget this anonymous message of faith in man which he received at the time of his deepest despair, and the alliterations of the words love/lovers will play an essential part in his semiotic adventure, 38 years later.

Jerusalem's wailing wall is usually perceived by the faithful as a metaphor of a state of mind, a mirror of the self, and a branching out to a transcendental calling. It is interesting to see how the metaphor of the wall has a dual effect on Stern. The wall looks at us, absorbing our solitude and our silence yet at the same time it resonates and sends out messages which envelop us in 'veils of words'. And in fact the semiotic adventure was immediately preceded by an iconic series of veils (1975-78). These veils were conceived in such a way as to circumvent the eye and lead its gaze further before allowing it to penetrate them; and it is in this narrow space that consciousness triggers off an emotion, pain, anxiety, hope, love. Stern has painted thus the moment when the human being who feels lonely wants to know why: from then on he connects himself to the full potentiality of an uncertain and anonymous communication circuit. Thus it is possible to 'see', if one so wishes, any landscape, any moment of the day, through the curtain. But one can also only see the veil, if one is not able to catch fate, the availability of chance.

If, to quote Marcel Duchamp, it is the onlookers who create art, how many onlookers have the talent to stop and see the happy strokes of luck, like Bernard

Stern during a winter's night in London in 1977: 'Why does a person paint on the wall of a bridge: "Pauline is our olive for ever and ever" and go back a few weeks later to add, 'not any more!'?'[6] Nowadays they are undoubtedly more numerous, and the increased sensitivity to the impulses sent out by those anonymous messages – no longer conceived as pathetic or derisive mysteries, but as recurrent manifestations of human normality as expressed by its difference – is one of the symptoms of the emotional mutation of post-modern consciousness.

An inclination to music is innate in Stern and a word for him is as much a bearer of meaning as of sound. After the transitory initiation period which culminated in a painting based on letters called 'In search of an ideal', Stern no longer felt it necessary to mediate the message. A major explosion took place, the frenzy of words transformed into free shouts. The luminous sulfurous paintings such as *Love* or *Changing Partners* require no comment. Stern's painting begins to scream, very naturally, and the double effect of accumulation and dissemination which affects the graphic weave reveals the emergence of an apparatus which recounts to this day the entire evolution of the semiotic adventure.

The awareness of urban nature as an audio-visual totality is the essential phenomenon that gives its mark to Stern's work. It is felt emotionally by the artist as the verification of an instinct and the living-out of destiny. How he conceives the relation between this awareness and memory is probably less clear. The system of differing repetition is founded on a precise aspect of memory. The memory which repeats the woven message of the graffiti and projects it in a ceaseless act of renewal out of the walls of the imaginary has totally found its place in the act of painting. It has become the *habitus* of Bernard Stern, his normal system of existential behaviour, and his operational memory. It has developed itself in a similar and autonomous way alongside his pure memory, which remembers, as it were, only the orbital fracture, the fractalisation of the process. The word *Love*, glanced at on a London wall during the 1940 blitz was frozen in Stern's pure memory, until the time when it set off the fractalisation of the 1978 works, *Love* and the whole series of the *Love Stories* until *Lovesick* (1979), which represents both an illusory and meaningful effort to stop the chain of self-similarities.

The sphere of the *habitus* is that of the permanent present, the reign of the *forma formans*. What is then to be done when normality becomes routine? The only solution is to fall back on pure memory, the central point of major generating impulses. At the beginning of 1979, Stern goes to Peru in order to clear his outlook and purify his vision. Through the Inca megaliths covered with posters, the shadows of times past can be glimpsed at under the sign Jesus-Cola. Pure memory reverberates the *habitus*: yesterday and today are part of the same present.

After the Peruvian muteness Stern explodes with the large series devoted to sports and cities, cycling and Central Park, and street life: joggers, crazy cyclists or bikers who knock themselves onto a background of fences covered in stencil inscriptions. The stencil is Stern's second graphic weave and in the end it will replace its calligraphy of gestures. Pure memory sends us back to the Covent Garden crates and this is actually a matter of operational choice. The stencilled letter is impersonal, it constitutes a basic element completely made into an object which can create extremely powerful effects of structural agglomerates. In *Central Park* or in *Sunday in Central Park* the accumulation of letters above the palisades creates the feeling of an autonomous graphic landscape: urban nature comes in to automatically obliterate the nature of the park. In the same way as graphic landscape has taken over from park landscape, erasing trees and lawns, the weave-stencil does not tolerate graffiti. In *The Great Race I* the movements, which seem peeled out of a black wood background, constitute an interruption in the density of the scriptural network. The density of the weave increases the feeling of effort and speed given by the cyclists in the foreground.

The stencil is the perfect language for differing repetition: each part can easily be taken for the whole, and the obviousness of the chain of self-similarities fractures the whole graphic weave. At such a rate uncertainty provokes vertigo and Stern got caught up in it. In *Applause*, *Violence*, *Crowd Noise* and *Cheering*, which depict scenes of American football, the vibrant weave unfolds itself from the palisades and buzzes around the players like a swarm of bees. The result is spectacular: the graphic weave takes off and disseminates itself in such a chaotic way as would not have been dismissed by the Italian Futurists with their 'free words'. The audio-visual meaning of urban nature here reaches its paroxysm: cacophony reaches its peak. Stern cannot stand any longer that violence which leads him to an unbearable mental state of upheaval. He questions his pure memory and the answer is immediate – music: 'I desperately wanted to start painting the sound of music about which I had been thinking . . . I wanted to find out if I was able to bring together in images not directly linked with figurative reality, both the sound of the music and the sheer beauty of a great performance.'[7]

A major error, owing no doubt to the lyrical nature and the musical culture of the artist. From 1981 to 1986, it resulted in a whole series of decorative and redundant compositions which were interesting to study linguistically. To introduce a graphic weave into the linear space of a musical partition is to bring too close together letter and note, by contracting the space of speech. In the first period, in the works of 1981 like *Rehearsal* or *Applause*, Stern has tried to give an impetus to the sanctimonious mish-mash of words by adding to them the imprints of hands or of serial violins in the style of Arman. The palisade has been replaced by the musical notebook. In this solemn and stymied context, the stencilled letters are exalted paradoxically in their formal rigour: they acquire the nobility of concise inscriptions. Two paintings done a year apart, in 1980 and 1981, have the same title: *Applause*. What a contrast between the first, inspired by sport, and the second whose inspiration this time was music: the difference lies in the life of the signs, between their dissemination and their amalgamation.

From 1982 onwards Stern carries on his musical series in Arman's quantitative weave: *Animato*, *2-4-6*, *Piano, Piano*, *Opening*, *Musical City* share, in their lower part, a reference to the serial imprints of musical instruments (pianos, horns and violins, violins, violins . . .) but the graphics of their audio-visual resonance resembles more and more closely the skyline of Manhattan. This is the change that takes place between *Musical City* (1986) and *Music City* (1989). In the lower part of the painting musical instruments replace the palisades covered by a trompe-l'oeil of lacerated posters.[8]

From then on, everything becomes clear, the scenario is set up and the urban series of 1989 is dedicated to Manhattan's iconography. It involves a composite iconography: the palisades mark out their weaves of stencilled trompe-l'oeil made up of silhouettes of Mickey Mouses and clowns dominated by a horizon of skyscrapers ruffled by stress that windsweeps the town. *Love it or leave it*; such is the title of a 1976 work, the above part of which corresponds well to this sketch.

And so it is that the repetitive memory has brought Stern back to New York, to Manhattan, to the Big Circus of the Great Apple . . . life is more like a circus than a symphony. It is a matter of good sense in the Kantian interpretation. Bernard Stern has found again in metropolitan urban nature the *forma formans* of his vision, common sense par excellence, and he is exulting. He knows that the common sense of the *forma formans* is part of a fracted whole of which we are – him and I, he and you, he and the other – self-similar particles. We can identify *ad infinitum* with the overall picture, we are doomed to the identical, and it is in this fatality of the identical that Bernard Stern has found the source of his exultation.

Such is the great game of life, and after having overcome the dizziness of it, Bernard Stern decided to dramatise its fractalisation. Starting from the New York iconography of palisades he has constructed a basic typology (that of common sense) – movie stars, emblematic effigies, Walt Disney's bestiary, posters and the repertoire of graphic slogan-clichés. The combination of this itemised language has enabled him to execute three different mother-compositions on the three faces of ten triangles. These triangles pivot individually, or altogether on demand. Simultaneous pivoting makes it possible for the viewer to see the three compositions in turn. This is the way the first fractalised triptych by Bernard Stern, *Many Happy Returns*, presents itself. The three mother-compositions represent different key characters, among them Mickey Mouse and Donald Duck, a lion's jaws and two sandwich-men carrying a panel which is covered with a stencilled inscription: 'Art is funny whoppee', as is the first composition. In the second composition, the key character is a symbol, the Statue of Liberty, whose starred head emerges from a wall of palisades inscribed with a frenzied Donald Duck and the effigy of a killer brandishing his gun. The sandwich-men carry a poster saying, 'Welcome to Dodge City'. The key characters of the third composition are famous couples, lovers from the movies, in passionate embrace. The poster carried by the sandwich-men says: 'We love the movies. Many Happy Returns'.

Here are three images subject to the manipulation of the spectator-actor. The individual pivoting of each face of the ten triangles brings about an almost unlimited number of surprising mutations. Interactivity creates a metamorphosis in the line of differing repetition. Each face of the ten triangles is a part taken for the whole. The succession of the differing self-similarities does not alter in any way the internal similarities of the repetitive process.

At the beginning of 1990 Stern executed another series of fractalisations of the same type which he called 'paintings in three acts'. *Welcome to the Big Circus*, his second fractalised triptych recaptures in its three mother-compositions a basic typology close to that of *Many Happy Returns*. The second composition presents an extremely scriptural weave made up of slogans based on sales, bank credit and consumption frenzy. The third introduces the worm in the fruit – a dialectic alienation in its opposition to the two preceding global images. Two little black girls dressed in their Sunday best contemplate a closed palisade painted with the emblematic effigy of 'Stars and Stripes'. Mickey vainly tries to get in: No way in! Shouldn't everybody be entitled to enter the Big Circus? Incorrigible Bernard, who can't help introducing a bitter pill at the joyful feast! Lucid exultation – again a matter of common sense . . .

One of the latest photographs that Stern sent me of *Welcome* to *the Big Circus* represents a bedevelled visual chaos. Each triangular element is stopped when it pivots on an edge and not on a side. The self-similarities take the shape of zig-zags and we witness the staging of a fractal chaos. There again we see trueness to life coming out of the circus, says pure memory, while smiling conspiringly to repetitive memory.

A conspiring smile, which is not innocent either. The process of changing the scenery by pivoting bedevelled elements was standard in the days of the Italian Commedia dell'Arte or of the Lyons Punch and Judy shows. The *Teatrini* executed by Lucio Fontana during the 60s which are contemporary with his series of oval *Buchi* called *La Fine di Dio* recall the metamorphic tradition liked by Baroque art. We find ourselves at this point on the razor's edge, in-between presentation and representation, and may be right in the middle of both, in an unstable situation between pure memory and repetitive memory. The equilibrium of the *forma formans* can only be preserved thanks to an implicit pact, that of stopping relative time. Our post-modern epoch is precisely that of the permanent present. The ambitious design of Bernard Stern unveils itself under our eyes in a post-Kantian perspective which would lead from Derrida and Deleuze to Mandelbrot: it is by fracturing his repetitive vision of urban nature that the artist tries to escape from the inexorable grip of the modern sense of time.

In a very scriptural piece dated 1978 – and how premonitory at that – Stern manages to bring out of the epigraphic field a true declaration of intents: 'Poets have lost their words'. He has been intent on making out of these words that he picked from city walls, like many others, the fractal object-subject of his paintings. Unlike Michaux or Bryen, Bernard Stern paints in order to go on writing.

Notes

1　*International Herald Tribune*, Paris, June 1970.
2　'Un maître de la transfiguration', J.P. Hodin's preface for the exhibition 'Bernard Stern, Thèmes et variations', Petit Palais, Geneva, 1975.
3　*The Connoisseur*, London, March 1975.
4a On the 27th October 1960, at Yves Klein's residence in Paris, Pierre Restany founded the *Nouveaux Réalistes* group: Arman, Dufrêne, Hains, Klein, Raysse, Spoerri, Tinguely, Villeglé were present. César and Rotella who were invited, were unable to attend the constitutive meeting but were part of the joint action. Niki de Saint-Phalle, Christo and Deschamps joined them subsequently.
b　On the concept of 'Nature Moderne' cf. P. Restany, *Les Nouveaux Réalistes*, Planète/Denoël, Paris 1968, *Le Nouveau Réalisme*, Christian Bourgois, Paris 1978 (Collection 10/18) or *L'autre face de l'art*, ed. Domus, Milan et Galilée, Paris 1979.
5　'The Power of Words', preface by Jean Antoine for the book *Bernard Stern*, Academy Editions, London 1981, p. 5.
6　'Obsessions', text by Bernard Stern in op. cit., p. 20.
7　Ibid, p. 24.
8　The catalogue of Bernard Stern's exhibition at the Fuji Art Gallery in Tokyo illustrates this passage very clearly. The reader should unfortunately only refer to the photographic documentation, my introductory text having been distorted by the translation (author's note).

L'œuvre de Bernard Stern est longue, divisée en périodes et riche en changements de caps; elle s'identifie totalement à la projection existentielle de l'homme, au point qu'Edward Lucie-Smith a pu écrire dans sa préface à une exposition qui a eu lieu à New York en 1987: 'What most impresses me about the pictorial idiom which Bernard Stern has evolved is its flexibility – not only the fact that it reaches out beyond art, but the fact that it can deal with a very wide range of subject matter without losing pictorial identity'. De cette identité picturale tous azimuts, la critique en a abondamment parlé. 'Bernard Stern peint comme vole l'oiseau ou comme nage le poisson' nous dit Max Wykes-Joyce[1]. J.P. Hodin renchérit: '. . . nous pouvons dire que l'œuvre récente de Stern est un défi à tous les systèmes d'art offerts aujourd'hui par les promoteurs des nouveaux "ismes". . .'[2], et à la même époque où Hodin écrivait le texte précédent, c'est à dire en 1975, Louise Collis n'hésitait pas à déclarer: 'La carrière de peintre de Bernard Stern ne fait que commencer.'[3]

Voilà qui me réjouit, moi qui suis l'un des promoteurs 'des nouveaux ismes qui – selon Hodin, correspondent à la pollution de la nature plus qu'à la communication humaine'. Le mouvement des Nouveaux Réalistes que j'ai créé à Paris en 1960 repose effectivement sur le sens de l'immense virtualité auto-expressive de la nature moderne, notre nature urbaine, industrielle et médiatique.[4] Et comme j'ai pris l'œuvre de Stern en marche, comme on saute dans un train, je peux affirmer avec Louise Collis, que son œuvre ne fait que commencer. Pour moi elle ne ferait que commencer en 1989 et en 1990 avec les deux séries cinétisées de compositions pivotantes et métamorphiques, *Many Happy Returns* et *Welcome to the Big Circus*. Et je pourrais convaincre aisément Stern du bien fondé de mon affirmation, car tous les peintres sont persuadés que leur dernière œuvre est un éternel recommencement. Mais ce serait une injustice et une aberration que de lui faire gommer de sa mémoire cet immense travail de sémiologie urbaine et de radioscopie de la peau des murs entrepris depuis 1978: une marée de signes qui constituent par leurs homothéties internes en cascades et la prolifération de leurs chaînes d'auto-similarités, la trame organique et le tissu moléculaire des actuelles fractalisations.

Plus avant encore, il y a la mémoire de la mémoire, toute la sédimentation icônique d'une expérience de vie inscrite dans le regard, le regard de Stern, un regard intemporel, celui d'un sage, effleuré par la folie du témoignage. Cette mémoire de la mémoire, encore fallait-il qu'il y ait quelqu'un qui soit capable de l'enregistrer, hors-cadre, dans le jeu d'un caméra mentale. Stern a trouvé en la personne du cinéaste Jean Antoine, notre ami commun, le témoin du témoignage. Et Jean Antoine nous dit: 'Quarante ans de travail, la lente maturation d'un métier et d'une technique, l'investigation presque systématique des domaines électifs: la femme, la famille, les clowns, les présidents, les fruits, les arbres et les villes, n'auront pas été de trop pour que Bernard Stern osât enfin entreprendre sa première composition sur des graffiti.'[5]

Pourquoi avoir attendu si longtemps, alors que les Nouveaux Réalistes avaient généralisé la pratique du 'décollage' d'affiches et leur transfert par pans entiers sur les cimaises des galeries et des salons, alors que Hains et Villeglé à Paris, Rotella à Rome, nous avaient donné à voir la peau des murs de nos villes comme le musée-journal quotidien de notre modernité? Bernard Stern n'aura pas été non plus le précurseur du graffiti art ni le premier à prendre pour motif la réalité sémiotique du paysage urbain new-yorkais. Le dialogue avec les murs est l'expression chez l'artiste du plus profond de la conscience d'être. C'est un souvenir global qui synthétise sa vie difficile à Londres en 1940, dans le blitz et les alertes, alors qu'il crevait de faim et travaillait comme dé-bardeur de fruits et légumes à Covent Garden. Les cageots qu'il coltinait étaient constellés de marques au pochoir, lettres caractéristiques qui feront leur réapparition massive dans sa peinture dès le début des années 80.

Le genre de souvenir globalisant se greffe aisément sur la légende personnelle et les mythes à usage interne. Un jour, dans la pénombre et le hululement des sirènes, avant de s'engouffrer dans le premier abri venu, il prend le temps de s'arrêter devant un mur lépreux et d'y lire les quatre lettres du mot *love* tracées à la craie. Stern n'oubliera jamais ce message anonyme de foi dans l'homme qu'il a reçu au moment du plus grand désespoir et les alliterations *love/lovers* – amour/ amants prendront une place déterminante dans son aventure sémiotique, 38 ans plus tard.

Le mur des lamentations à Jérusalem est perçu par la plupart des fidèles comme la métaphore tangible d'un état d'âme, le miroir de soi et le branchement sur un appel transcendantal. Il est significatif de voir combien la métaphore du mur agit sur Stern de façon binaire. Le mur nous regarde et absorbe notre solitude et notre silence mais en même temps il résonne et émet des messages qui nous enveloppent dans un 'rideau de paroles'. Et en fait l'aventure sémiotique est immédiatement précédée d'une série icônique de rideaux (1975-78). Ces rideaux sont conçus de façon à entourer le regard et le pousser à voir au delà. Ils arrêtent l'œil avant de se laisser pénétrer par lui. Et c'est dans cet espace interstitiel que la conscience introduit le déclic d'une émotion, douleur, angoisse, espoir, amour. Stern a peint là le moment où l'être qui se sent seul veut savoir pourquoi: dès lors il se branche sur la pleine virtualité d'un circuit de communication aléatoire et anonyme. On peut 'voir' ainsi, si l'on veut, n'importe quel paysage ou n'importe quel moment de la journée, à travers le rideau, mais on peut aussi ne voir que le rideau, si l'on n'a pas saisi la chance, la disponibilité du hasard.

Si ce sont les regardeurs qui font l'art, comme l'a dit Marcel Duchamp, combien de regardeurs savent tomber en arrêt devant les bonheurs du hasard, comme Bernard Stern durant une nuit d'hiver à Londres en 1977: 'Qu'est-ce qui pousse un être à écrire sur le parapet d'un pont: Pauline is our olive for ever and ever . . . et à venir y ajouter quelques semaines plus tard: not any more!'[6] Ils sont sans doute de plus en plus nombreux aujourd'hui, et cette sensibilité accrue aux pulsions de ces messages anonymes – conçus non plus comme des mystères pathétiques ou dérisoires, mais comme des récurrences de la normalité de l'humain dans l'expression de sa différence – est l'un des symptômes annonciateurs de la mutation affective de la conscience post-moderne.

La propension musicale est innée chez Stern et le mot est chez lui tout autant porteur de sens que de son. Après la transition initiatique qui culmine avec un tableau sur fond de lettres intitulé 'A la recherche d'un idéal', Stern n'éprouvera plus le besoin de médiatiser le message. Ce sera la grande explosion immédiate, la frénésie des mots devenus des cris en liberté. Les tableaux lumineux et. sulfureux tels que 'love' ou 'changing partners' se passent de commentaires. La peinture de Stern se met à hurler, tout naturellement, et l'effet double d'accumulation et de dissémination qui affecte la trame graphique révèle l'émergence d'un dispositif de répétition différente qui rend compte jusqu' à ce jour de l'entière évolution de l'aventure sémiotique.

La prise de conscience de la nature urbaine comme une totalité perceptive audio-visuelle constitue le phénomène capital dans l'œuvre de Stern. L'artiste le ressent de façon affective, comme la vérification d'un instinct et l'accomplissement d'un destin. Ce qu'il conçoit peut-être de façon moins claire, c'est le rapport de ce constat à la mémoire. C'est sur un aspect précis de la mémoire que se fonde le dispositif de répétition différente. La mémoire qui répète le message tramé des graffiti et le projette en un incessant renouveau hors des murs de l'imaginaire, s'est totalement normalisée dans l'acte de peindre. Elle est devenue l'*habitus* de Bernard Stern, son système habitudinaire de comportement existentiel, sa mémoire opérationnelle. Elle s'est développée de façon analogique et autonome par rapport à sa mémoire pure qui elle ne retient que la fracture orbitale, la fractalisation du processus. Le mot 'love', entrevu sur un mur de Londres durant le blitz de 1940 a été gelé dans la mémoire pure de Stern, jusqu'au moment où il a déclenché la fractalisation des œuvres de 1978, 'love' et toute la série des *Love Stories* jusqu'à *Lovesick* (1979), qui constitue une tentative aussi illustoire que significative d'arrêt dans la chaîne des auto-similarités.

La sphère de l'*habitus* est celle du présent permanent, le règne de la *forma formans*. Que faire lorsque la normalité devient routine? La seule solution réside dans le recours à la mémoire pure, siège des grandes pulsions génératrices. Au début de 1979 Stern va au Perou pour y blanchir son regard et purifier sa vision: les mégalithes incas tapissés d'affiches publicitaires laissent entrevoir les ombres des anciens temps sous le signe Jésus-Cola. La mémoire pure renvoie à l'*habitus*: hier et aujourd'hui font partie du même présent.

Après la sourdine péruvienne Stern s'éclate avec les grandes séries sportives et urbaines, le cyclisme et Central Park, la vie de la rue: des joggers, des fous à velo ou en moto se défoncent sur un fond de palissades saturées d'inscriptions au pochoir.

Le pochoir constitue la seconde trame graphique de Stern et elle finira par se substituer à sa calligraphie gestuelle. La mémoire pure nous renvoie aux gageots de Covent Garden. En fait il s'agit d'un choix opérationnel. La lettre au pochoir est impersonnelle, elle consitue un élément de base totalement objectif qui se prête à des effets d'agglomérats structurels extrèmement puissants. Dans *Central Park*, ou dans *Sunday in Central Park*, l'accumulation des œuvres superposées sur les palissades crée la sensation d'un paysage graphique autonome: la nature urbaine vient automatiquement oblitérer la nature du parc. De même que le paysage graphique s'est substitué au paysage du parc, gommant les arbres et les pelouses, la trame-pochoir ne tolère pas les graffiti. Dans *The Great Race I*, les traces gestuelles, qui semblent grattées sur un fond de bois noir, constituent une brèche dans la densité du réseau scriptural, la densité de la trame accentue la sensation d'effort et de vitesse que nous donnent les cyclistes du premier plan.

Le pochoir est le langage par excellence de la répétition différente: chaque partie peut aisément être prise pour le tout, et l'évidence des auto-similarités en chaîne fractalise la trame graphique toute entière. A ce rythme l'aléatoire donne le vertige, et Stern s'y est laissé prendre. *Dans Applause, Violence, Crowd Noise, Cheering*, qui figurent des scènes de foot-ball americain, la trame en folie se détache des palissades pour virevolter autour des joueurs comme un essaim d'abeilles. L'effet est spectaculaire: la trame graphique s'emballe et donne lieu à une dissémination chaotique que n'auraient pas reniée les futuristes italiens dans leurs 'Mots en liberté'. Le sens audio-visuel de la nature urbaine atteint là son paroxysme. La cacophonie atteint son comble. Stern ne supporte plus cette violence qui le met dans un état d'agitation mentale insoutenable. Il interroge la mémoire pure, et la réponse est immédiate: la musique. 'Je voulais à tout prix entreprendre un travail sur les sons musicaux qui occupaient mes pensées . . . je voulais savoir si j'étais capable de rassembler et de concrétiser, sous formes d'images qui ne seraient pas liées directement à une réalité figurative, à la fois le son et la beauté d'une grande interprétation musicale.'[7]

Grave erreur, imputable sans aucun doute à la nature lyrique et à la culture musicale de l'artiste, il en résultera, de 1981 à 1986, toute une série de compositions décoratives et redondantes qui sont intéressantes à étudier sur le plan du système linguistique. Introduire la trame graphique dans l'espace linéaire d'une page de partition musicale, c'est forcer un peu trop l'analogie entre la lettre et la note, en tétanisant l'espace du discours. Dans un premier temps, dans des œuvres de 1981, comme *Rehearsal* ou *Applause*, Stern a cherché à dynamiser la béate bouillie des mots en y adjoignant des empreintes de mains ou de violons sériels dans le style d'Arman. La palissade a fait place au cahier de musique. Dans ce contexte solennel et coincé les lettres au pochoir sont paradoxalement exaltés dans leur rigueur formelle: elles acquièrent la noblesse des inscriptions lapidaires. Deux toiles exécutées à un an de distance, 1980 et 1981, portent le même titre, *Applause*. Quel contraste entre la première, d'inspiration sportive, et la seconde, d'inspiration musicale: toute la différence réside dans la vie des signes, entre leur dissémination et leur amalgame.

A partir de 1982 Stern poursuit sa série musicale dans le sillage quantitatif d'Arman: *Animato*, *2-4-6*, *Piano*, *Piano*, *Ouverture*, *Musical City* ont en commun, dans leur partie inférieure la référence aux empreintes sérielles d'instruments de musique (Pianos, cors, et violons, violons, violons…). Mais la graphie de leur résonance audio-visuelle en élévation prend de plus en plus l'allure du skyline de Manhattan. C'est ainsi que s'opère le passage de *Musical City* (1986) à *Music City* (1989). Dans la moitié inférieure du tableau de 1989 les instruments de musique font place aux palissades recouvertes d'un trompe-l'œil d'affiches lacérées.[8]

Désormais tout s'éclaire, le scénario se met en place, et la série urbaine de 1989 est dédiée à l'iconographie de Manhattan. Iconographie composite. Les palissades egrènent leur trames-pochoirs en trompe-l'œil de silhouettes de Mickey Mouses ou de clowns, et au dessus d'elles trône l'horizon des gratte-ciels ébouriffés par le stress soufflant en tempête sur la ville. *Love it or leave it!*, tel est le titre d'une œuvre de 1976 dont la partie supérieure correspond bien à ce schéma.

Et c'est ainsi que la mémoire répétitive a ramené Stern à New York, à Manhattan, au Big Circus du Great Apple… la vie se rapproche plus du cirque que de la symphonie, c'est une question de bon sens dans le sens kantien du terme. Bernard Stern a retrouvé dans la nature urbaine metropolitaine la *forma formans* de sa vision, le sens commun par excellence. Et il en jubile. Il sait que le sens commun de la *forma formans* fait partie d'un tout fractal dont nous sommes lui et moi, lui et vous, lui et l'autre, des particules auto-similaires. Nous retrouvons en nous à l'infini la figure du tout, nous sommes voués à l'identique, et c'est dans cette fatalité de l'identique que Bernard Stern a trouvé la source de sa jubilation.

Il y va là du grand jeu de la vie, et après en avoir surmonté le vertige, Bernard Stern a décidé d'en théâtraliser la fractalisation. Partant de l'iconographie new-yorkaise des palissades, il a dressé une typologie de base (celle du sens commun)

– stars de cinéma, effigies emblématiques, bestiaire de Walt Disney, posters, répertoire de slogans-clichés graphiques. La combinaison de la langage 'répertorié' lui a permis de réaliser trois différentes compositions-mères sur les trois faces de dix triangles. Ces triangles pivotent individuellement, ou, à volonté tous ensemble. Le pivotage simultané permet de voir les trois compositions à tour de rôle. C'est ainsi que se présente *Many Happy Returns*, le premier tryptique fractalisé de Bernard Stern. Les trois compositions-mères figurent différents personnages-clés auxquels se mêlent Mickey Mouse et Donald Duck, la gueule d'un lion et deux hommes-sandwichs portant un panneau sur lequel figure l'inscription-pochoir: 'Art is funny whoopee'. Voilà pour la composition no. I. Dans la seconde, le personnage-clé est un symbole, la statue de la liberté dont la tête étoilée émerge d'un mur de palissades sur lequel s'incrit un Donald Duck en fureur et l'effigie d'un tueur brandissant son pistolet. Les hommes-sandwichs présentent une publicité: 'Welcome to Dodge City'. Les personnages-clés de la composition no. III sont des couples célèbres d'amants du cinéma en pleine étreinte passionnelle. Le poster des hommes-sandwichs déclare: 'We love the movies. Many Happy Returns.'

Voici donc trois images de départ soumises à la manipulation du spectateur-acteur. Le pivotage individuel de chaque face des dix triangles fait apparaître une quantité quasi-illimitée de mutations étonnantes. L'interactivité crée la métamorphose dans la ligne de la répétition différente. Chaque face des dix triangles est la partie prise pour le tout. La succession des auto-similarités dans la différence n'altère en rien les homothéties internes du processus répétitif.

Au début de 1990 Stern a réalisé une autre série de fractalisations du même type, qu'il a intitulée 'peintures en trois actes'. *Welcome to the Big Circus*, son second tryptique fractalisé reprend dans ses trois compositions-mères une typologie de base proche de celle de *Many Happy Returns*. La composition no. II offre une trame scripturale extrêmement dense de slogans basés sur les soldes, le crédit bancaire, la frénésie de consommation. La composition no. III introduit le ver dans le fruit, l'aliénation dialectique par rapport aux deux images globales précédentes. Deux petites filles noires en robe du dimanche contemplent une palissade close et peinte à l'effigie emblématique des 'Stars and Stripes', Mickey s'y heurte en vain: No way in! Tout le monde n'aurait-il pas droit à l'entrée au Big Circus? Incorrigible Bernard, qui ne peut s'empêcher de placer l'herbe amère à la table du festin de la joie! La jubilation est lucide, c'est encore une question de bon sens . . .

L'une des dernières photos que Stern m'a envoyé de *Welcome to the Big Circus* représente un chaos visuel biseauté. Chaque élément triangulaire est arrêté au moment où il pivote sur une arête et non sur une face. Les auto-similarités se reconstituent en zig-zag et nous assisstons à la mise en scène d'un chaos fractal. Voilà encore une vérité du cirque, dit la mémoire pure, en jetant un sourire complice à la mémoire répétitive.

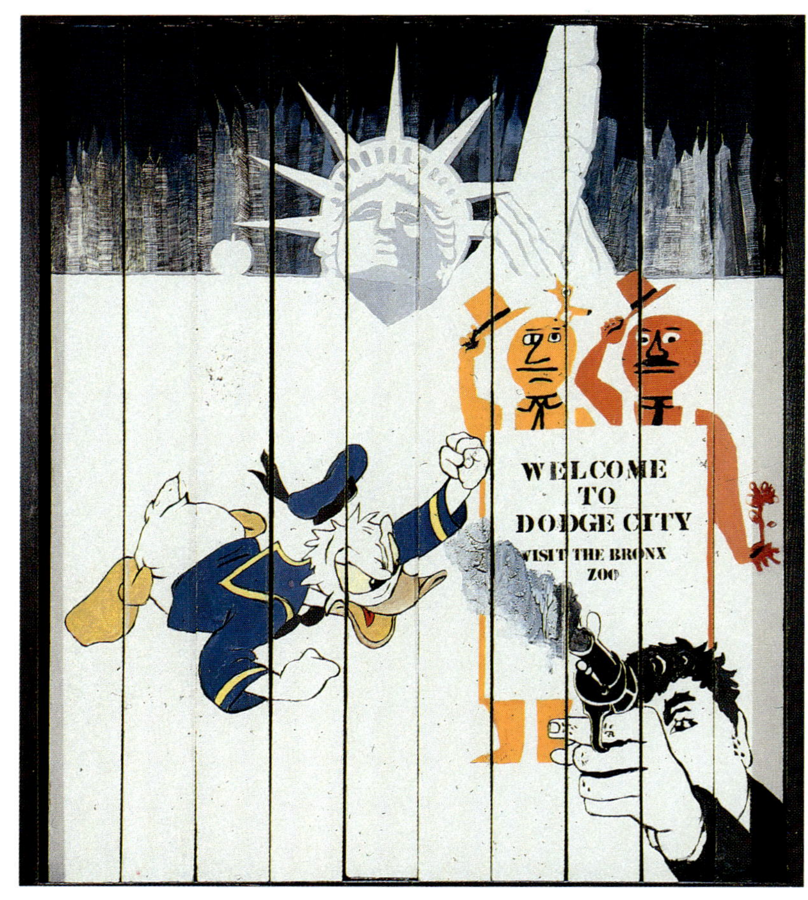

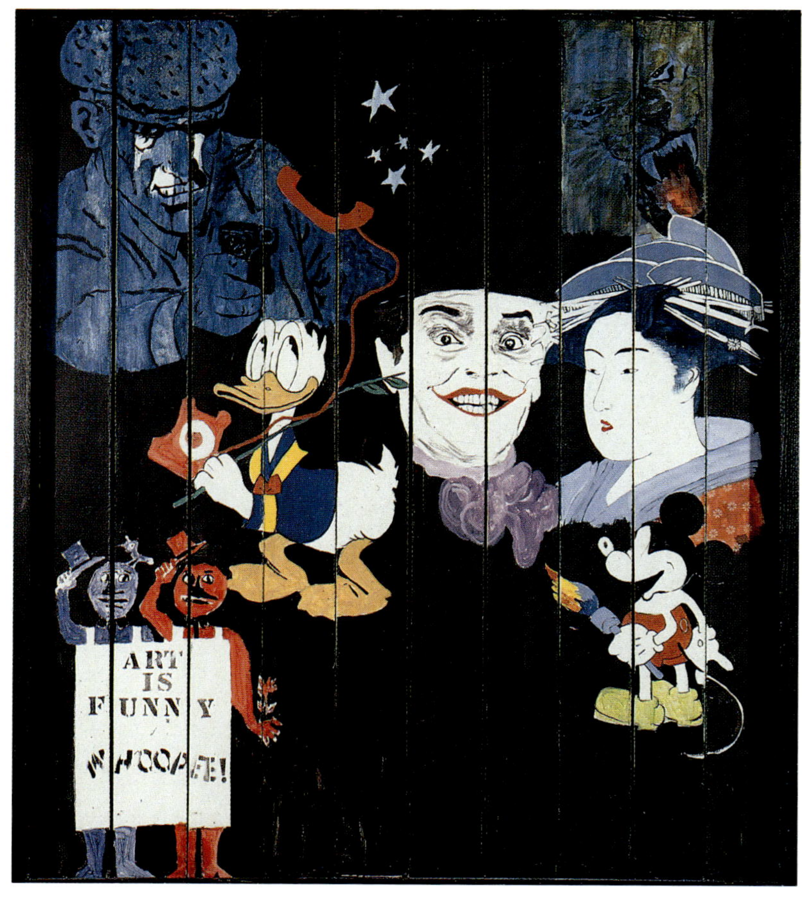

Many Happy Returns, 1989

20

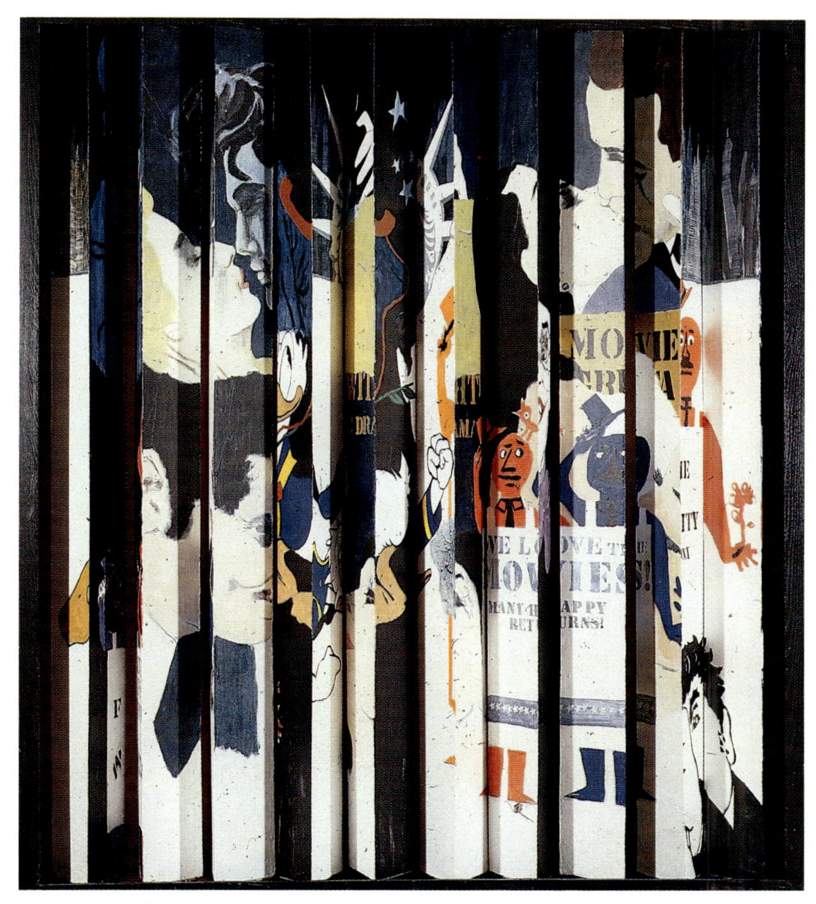

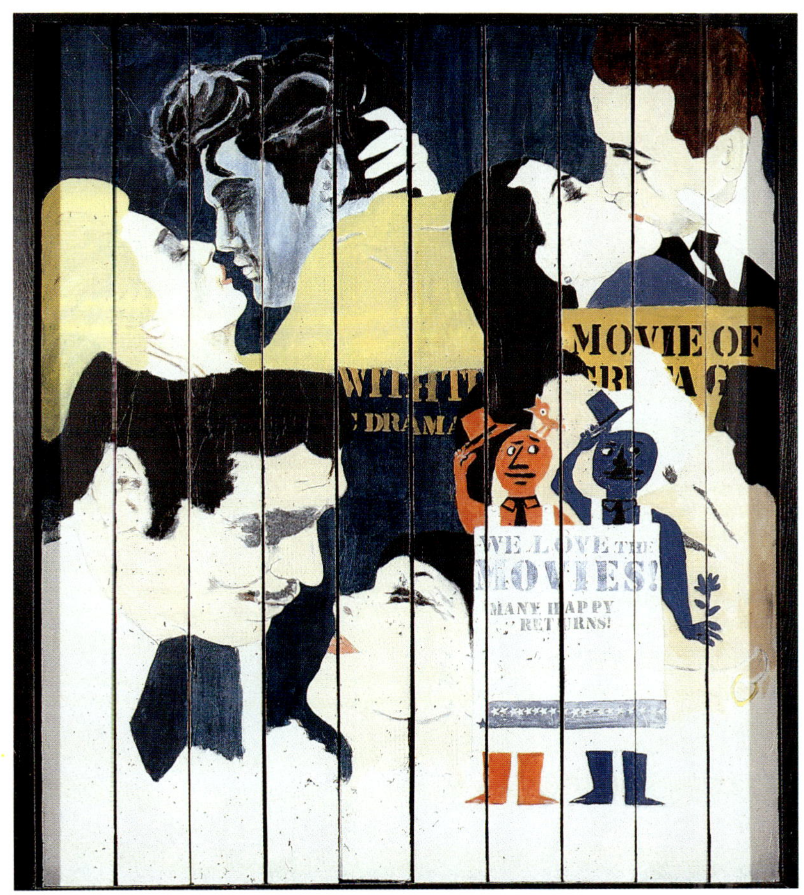

Many Happy Returns, 1989

Le sourire est complice et il n'est pas innocent non plus. Le procédé du changement de décor par pivotage d'éléments biseautés était courant à l'époque de la commedia dell' arte italienne ou du guignol lyonnais. Les *Teatrini* exécutés par Lucio Fontana durant les années 60, et qui sont contemporains de sa série des *Buchi* ovales intitulés *La Fine di Dio* sont un rappel de cette tradition métamorphique chère au baroque. Nous nous trouvons là sur le bord du rasoir, à la limite entre la présentation et la représentation, et peut-être bien en plein dans les deux. Nous sommes en équilibre instable entre la mémoire pure et la mémoire répétitive, et l'équilibre de la *forma formans* ne peut être préservé qu'au terme d'un pacte implicite, l'arrêt du temps relatif. Notre époque post-moderne est précisément celle du présent permanent. L'ambitieux dessein de Bernard Stern se dévoile à nos yeux, dans une perspective post-kantienne qui irait de Derrida et Deleuze jusqu'à Mandelbrot: c'est en fractalisant sa vision répétitive de la nature urbaine que l'artiste cherche à échapper à l'emprise inexorable de la durée moderne.

Dans une œuvre très scripturale de 1978, et ô combien prémonitoire, Stern fait emerger du champ épigraphique une véritable déclaration d'intentions: 'Les poètes ont perdu leurs paroles'. Ces paroles, qu'il est allé cueillir après tant d'autres sur les murs de la ville, il a tenu à en faire l'objet-sujet fractal de ses tableaux. A l'inverse d'un Michaux ou d'un Bryen, Bernard Stern peint pour pouvoir encore écrire.

Notes

1 *International Herald Tribune*, Paris, juin 1970.

2 'Un maître de la transfiguration', préface de J.P. Hodin pour l'exposition 'Bernard Stern, Thèmes et variations', Petit Palais, Genève, 1975.

3 *The Connoisseur*, Londres, mars 1975

4a Le 27 octobre 1960, à Paris au domicile d'Yves Klein, Pierre Restany a fondé le groupe des Nouveaux Réalistes: Arman, Dufrêne, Hains, Klein, Raysse, Spoerri, Tinguely, Villeglé étaient présents. César et Rotella, invités, n'avaient pu participer à la réunion constitutive, mais s'integrèrent à l'action collective. Niki de Saint-Phalle, Christo et Deschamps les rejoignèrent par la suite.

b Sur le concept de 'Nature Moderne' cf. P. Restany, *Les Nouveaux Réalistes*, Planète/Denoël, Paris 1968, *Le Nouveau Réalisme*, Christian Bourgois, Paris 1978 (Collection 10/18) ou encore *L'autre face de l'art*, ed. Domus, Milan et Galilée, Paris 1979.

5 'Le pouvoir des mots', préface de Jean Antoine pour le livre *Bernard Stern*, Academy Editions, Londres 1981, p. 8.

6 'Obsessions', texte de Bernard Stern in op. cit., p. 20.

7 Ibidem, p. 24.

8 Le catalogue de l'exposition Bernard Stern à la Fuji Art Gallery de Tokyo (1989) illustre très clairement ce passage. Le lecteur doit hélas se référer uniquement à la documentation photographique, mon texte de présentation ayant été dénaturé par la traduction (note de l'auteur.)

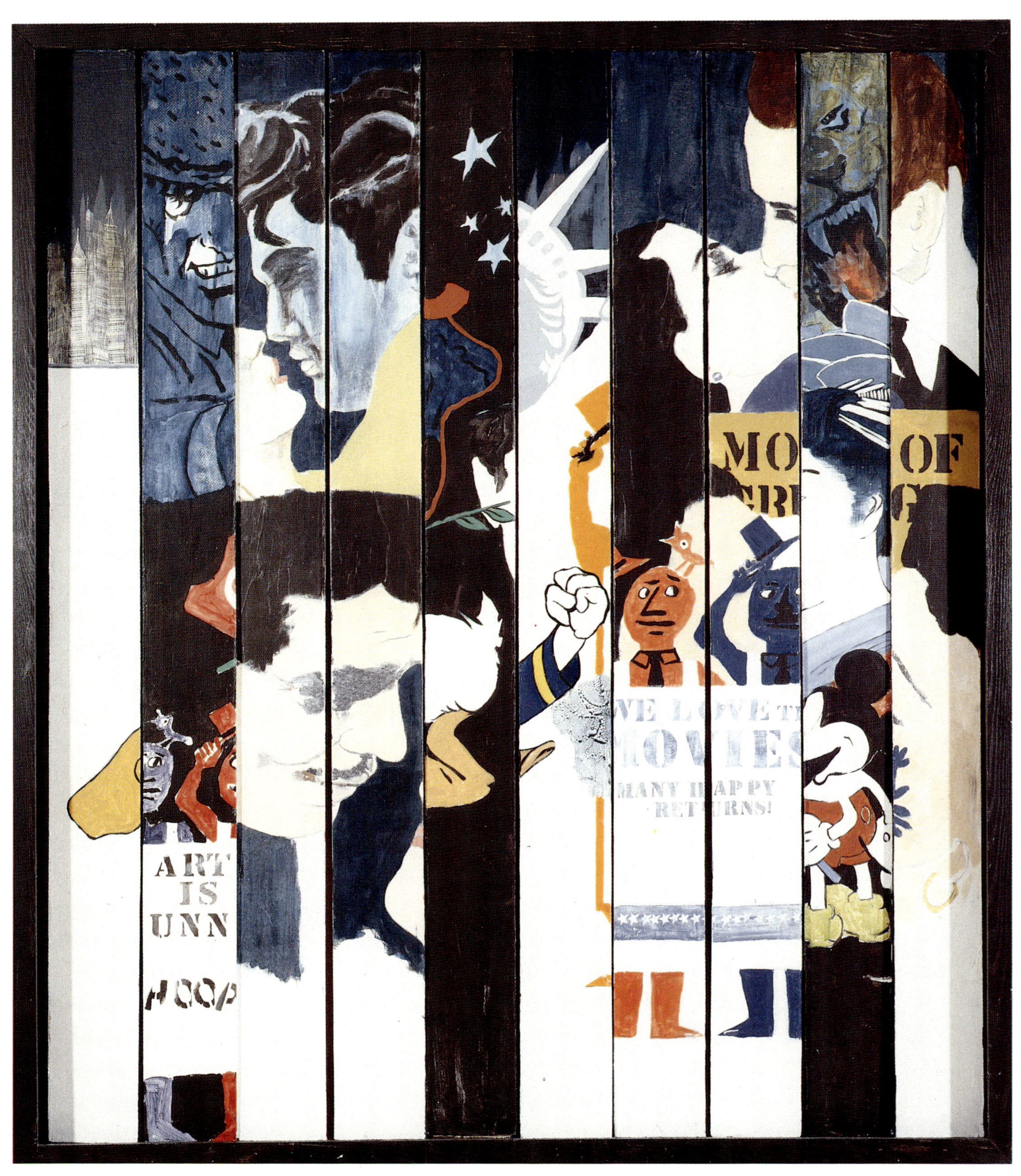

Many Happy Returns, 1989

THE PLATES

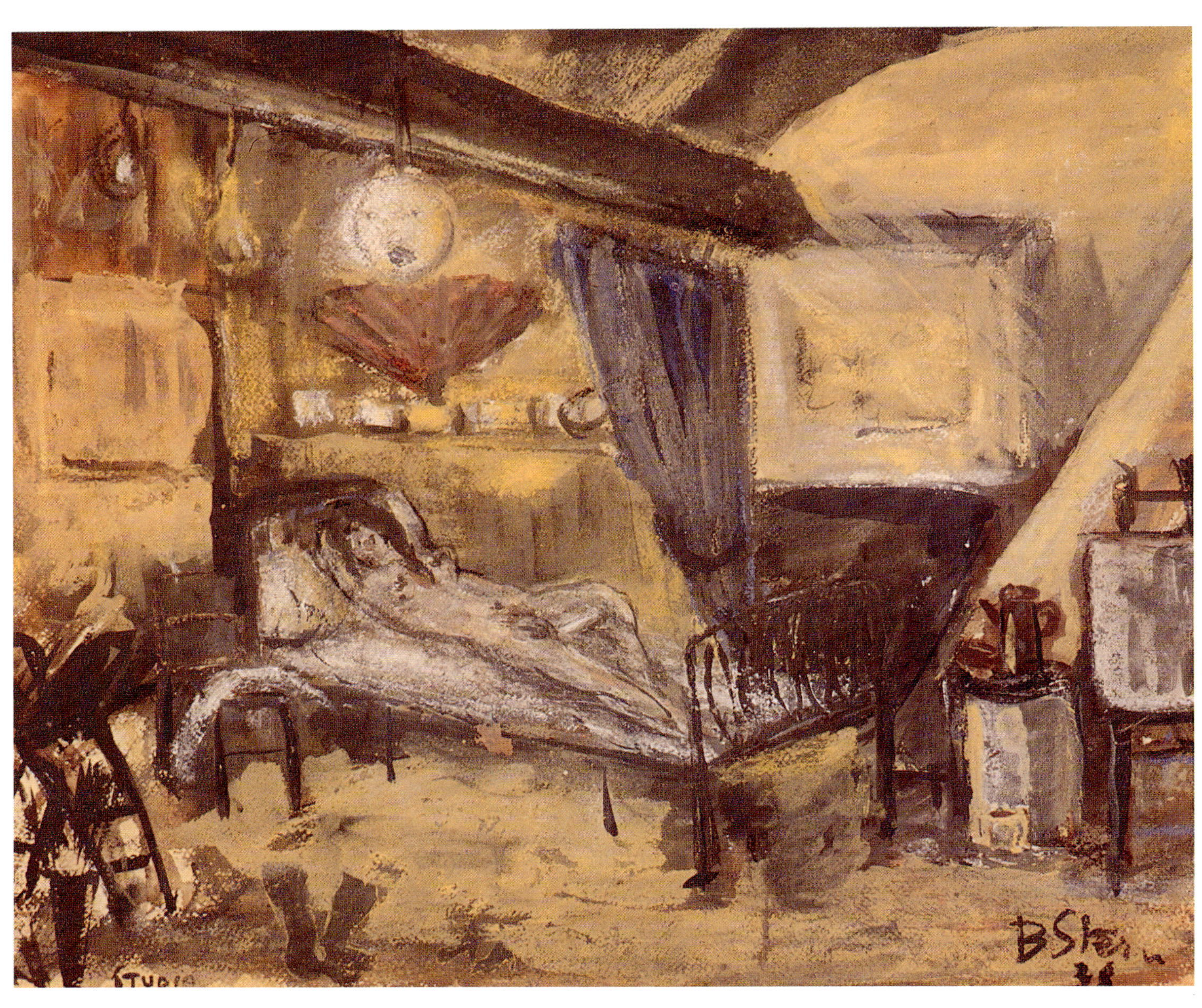

My Studio, 1938, pastel, 33x41cm, Artist's Collection

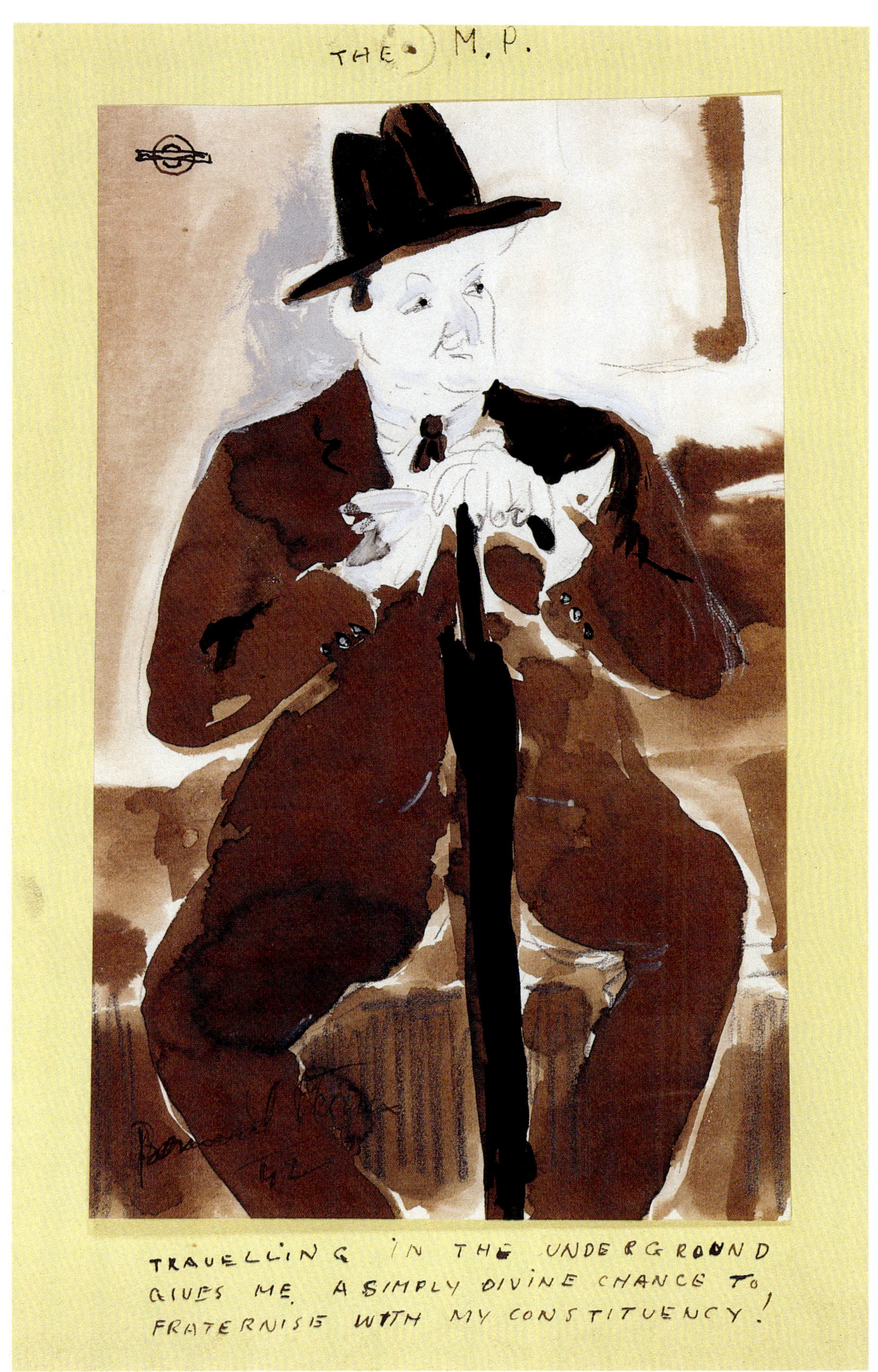

Man in Subway, 1942, ink/wash, 20x13cm, Private Collection, Paris

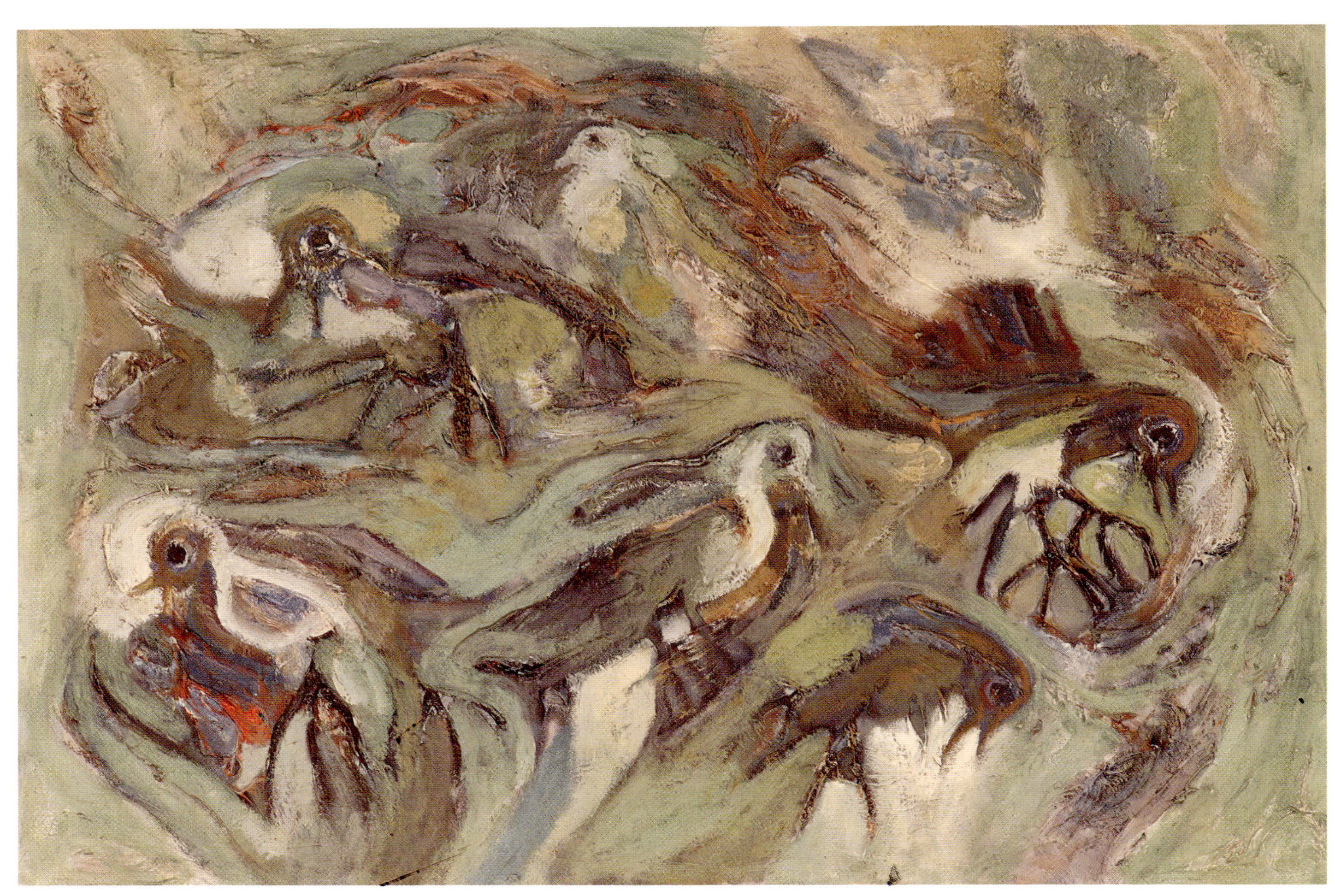

Birds on a Tree, 1952, oil on canvas, 102x153cm, Private Collection, Frankfurt

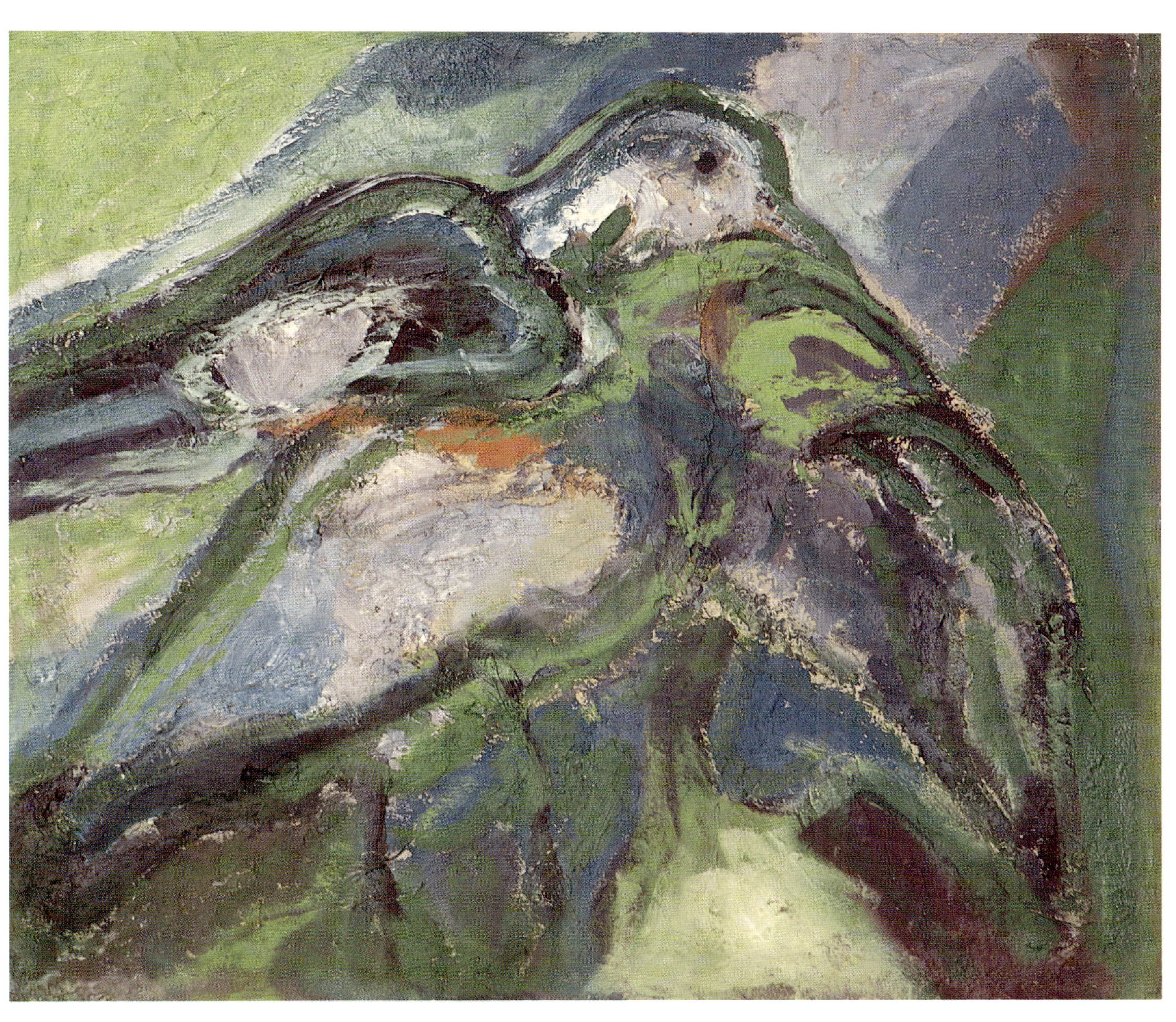

Birds Huddling, 1955, oil on canvas, 64x76cm, Private Collection, Tampa, Florida

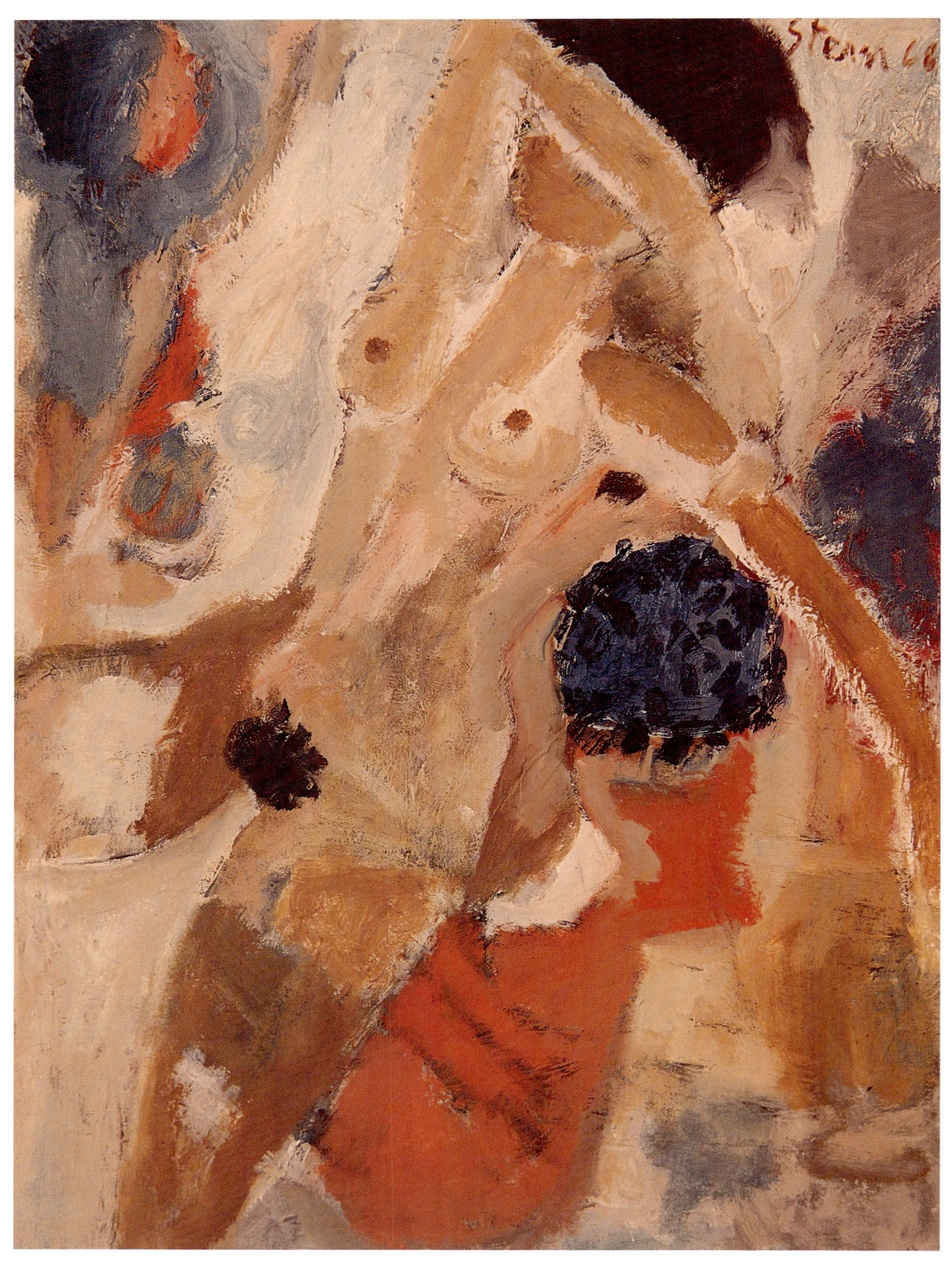

Sunlight on the Beach, 1968, oil on canvas, 112x86cm, J. Frye Collection, London

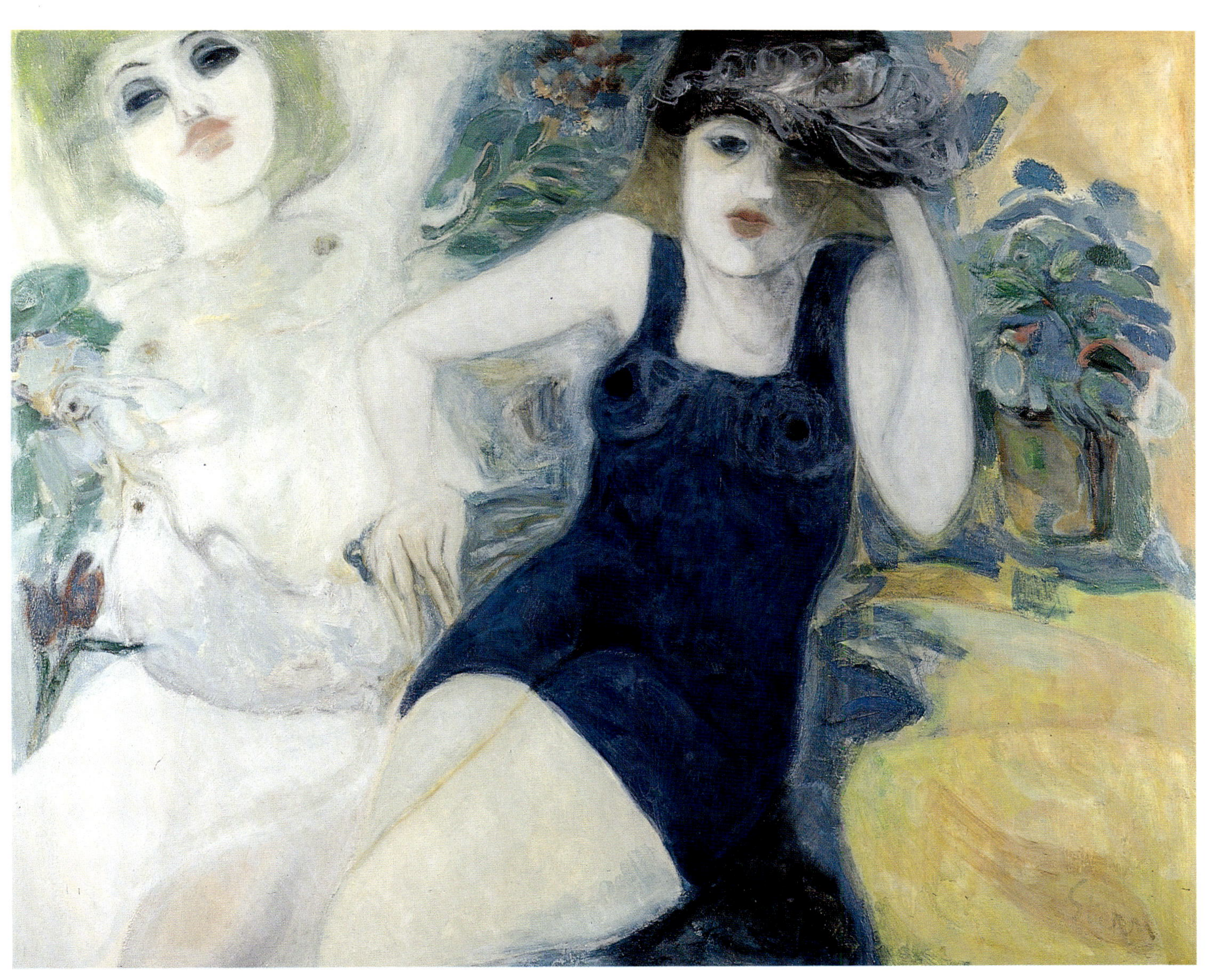

Dames au Salon, 1968, oil on canvas, 102×121cm, Ruth Orenstein Collection

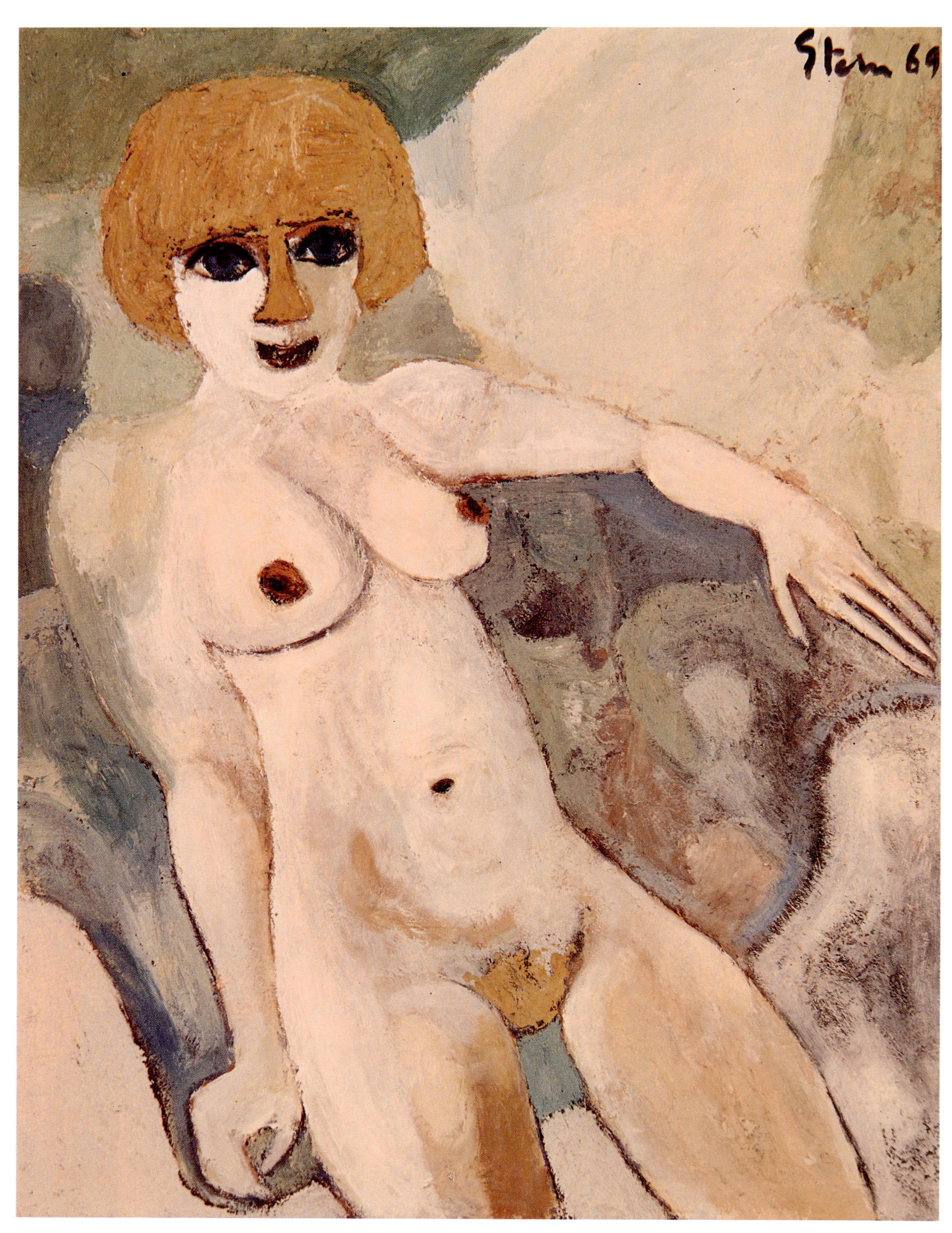

Nude, *Smiling*, 1969, oil on canvas, 122x97cm, A. Jugeau Collection, Paris

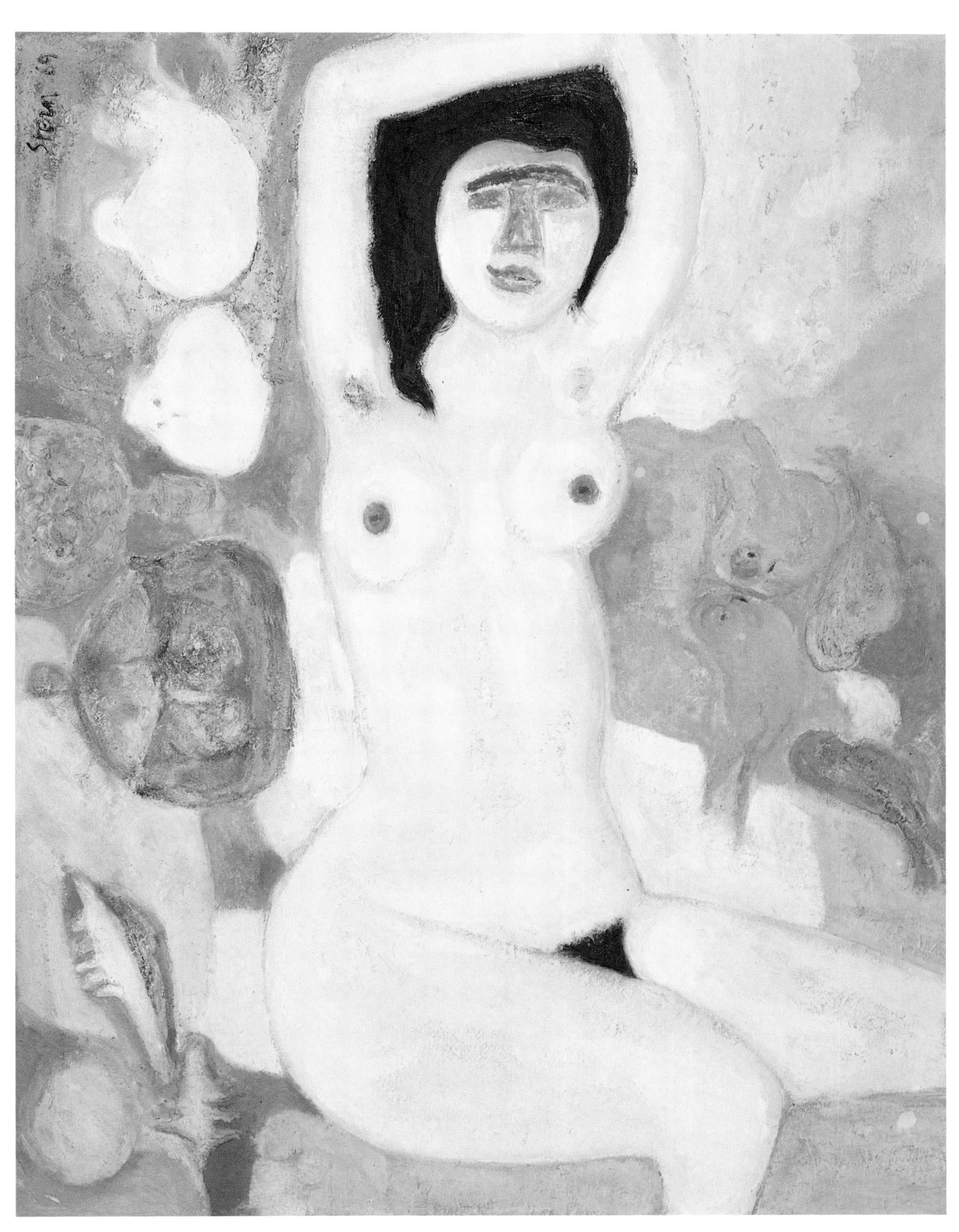

The Friends, 1969, oil on canvas, 102x127cm, McCririck Collection, Chichester

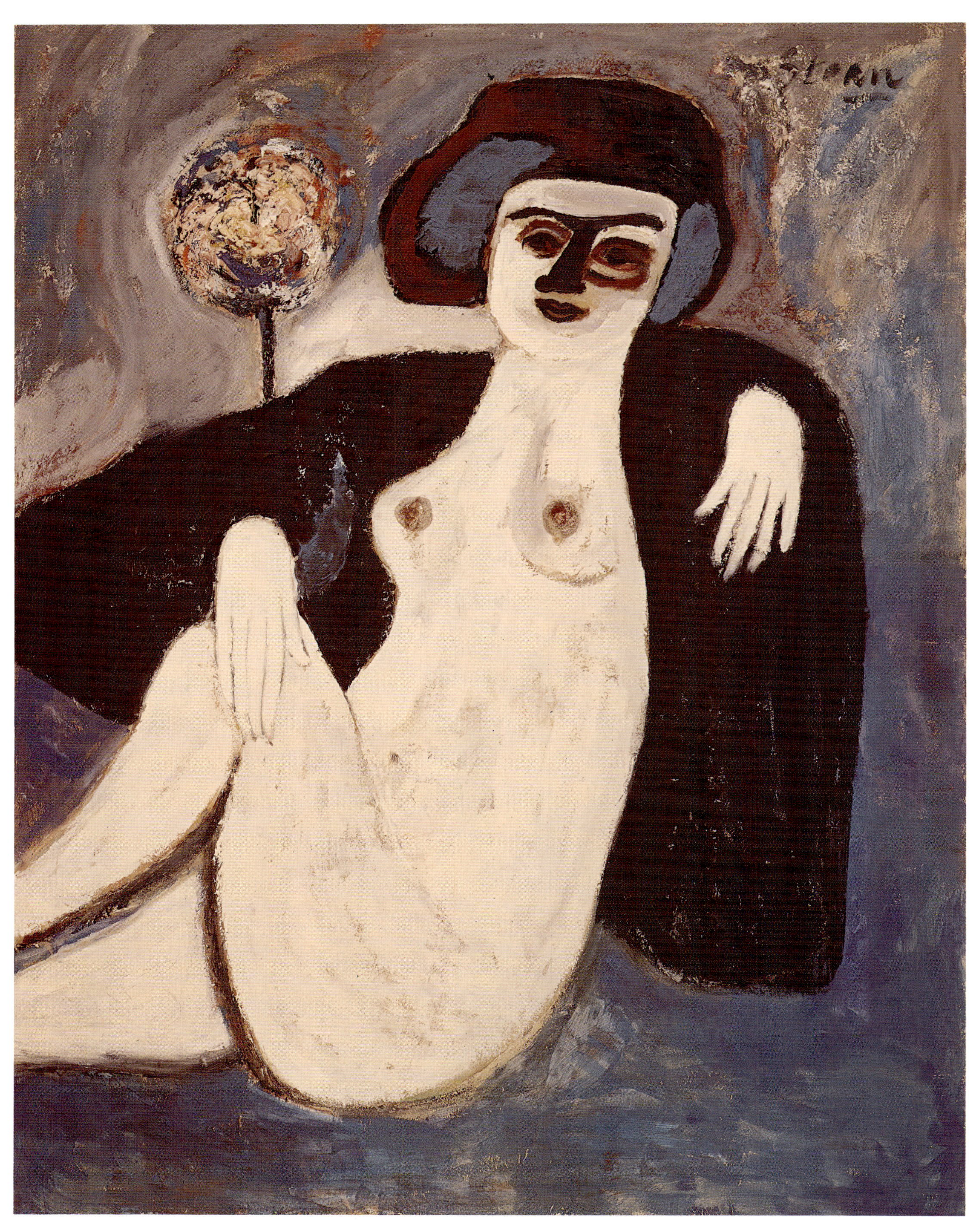

Socialite I, 1969, oil on canvas, 127×102cm, Klaus Heufer Collection, Caracas

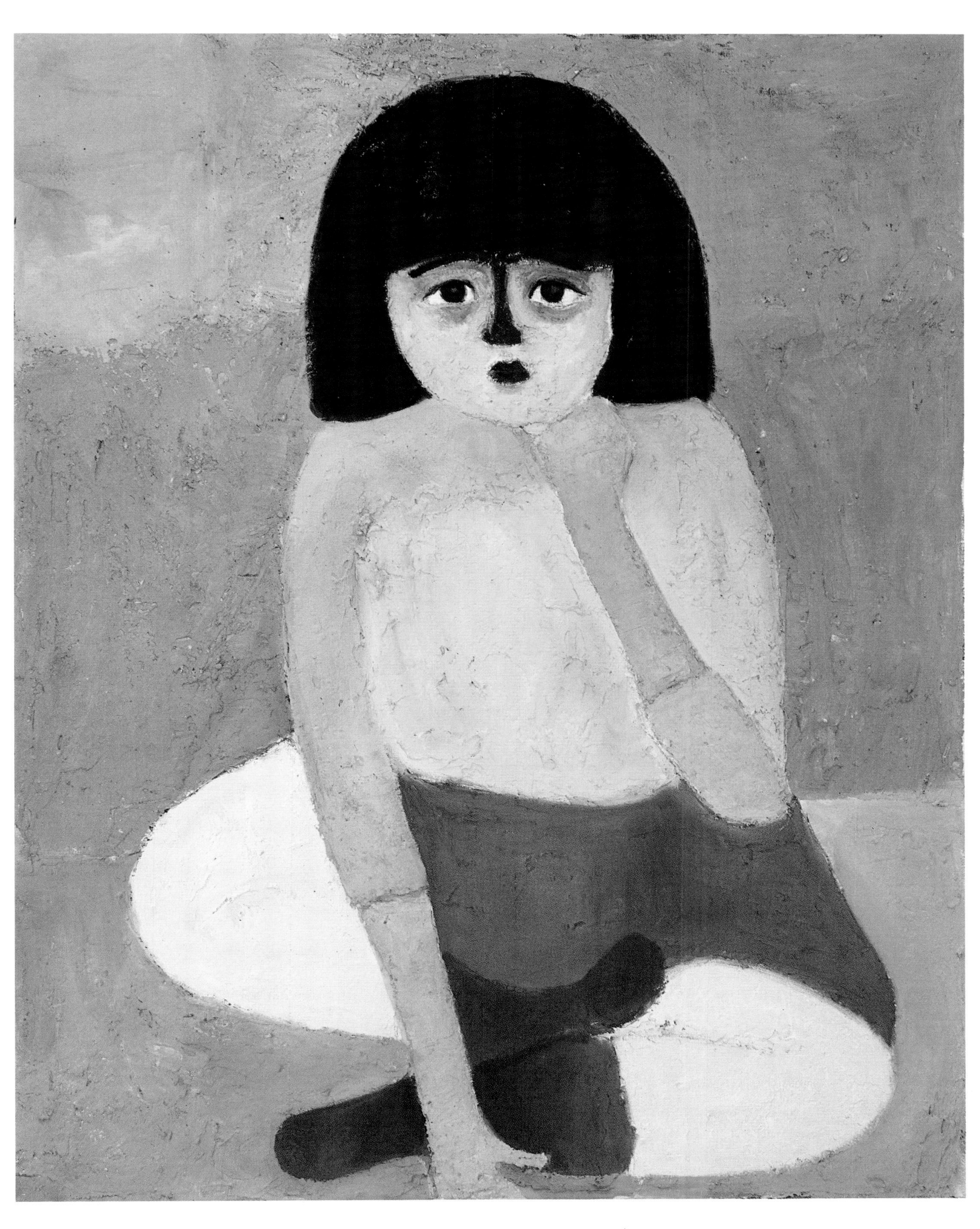

Fat Baby, 1969, oil on canvas, 76x64cm, Mr. & Mrs. Julius Collection, London

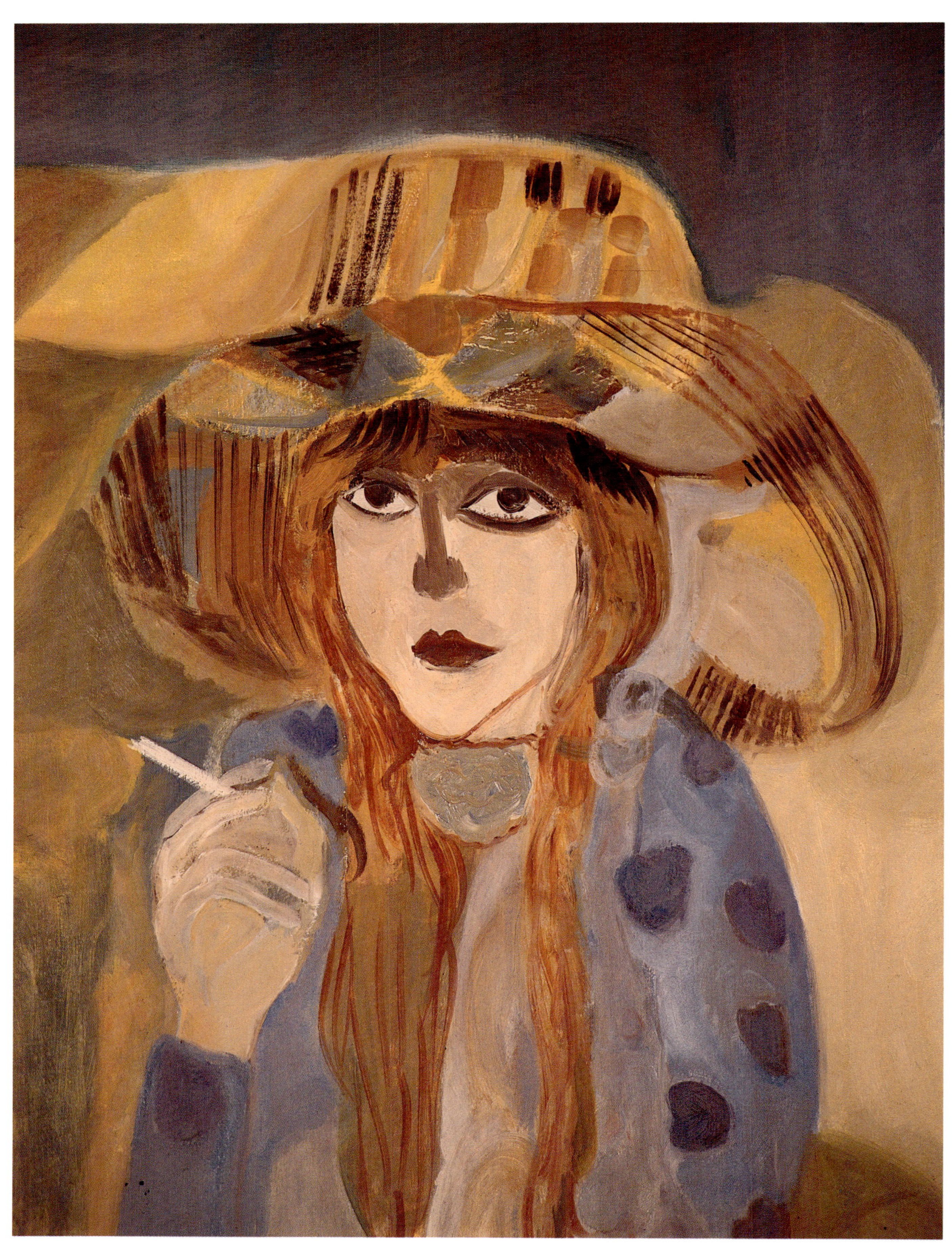

Sarah, 1970, oil on canvas, 81×71cm, Dr. Abraham Eisen Collection, Tel Aviv

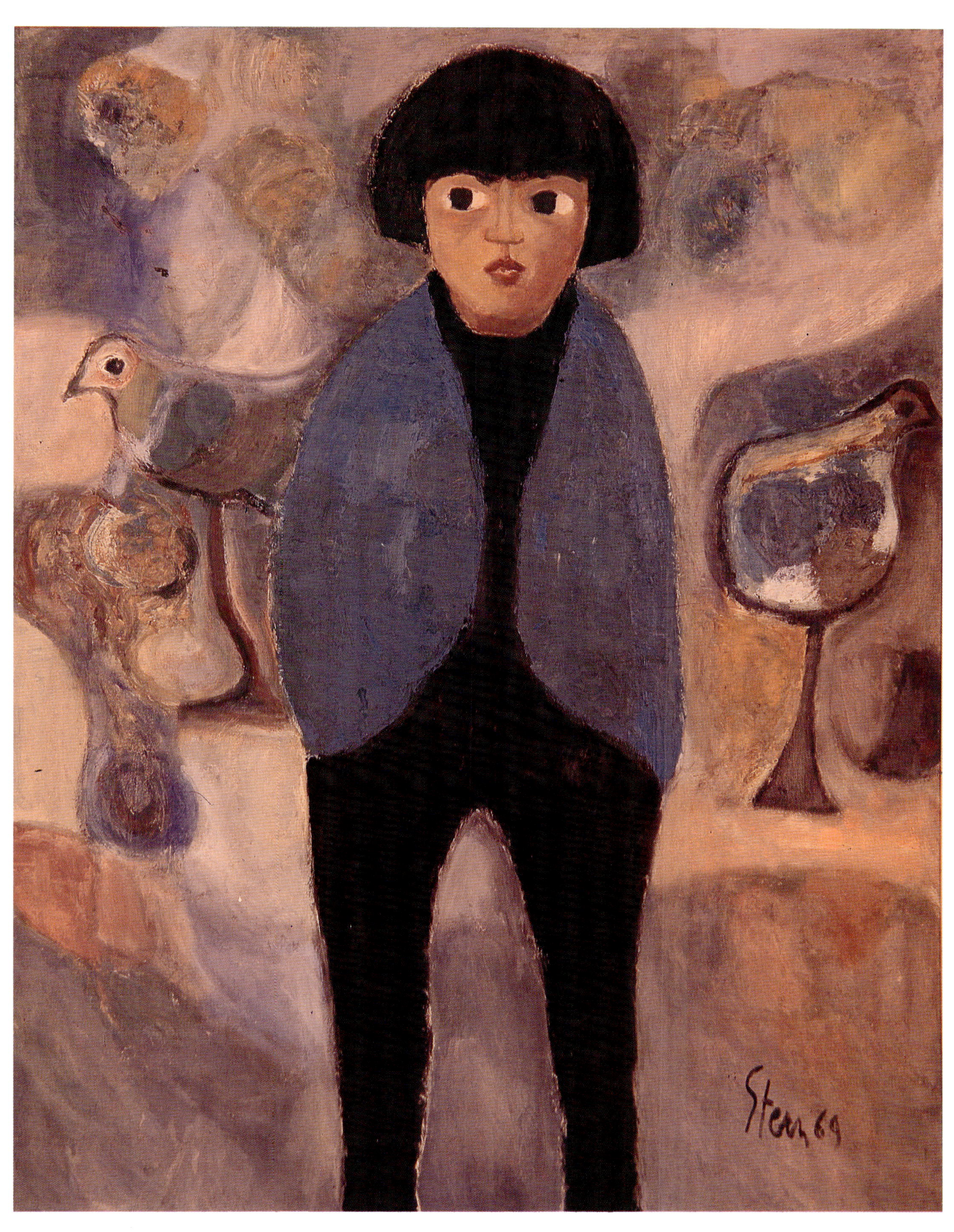

Kim in Mark's Clothes, 1969, oil on canvas, 127×102cm, Warren Spiess Collection, Caracas

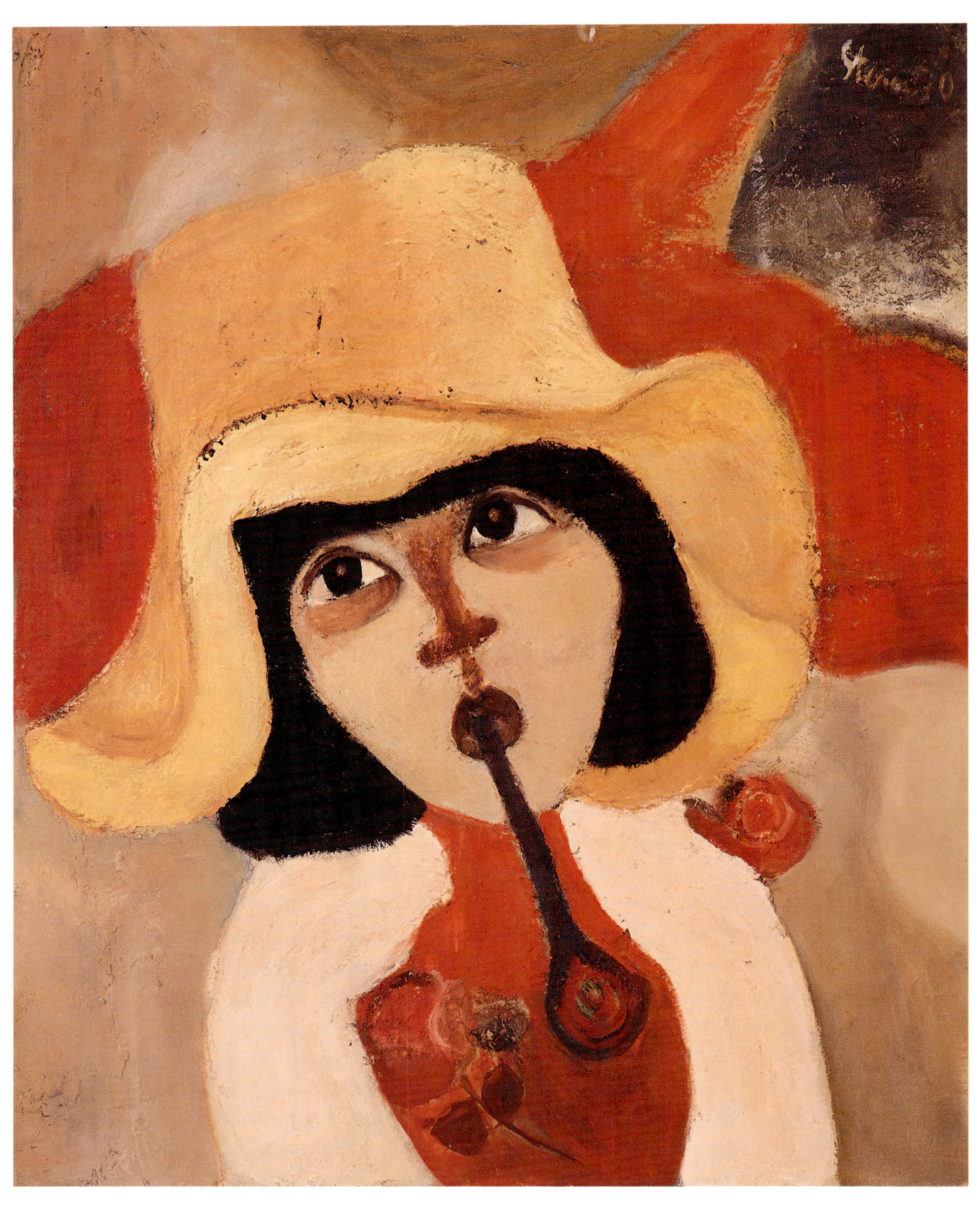

Sad Party Girl, 1969, oil on canvas, 76x64cm, Bert Cohen Collection, Amsterdam

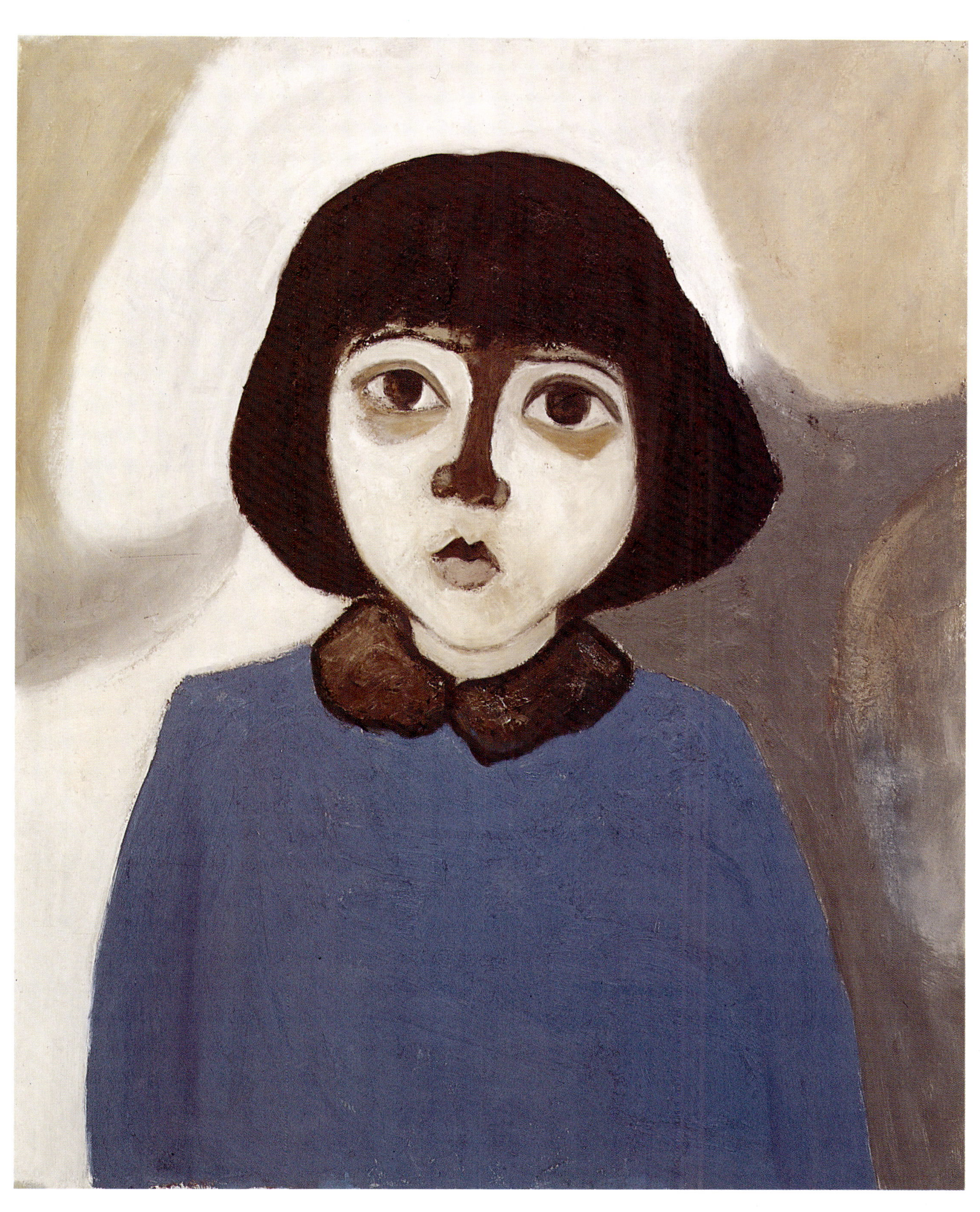

The Day the Dog Died, 1970, oil on canvas, 76x64cm, Mr. & Mrs. Melman Collection, London

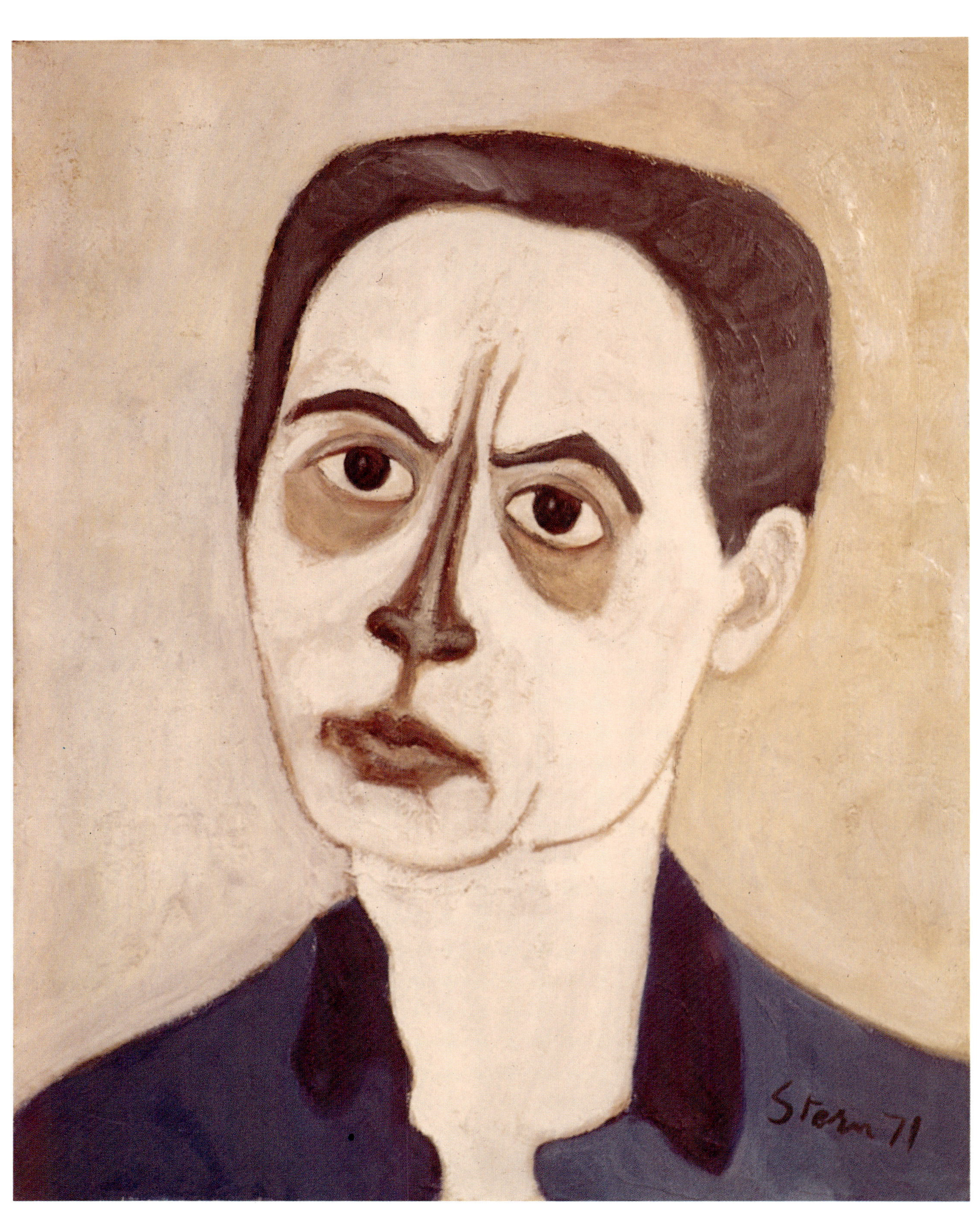

Self Portrait, 1971, oil on canvas, 76x64cm, Artist's Collection

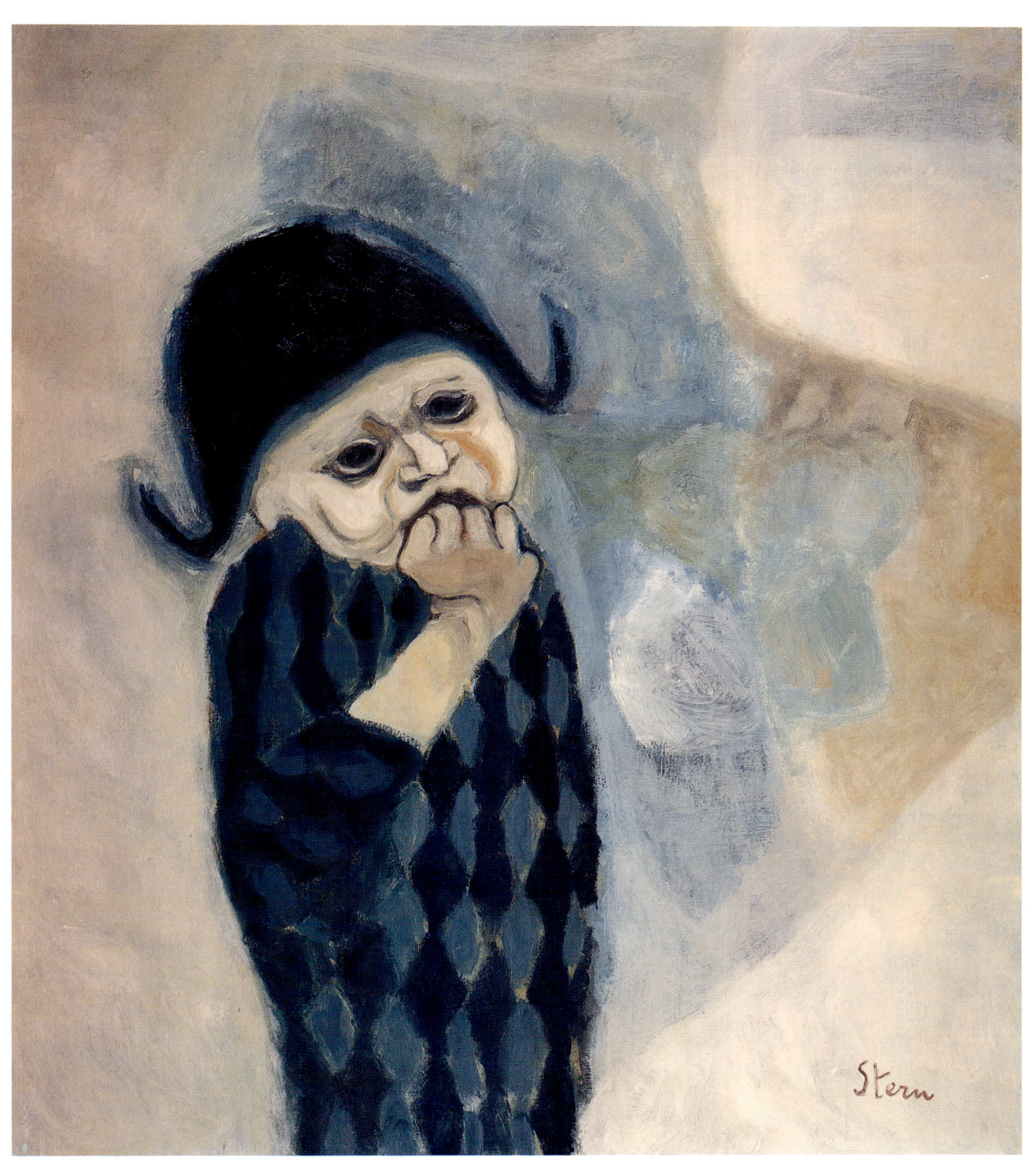

Burden of the Harlequin, 1973, oil on canvas, 102x91cm, Private Collection, Paris

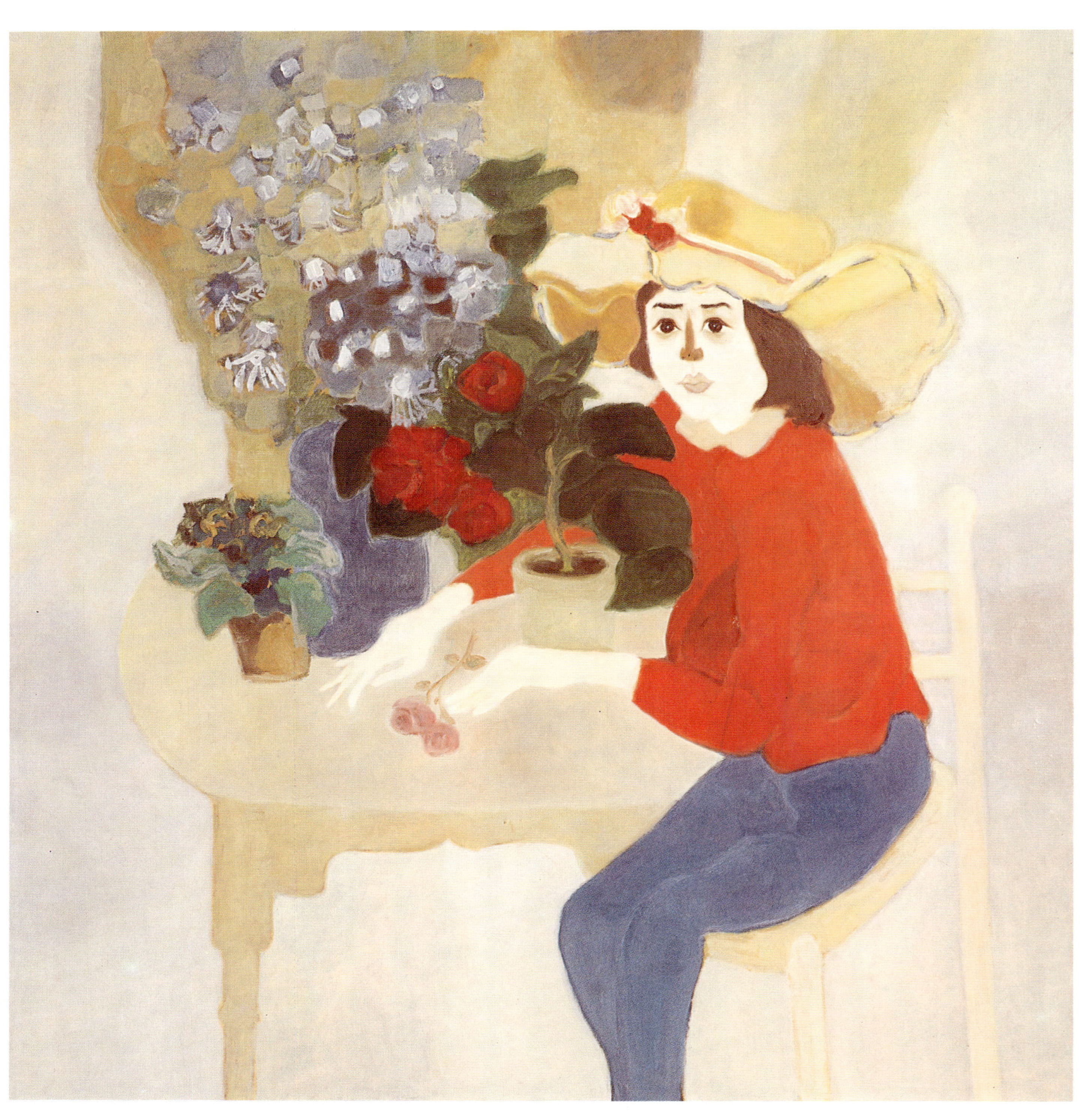

Girl in a Straw Hat, 1971, oil on canvas, 122x122cm, Dr. Abraham Eisen Collection, Tel Aviv

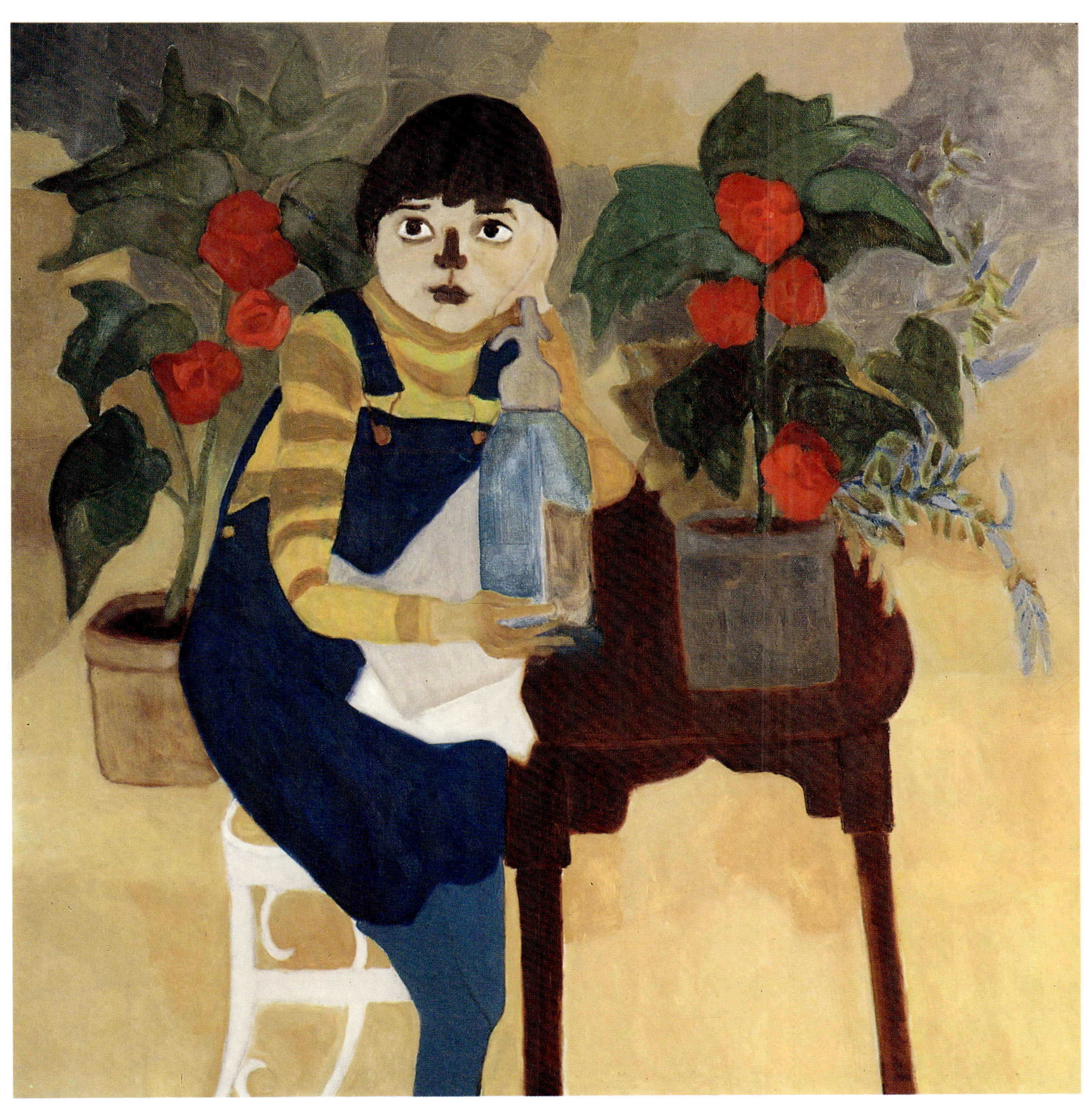

Boy with Begonias. 1971, oil on canvas, 122×122cm, Lindsay Bowman Collection, London

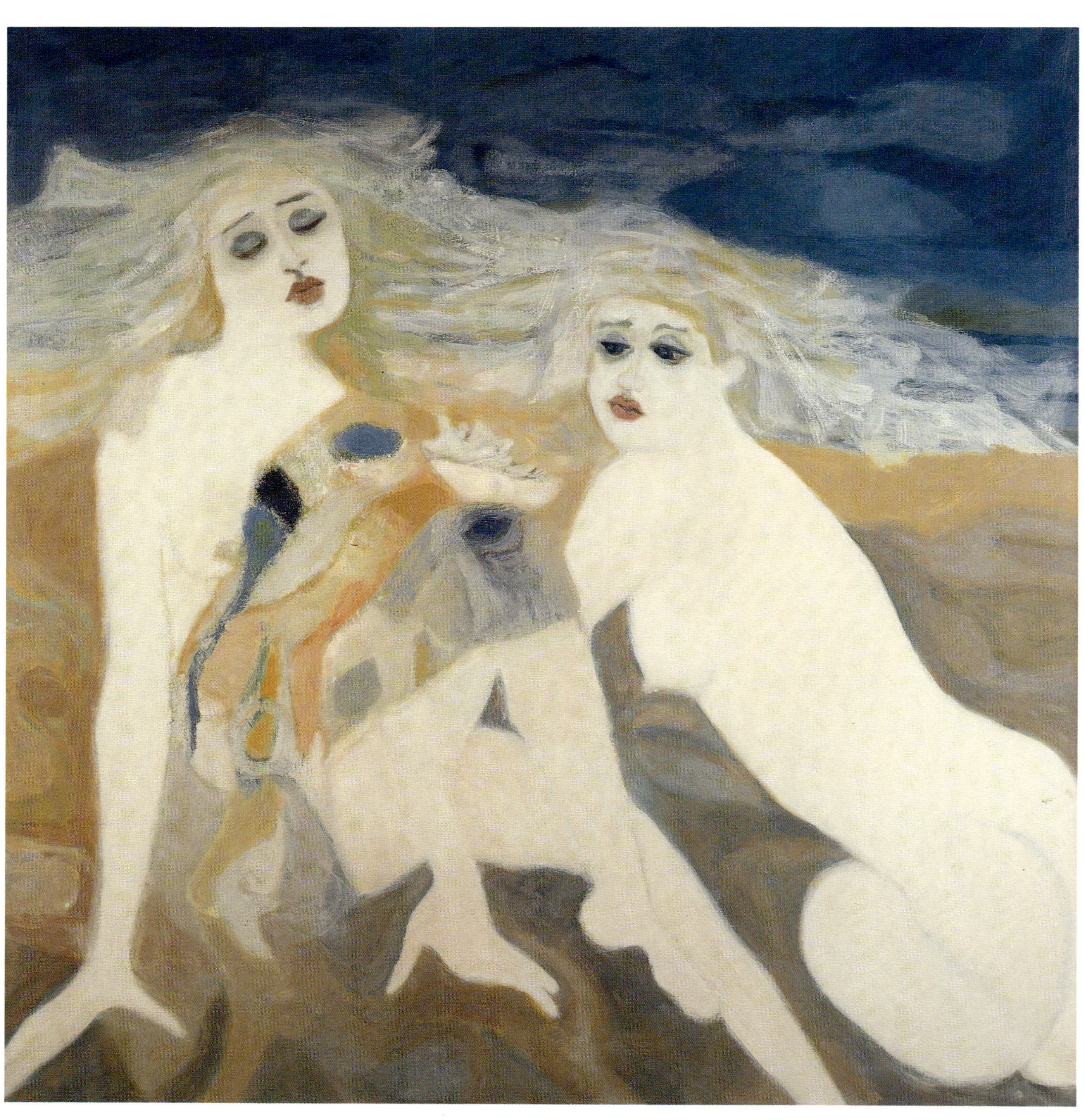

Girls on the Beach, 1971, oil on canvas, 122x122cm, H. Braasch Collection, New York

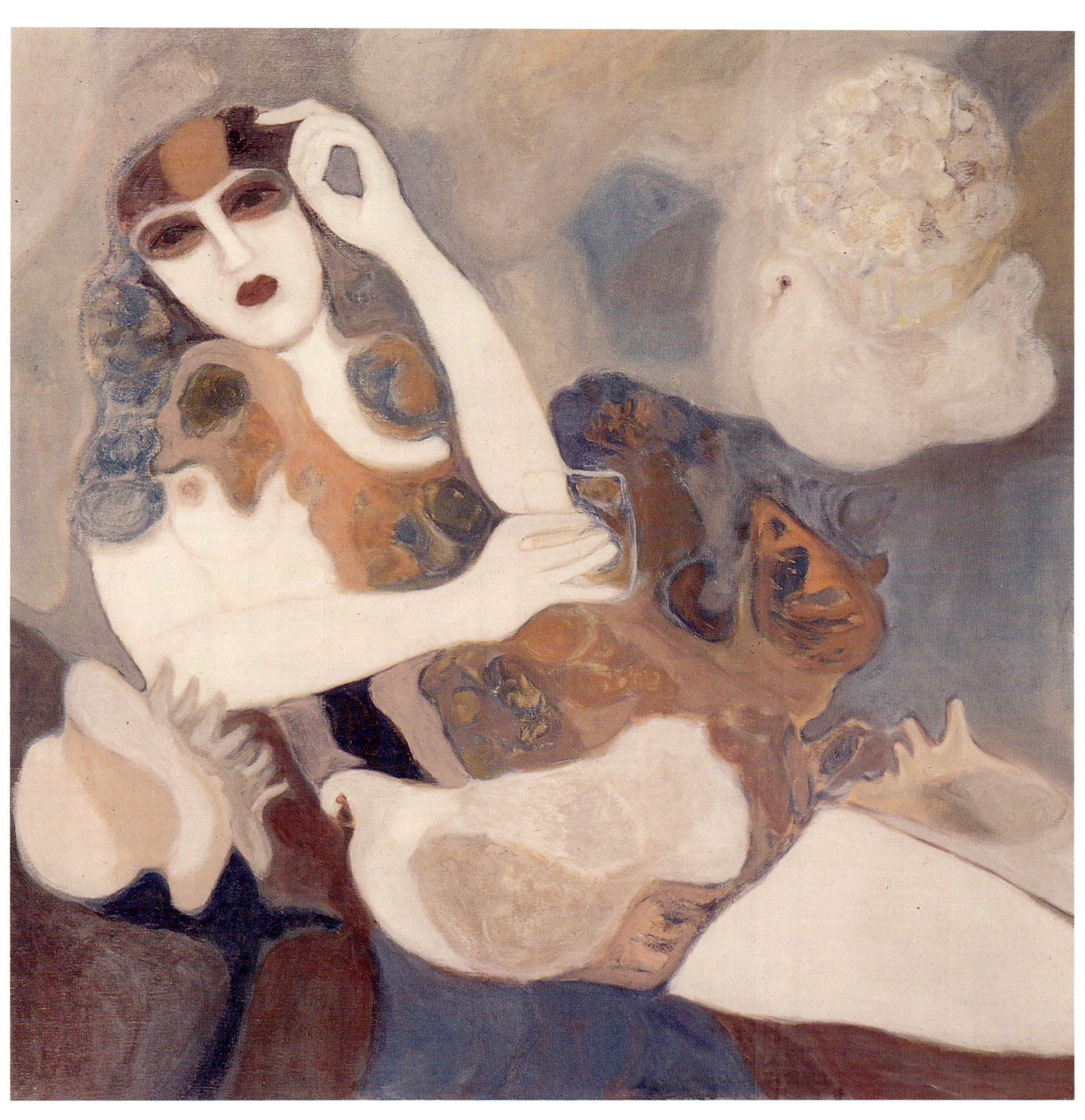

Odalisque, 1970, oil on canvas, 122x122cm, Alberto Torel Collection, London

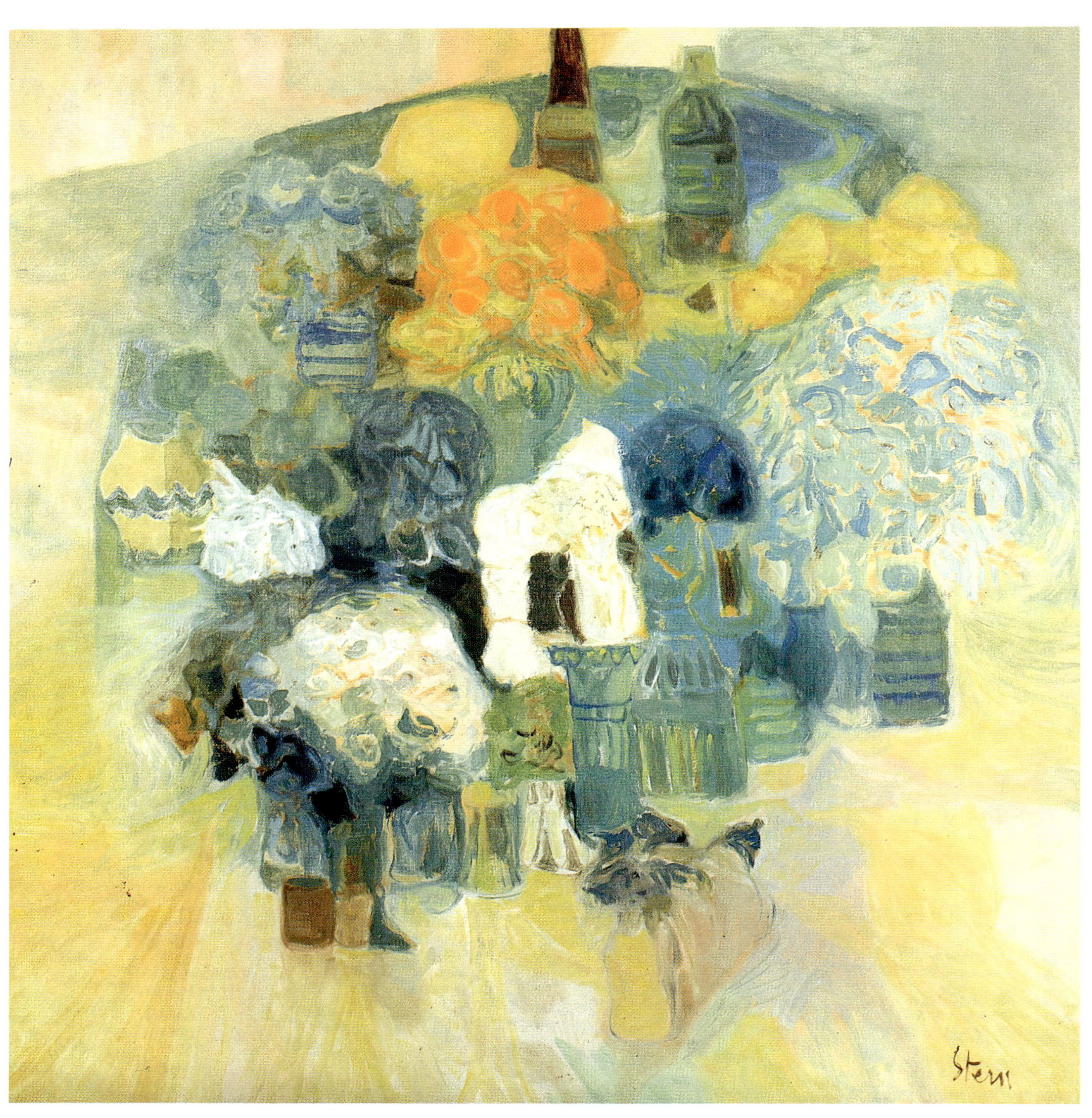

Multiple Bouquet, 1971, oil on canvas, 183x183cm, Makoto Iida Collection, Tokyo

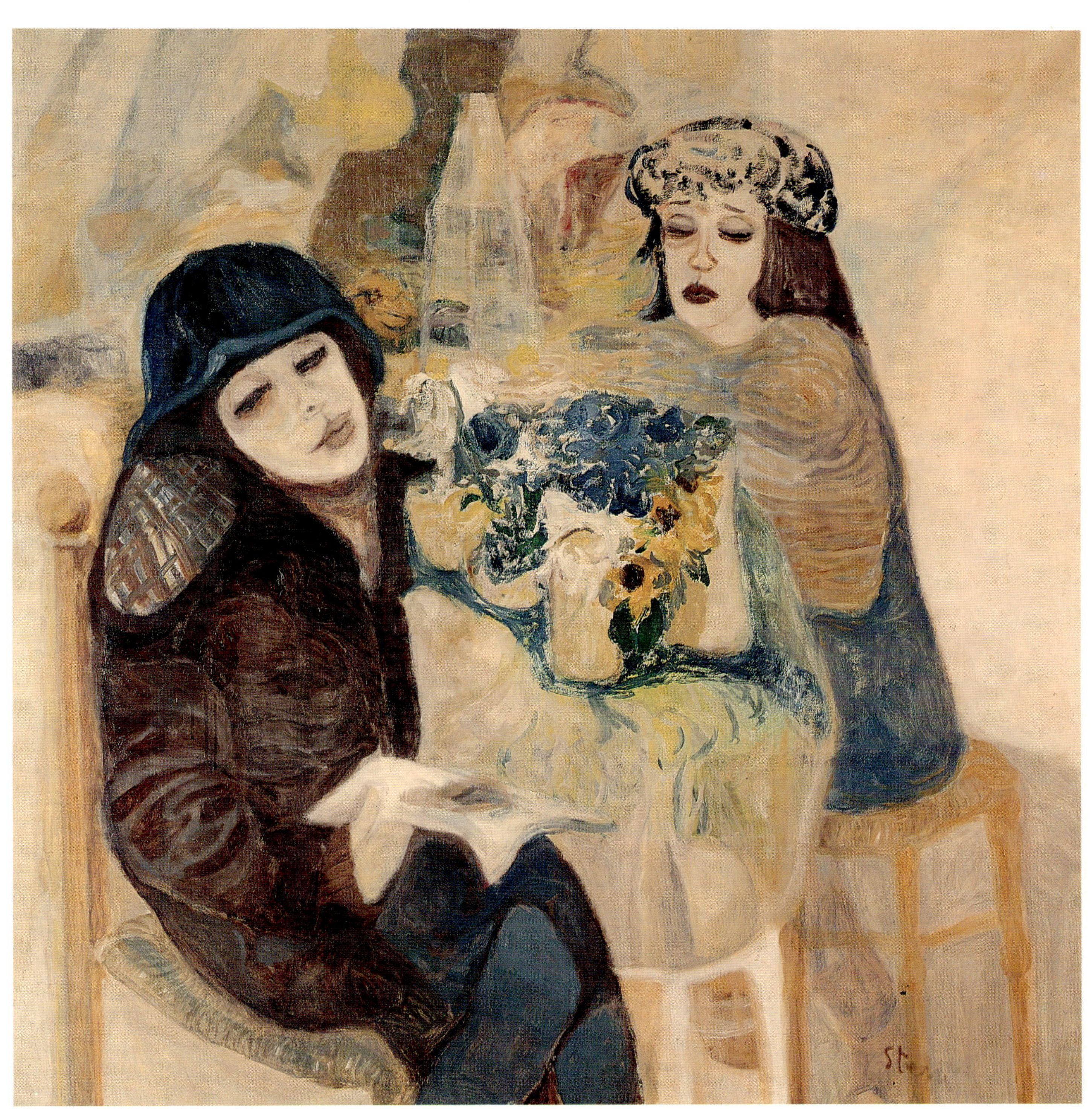

Afternoon Tea, 1972, oil on canvas, 122x122cm, Private Collection, Israel

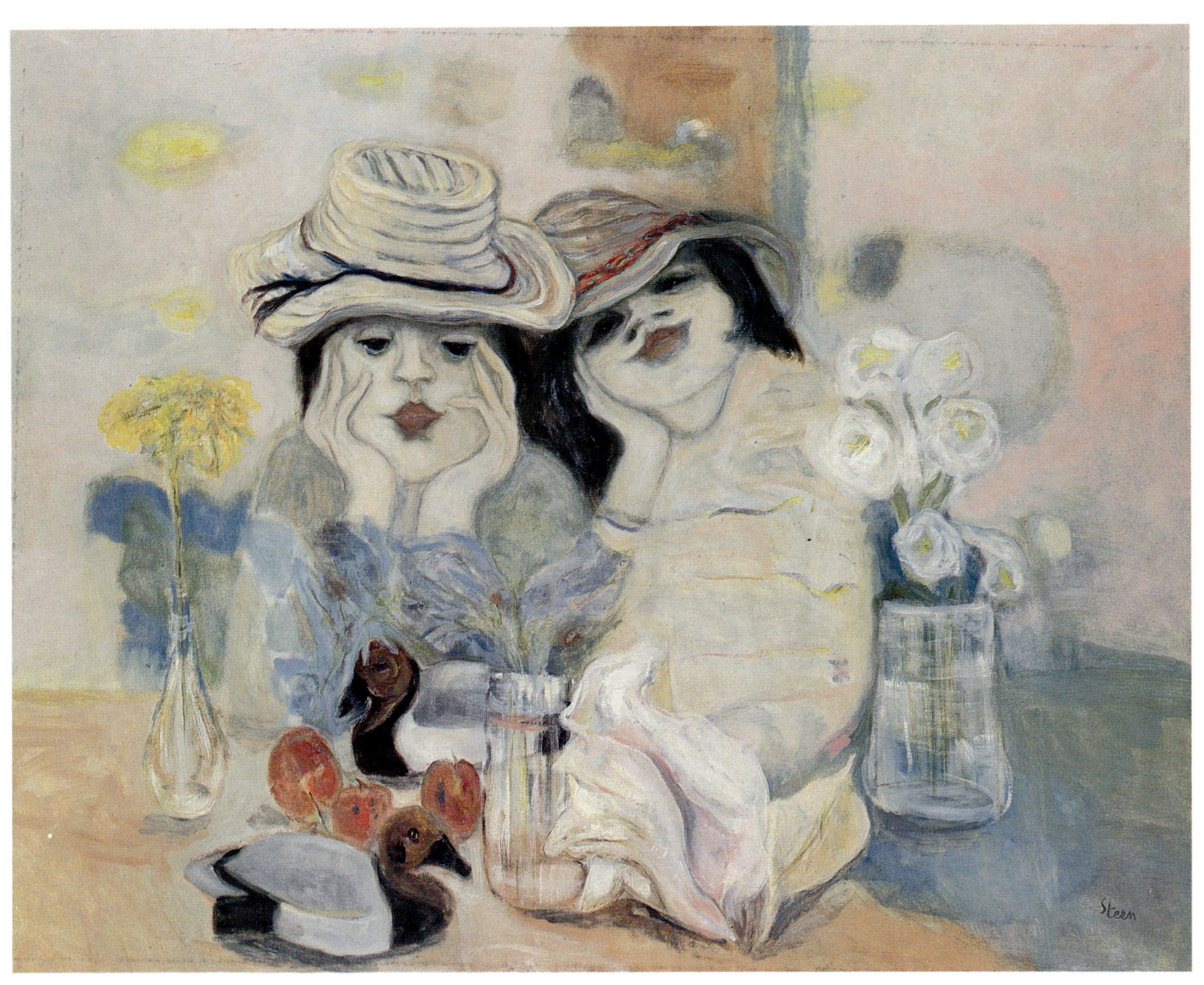

Fin de Vacances, 1972, oil on canvas, 92x122cm, Mrs. Muriel Kerr Collection, Dublin

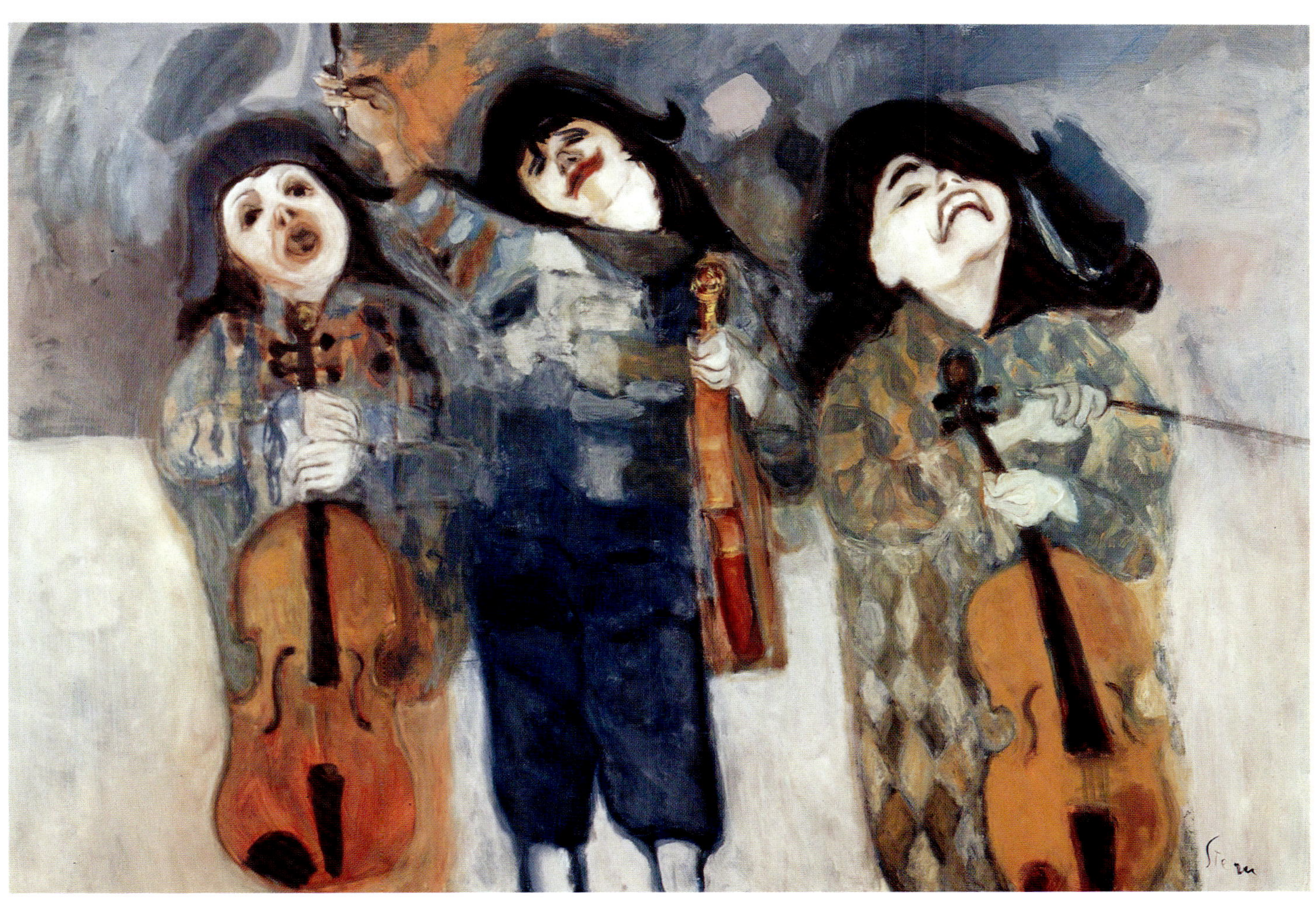

After the Concert, 1972, oil on canvas, 122x183cm, Robert Debbas Collection, Beirut

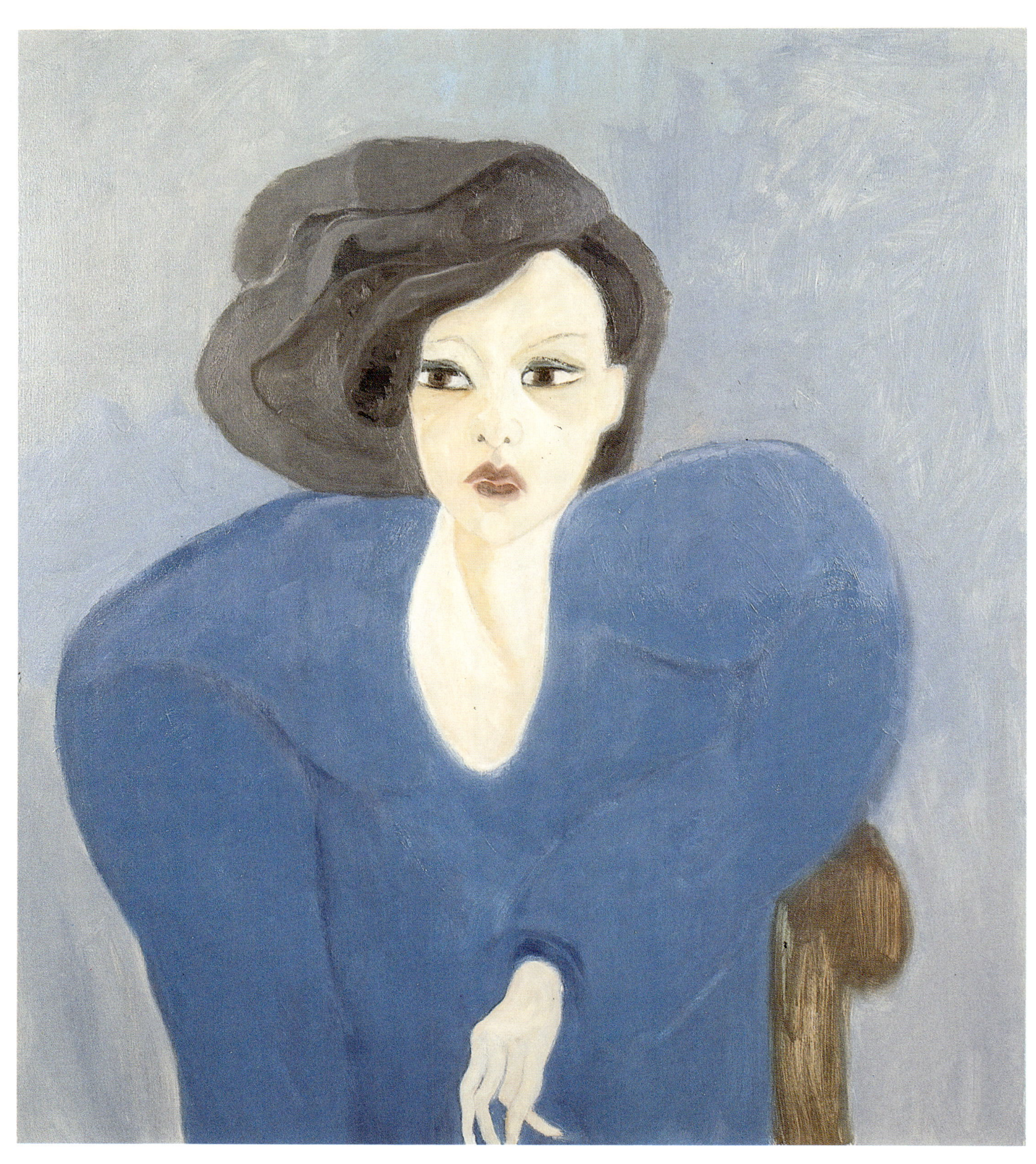

Japanese Lady, 1972, oil on canvas, 122x122cm, Nicoline Pon Collection, Zurich

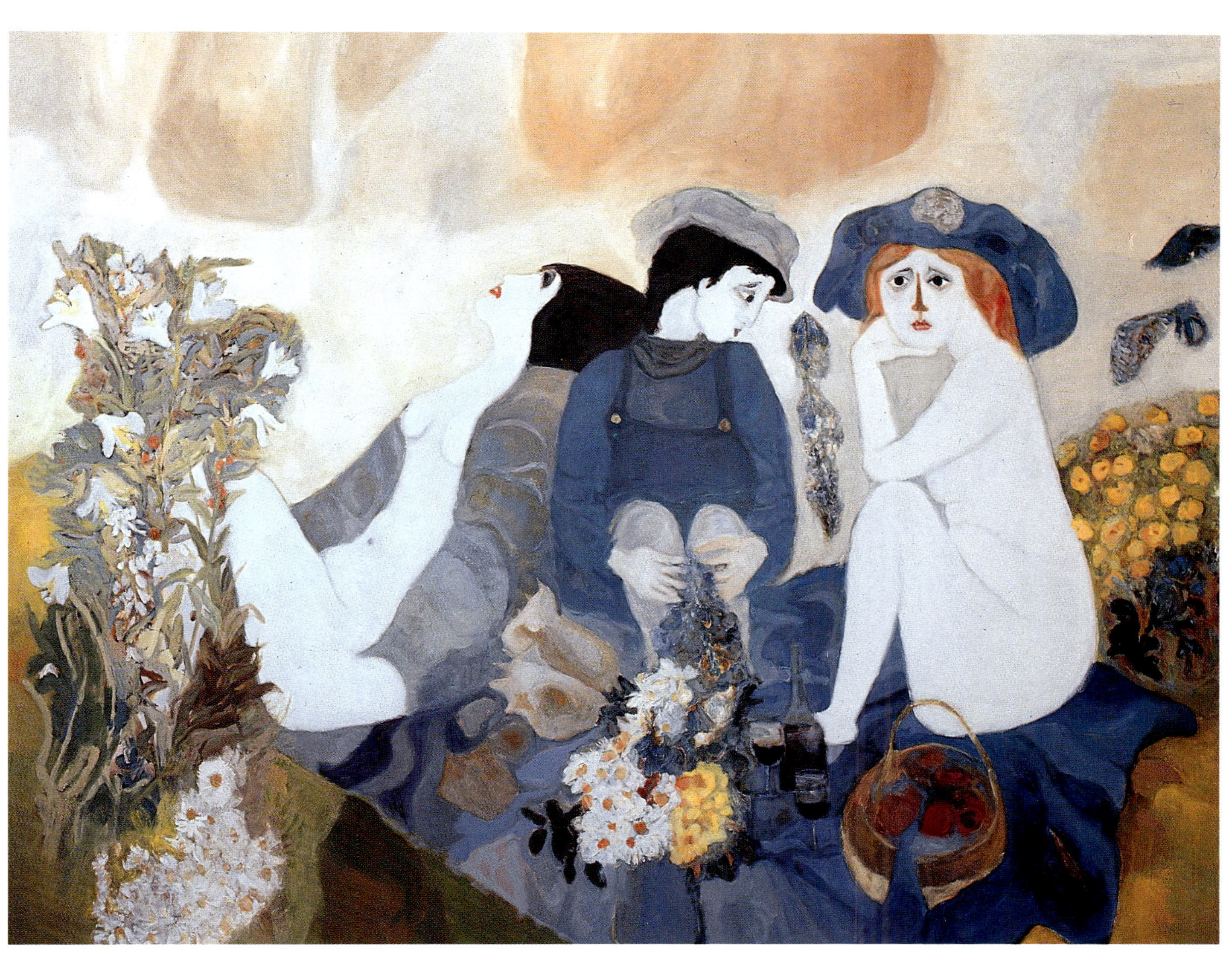

Déjeuner sur l'herbe Revisited, 1971, oil on canvas, 183x244cm, Private Collection, London

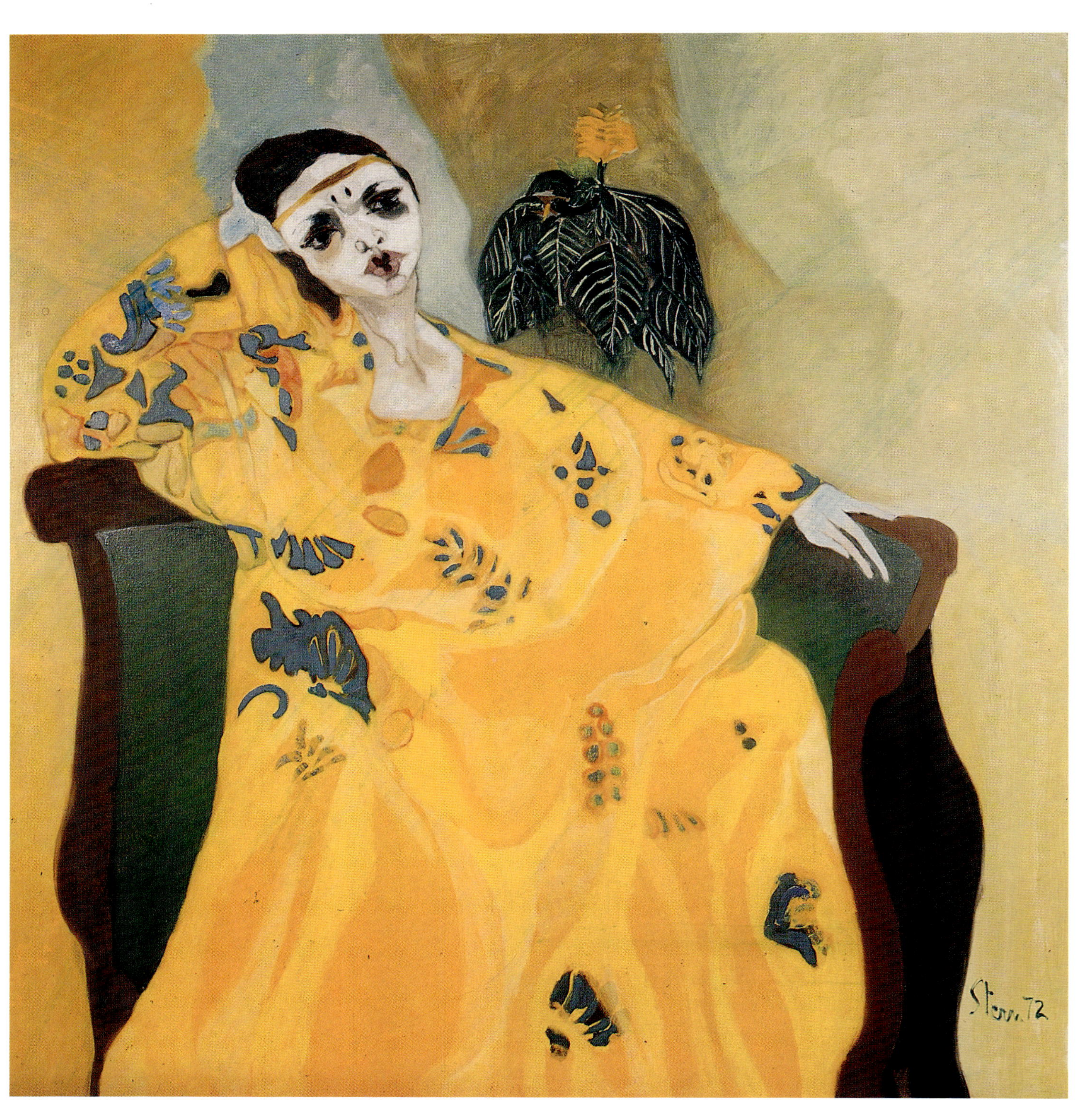

La Japonaise en jaune, 1972, oil on canvas, 183×183cm, Private Collection, London

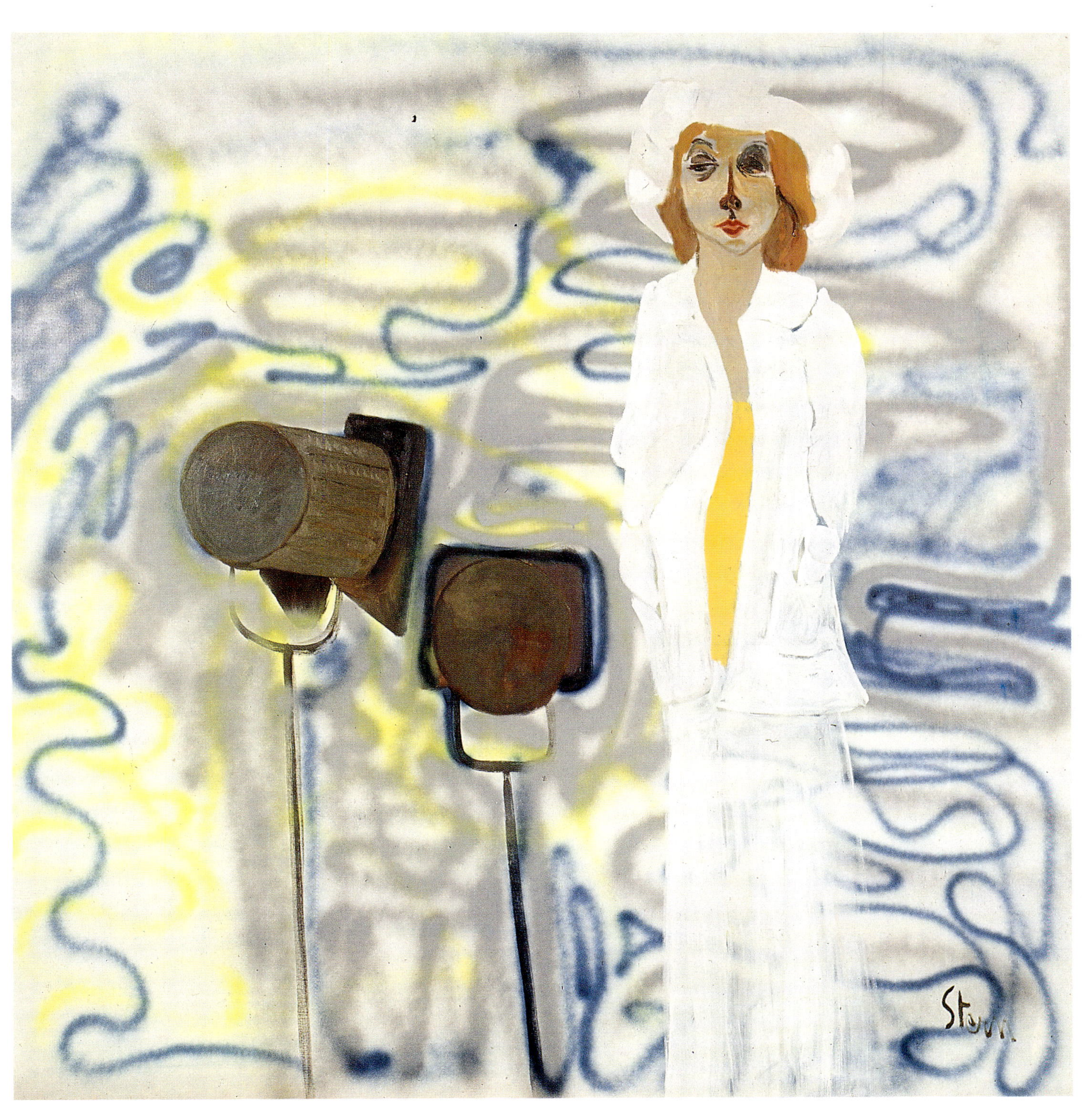

The Star, 1972, oil on canvas, 183x183cm, Artist's Collection

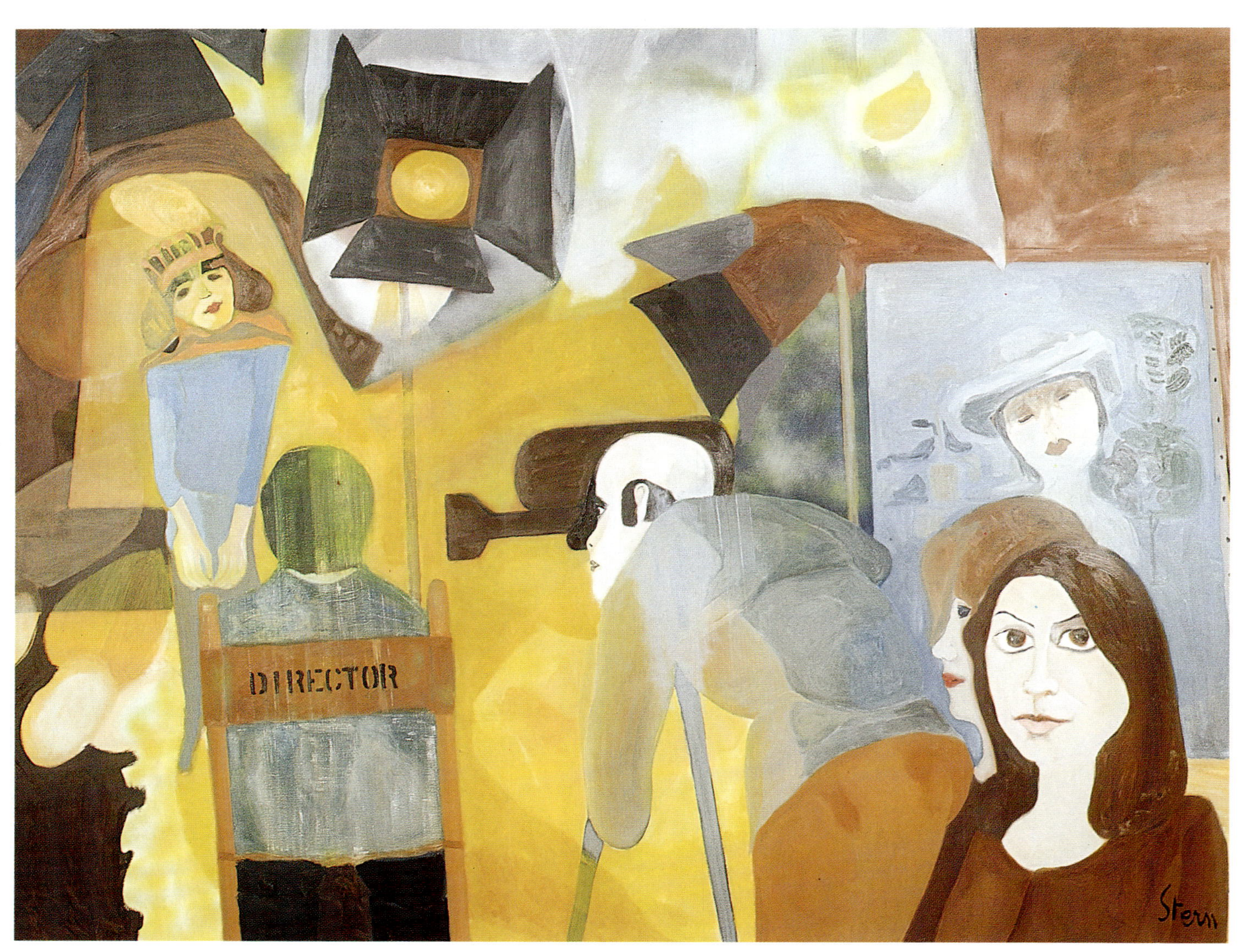

Movie Maker, 1972, oil on canvas, 183×244cm, Artist's Collection

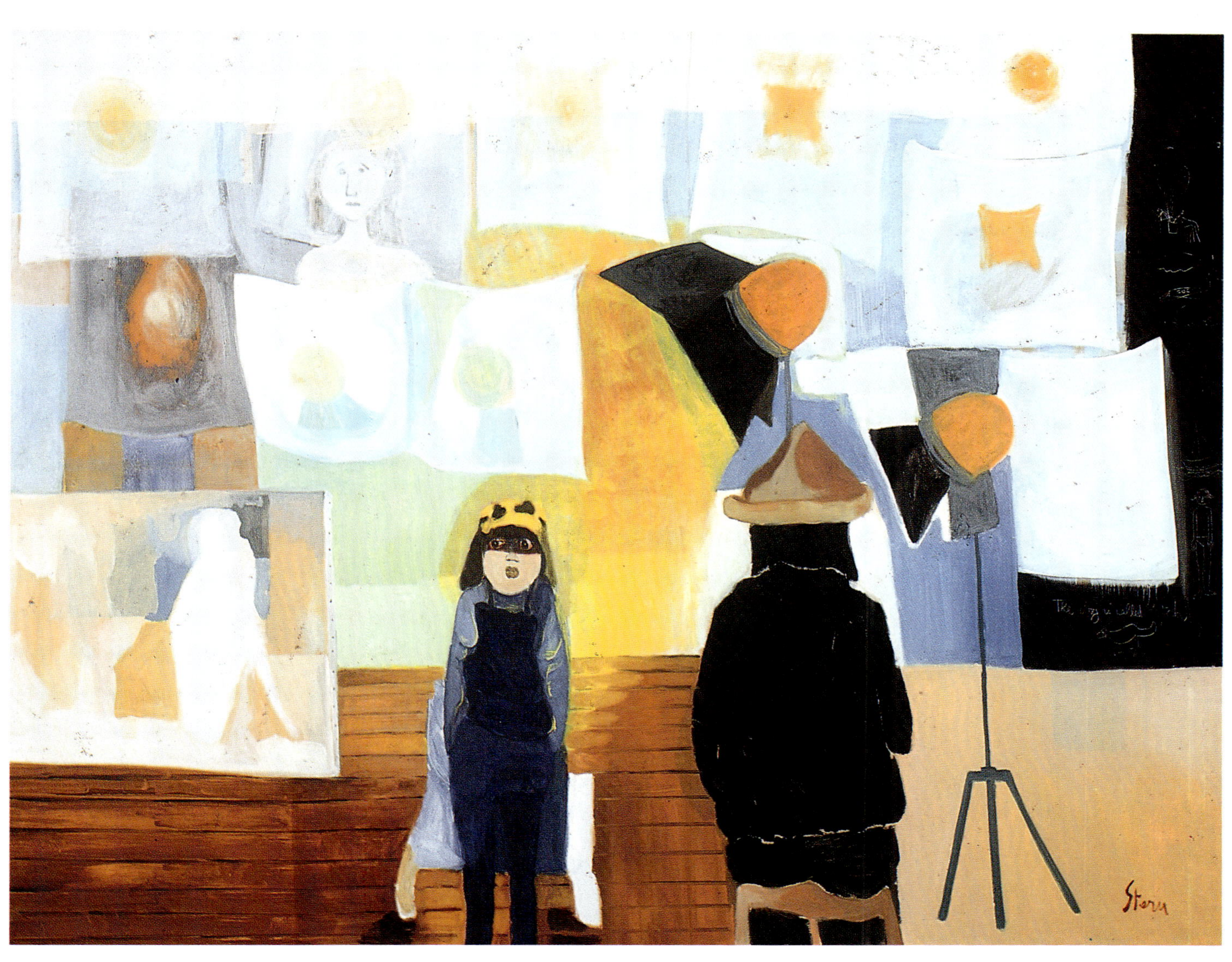

Making a Movie, 1972, oil on canvas, 183x244cm, Artist's Collection

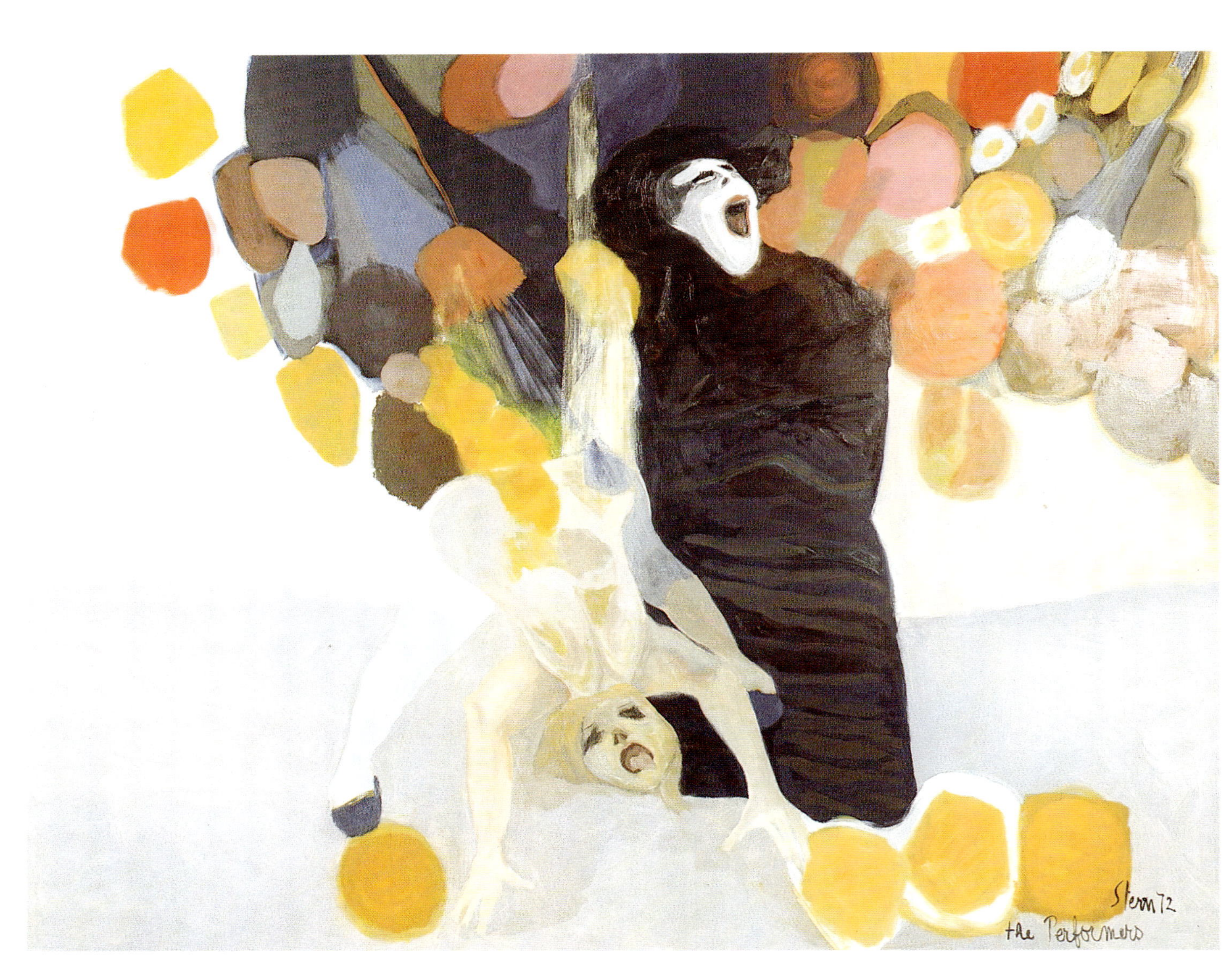

The Performers, 1972, oil on canvas, 183x244cm, Artist's Collection

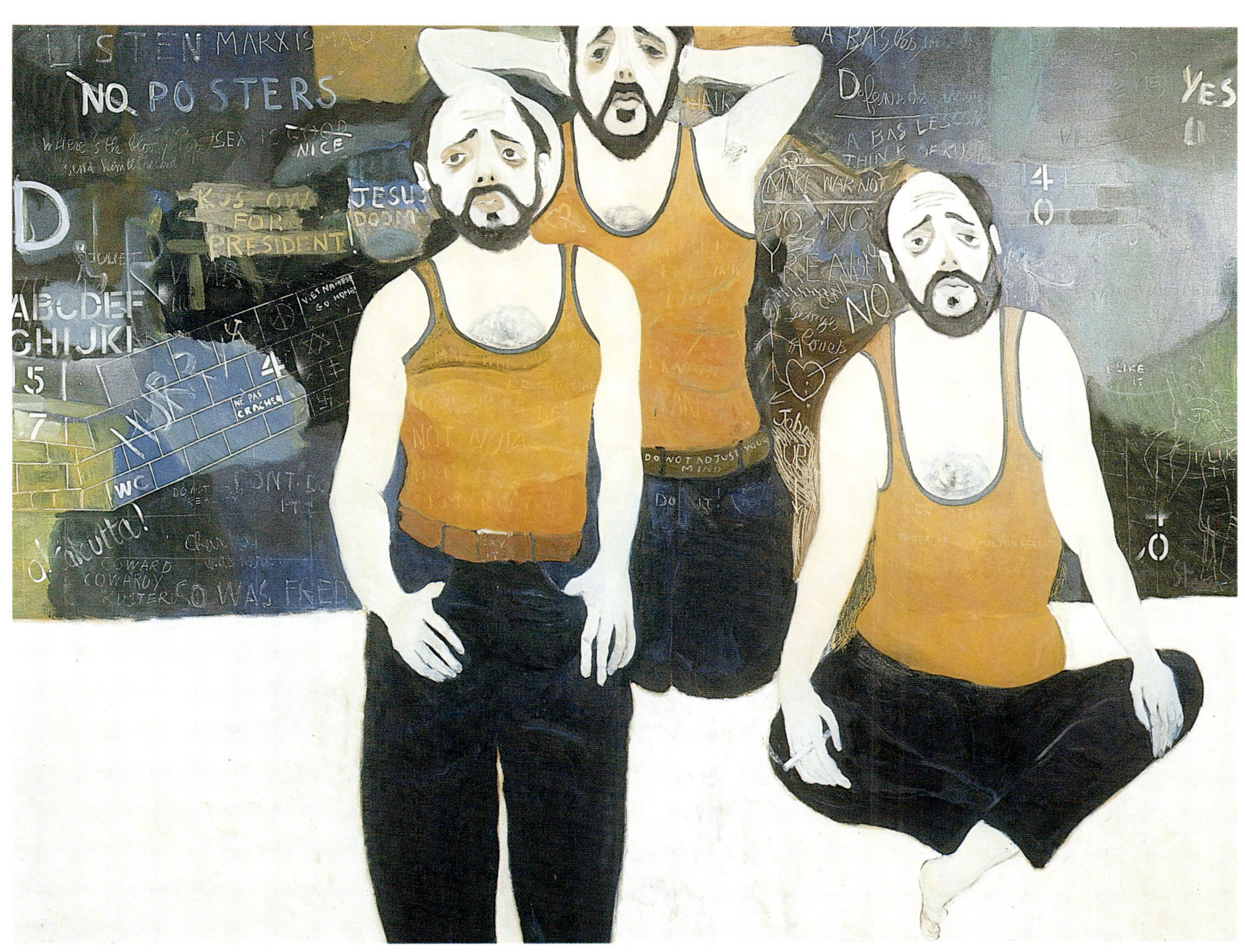

Cross Roads (Michael Kustow), 1972, oil on canvas, 183x244cm, Artist's Collection

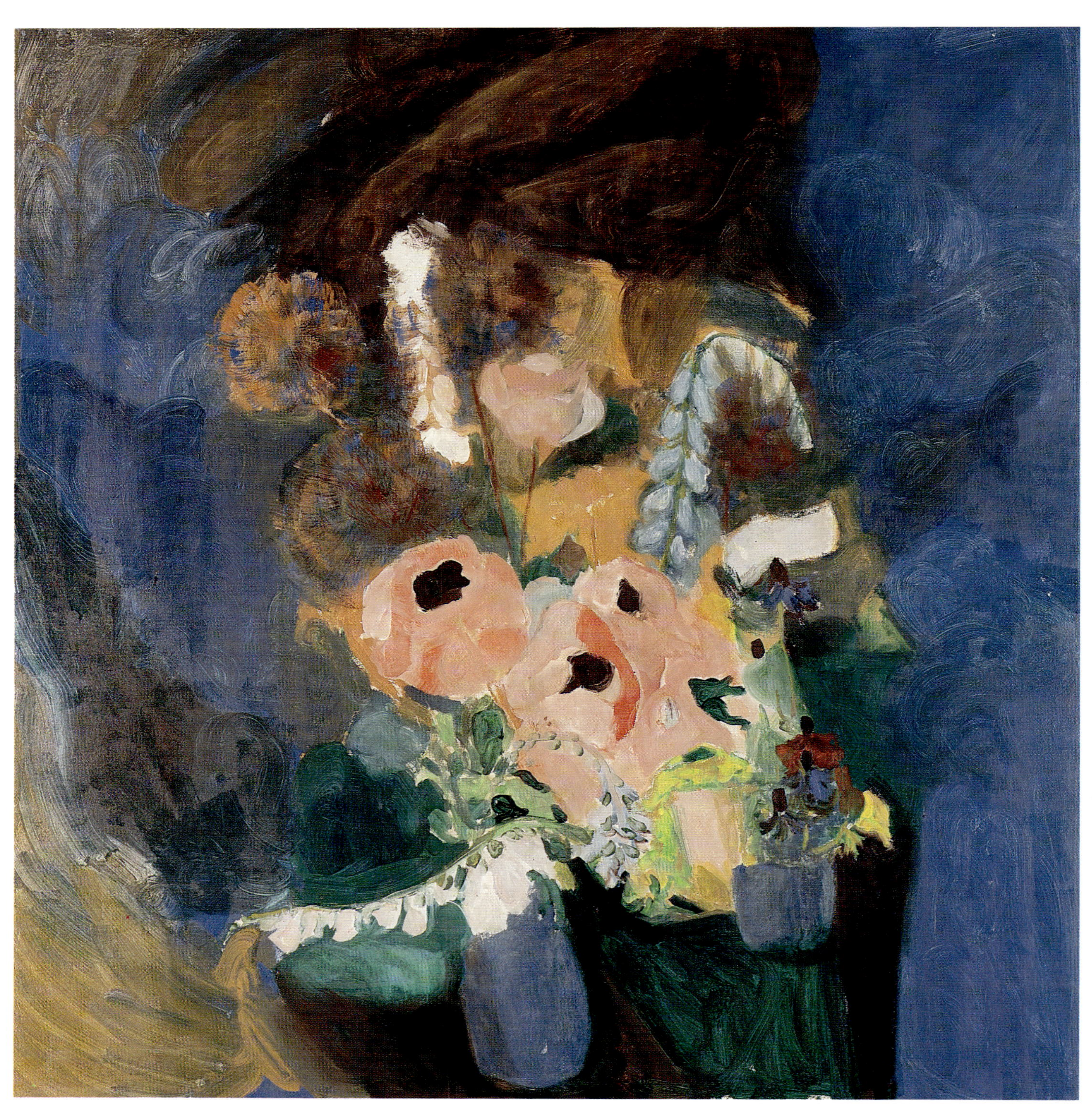

Flower Composition, 1972, oil on canvas, 122x122cm, Private Collection, Zurich

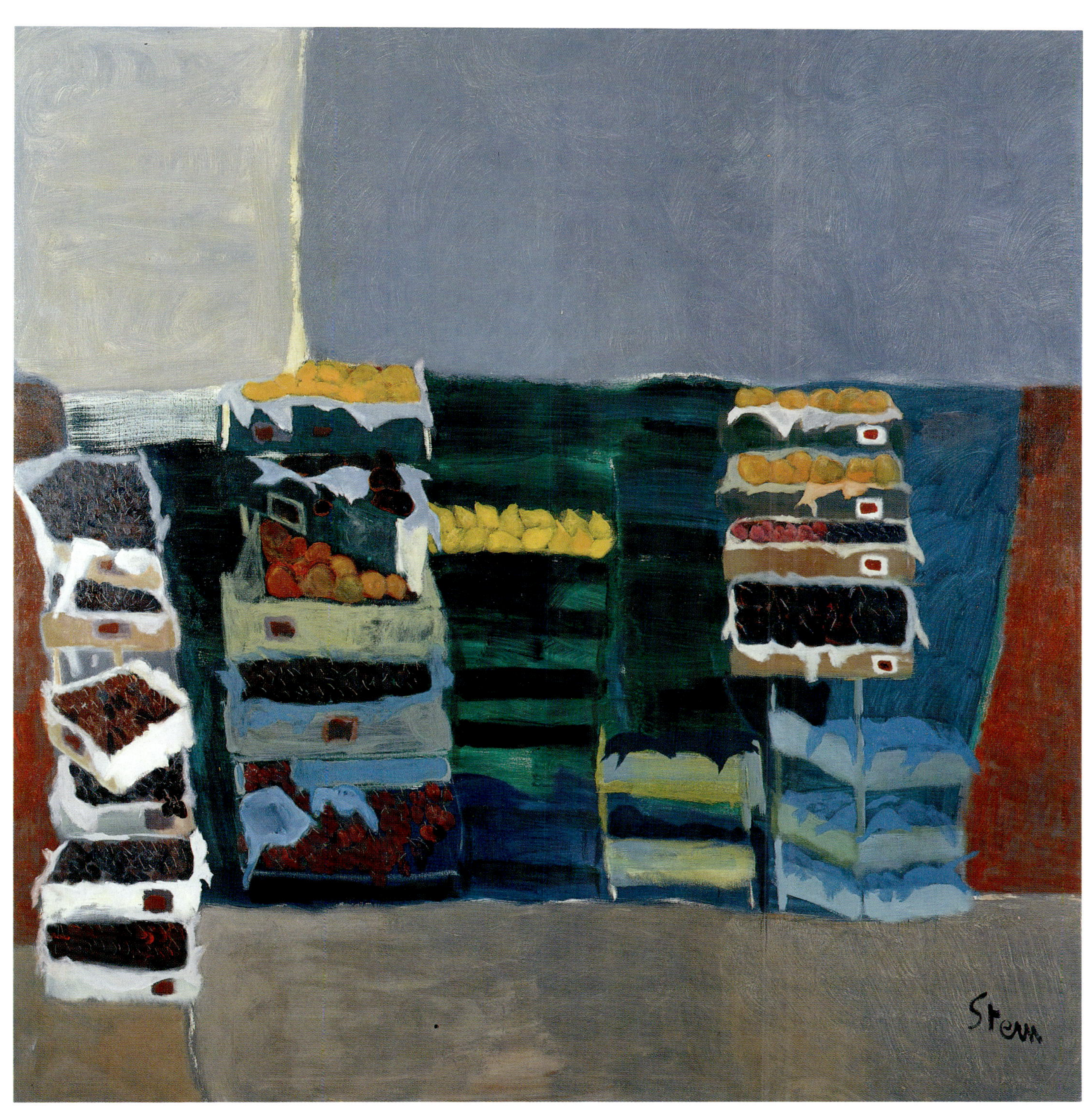

Fruit Crates III, 1972, oil on canvas, 183x183cm, Private Collection, New York

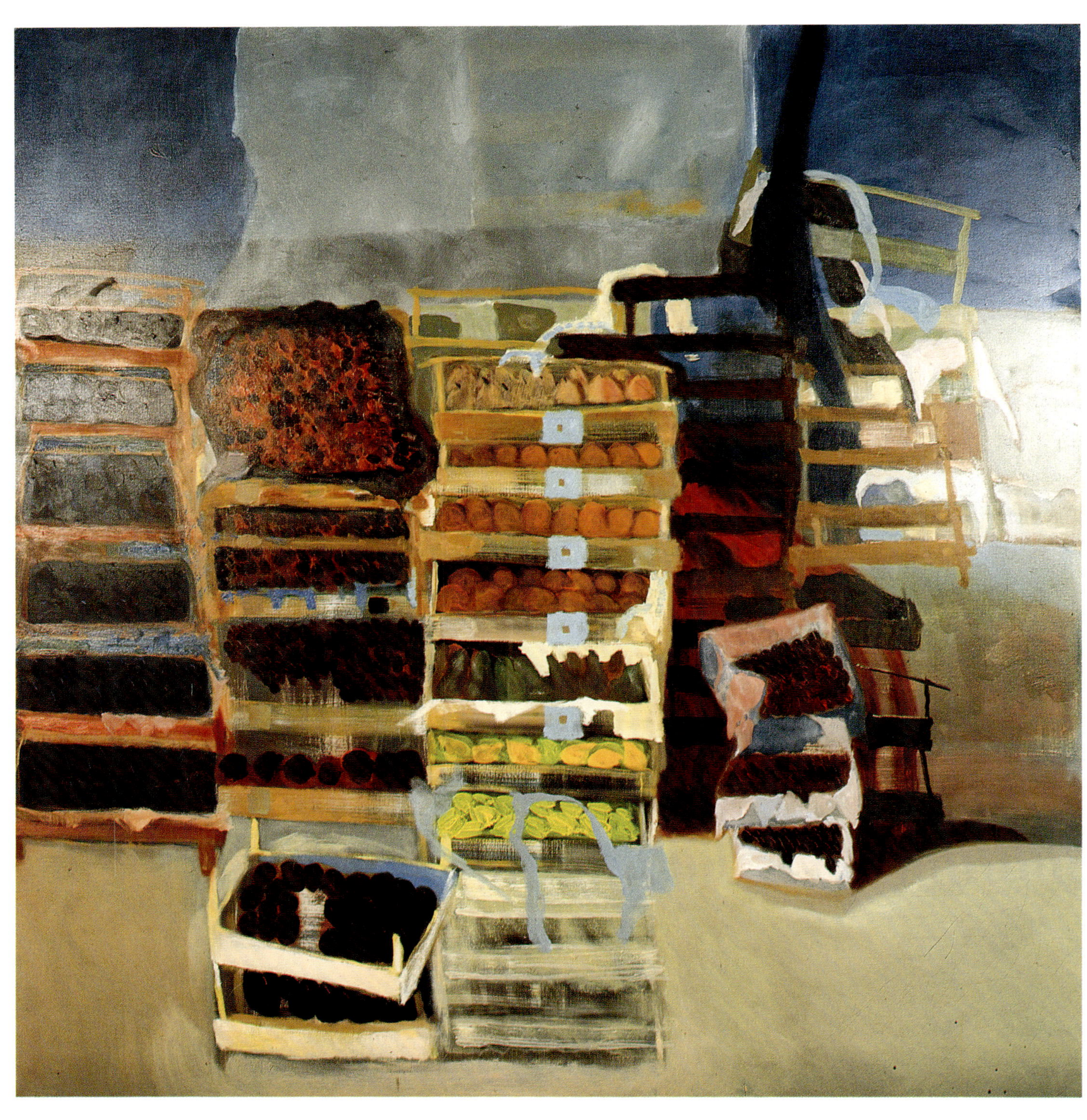

Fruit Crates in the Market, 1972, oil on canvas, 183x183cm, Sir Joseph Lockwood Collection, London

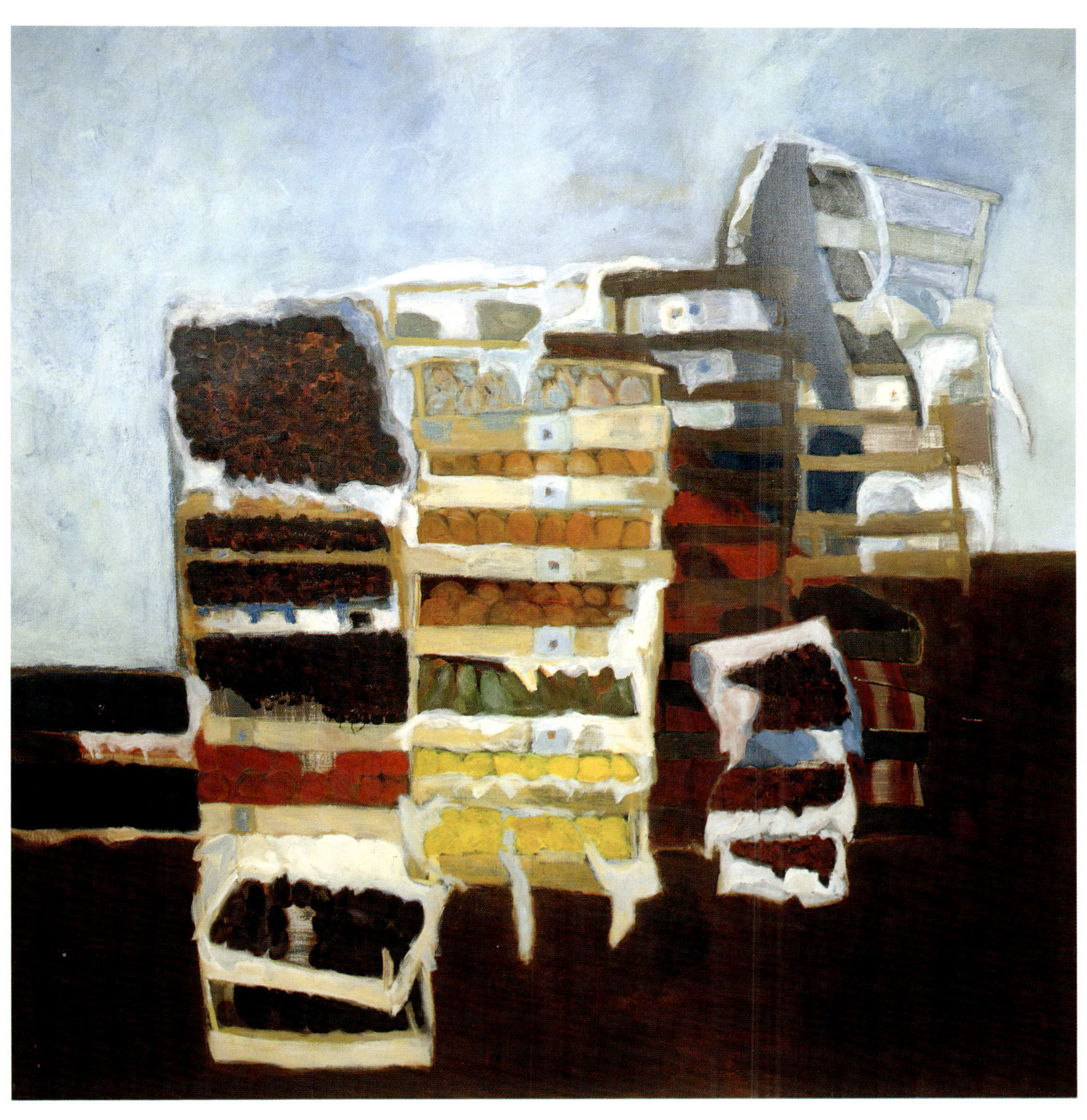

Fruit Crates, 1972, oil on canvas, 183x183cm, Mrs. Hedi Label Collection, Santa Cruz, California

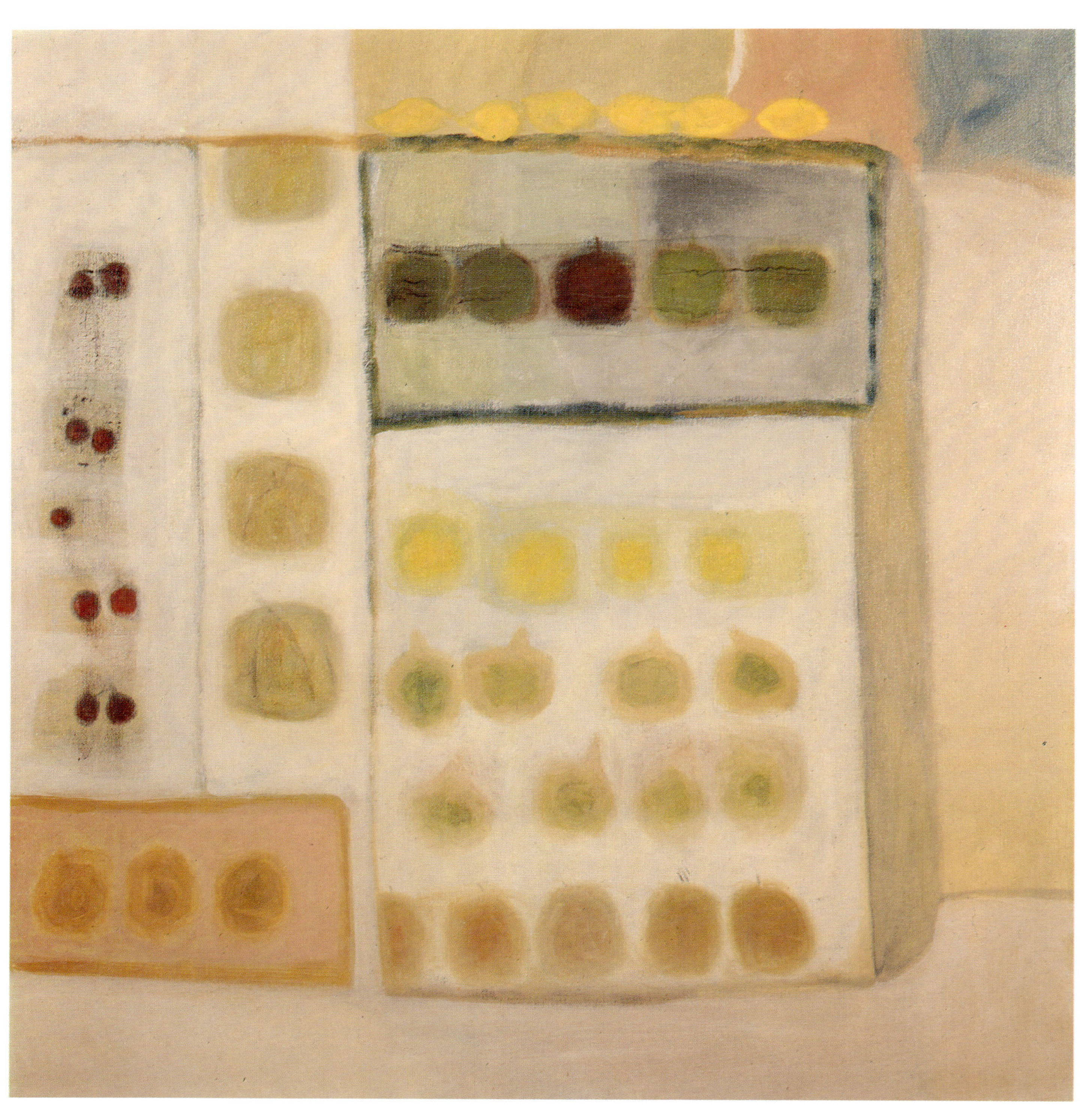

Music Machine, 1972, oil on canvas, 102x92cm, Manuel Solana Collection, Madrid

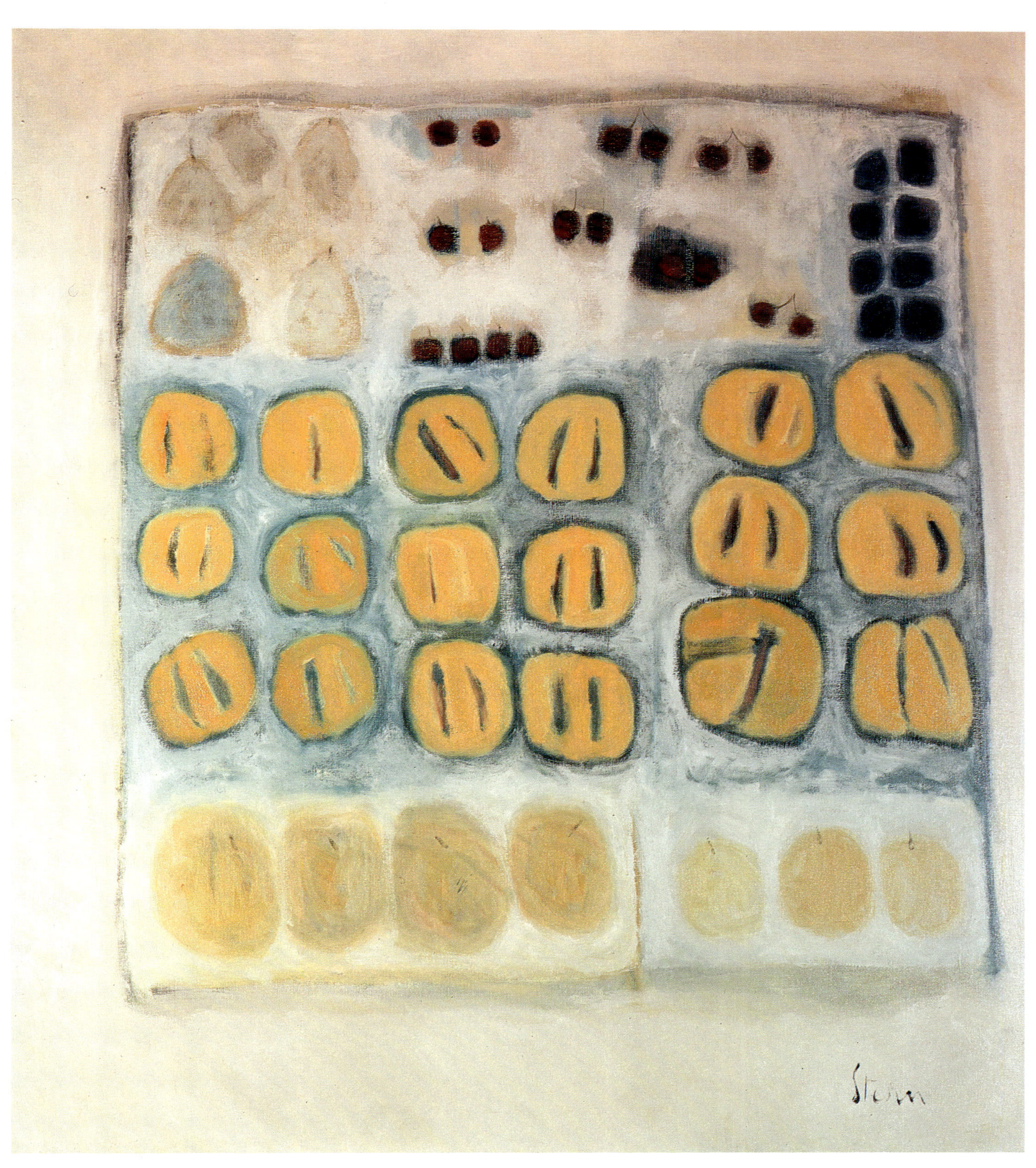

Musical Notes, 1973, oil on canvas, 102x91cm, Petit Palais Collection, Geneva

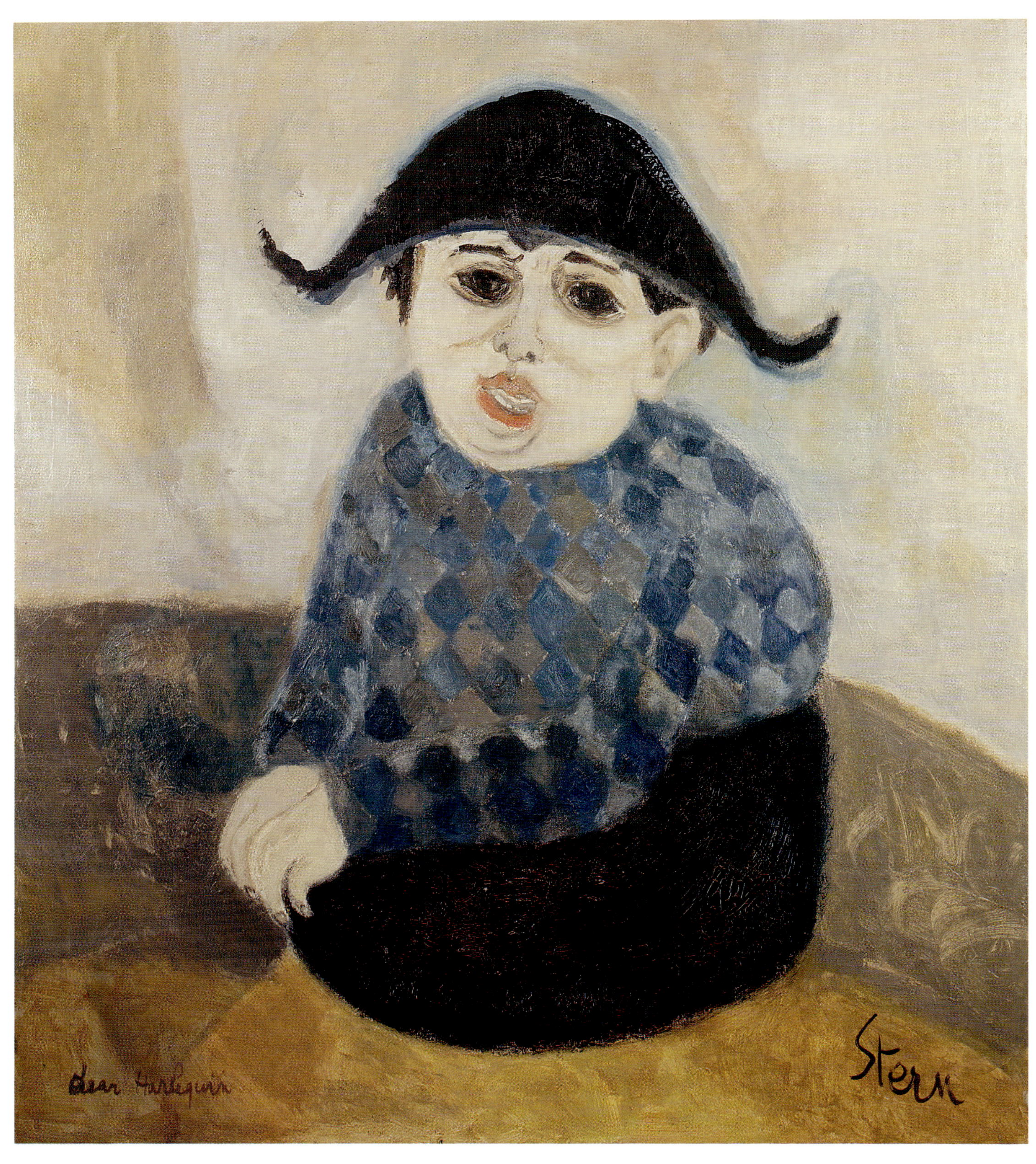

Born a Harlequin, 1973, oil on canvas, 102x91cm, Artist's Collection

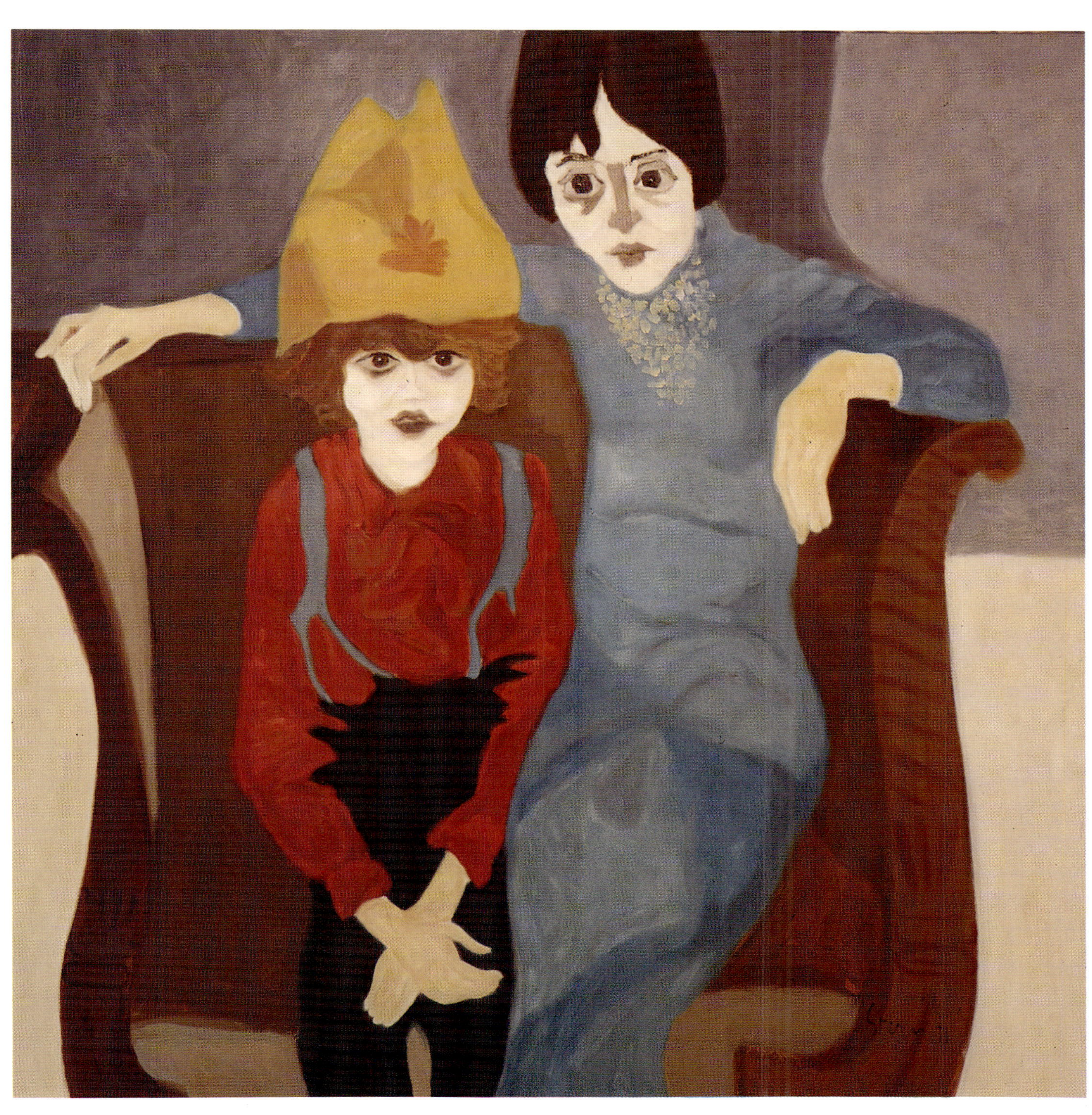

Fête des Rois, 1973, oil on canvas, 122x122cm, Luciano Zucchi Collection, London

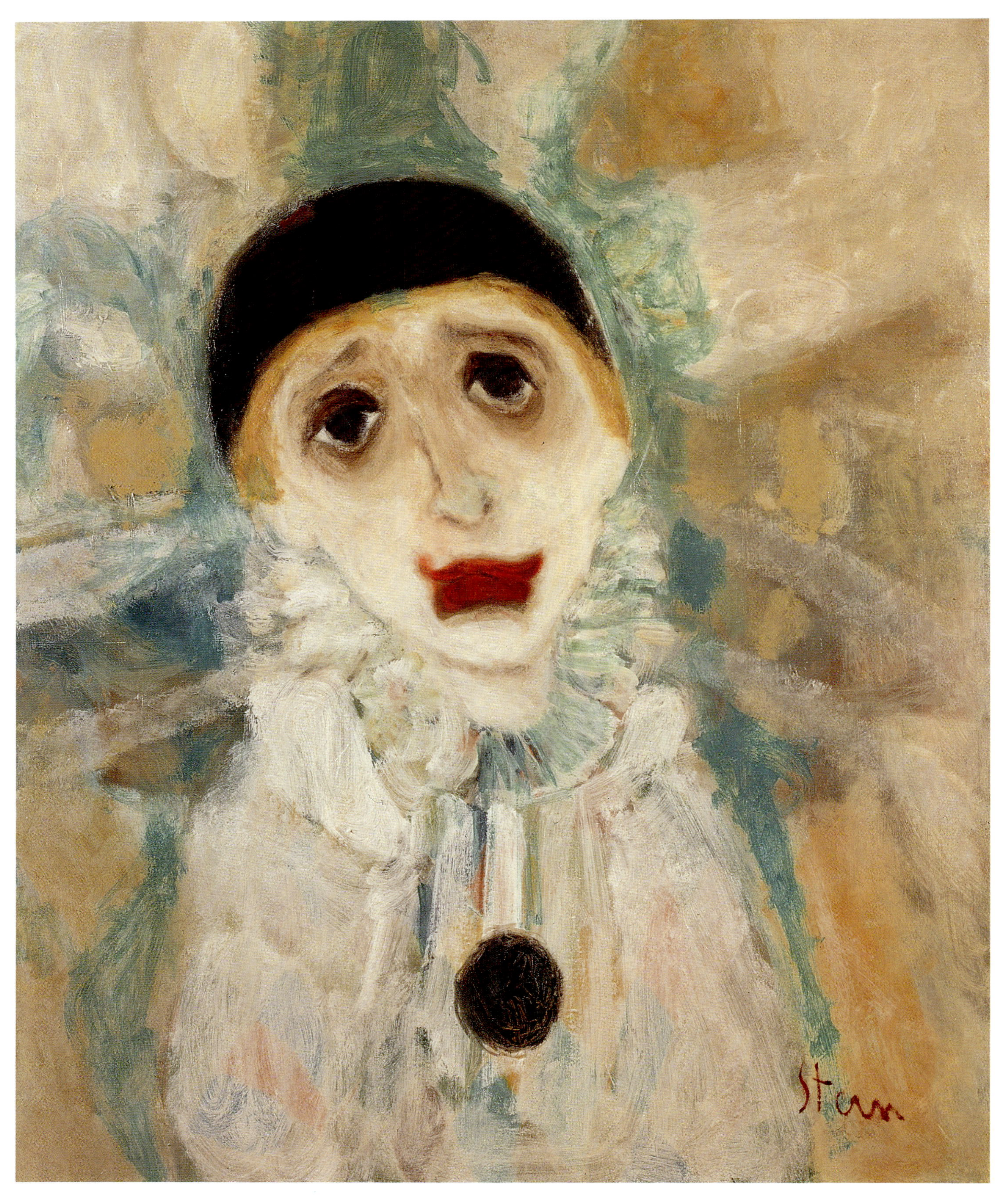

Pierrot, 1973, oil on canvas, 76x64cm, Private Collection, Israel

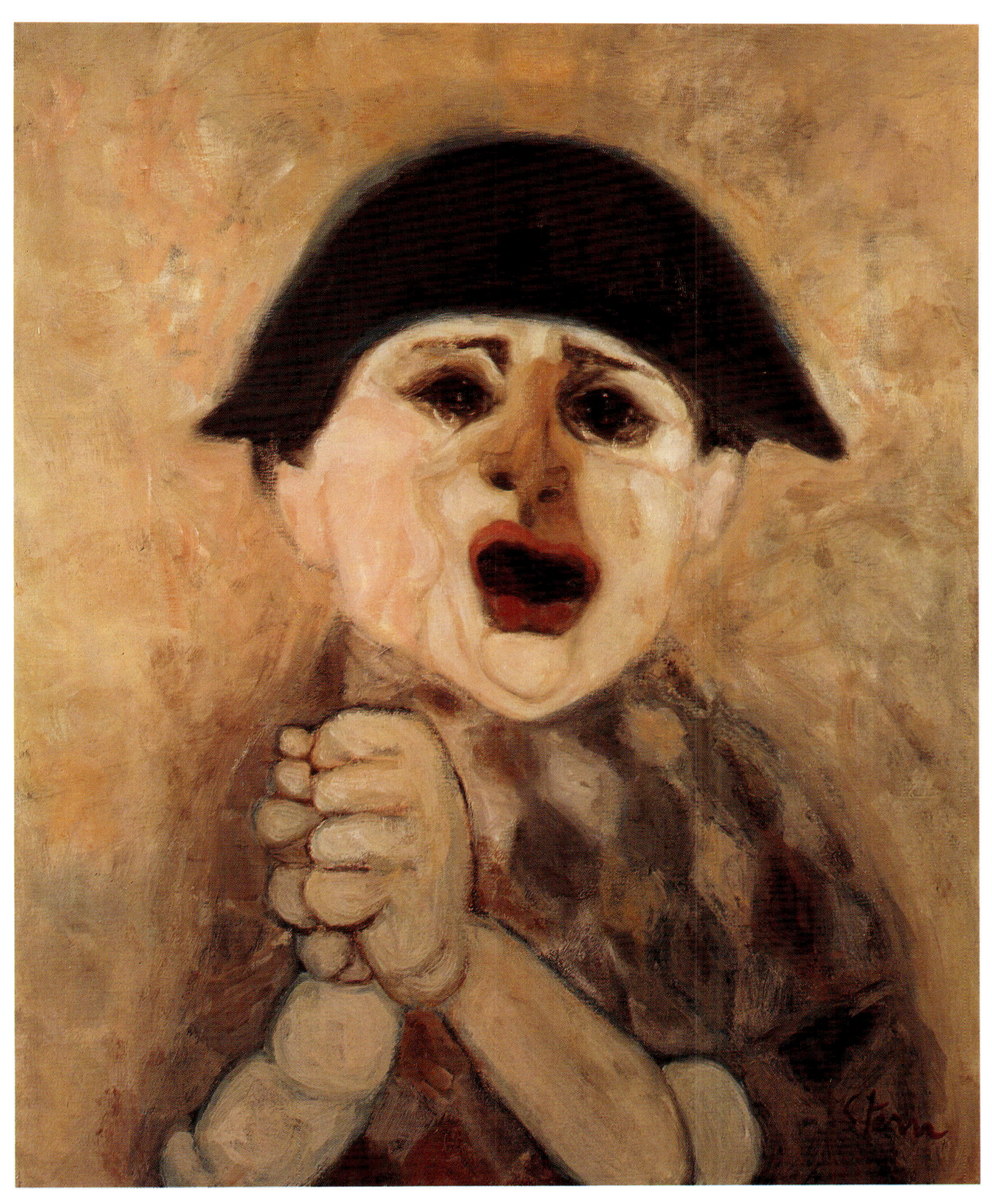

Sad Harlequin, 1973, oil on canvas, 76x64cm, Private Collection, Israel

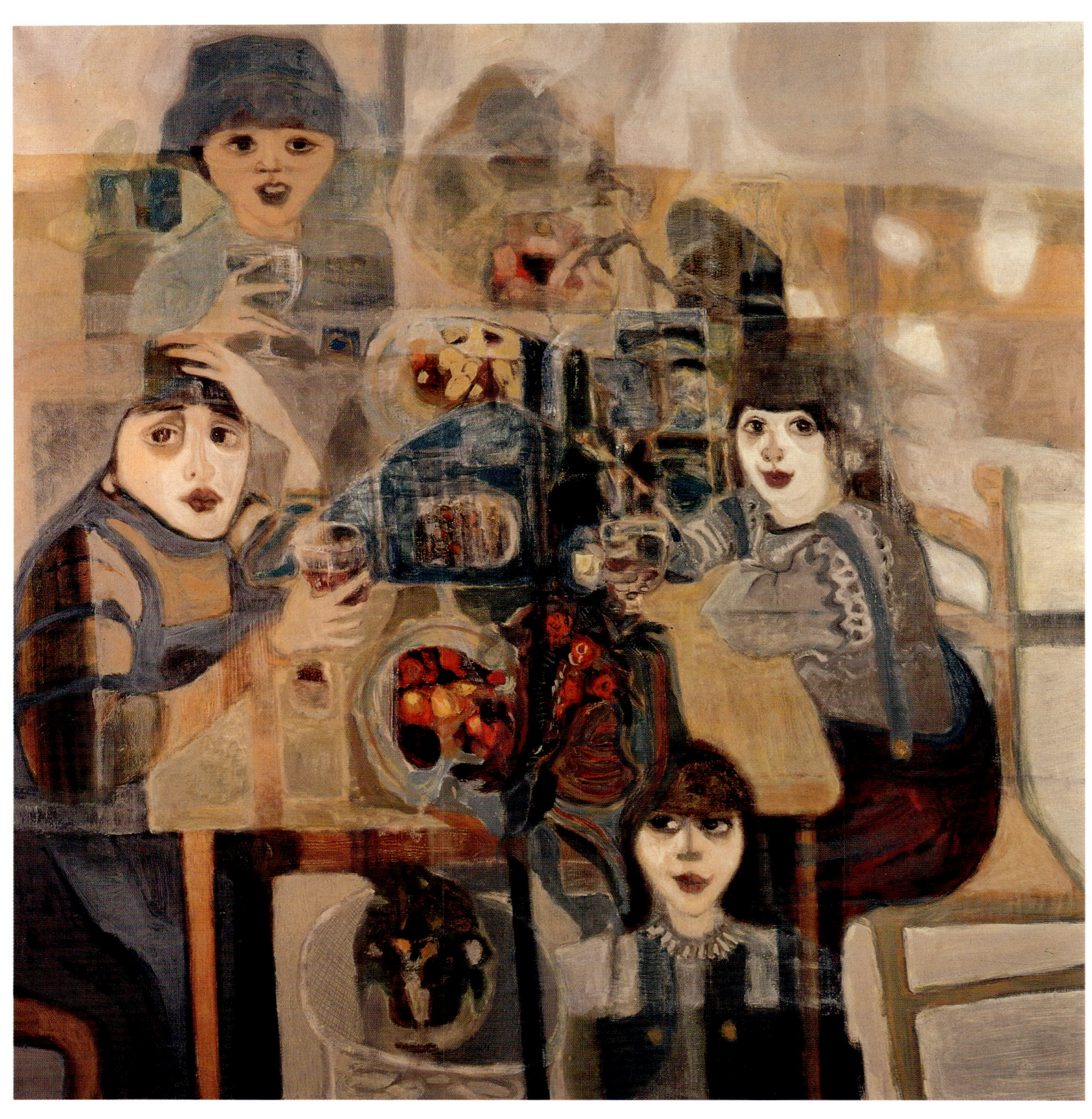

Double Exposure, 1973, oil on canvas, 152x152cm, David Weisz Collection, Caracas

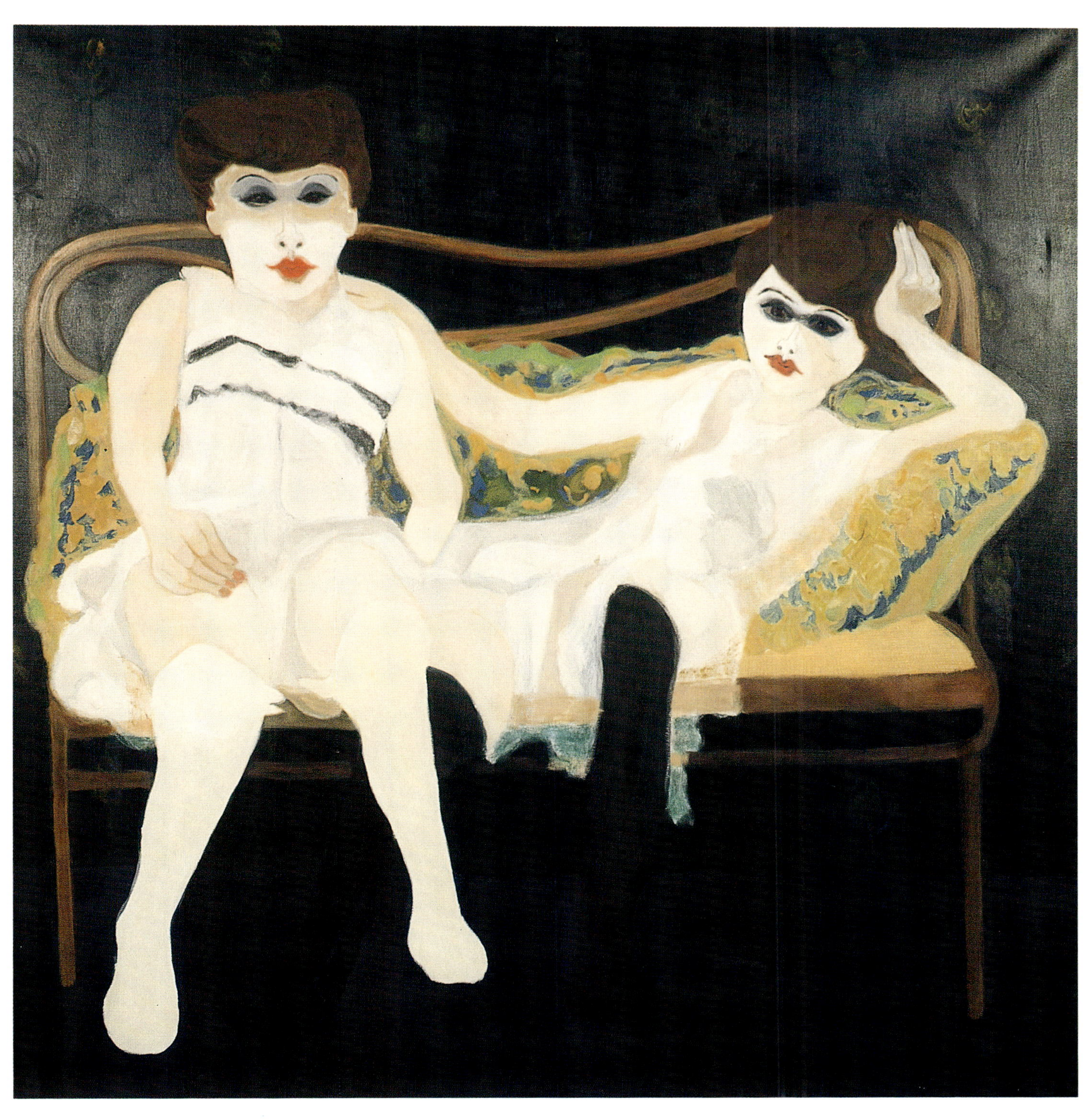

Dames au Salon, 1973, oil on canvas, 152x152cm, Private Collection, Munich

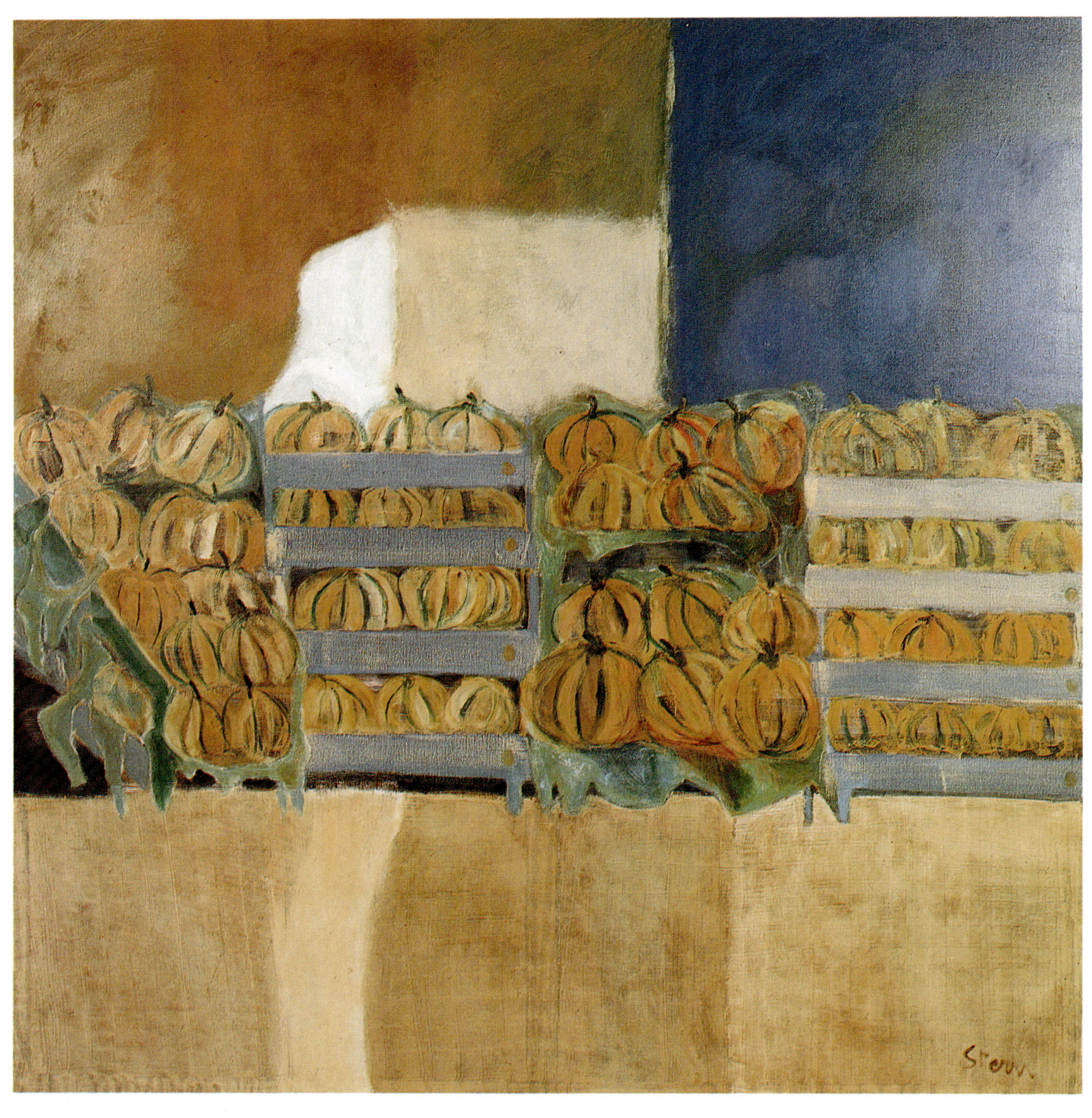

Melon Crates, 1973, oil on canvas, 183x183cm, Sir Joseph Lockwood Collection, London

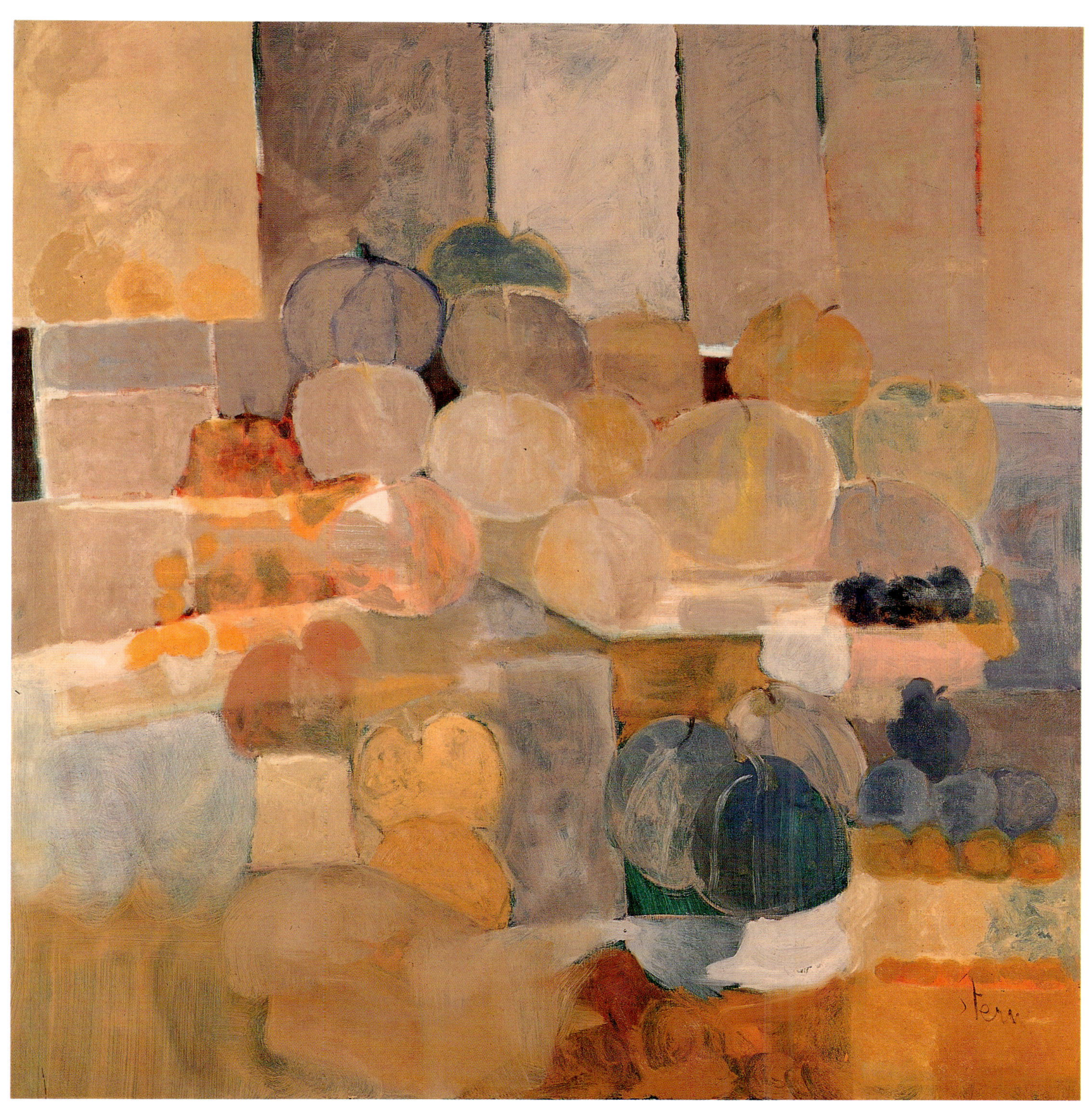

Still Life With Crates, 1973, oil on canvas, 152x152cm, Nicoline Pon Collection, Zurich

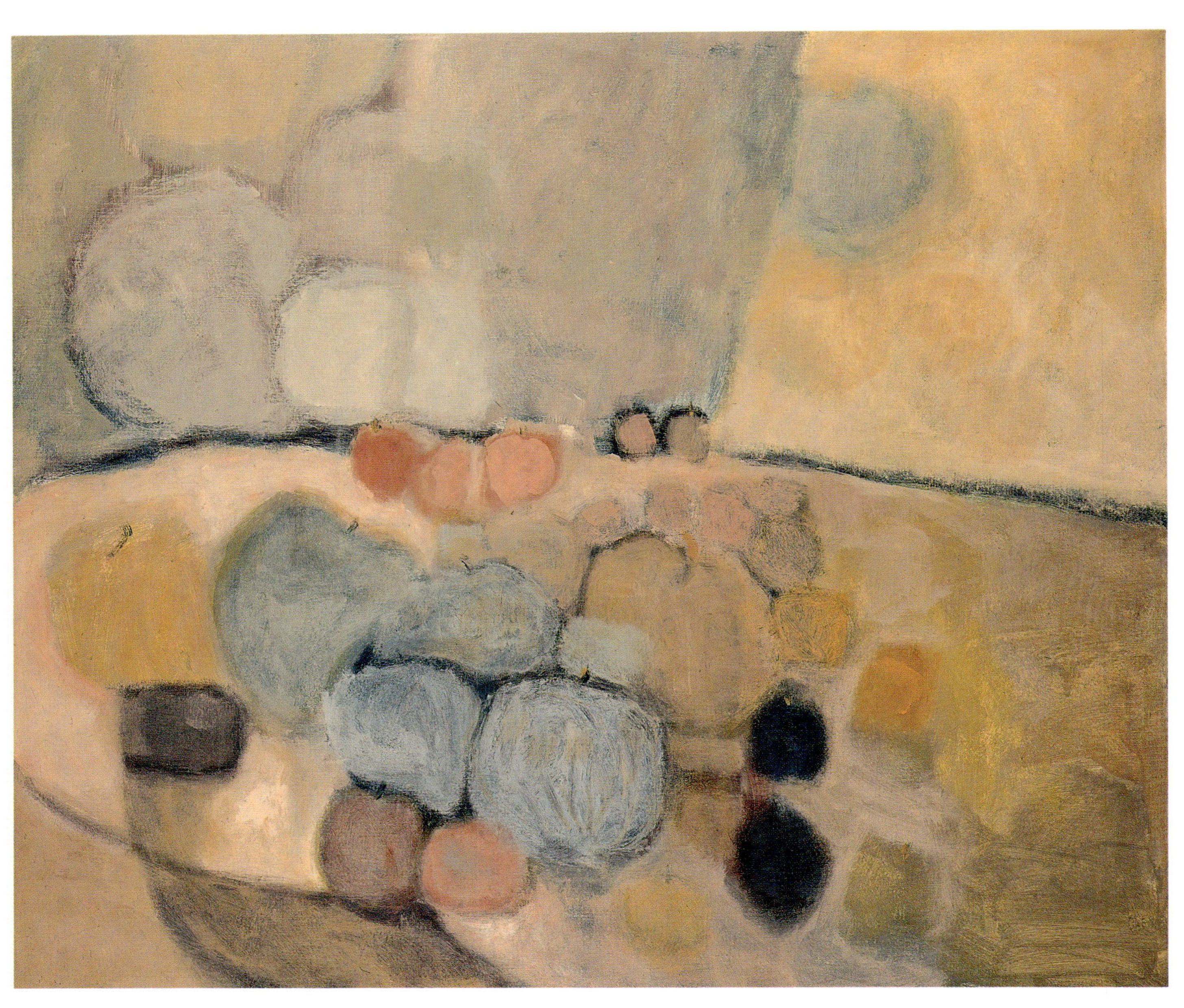

Paysage Fruité, 1973, oil on canvas, 64x76cm, H. Recanati Collection, Buenos Aires

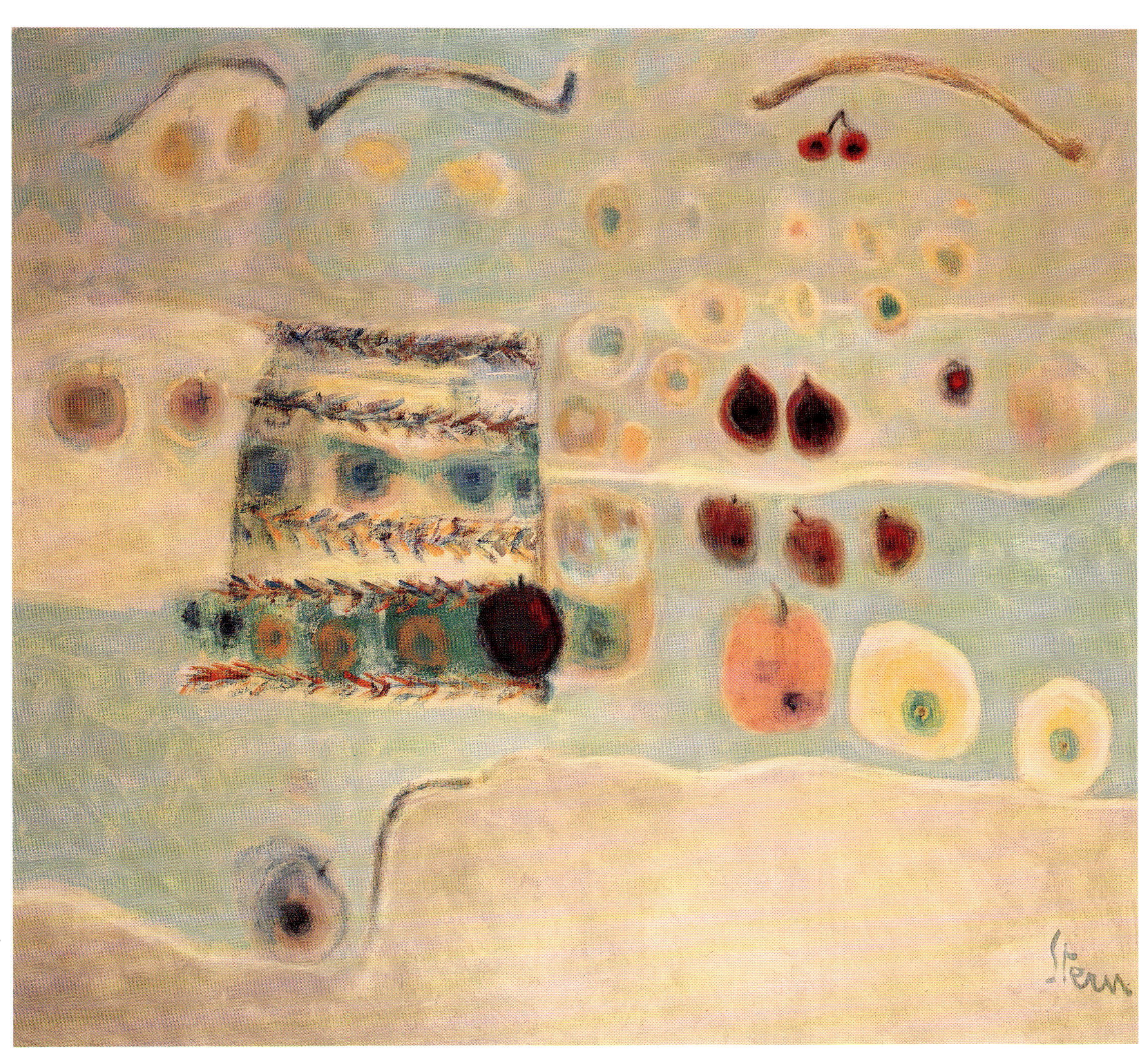

Festival, 1974, oil on canvas, 91x102cm, Petit Palais Collection, Geneva

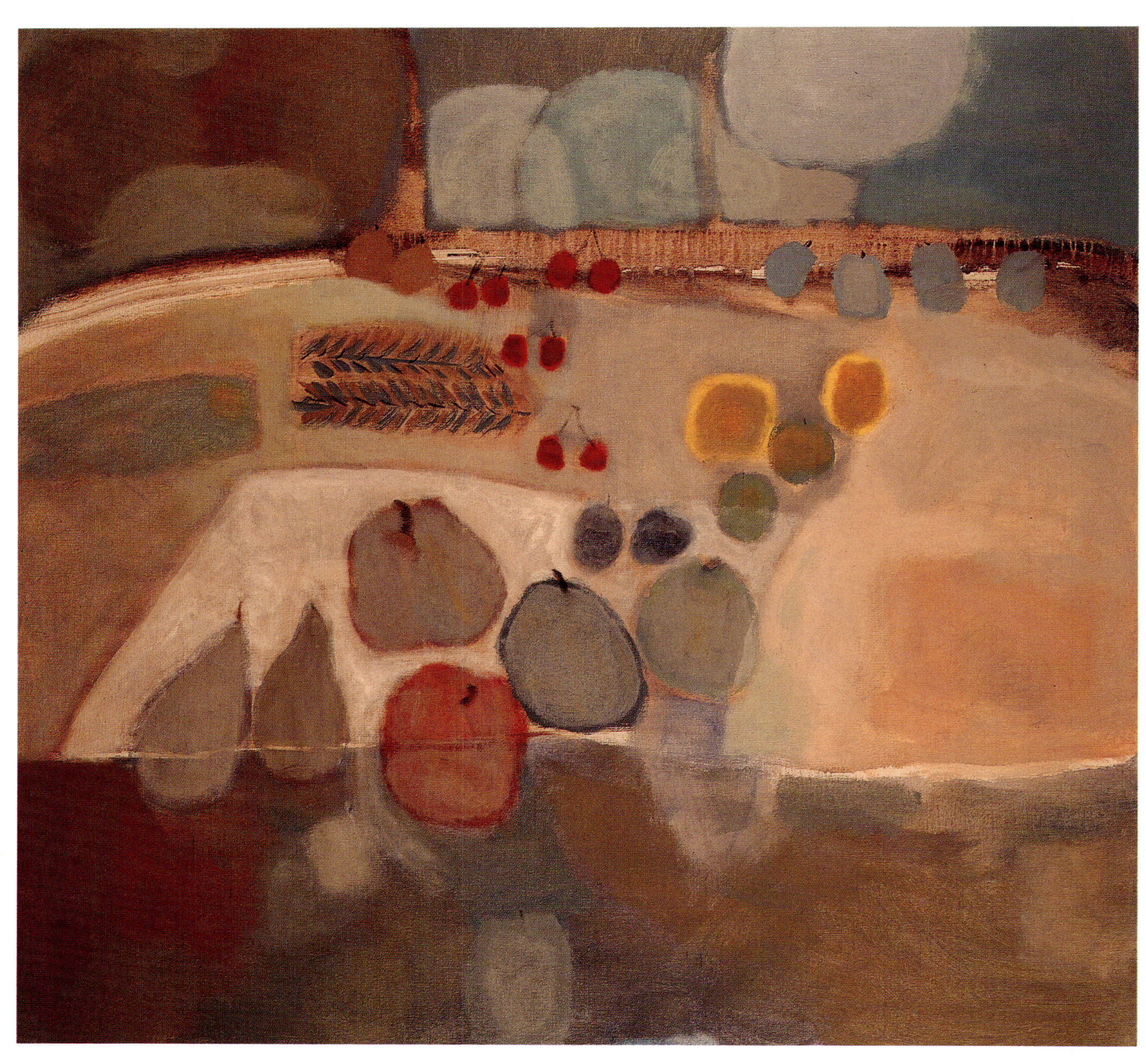

Country Walk, 1973, oil on canvas, 91x102cm, Makoto Iida Collection, Tokyo

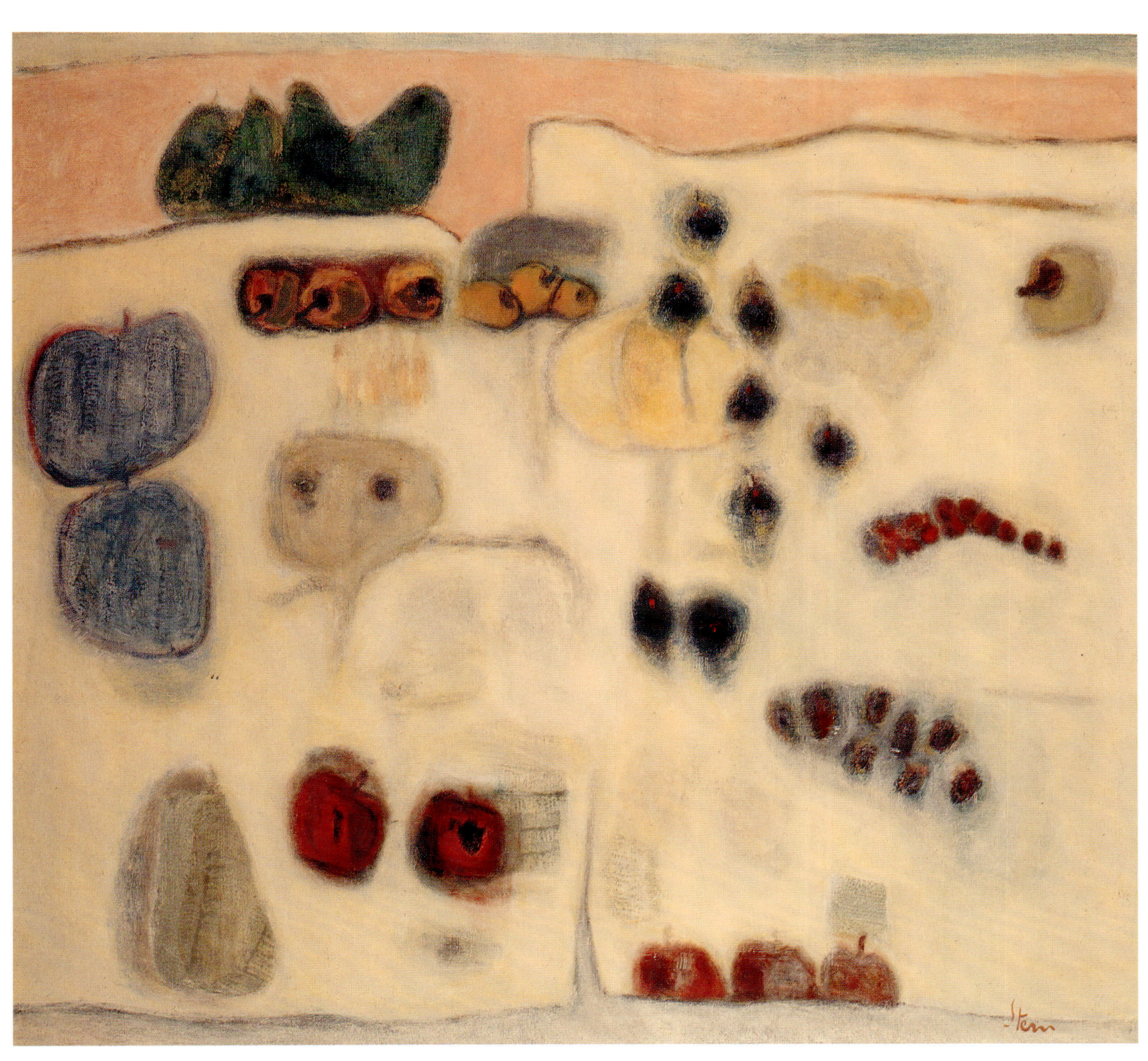

Fruit Lovers 1st Picnic, 1974, oil on canvas, 91×102cm, Mr. & Mrs. Cervellini Collection, Paris

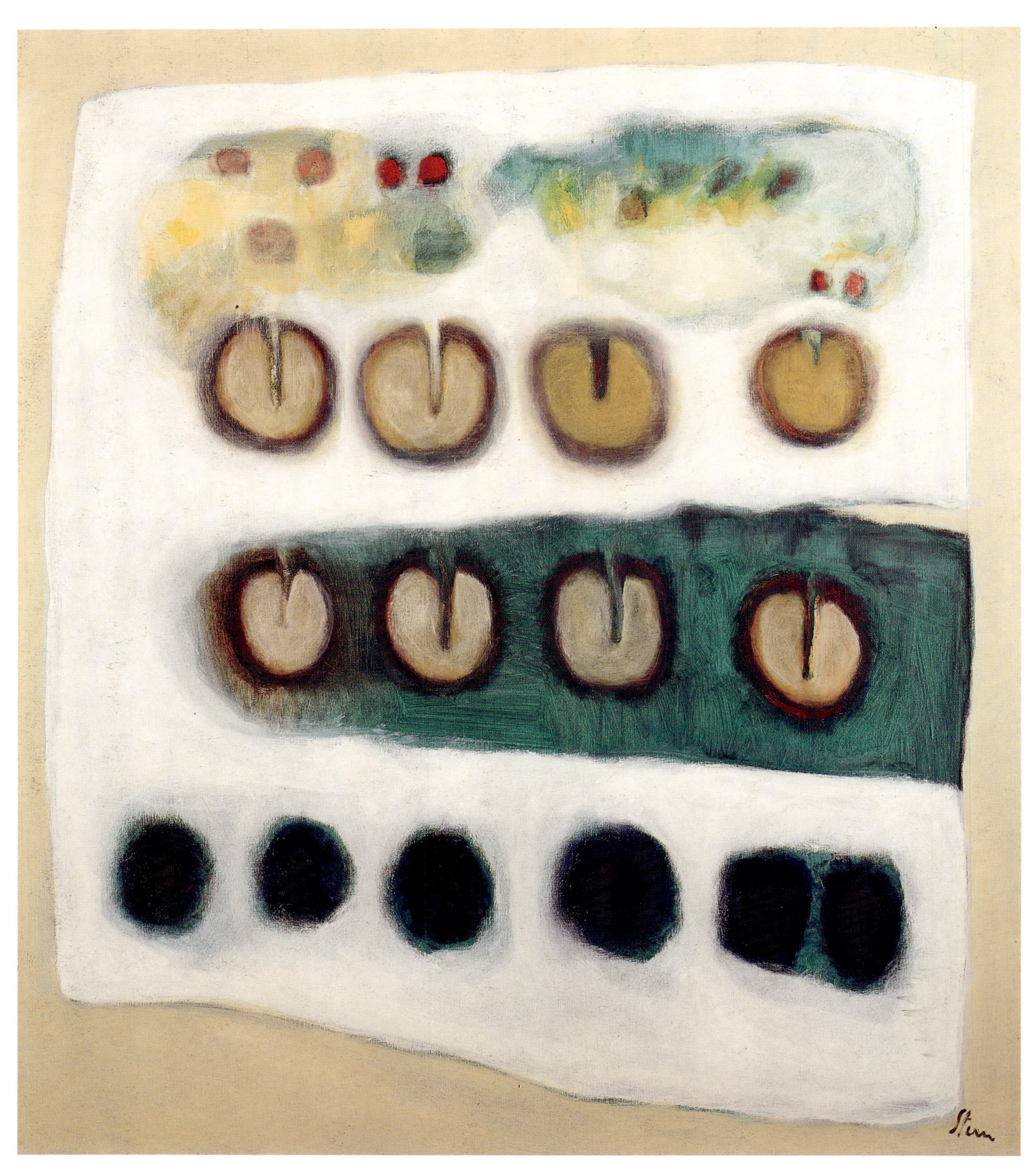

Drum Beat, 1974, oil on canvas, 102x91cm, Petit Palais Collection, Geneva

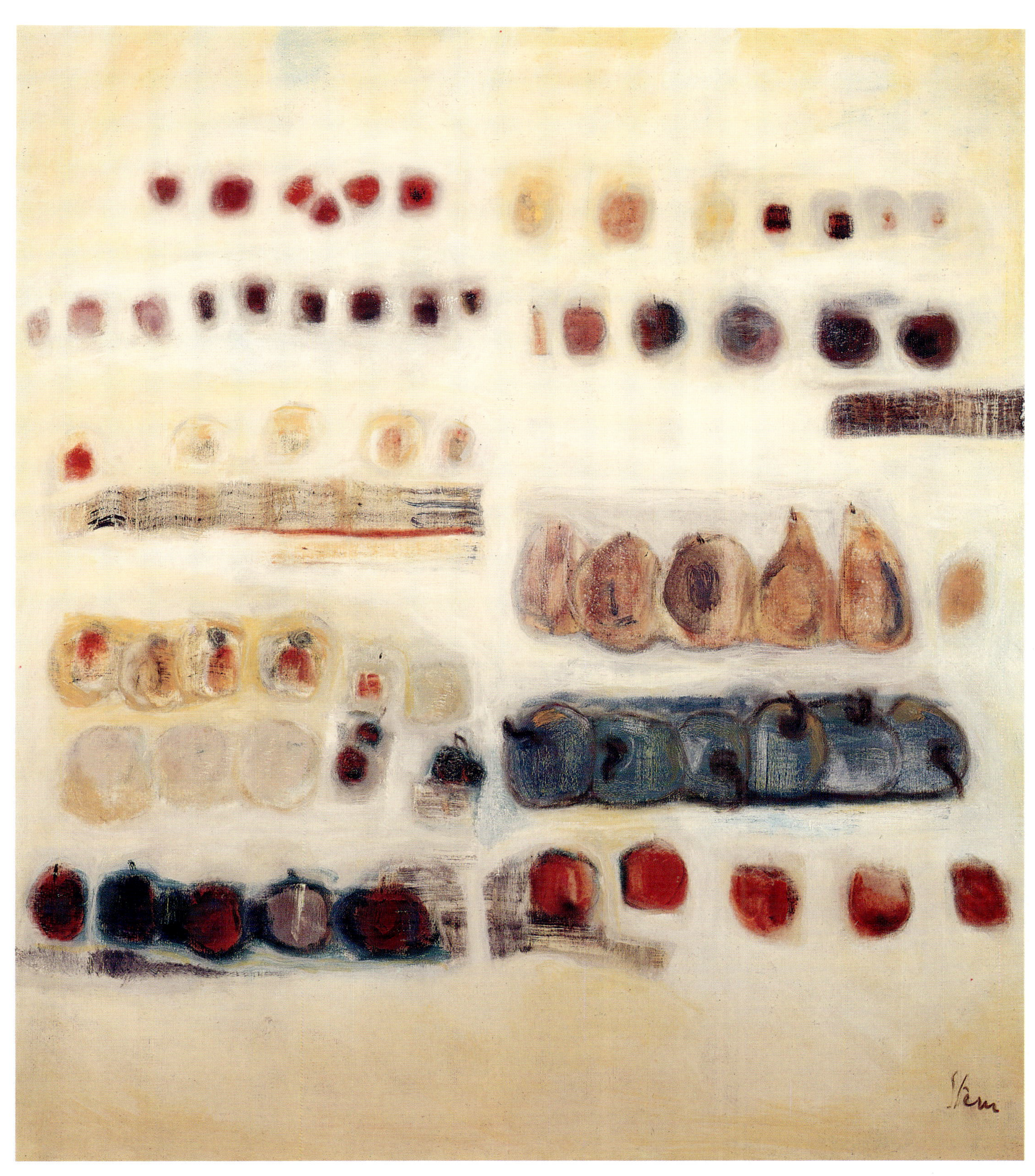

Adagic, 1974, oil on canvas, 102x91cm, Ashkenazy Collection, Los Angeles

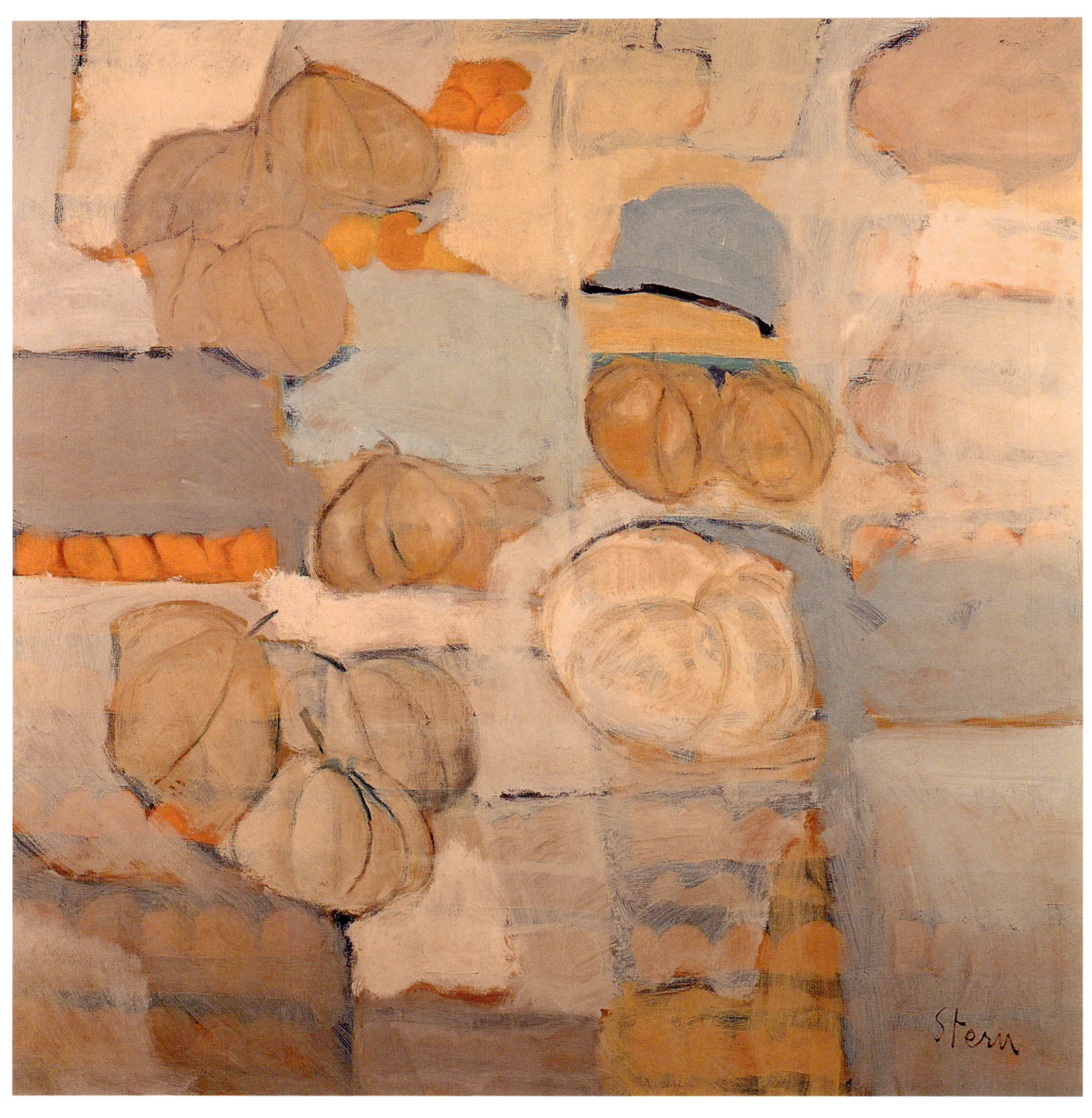

Crates, 1974, oil on canvas, 152x152cm, Artist's Collection

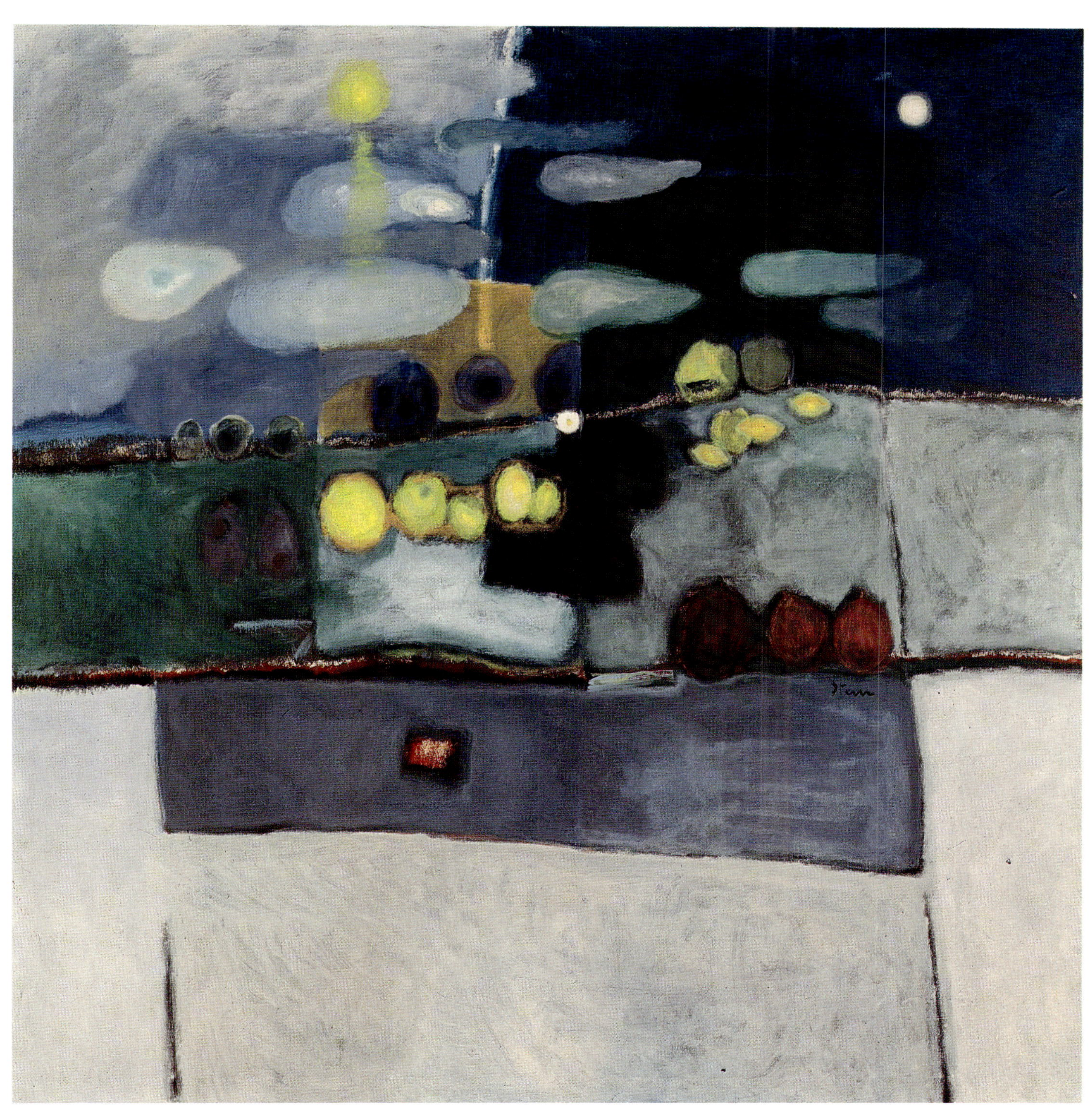

Day and Night, 1974, oil on canvas, 152x152cm, Mrs. Hedi Label Collection, Santa Cruz, California

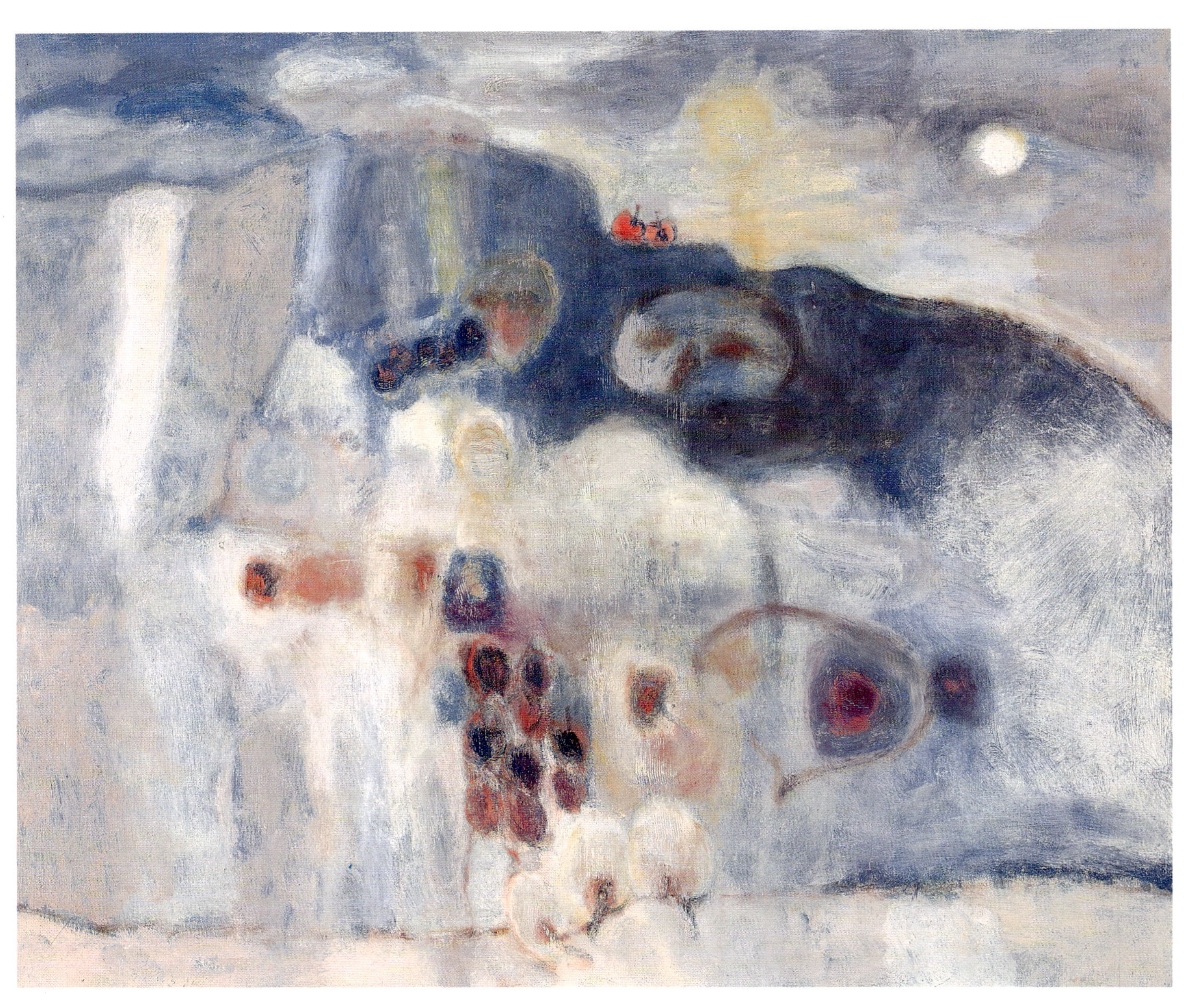

Wagnerian Poem, 1974, oil on canvas, 64x76cm, Manuel Solana Collection, Madrid

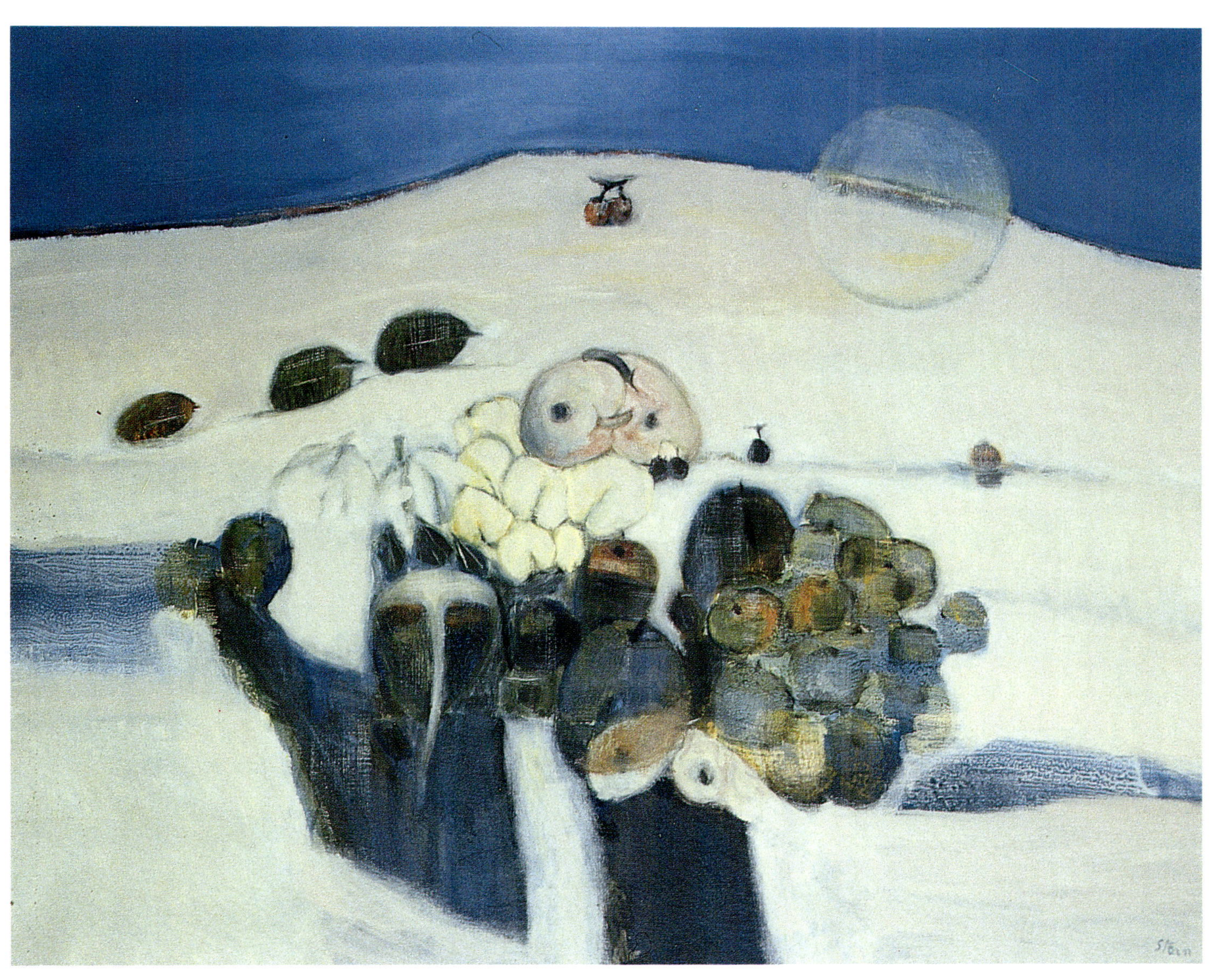

Noah's Ark Landing in Yucatan, 1974, oil on canvas, 91x122cm, Musée d'Art Moderne Collection, Ostend

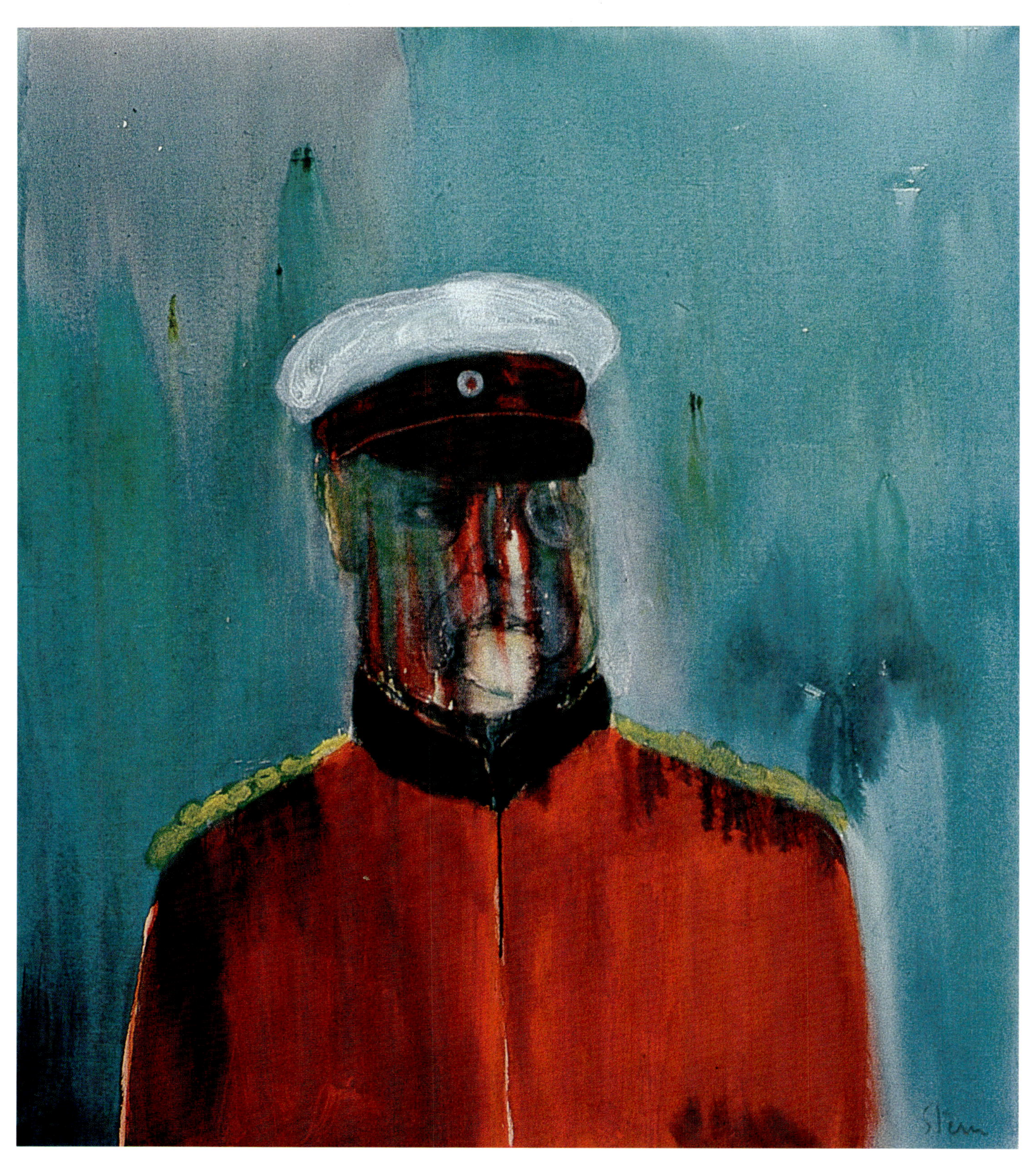

Le Conquérant, 1975, acrylic on canvas, 102x91cm, Ashkenazy Collection, Los Angeles

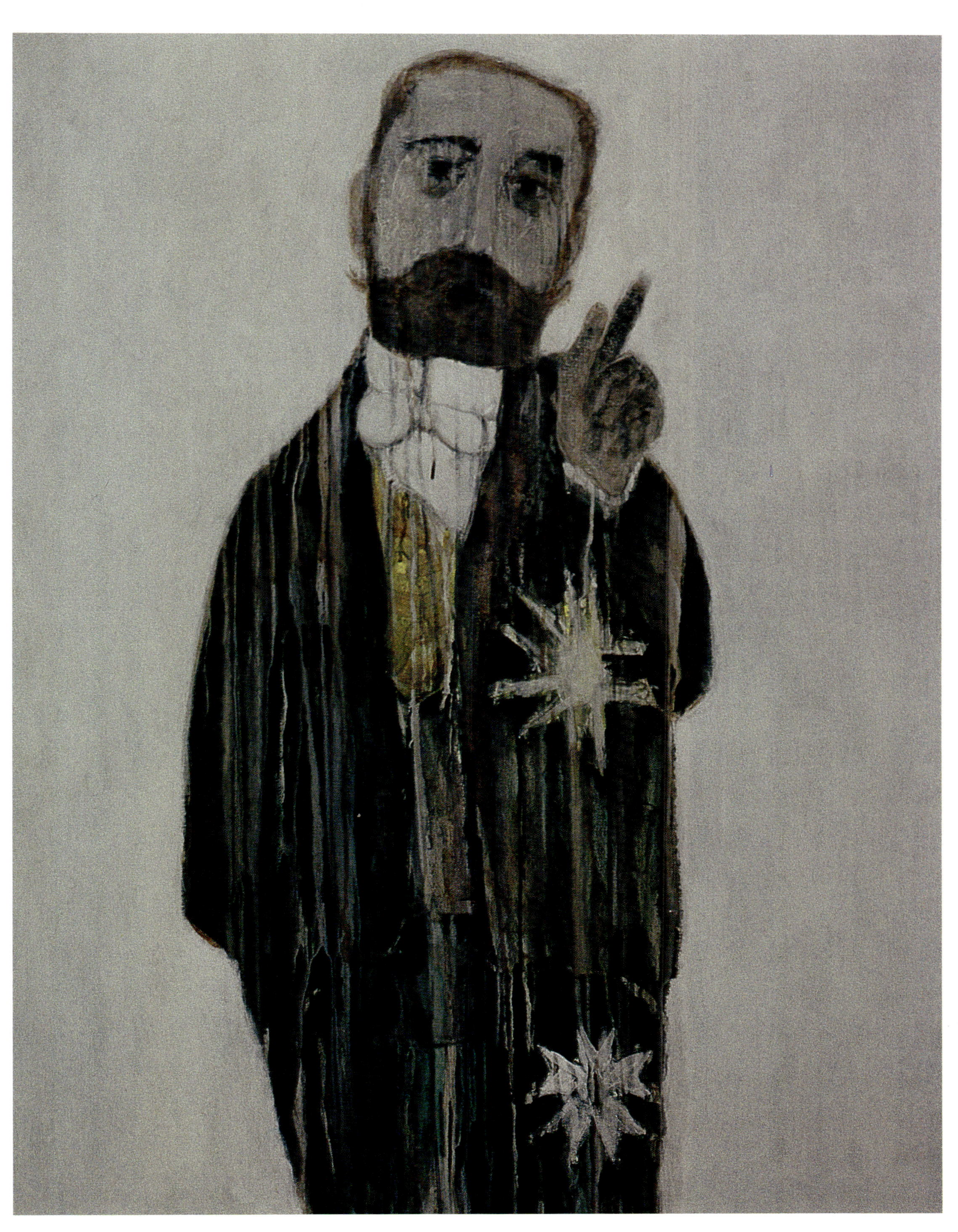

Les Promesses du Député, 1975, oil on canvas, 122x97cm, Private Collection, Reims

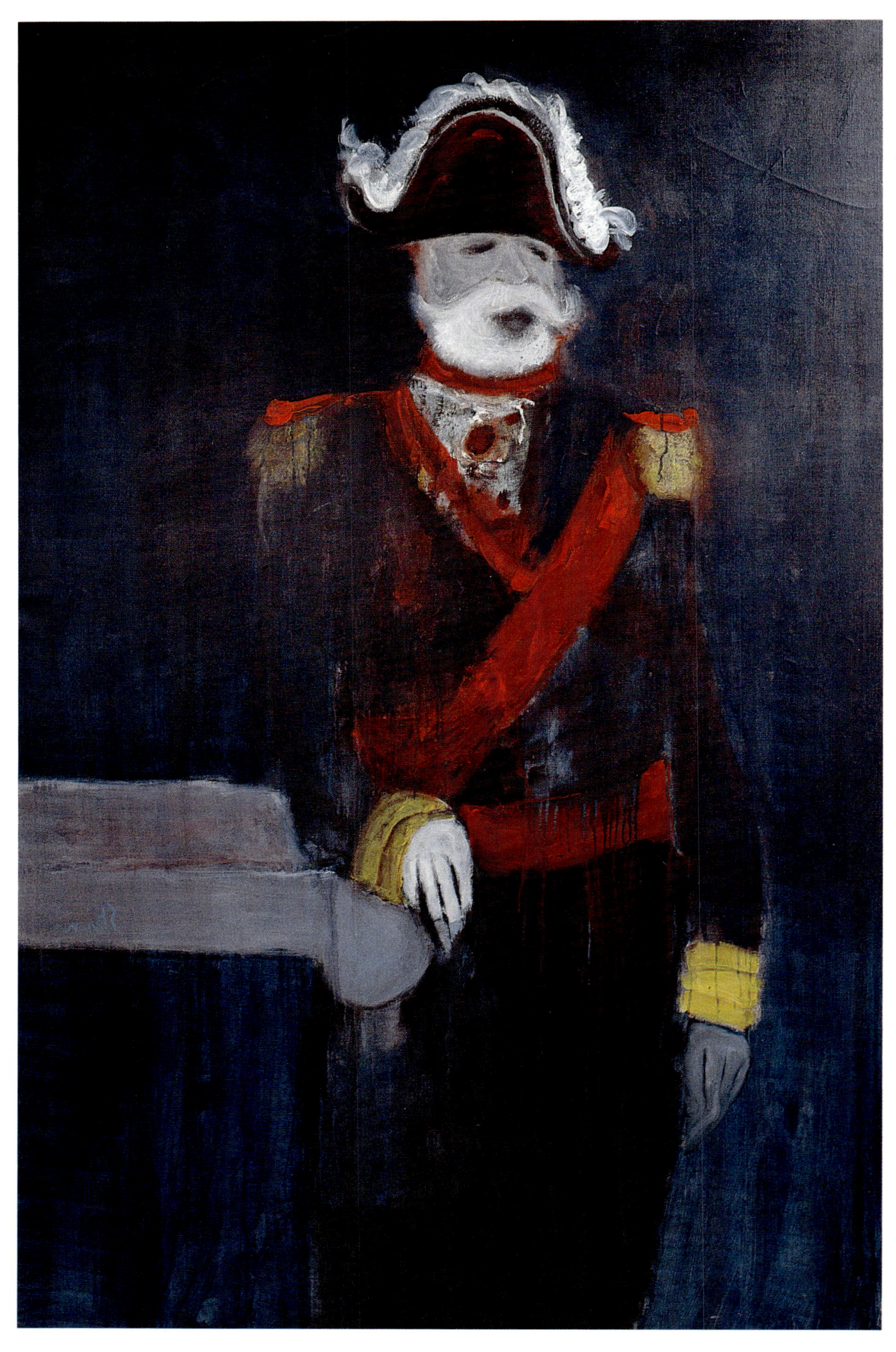

Le Général, 1975, oil on canvas, 183x122cm, Mrs. Hedi Label Collection, Santa Cruz, California

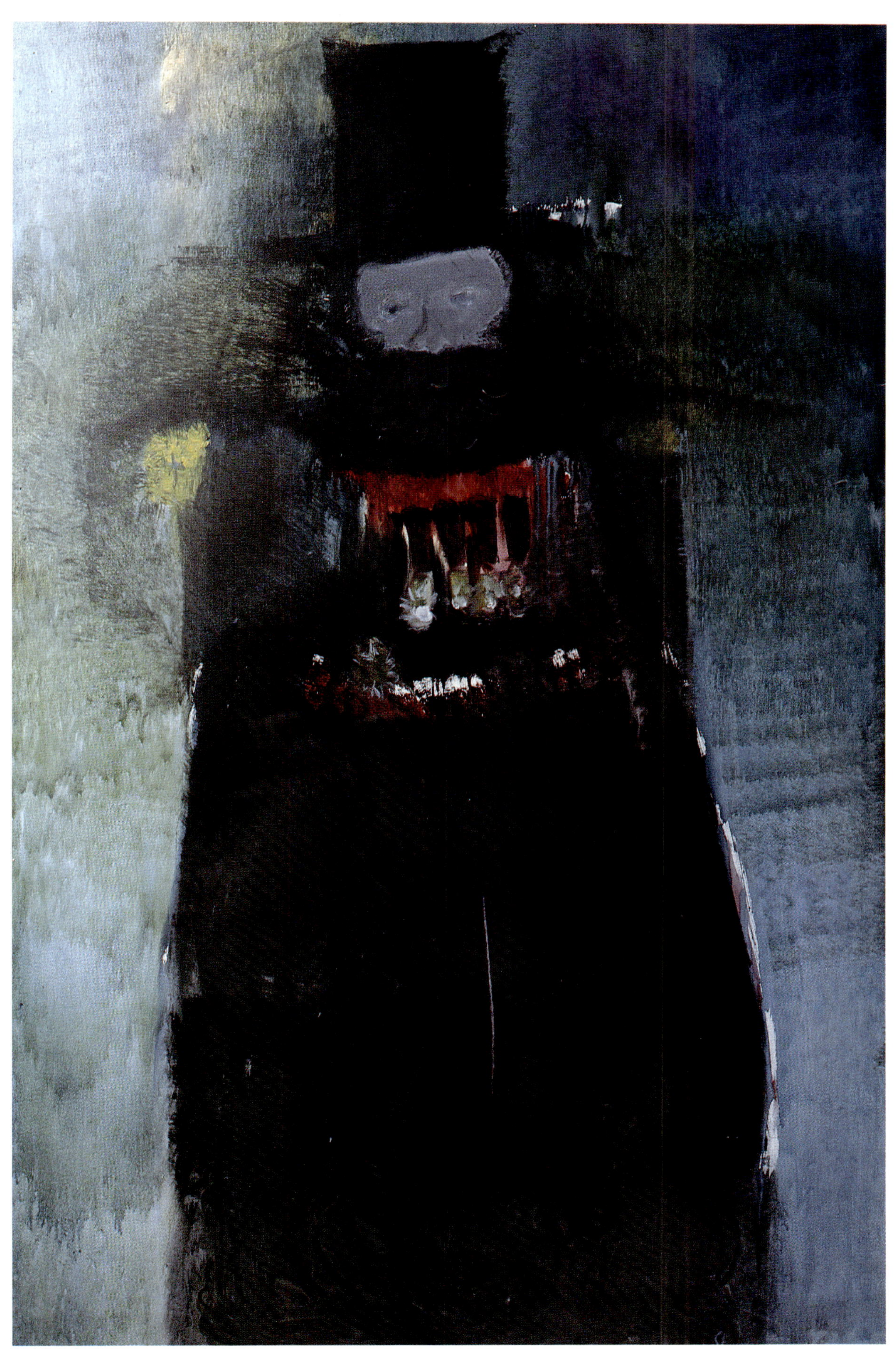

L'Anarchiste Arrivé, 1975, oil on canvas, 183x122cm, Mrs. Hedi Label Collection, Santa Cruz, California

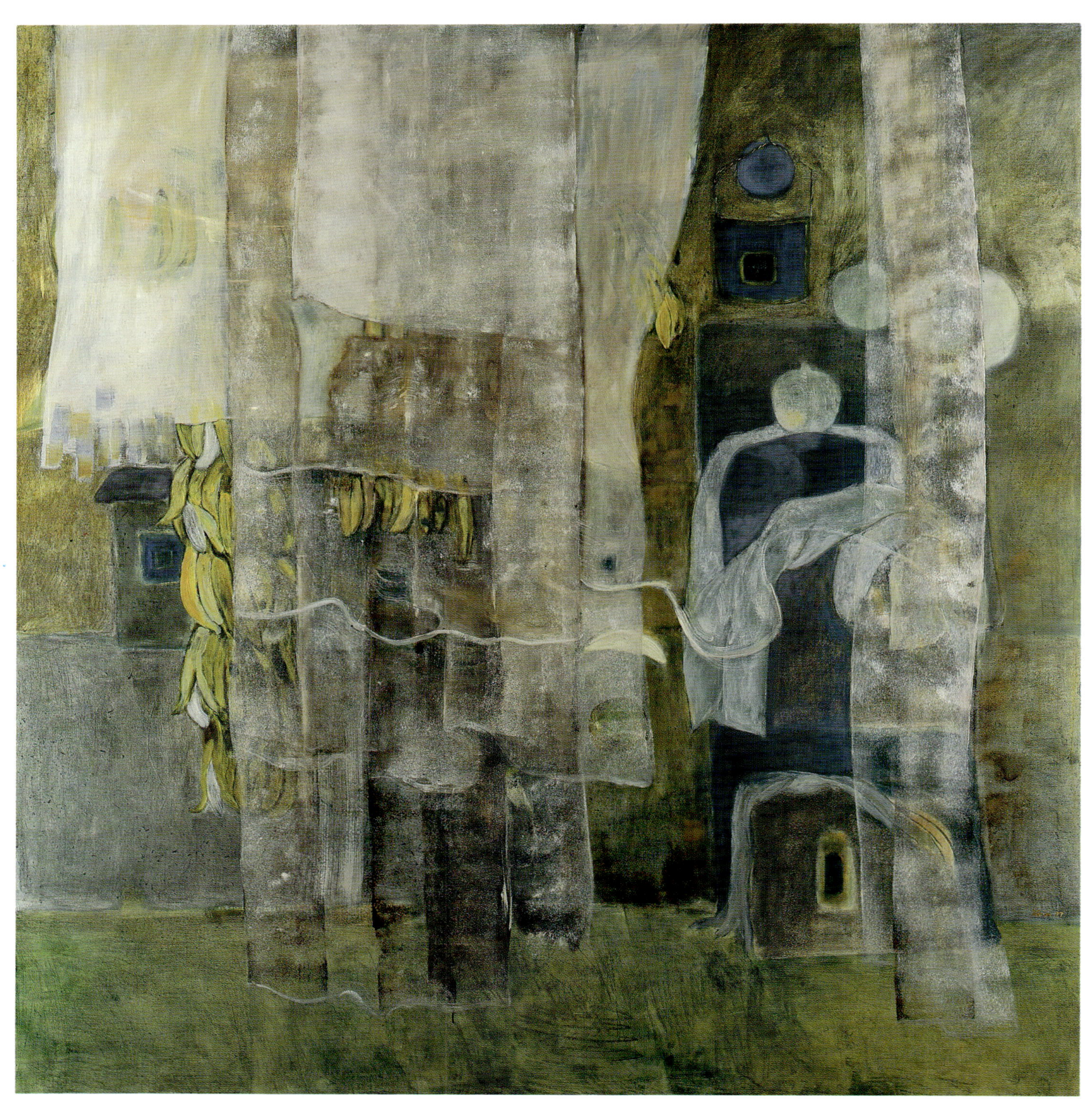

Bananas in Yucatan, 1976, oil on canvas, 183x183cm, Mrs. Hedi Label Collection, Santa Cruz, California

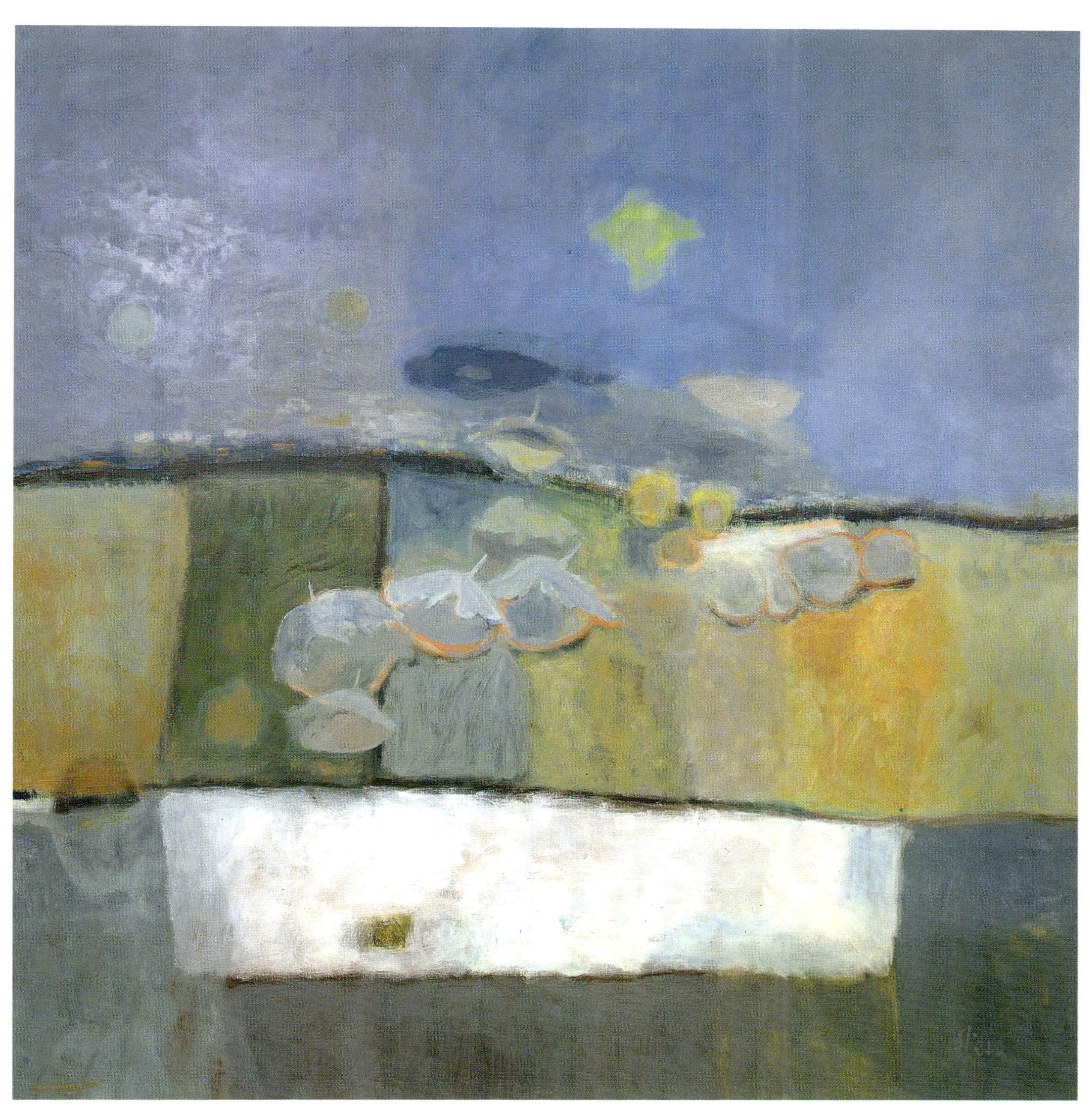

Summer, 1976, oil on canvas, 152×152cm, Mrs. Hedi Label Collection, Santa Cruz, California

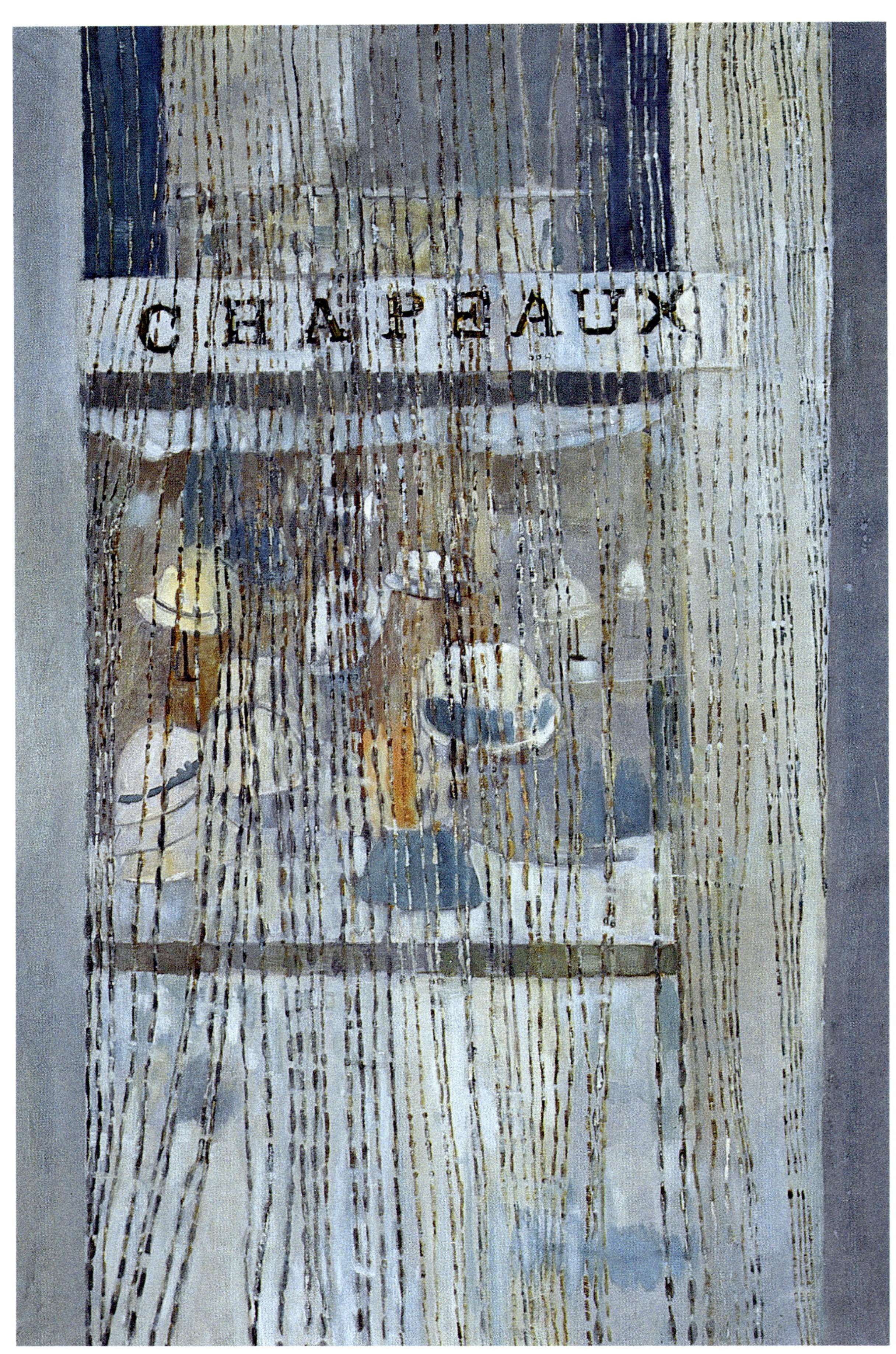

Hat Shop, 1976, oil on canvas, 150x100cm, Private Collection, Paris

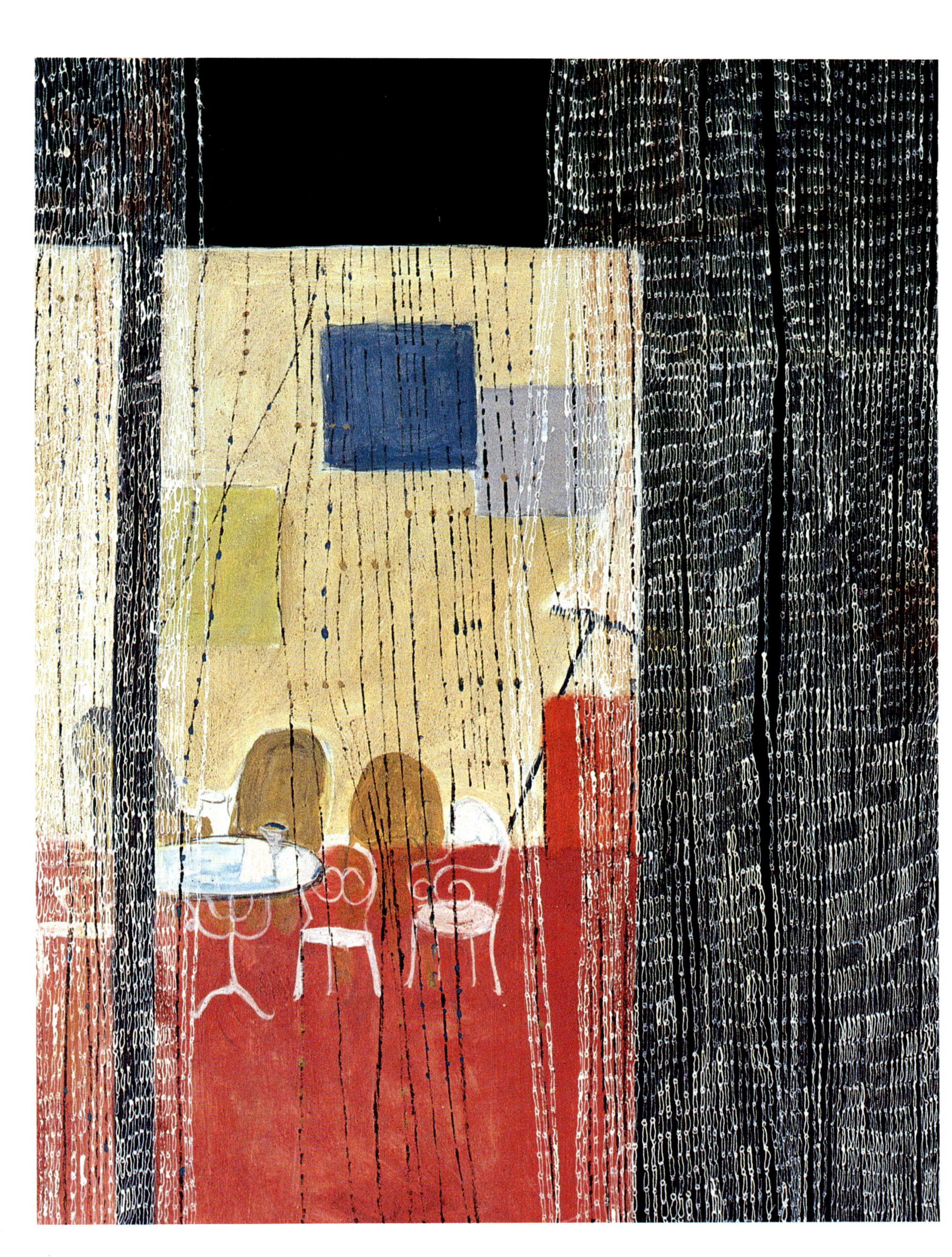

Le Calme de la Bourgeoisie, 1976, oil on canvas, 90x77cm, Private Collection, Basel

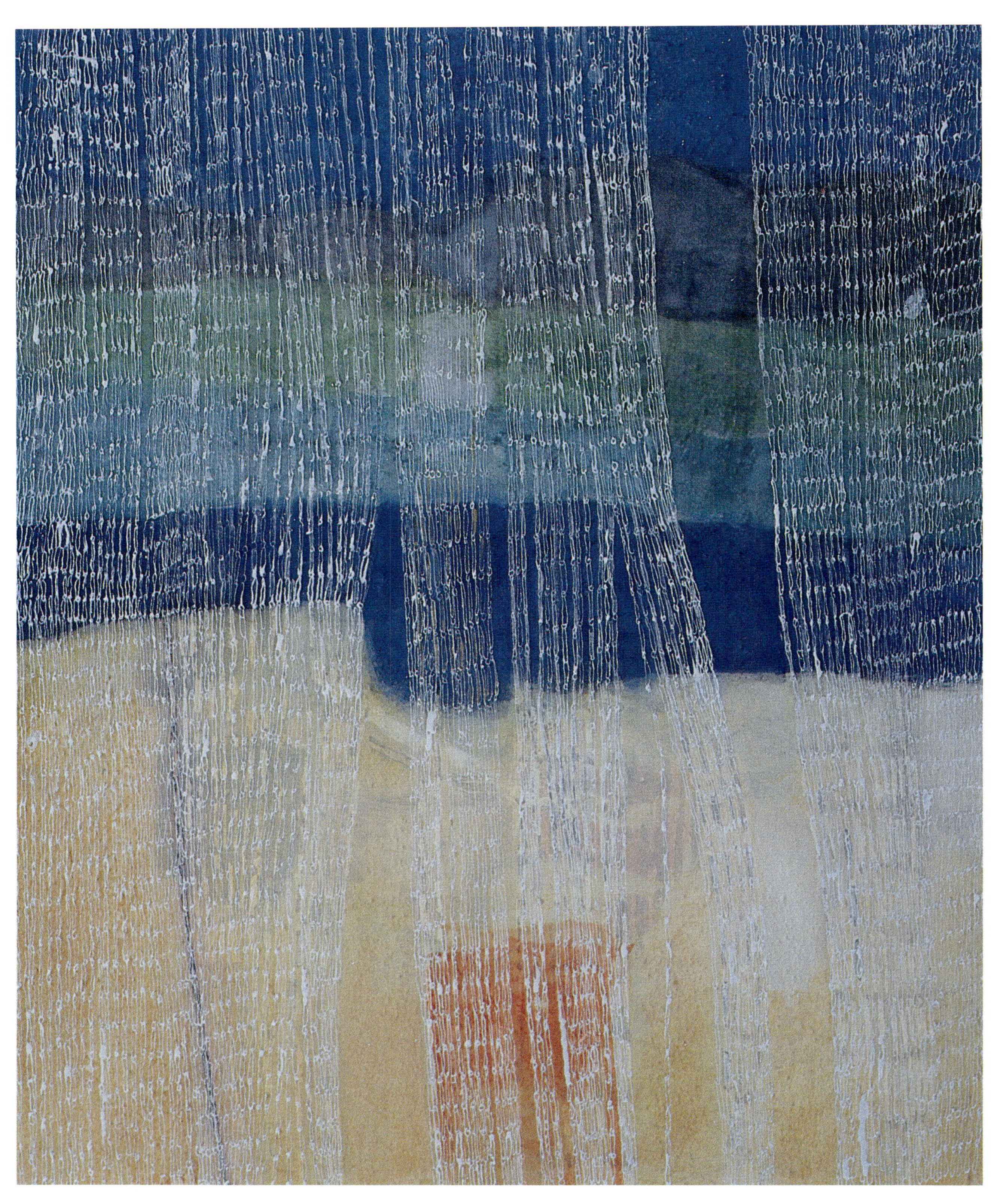

Curtain on a View, 1975, oil on canvas, 72×60cm

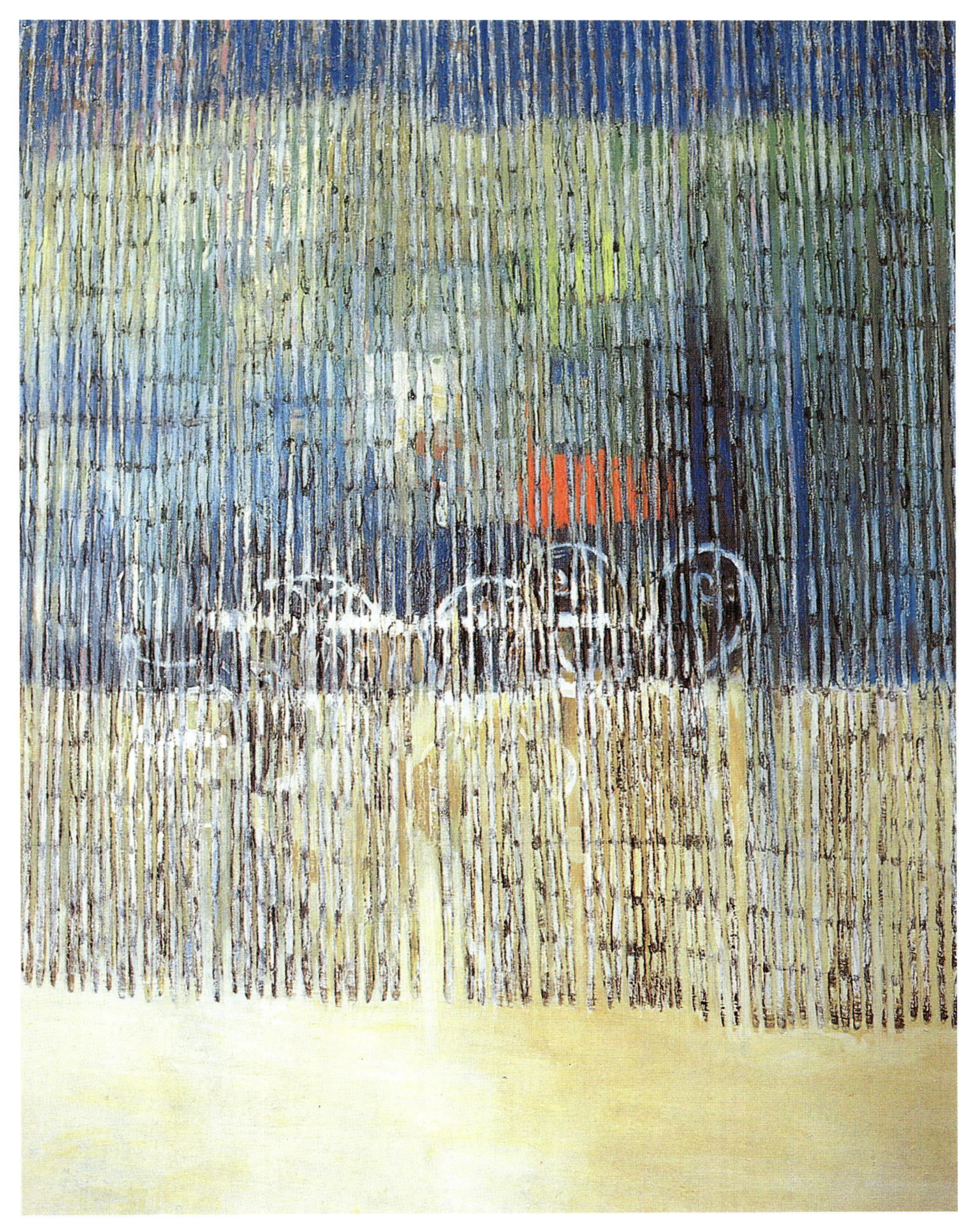

Les Rideaux, 1978, oil on canvas, 92x73cm

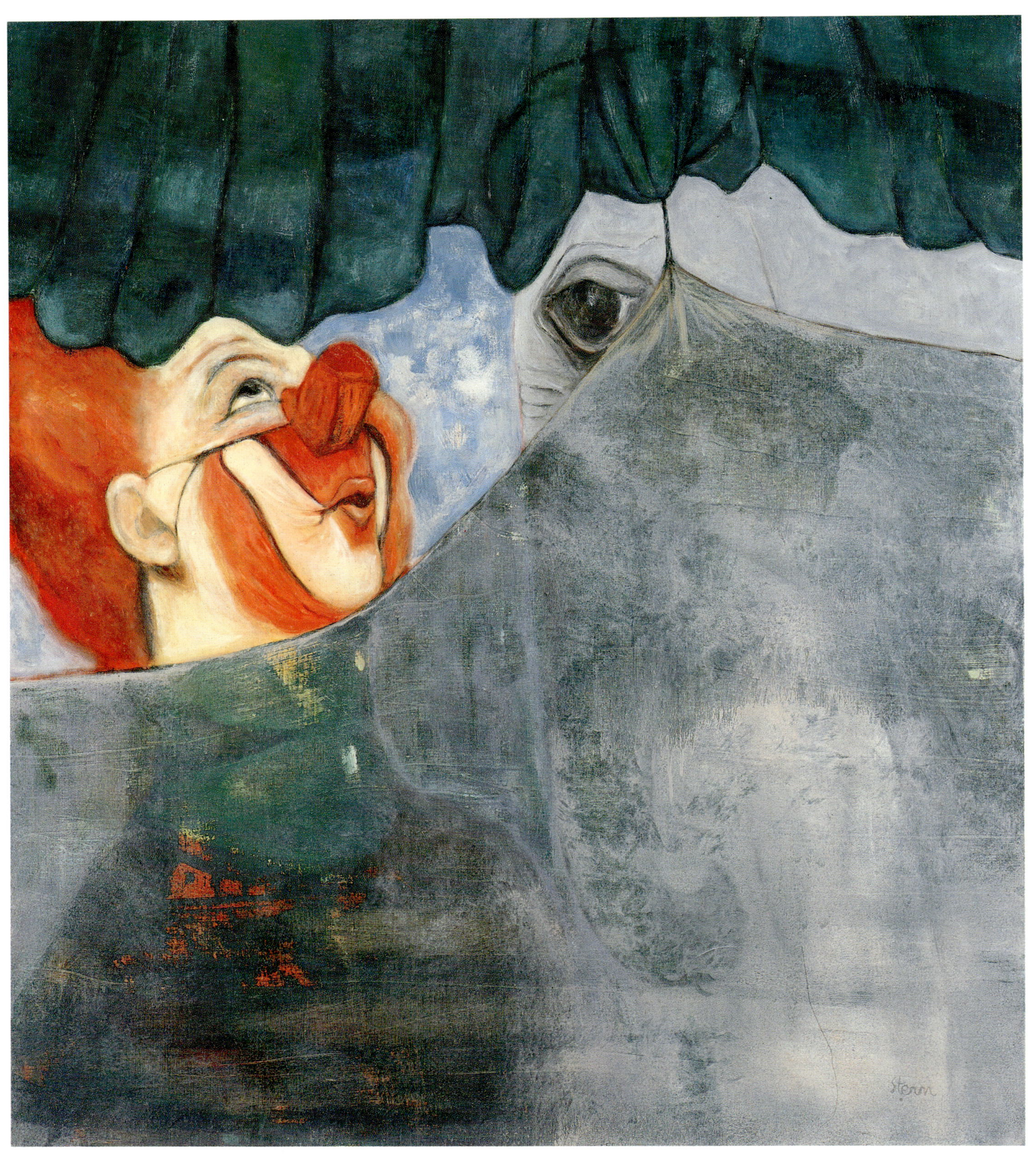

Colleagues, 1977, oil on canvas, 102x92cm, Giulio Castelli Collection, Milan

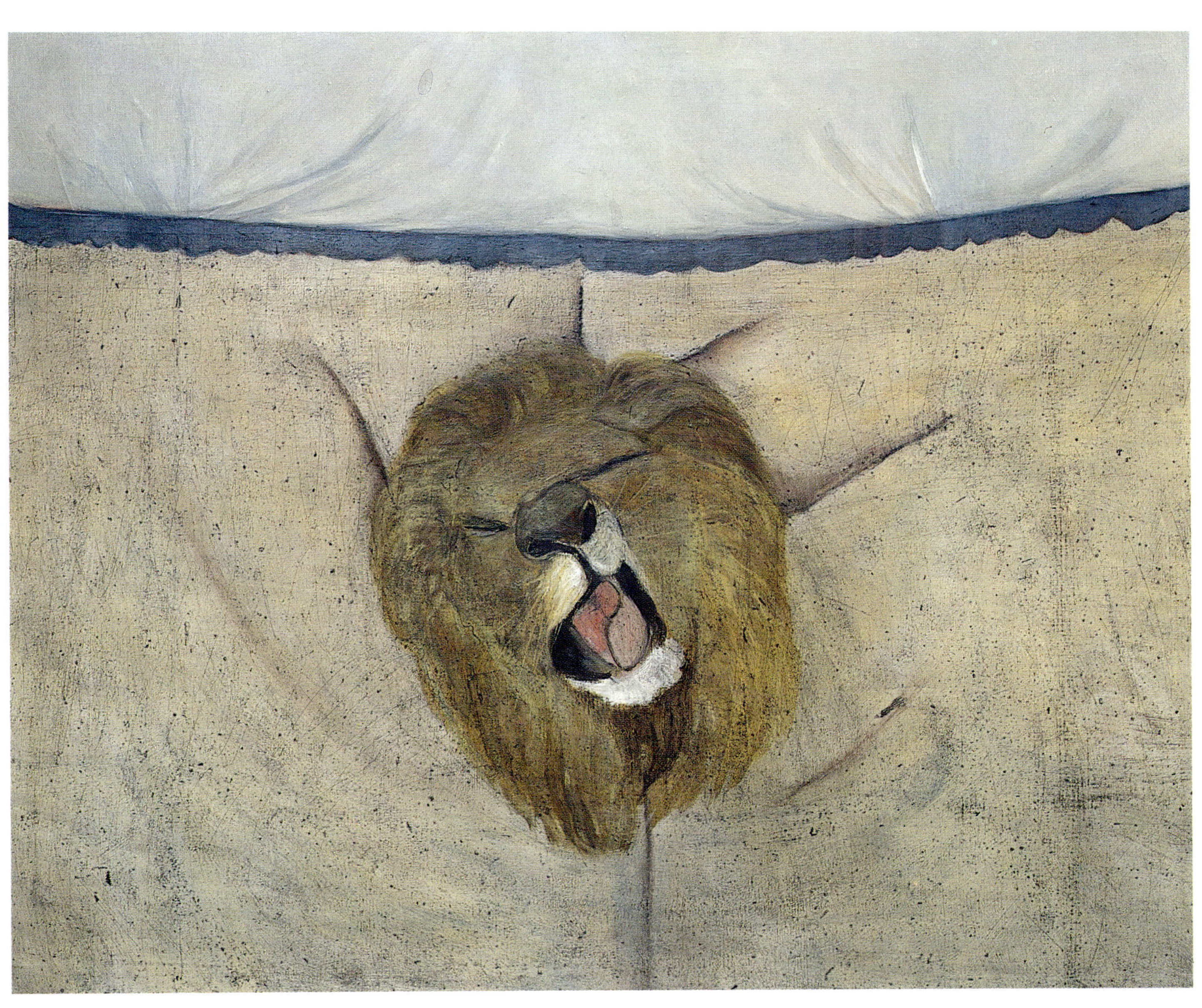

Side Show, 1977, oil on canvas, 96x21cm, Della Turca Collection, Paris

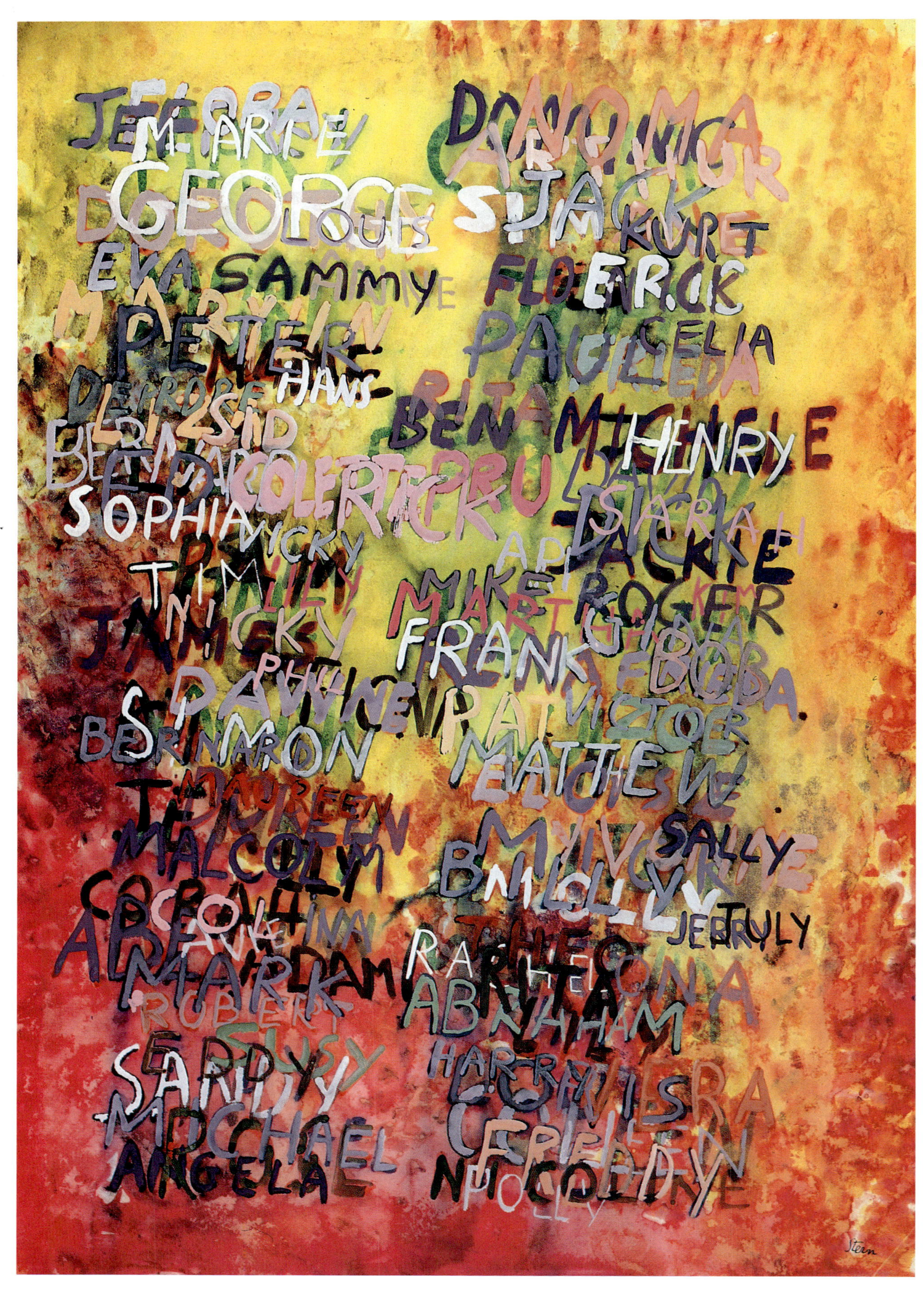

Changing Partners, 1978, mixed media on paper, 80x57cm, Artist's Collection

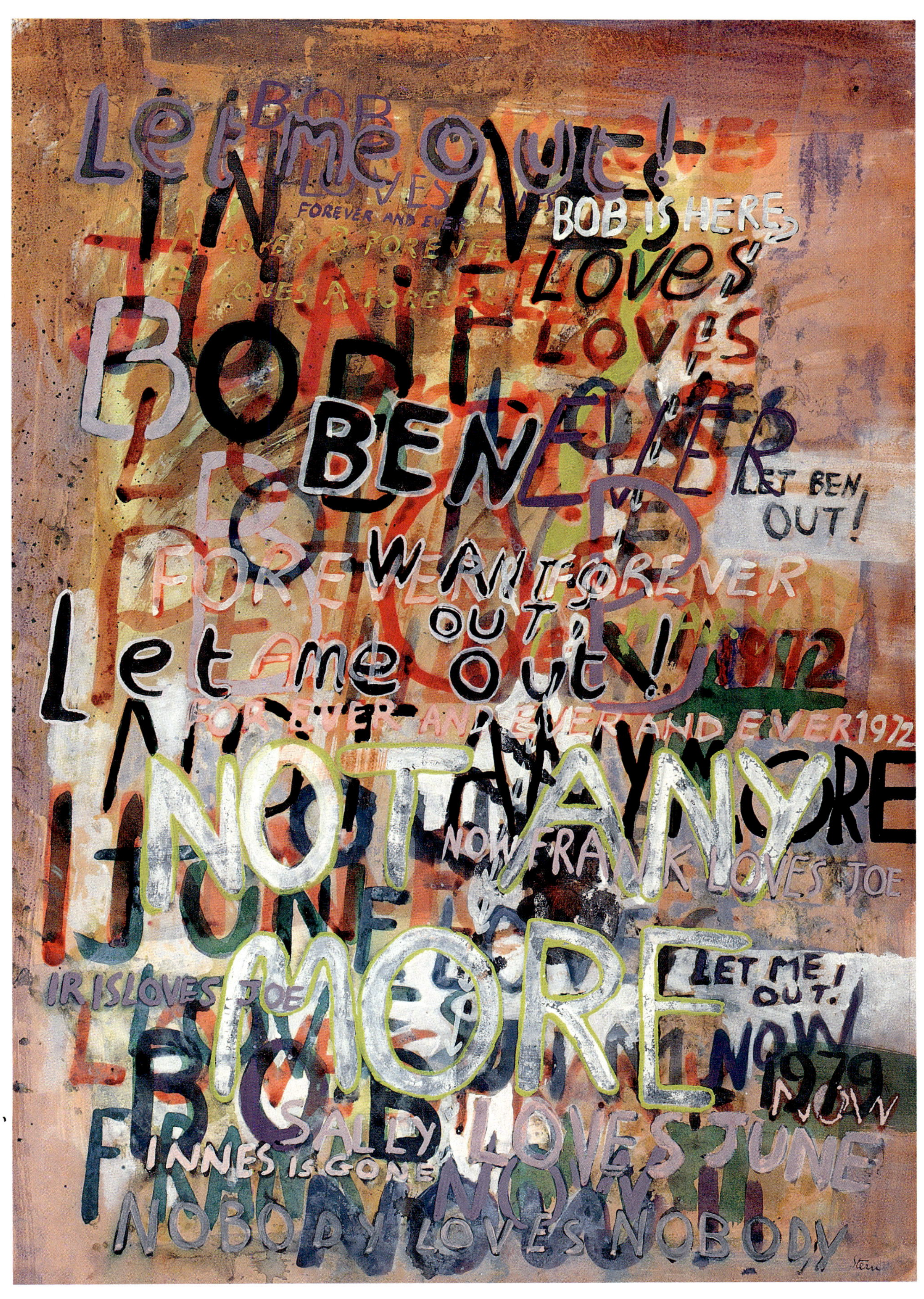

Not Any More, 1978, mixed media on paper, 80x57cm, Artist's Collection

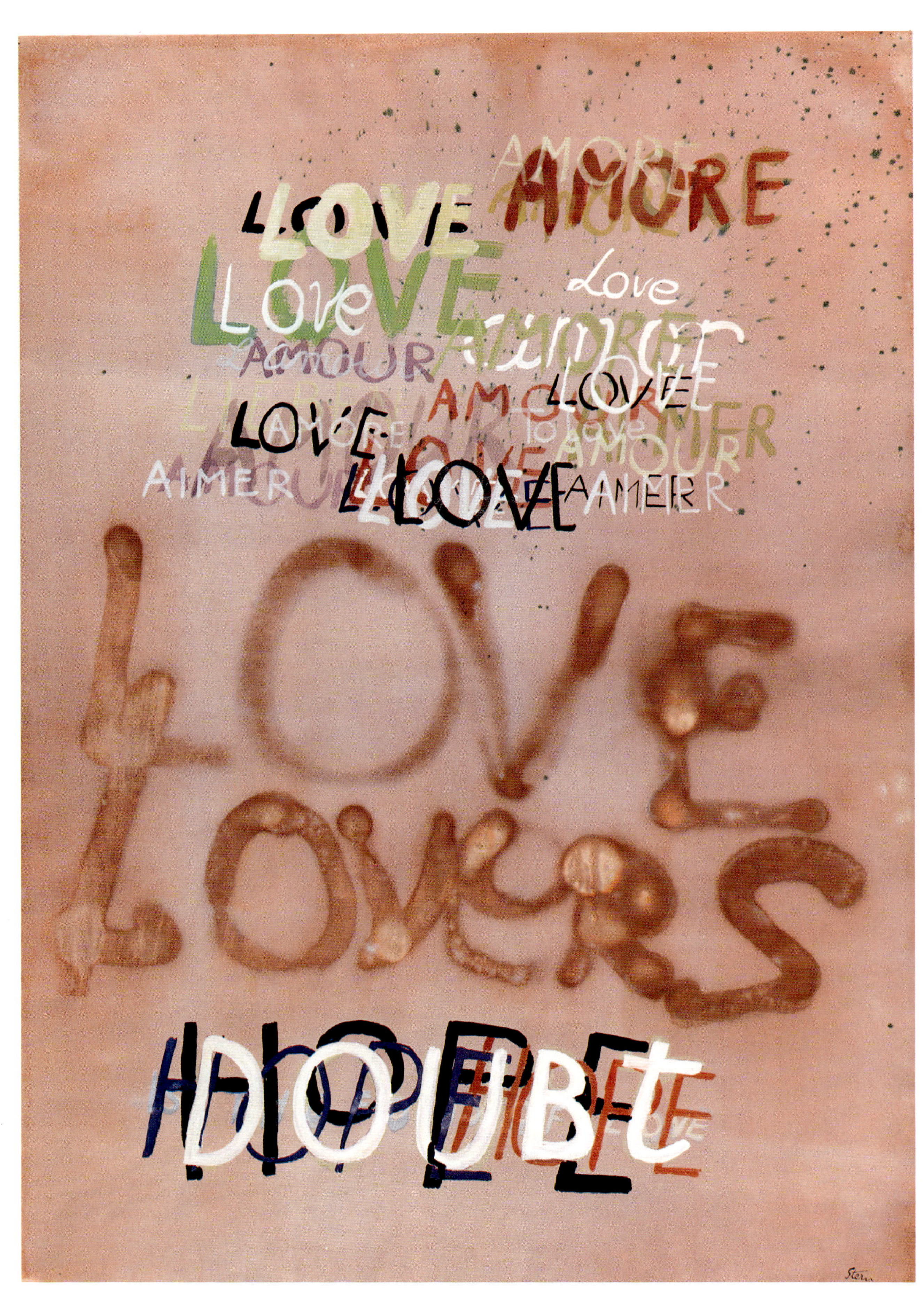

Love Story, 1978, mixed media on paper, 60x45cm, Artist's Collection

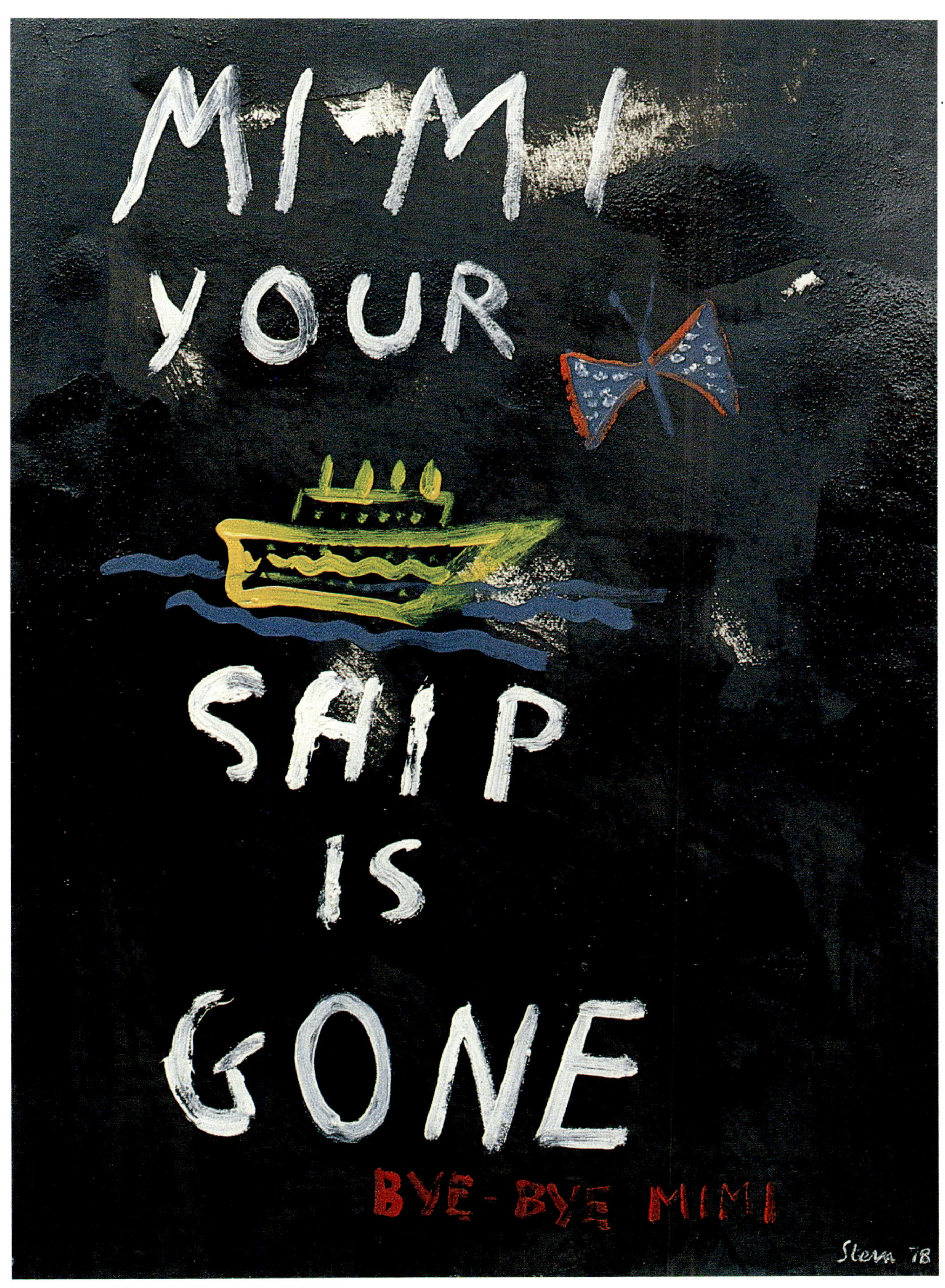

Mimi, Your Ship is Gone, 1978, mixed media on paper, 80x57cm, Artist's Collection

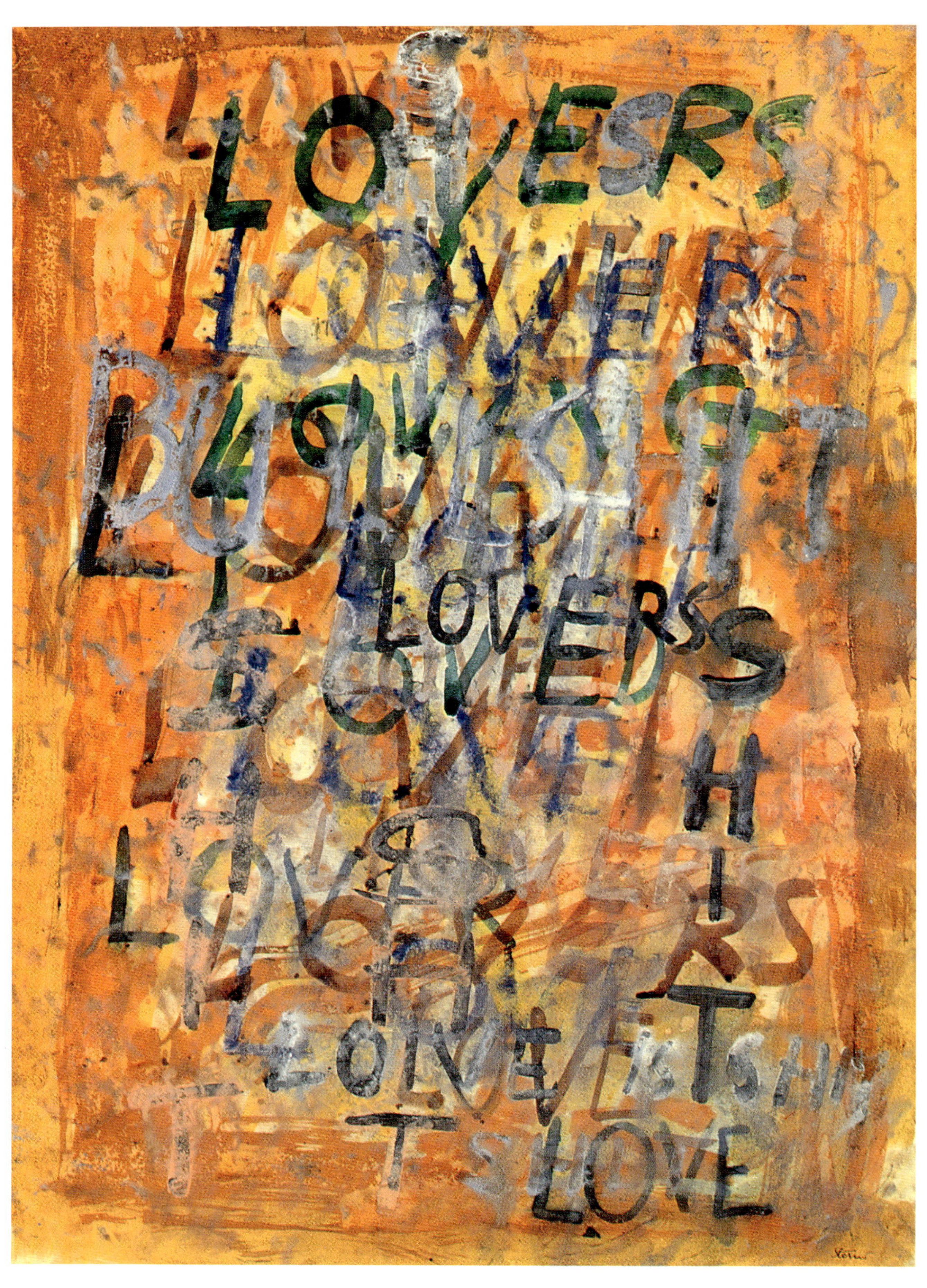

Love, 1978, mixed media on paper, 79x58cm, Artist's Collection

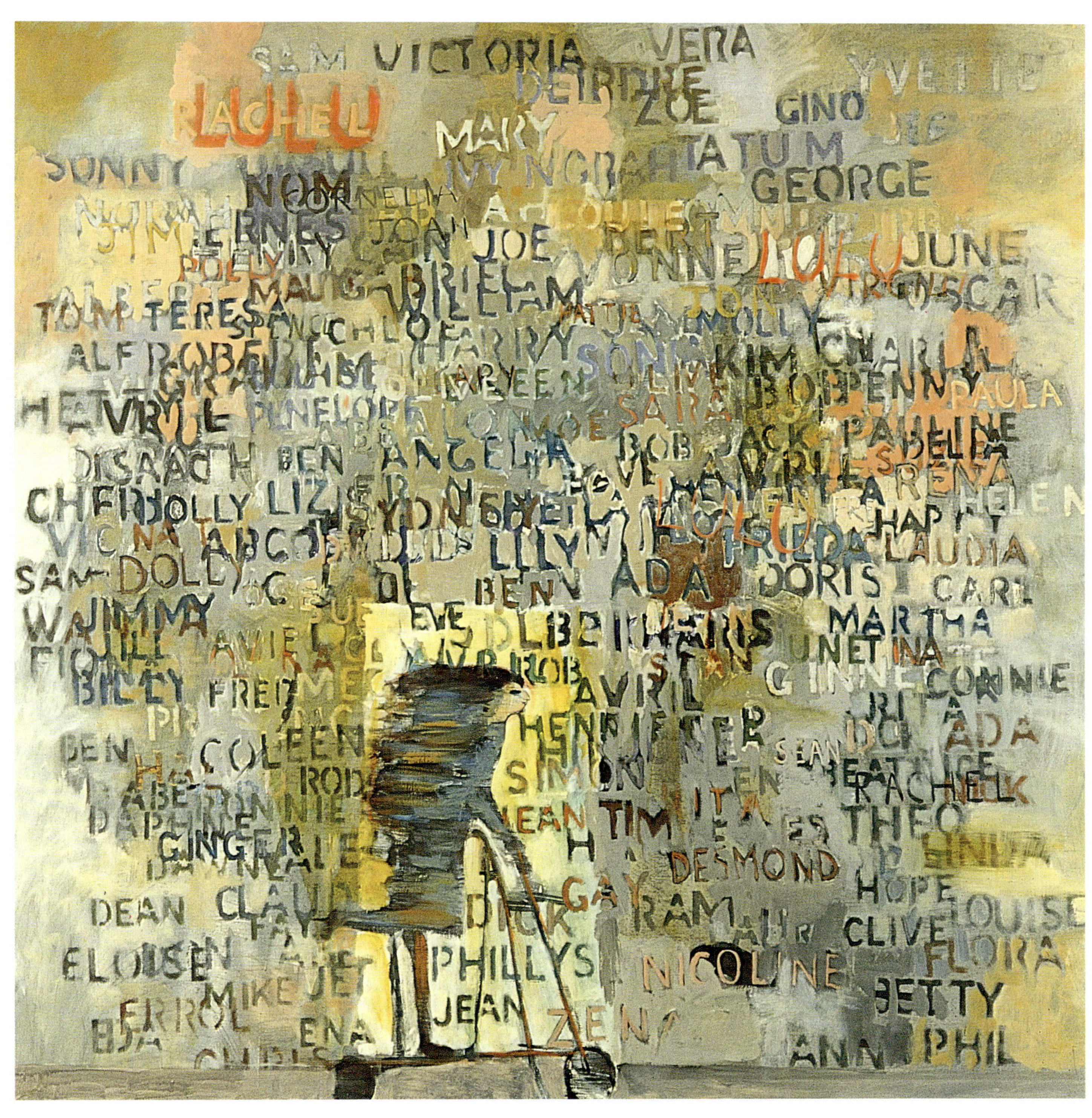

Self Portraits, 1978, oil on canvas, 152x152cm, Artist's Collection

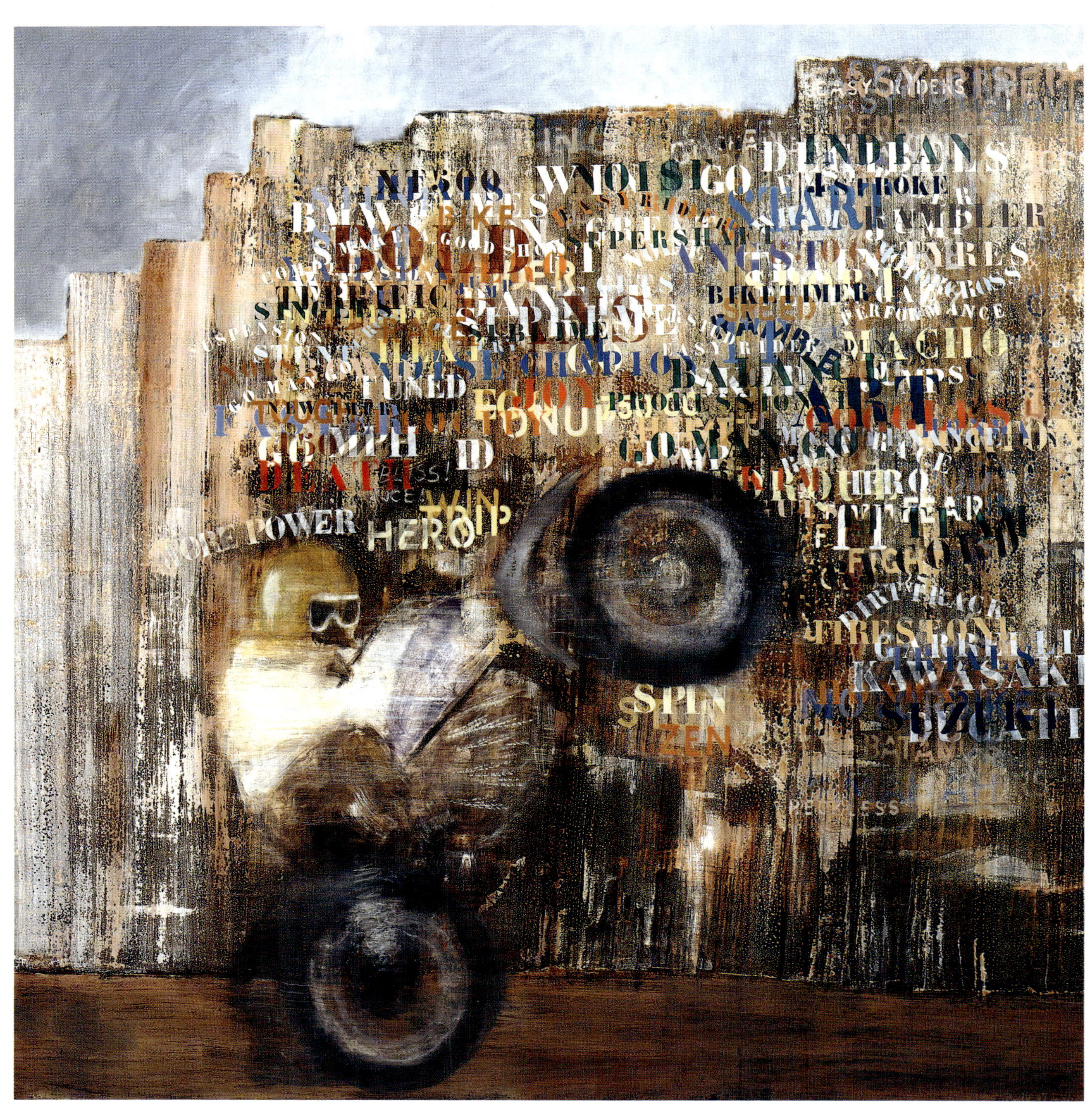

Easy Rider II, 1978, oil on canvas, 183×183cm, Makoto Iida Collection, Tokyo

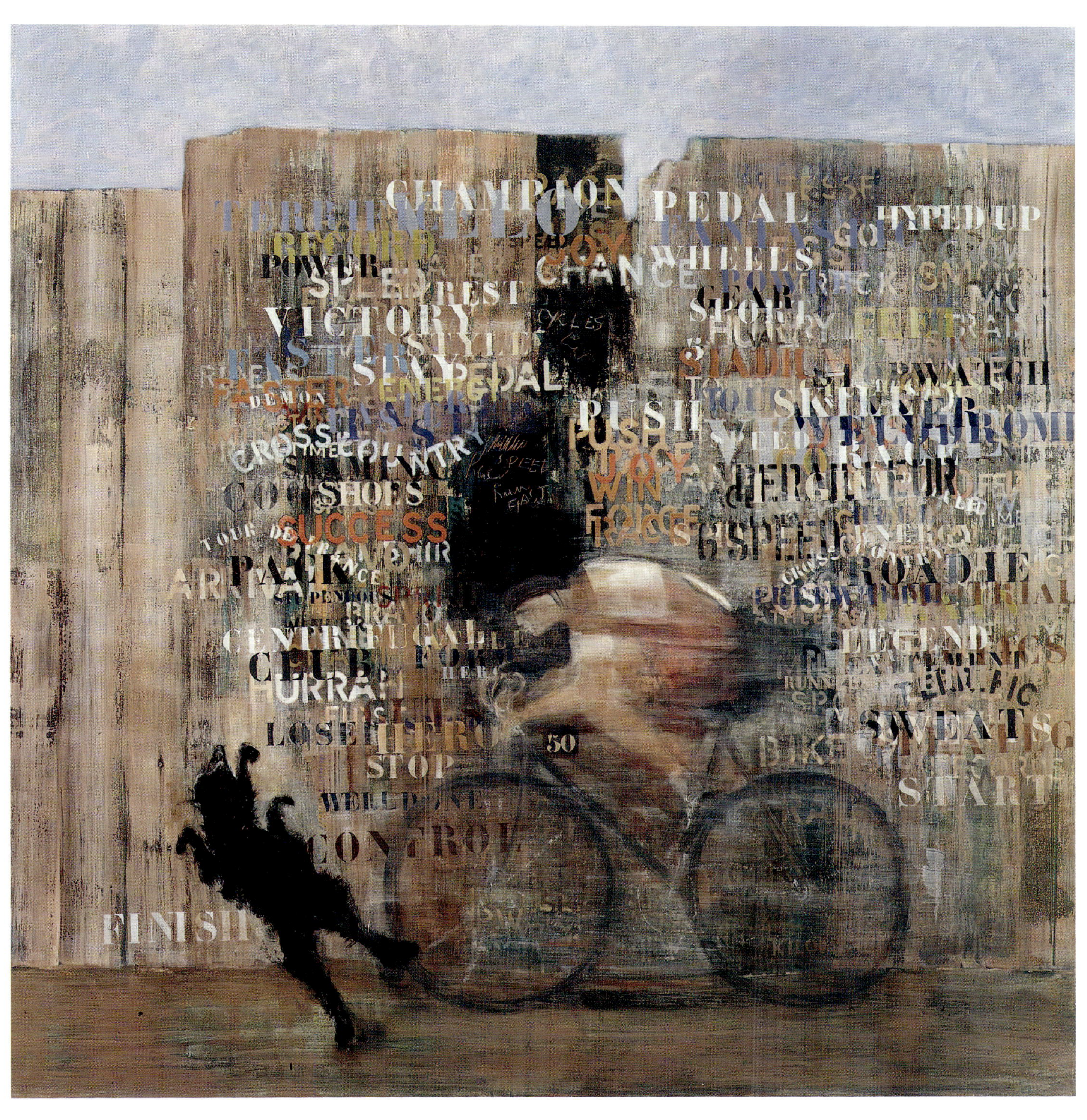

The Great Race I, 1978, oil on canvas, 183×183cm, Artist's Collection

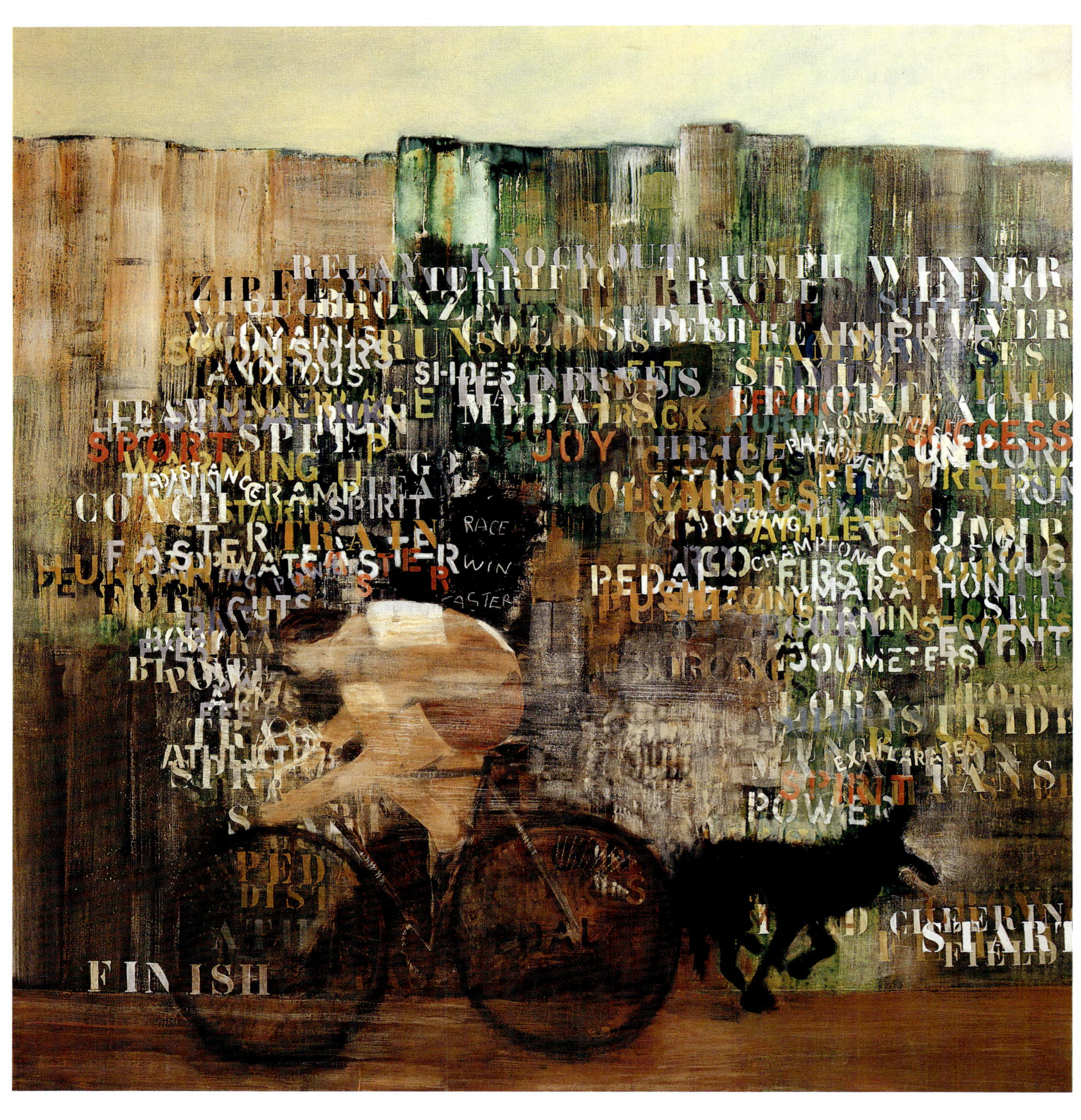

The Great Race II, 1978, oil on canvas, 183x183cm, Makoto Iida Collection, Tokyo

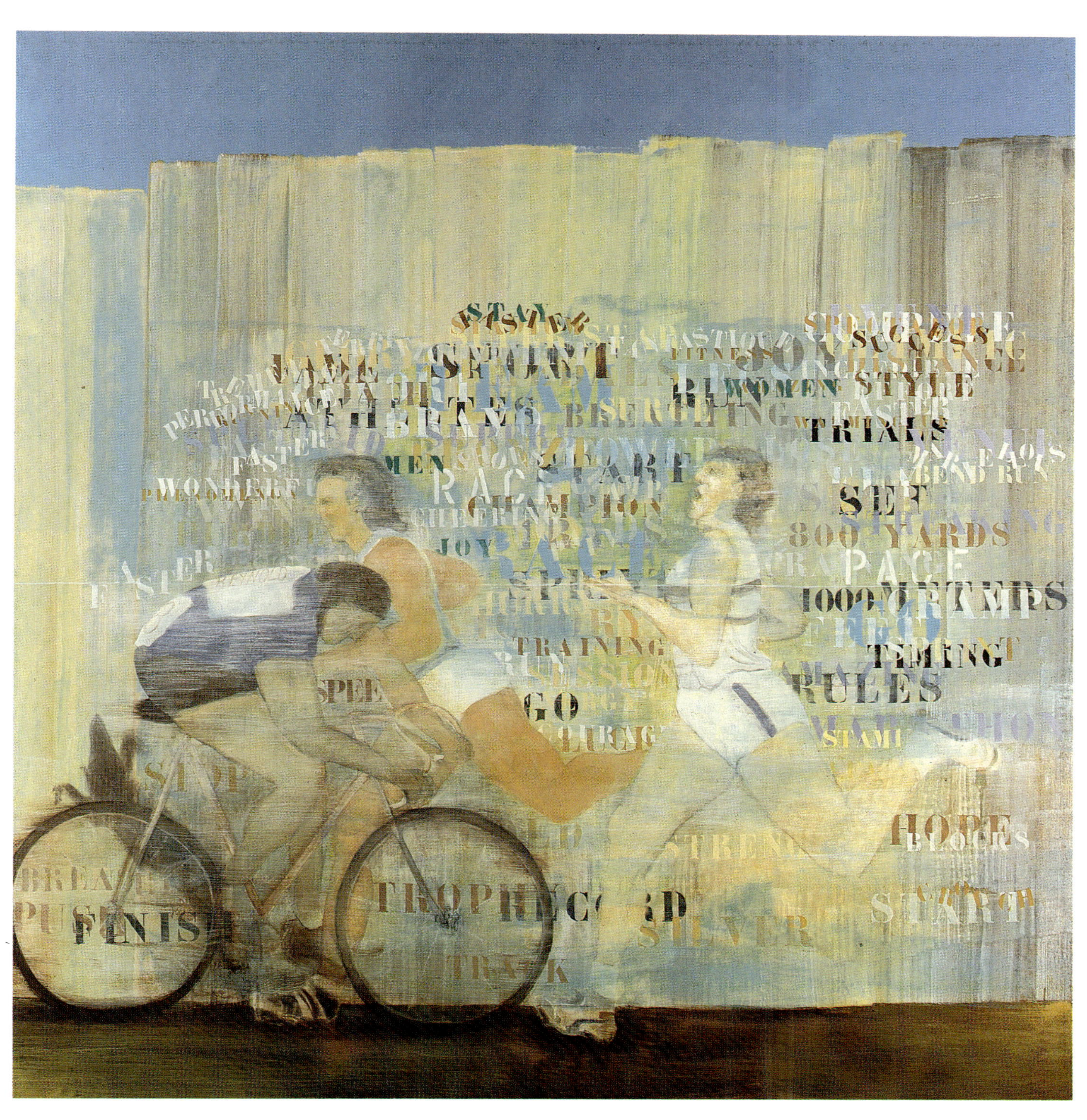

Sunday in Central Park, 1979, acrylic on canvas, 183x183cm, Private Collection, New York

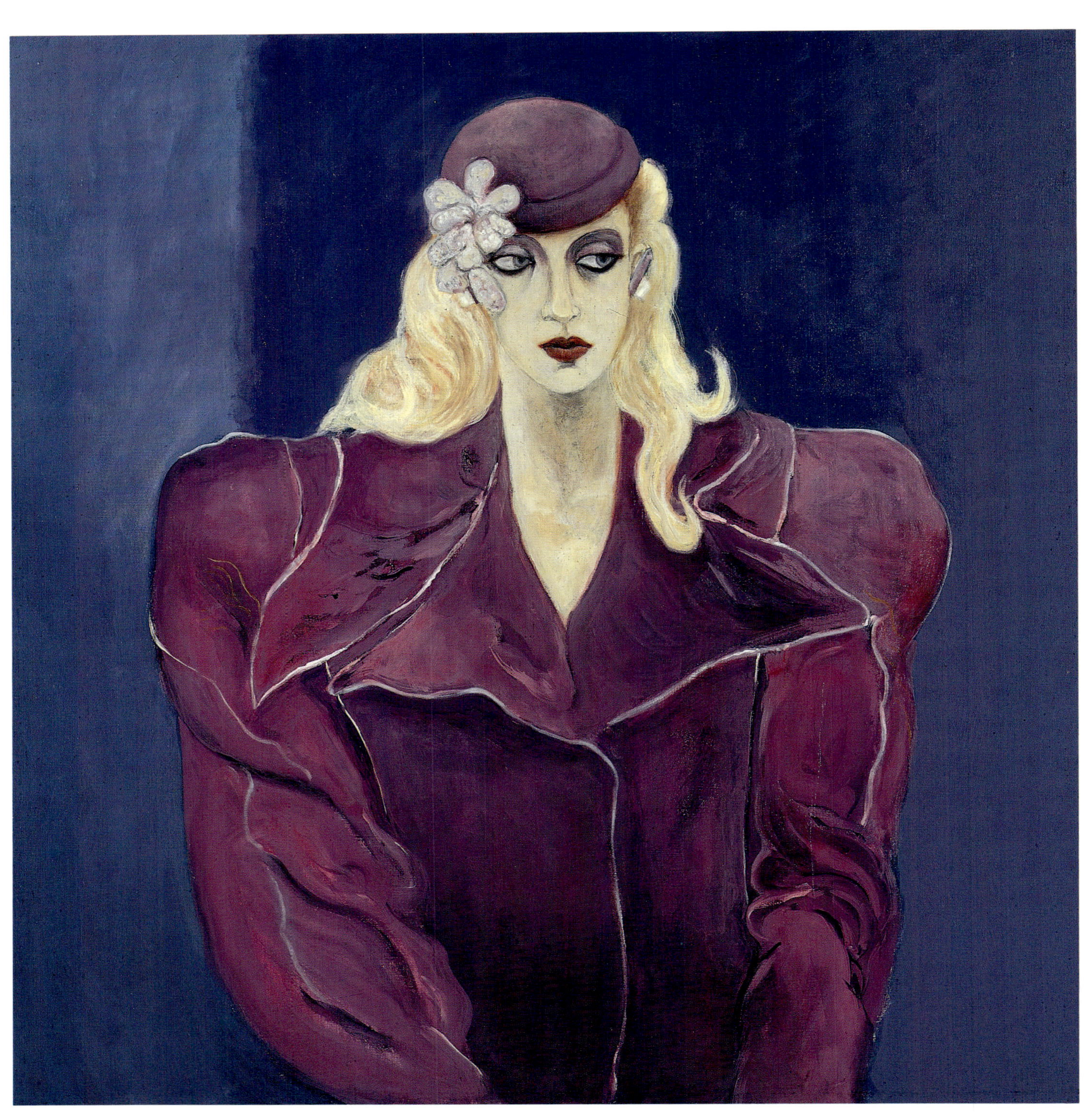

Portrait of Sarah Medway, 1979, oil on canvas, 152x152cm, Medway Collection, London

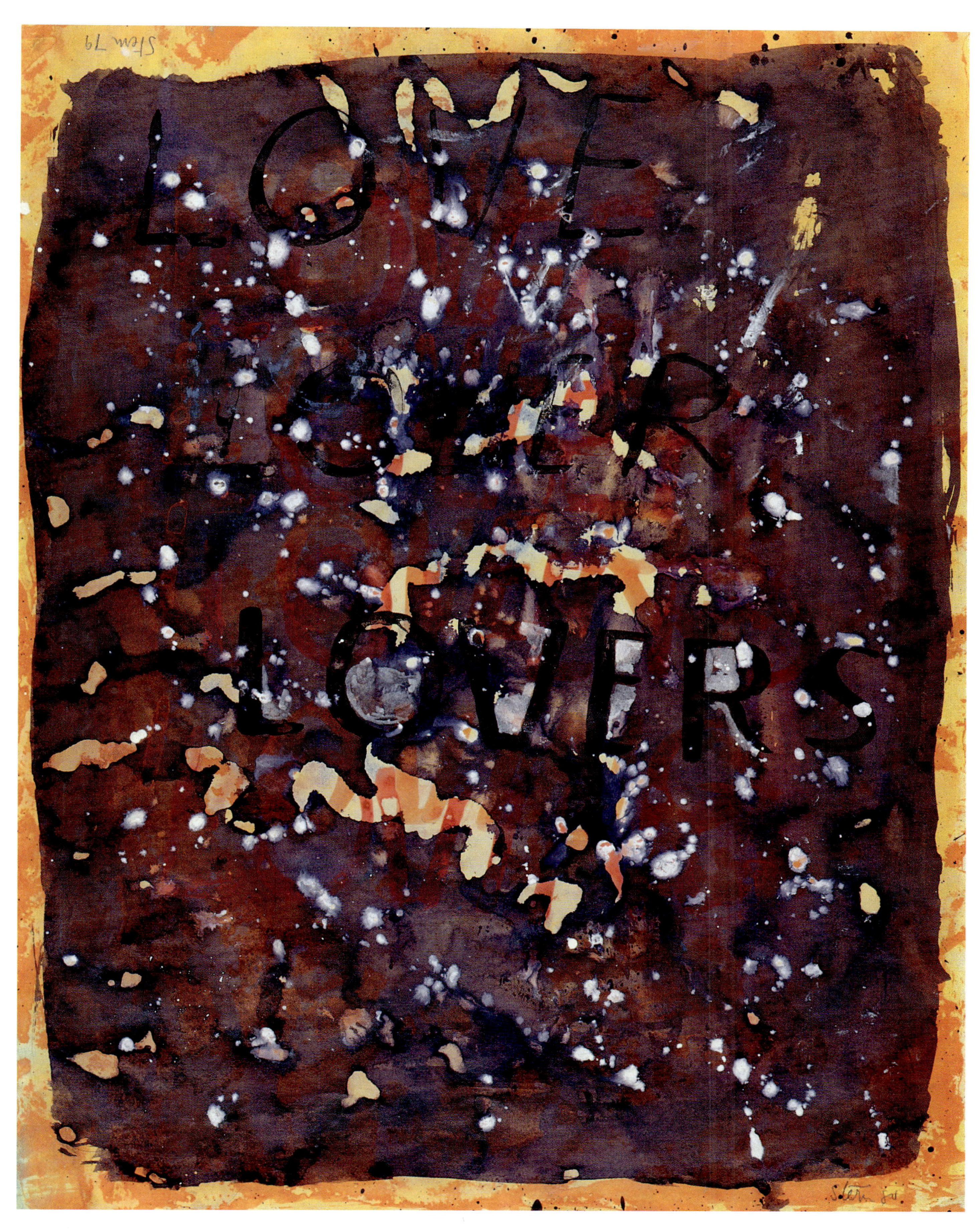

Starry Night, 1980, mixed media on paper, 57x46cm, Artist's Collection

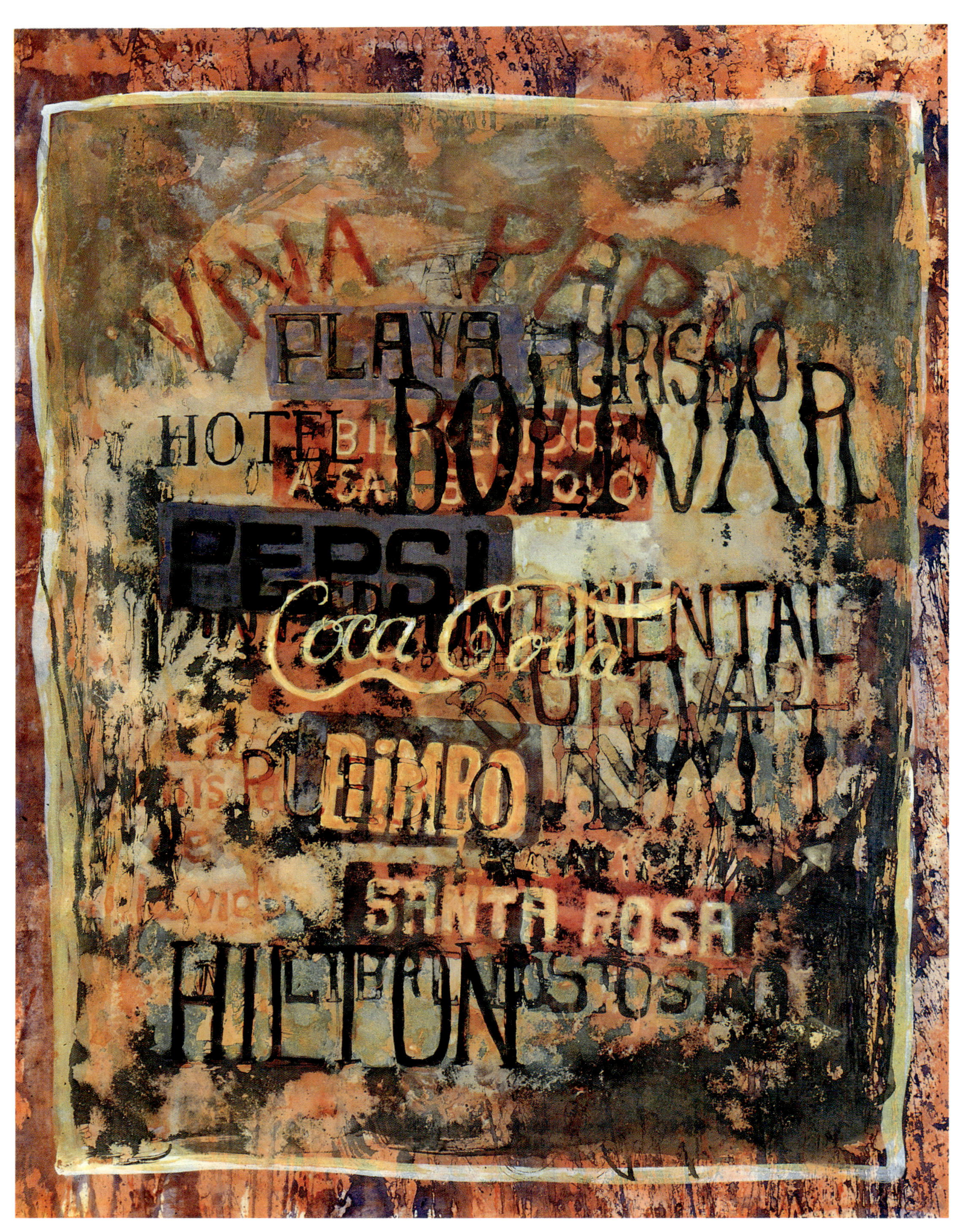

Bolivar, etc, 1979, mixed media on paper, 57x45cm, Artist's Collection

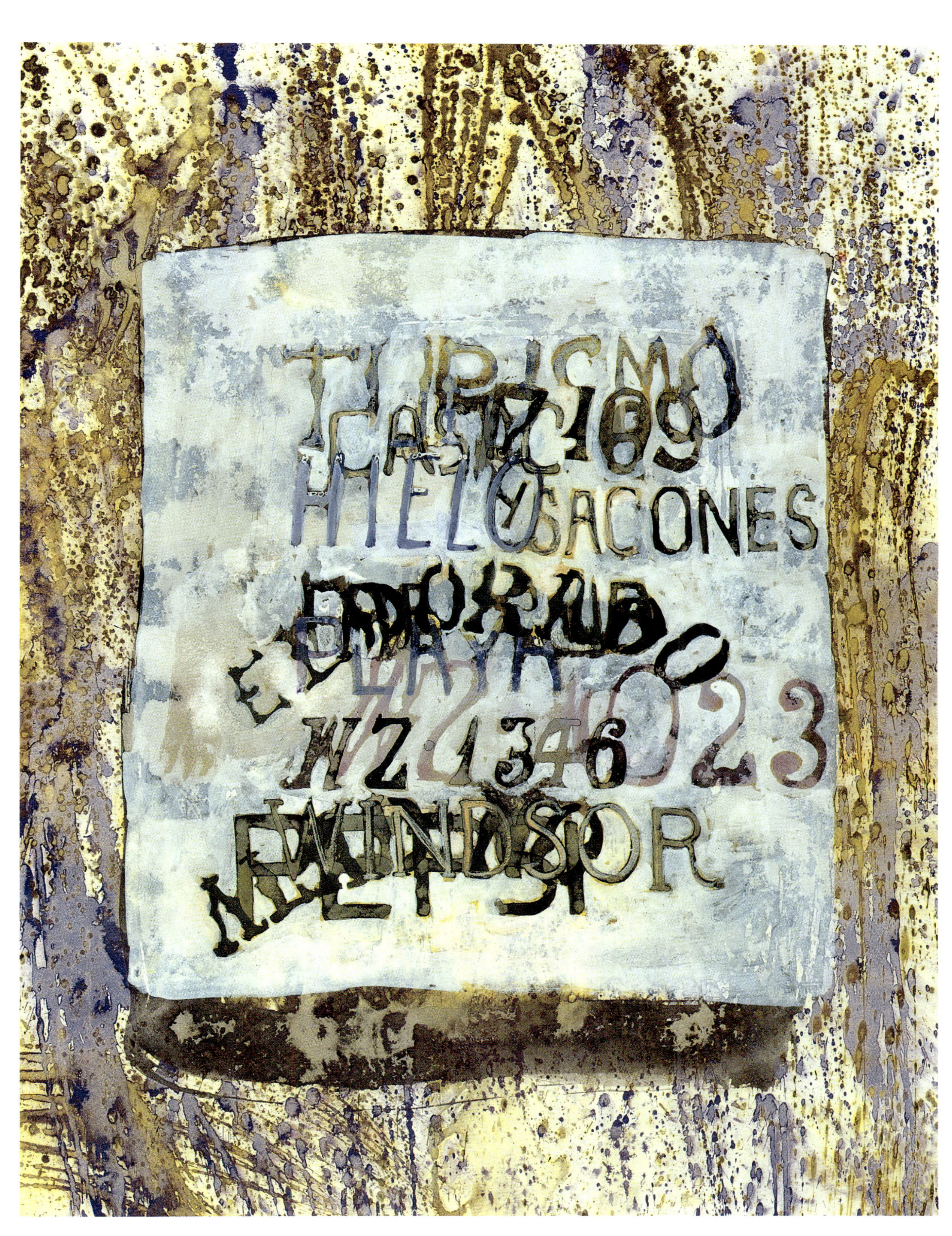

Turismo, 1979, mixed media on paper, 57x45cm

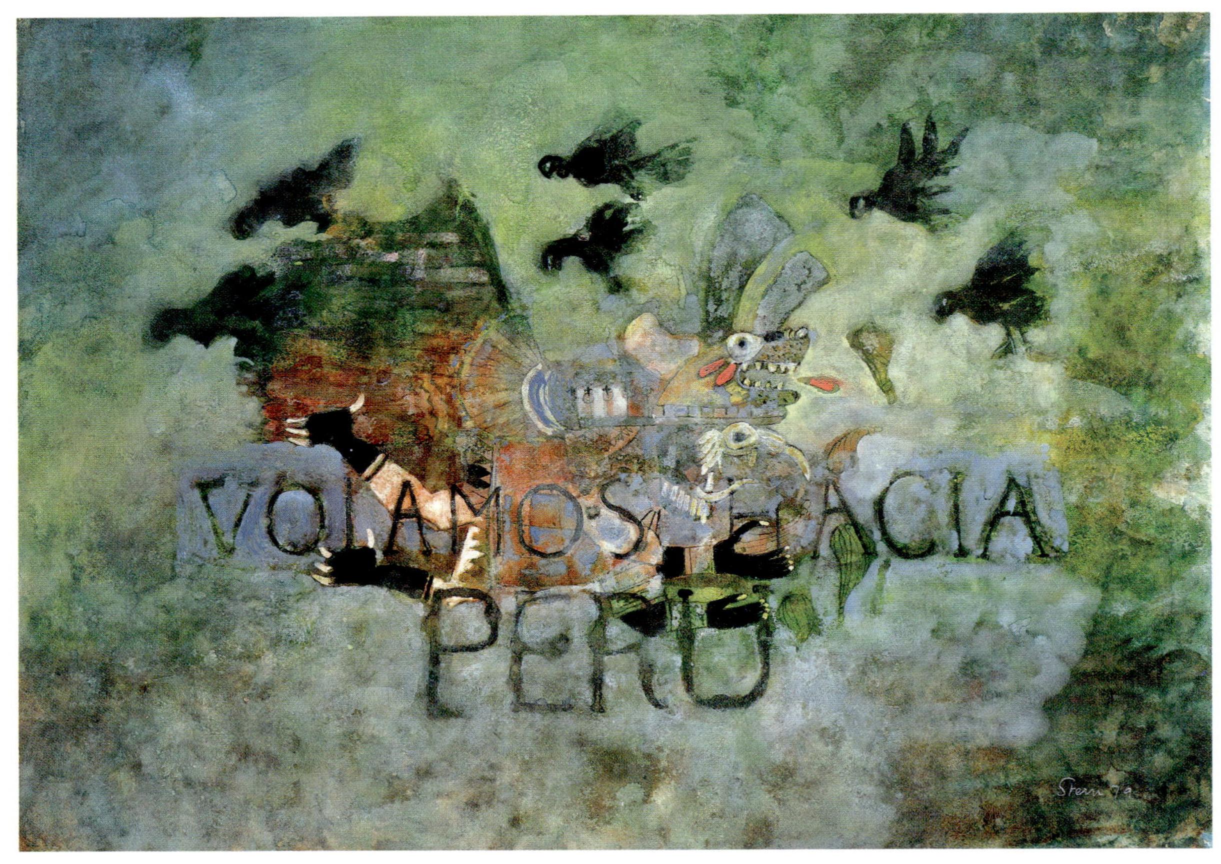

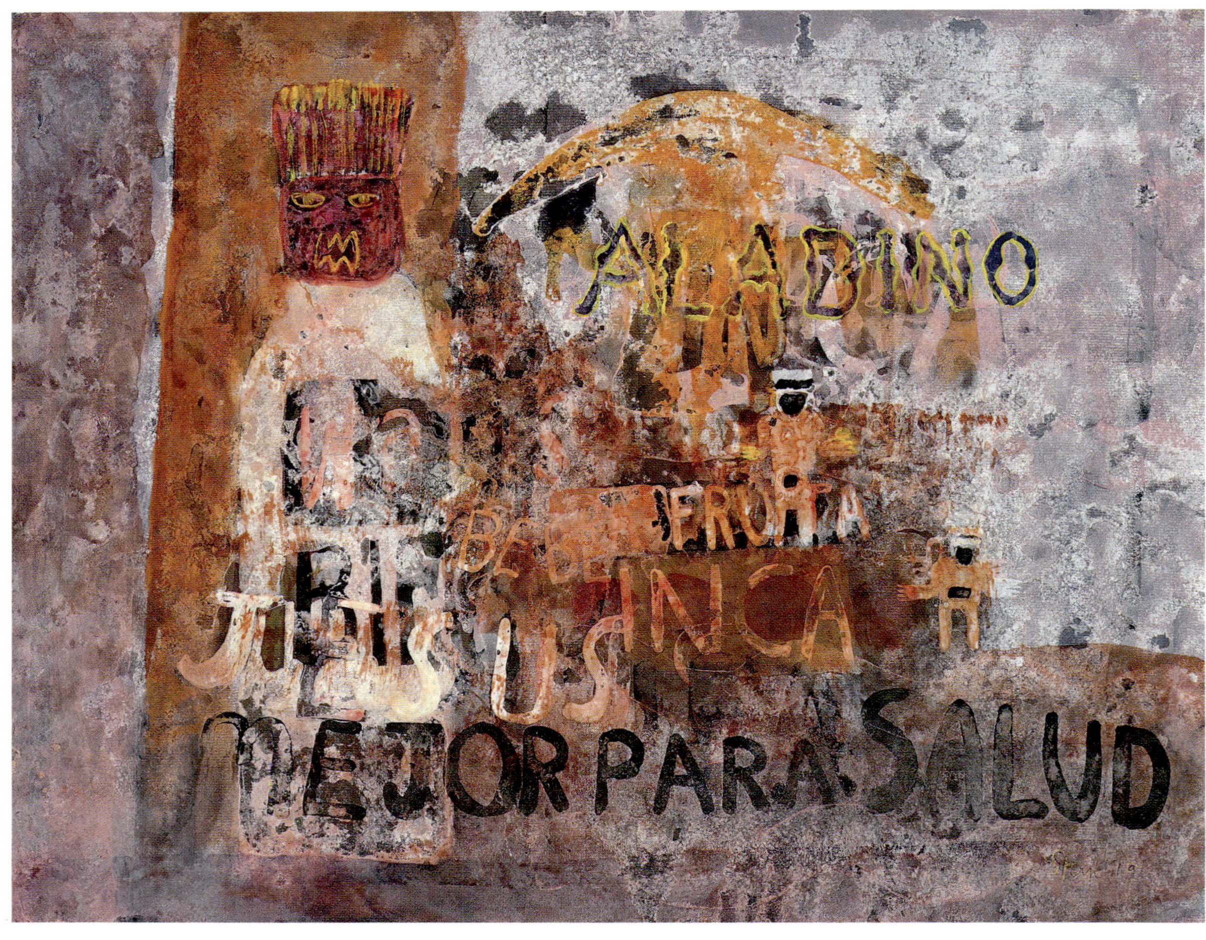

Volamos, 1979, mixed media on paper, 55x79cm, J. Woods Collection, London
Aladino II, 1979, mixed media on paper, 59x45cm, Alain Berrier Collection, Paris

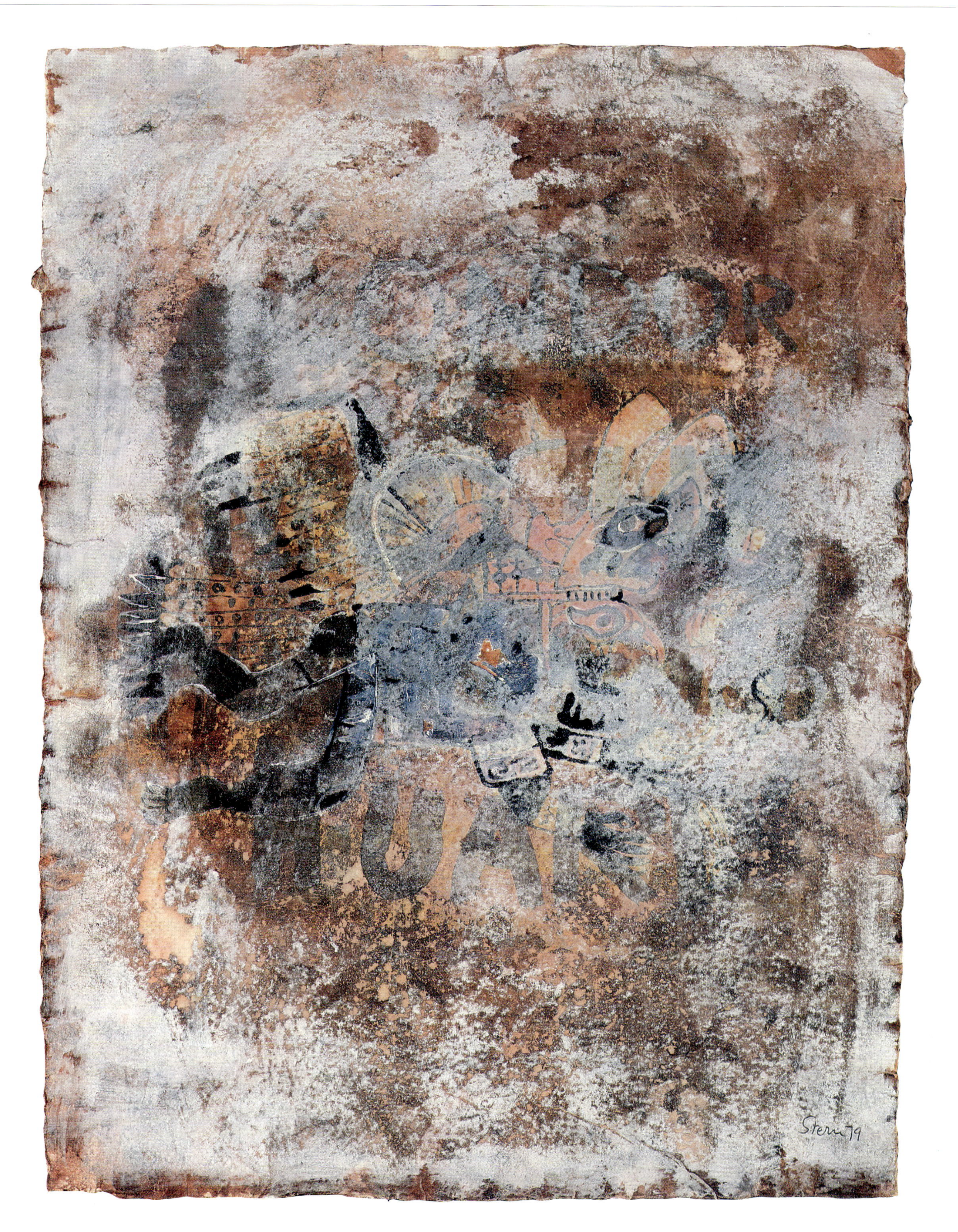

Battle Confusion, 1979, mixed media on paper, 59x44cm, Artist's Collection

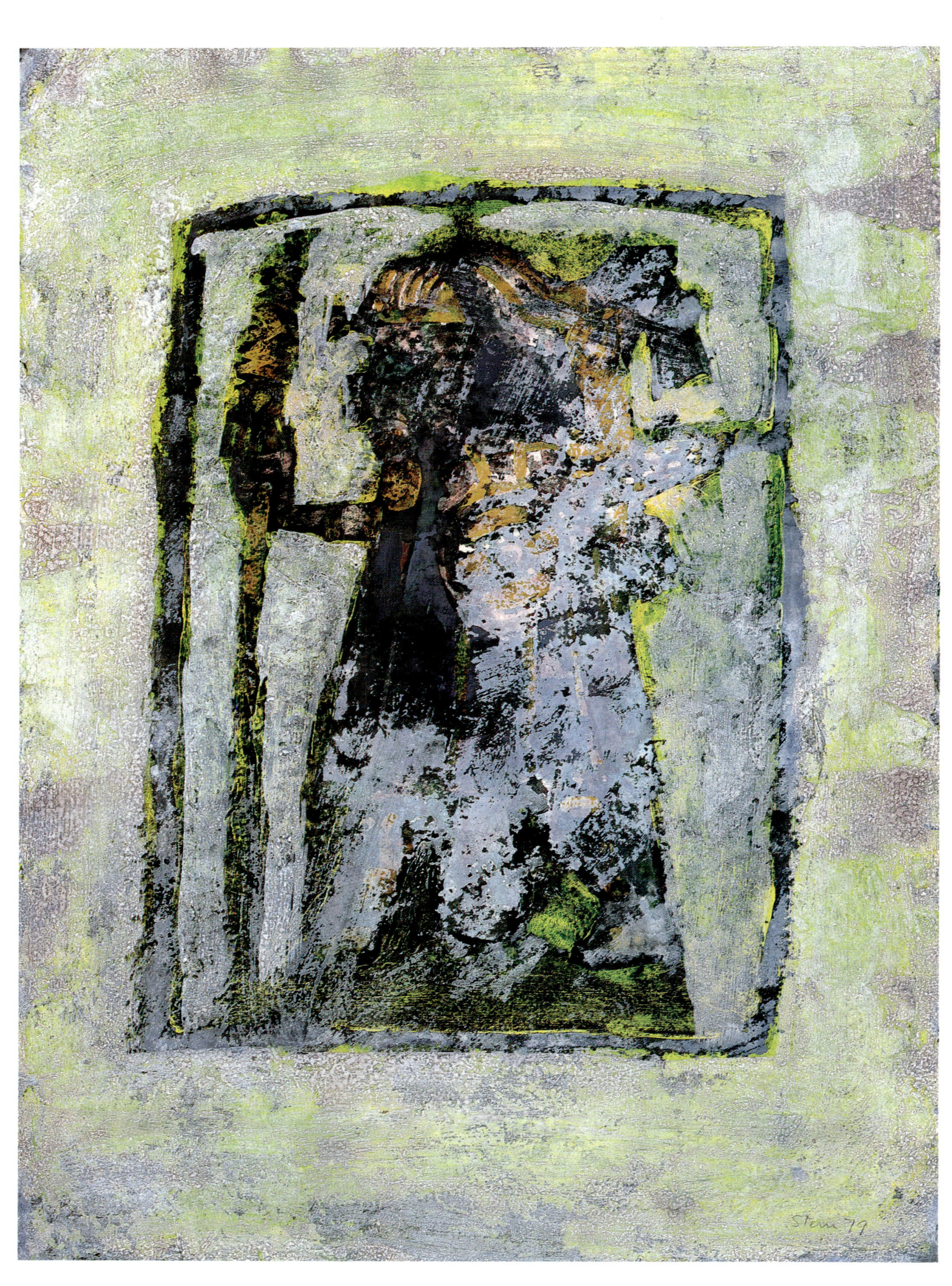

The Leader, 1979, mixed media on paper, 59x45cm, Artist's Collection

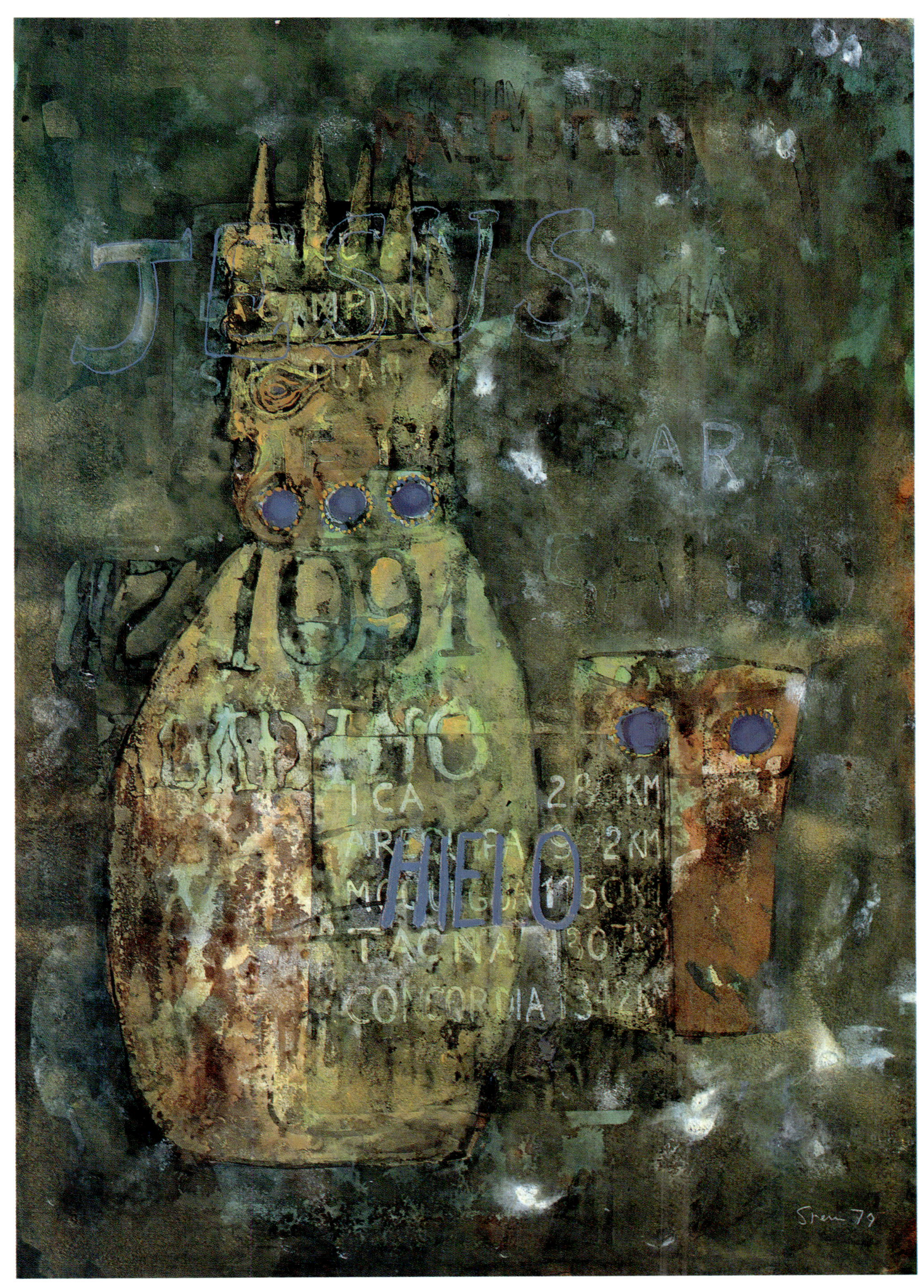

Aladino I, 1979, mixed media on paper, 57x80cm, Alain Berrier Collection, Paris

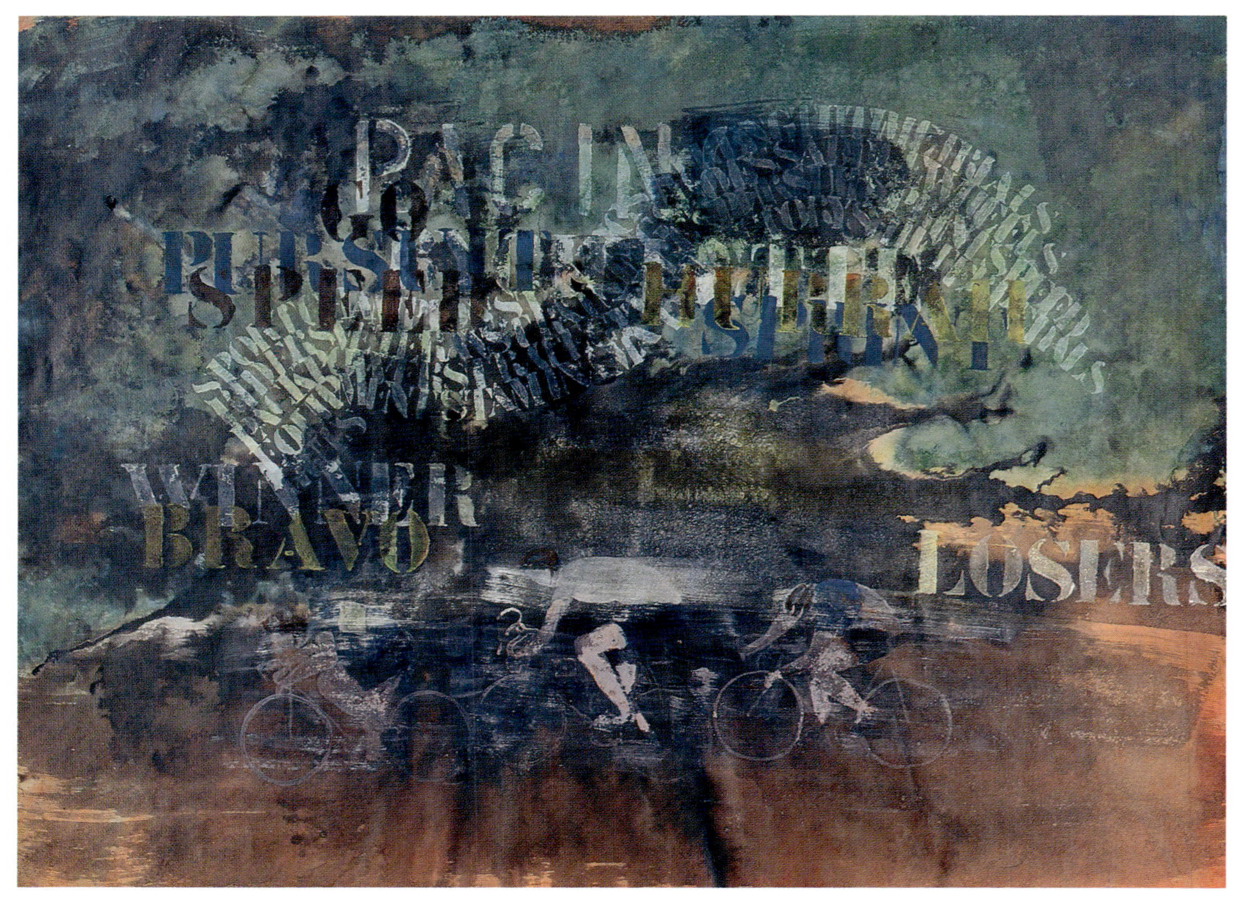

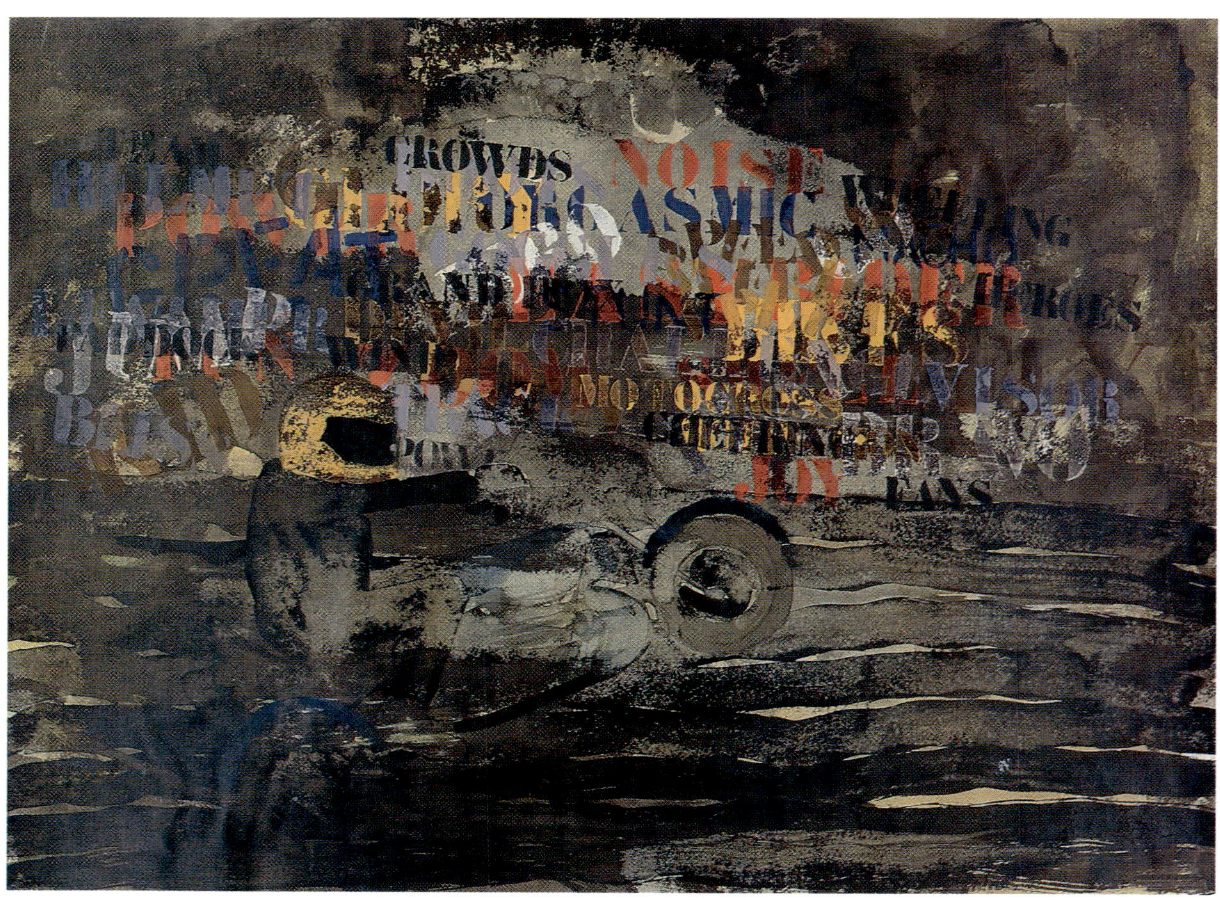

Racing!, 1980, mixed media on paper, 57x80cm, Lou Morgan Collection, Chicago
Speedster, 1980, mixed media on paper, 57x80cm, Hans Ulrich Collection, Frankfurt

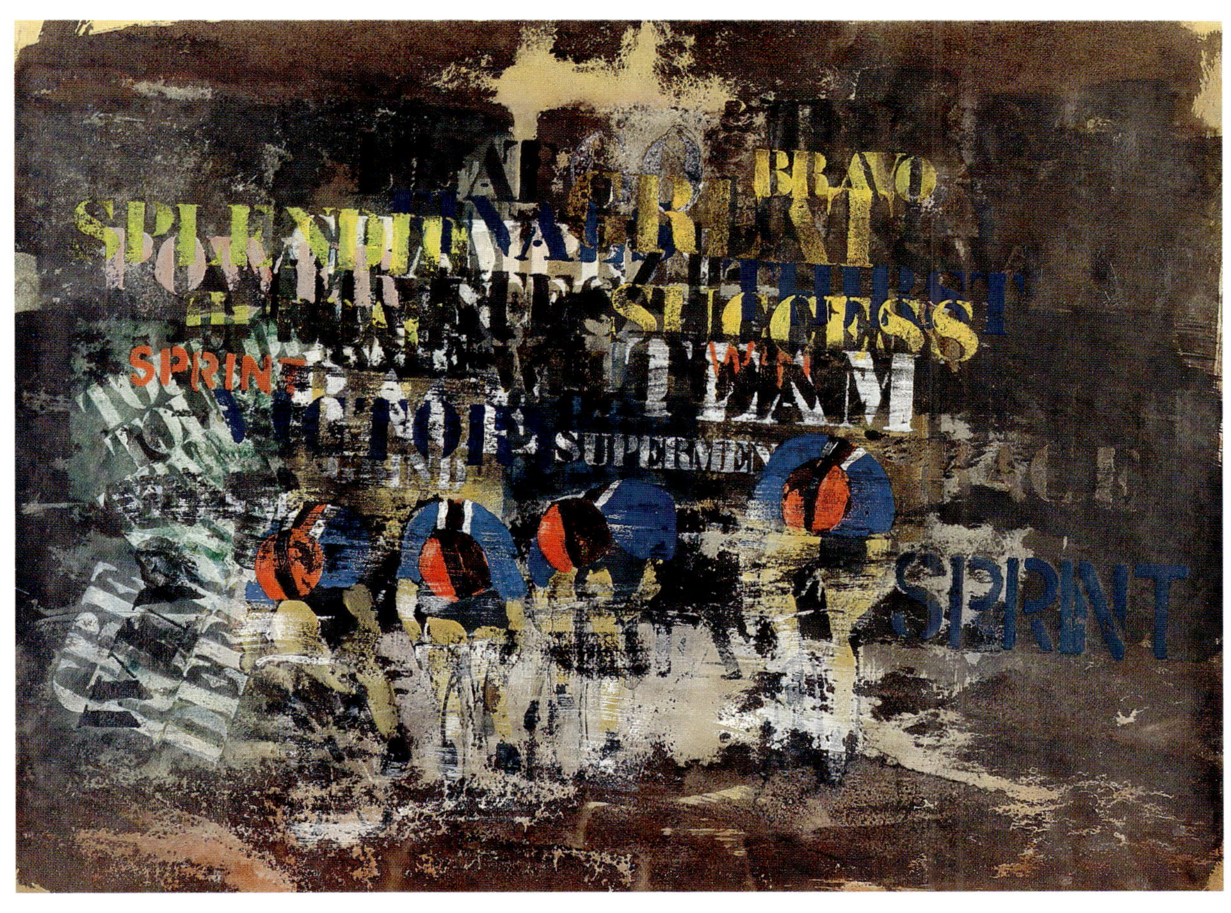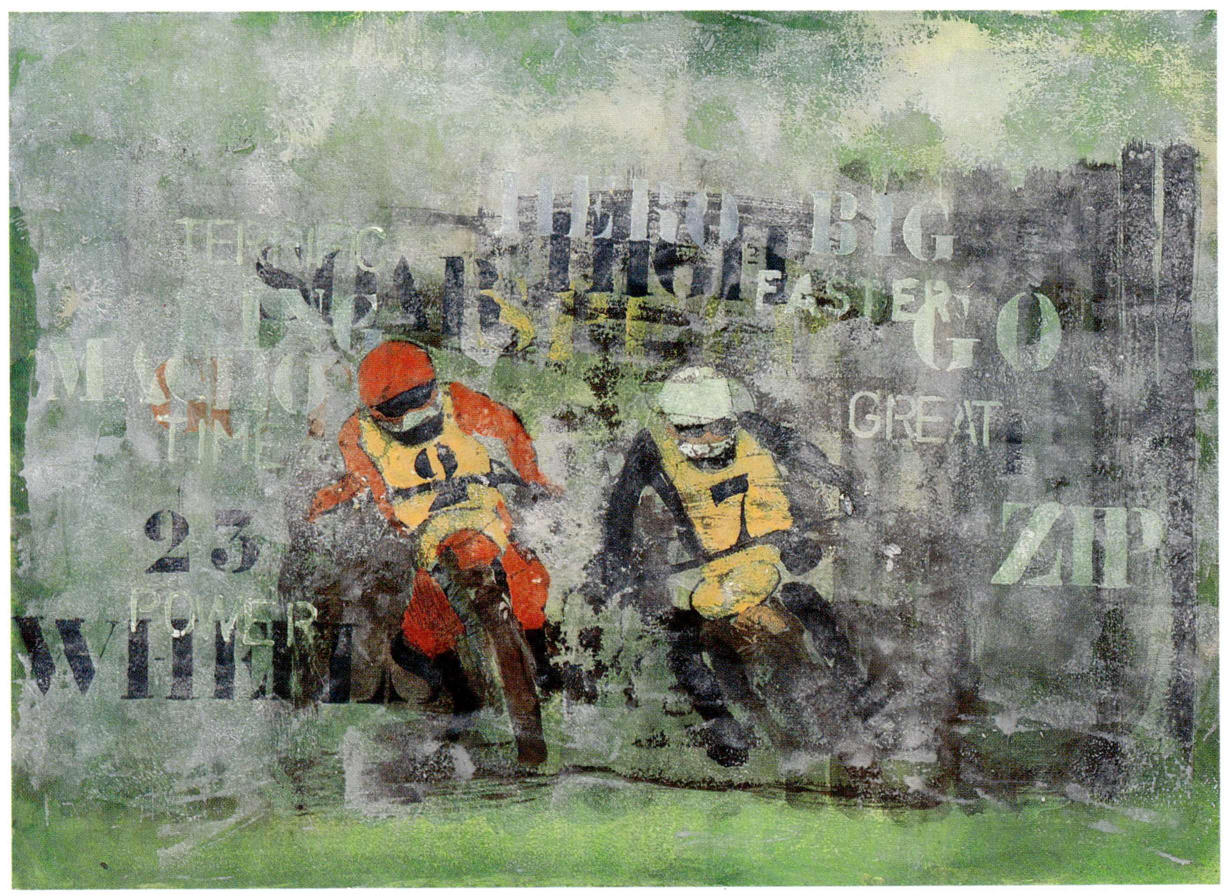

Teamwork, 1980, mixed media on paper, 57x80cm, Lou Morgan Collection, Chicago
Race, 1980, mixed media on paper, 57x80cm, H. Braasch Collection, New York

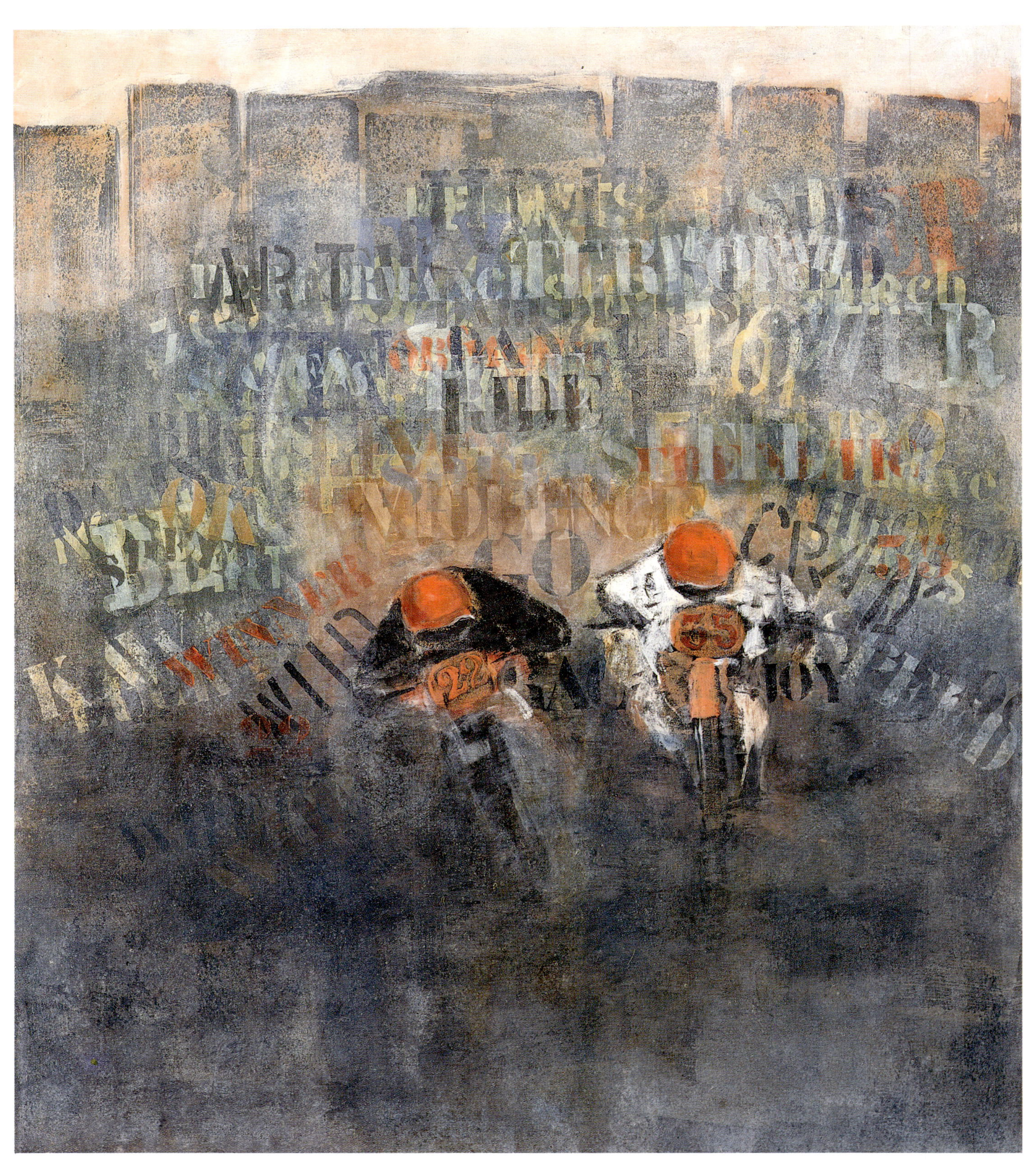

Vroom!, 1980, oil on canvas, 102x92cm, Stephen Lazzaro Collection, New York

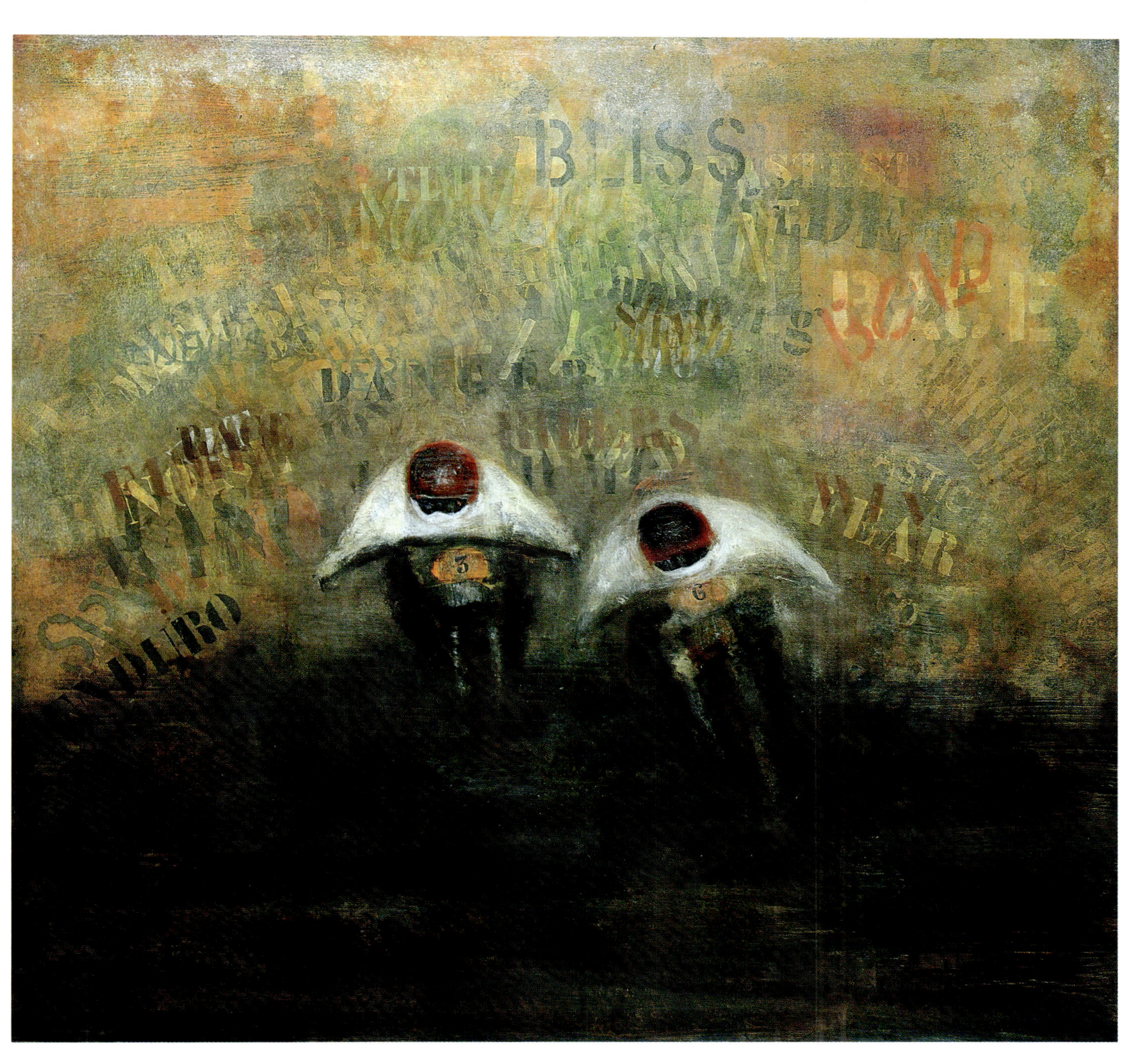

Speed, 1980, oil on canvas, 102x92cm, Private Collection, Frankfurt

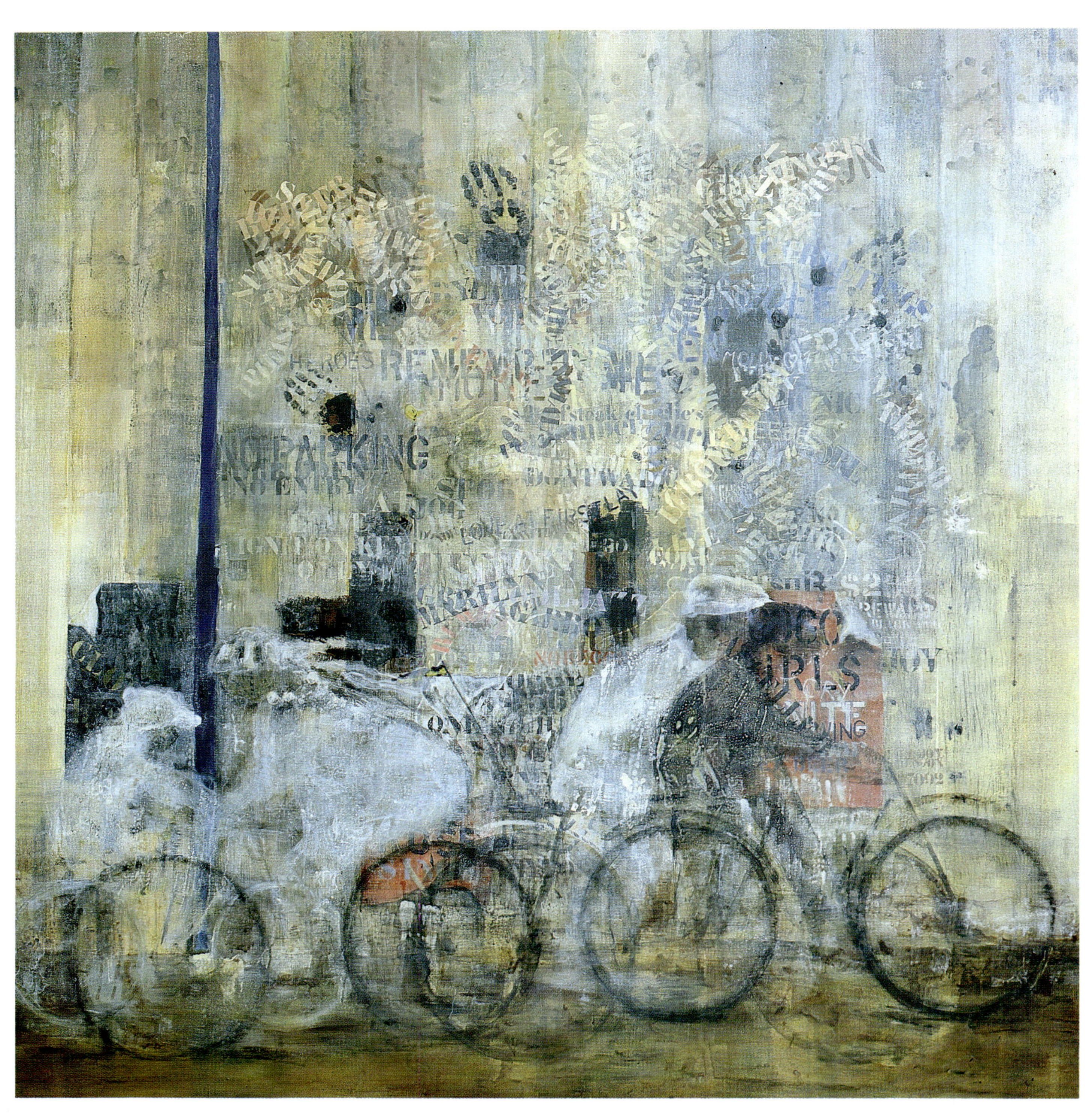

Washington Square, 1980, acrylic on canvas, 183x183cm, Private Collection, New York

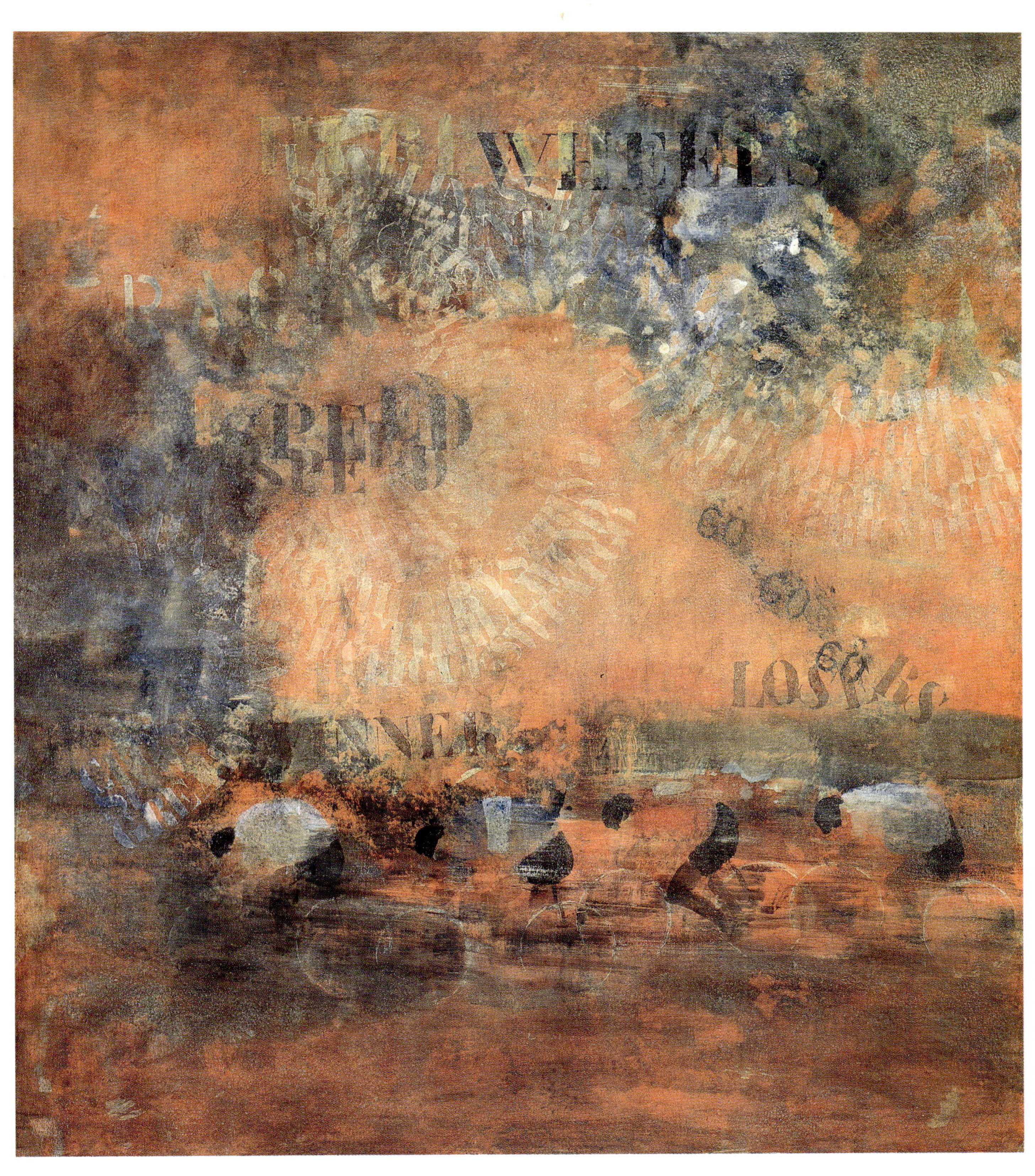

Last Effort, 1980, oil on canvas, 102×92cm, R. D'Ieteren Collection, Brussels

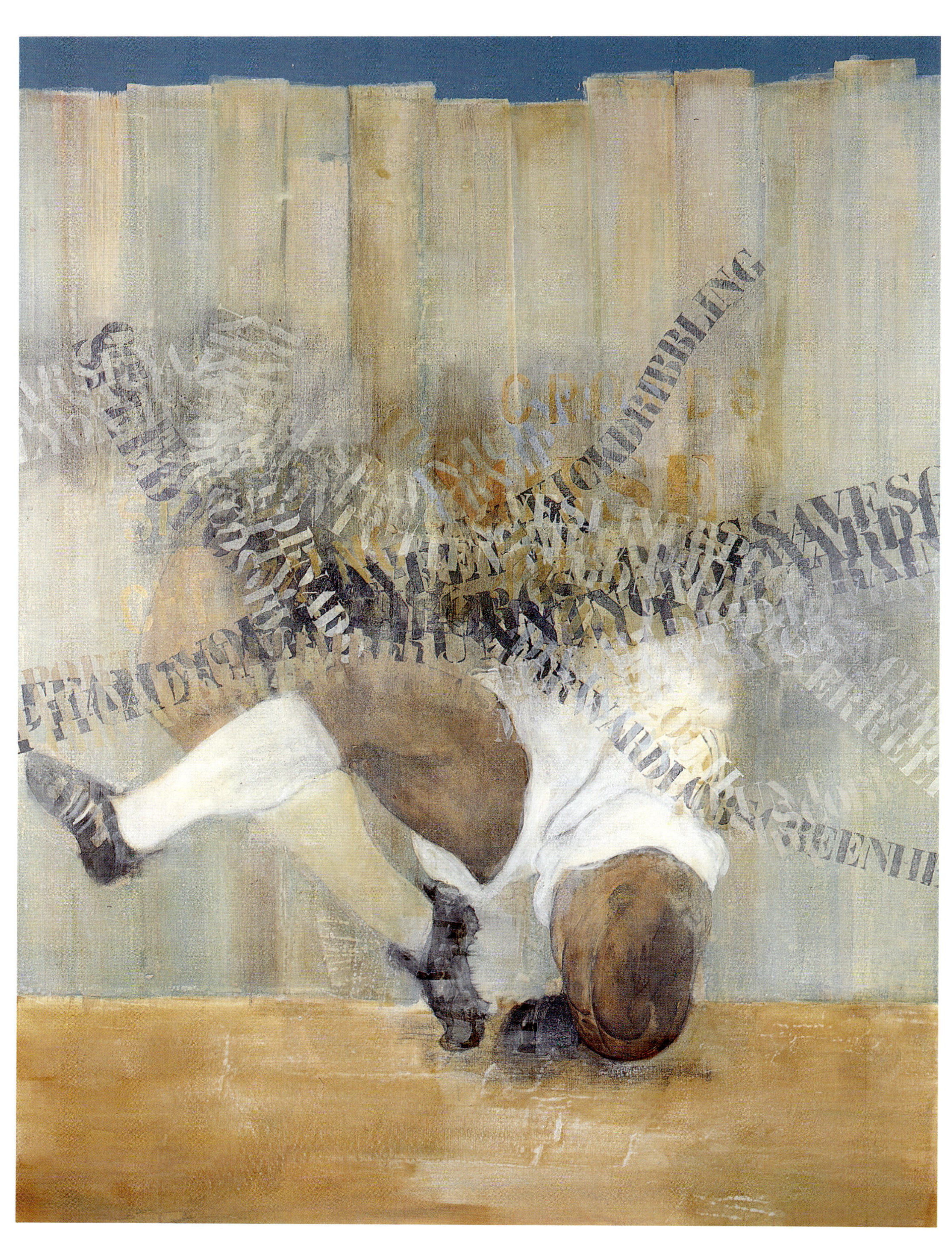

Power and Noise, 1980, oil on canvas, 146x114cm, Ashkenazy Collection, Los Angeles

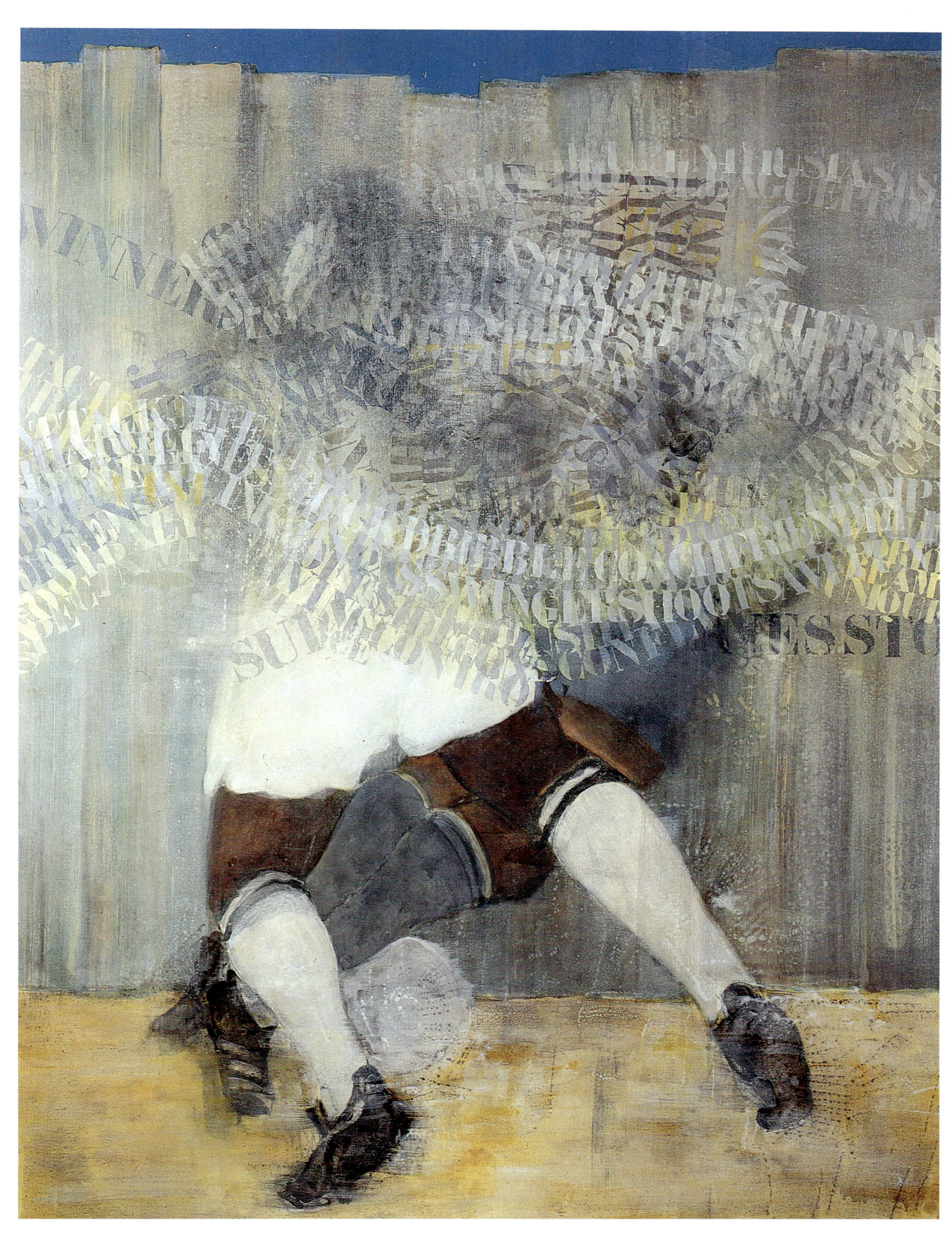

Crowd Noise IV, 1980, oil on canvas, 146x114cm, M. Henochsberg Collection, Paris

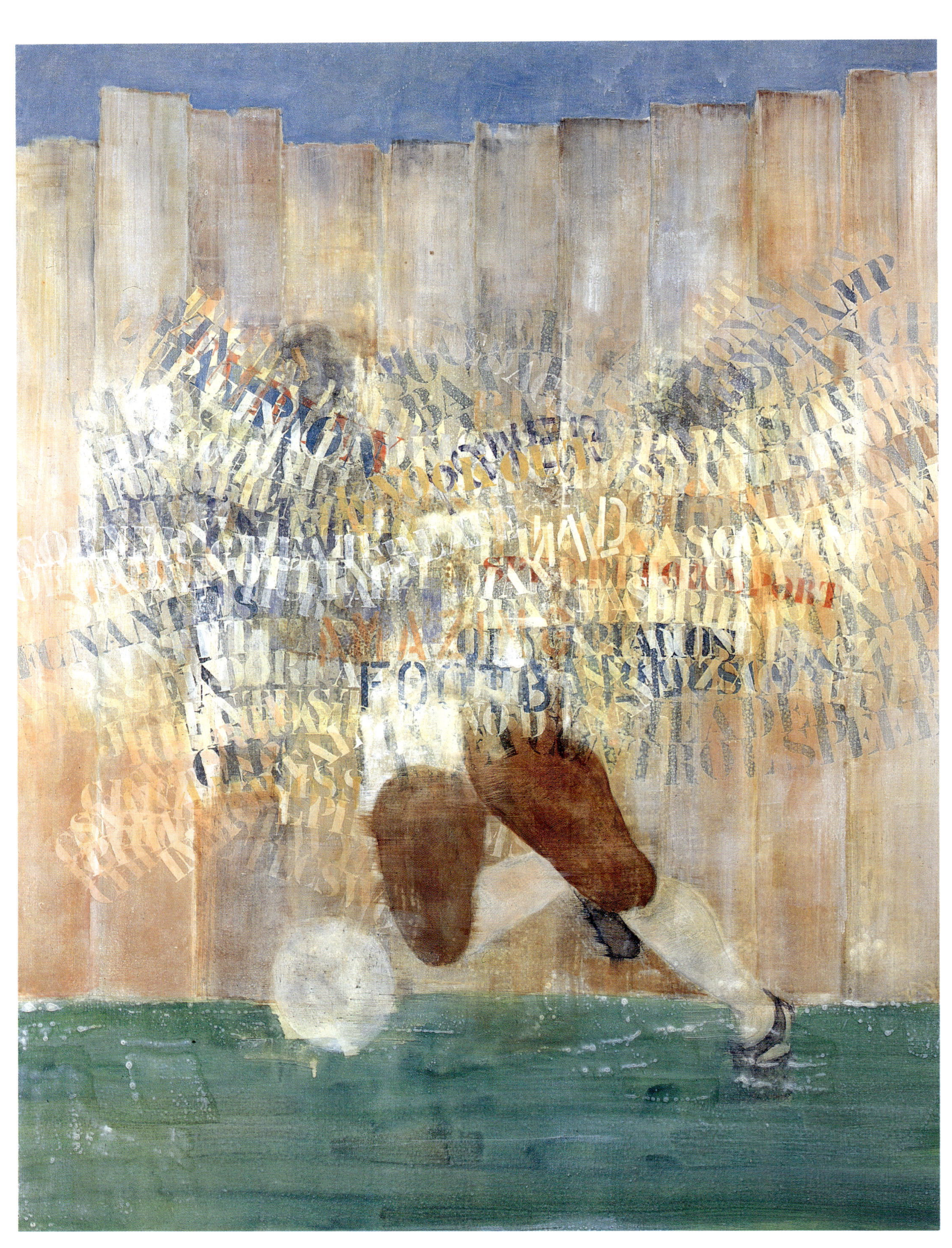

Crowd Noise I, 1980, acrylic on canvas, 146x114cm, Ashkenazy Collection, Los Angeles

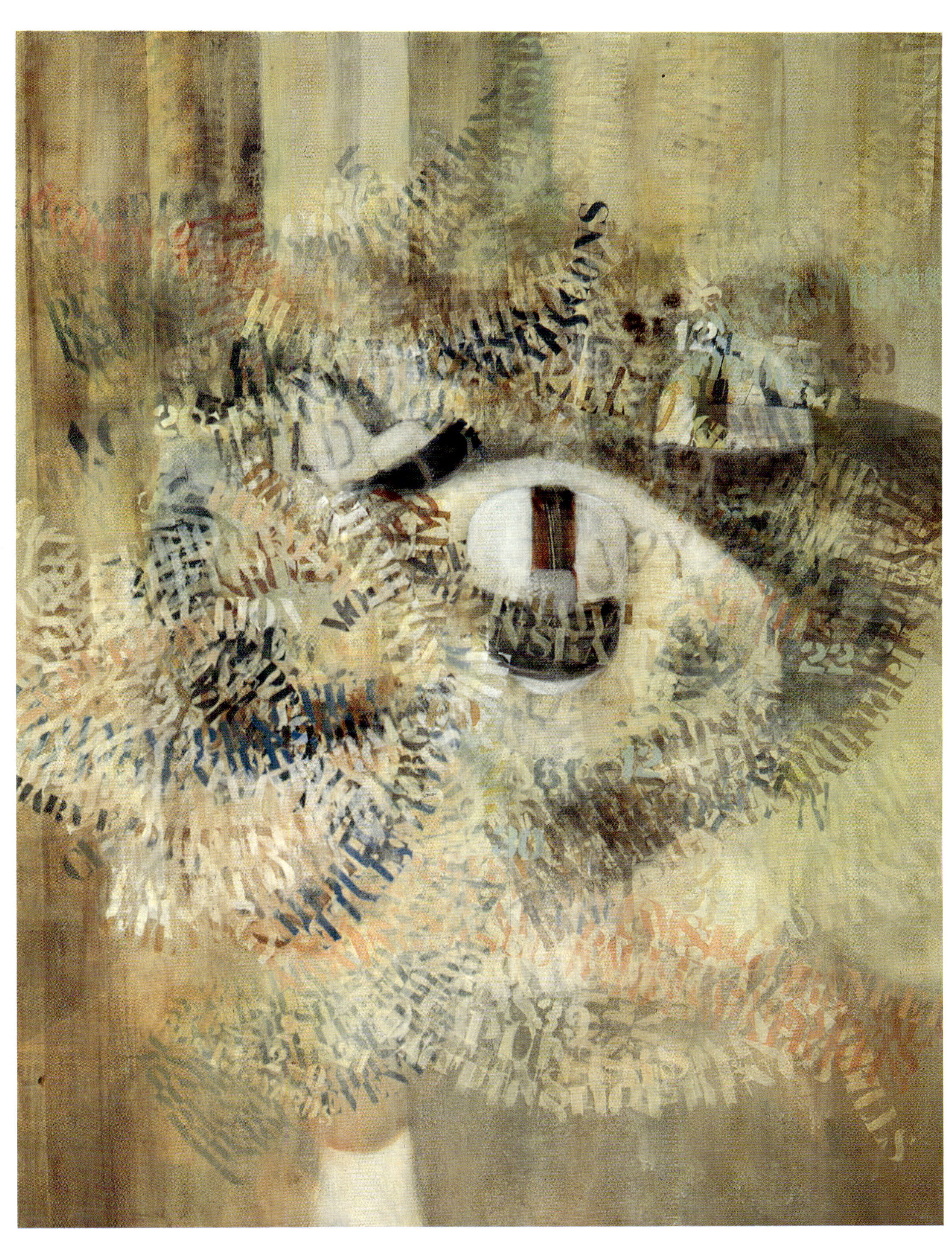

Cheering, 1980, oil on canvas, 146x114cm, Private Collection, Palm Beach, Florida

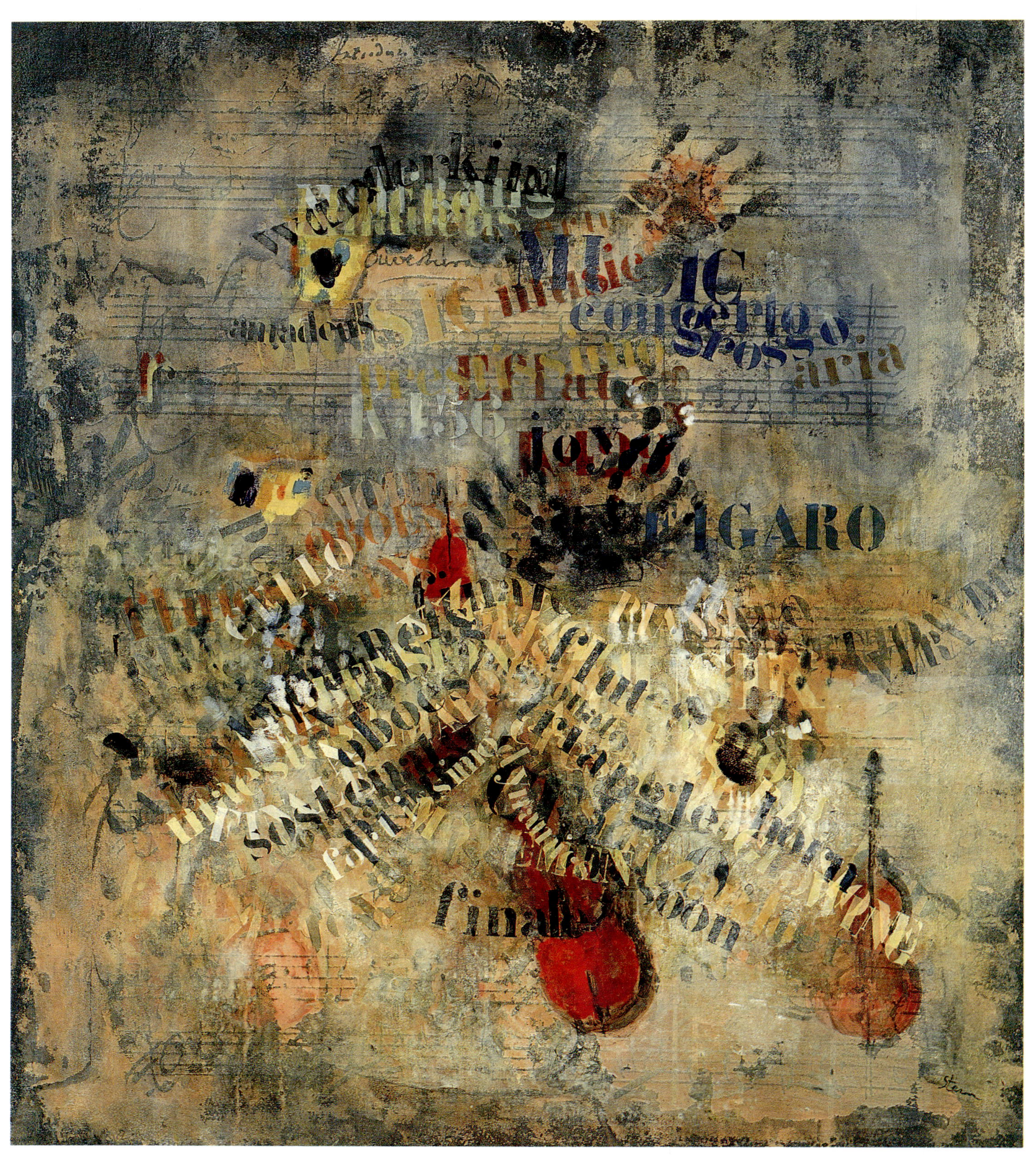

Concerto, 1981, acrylic on canvas, 102×92cm

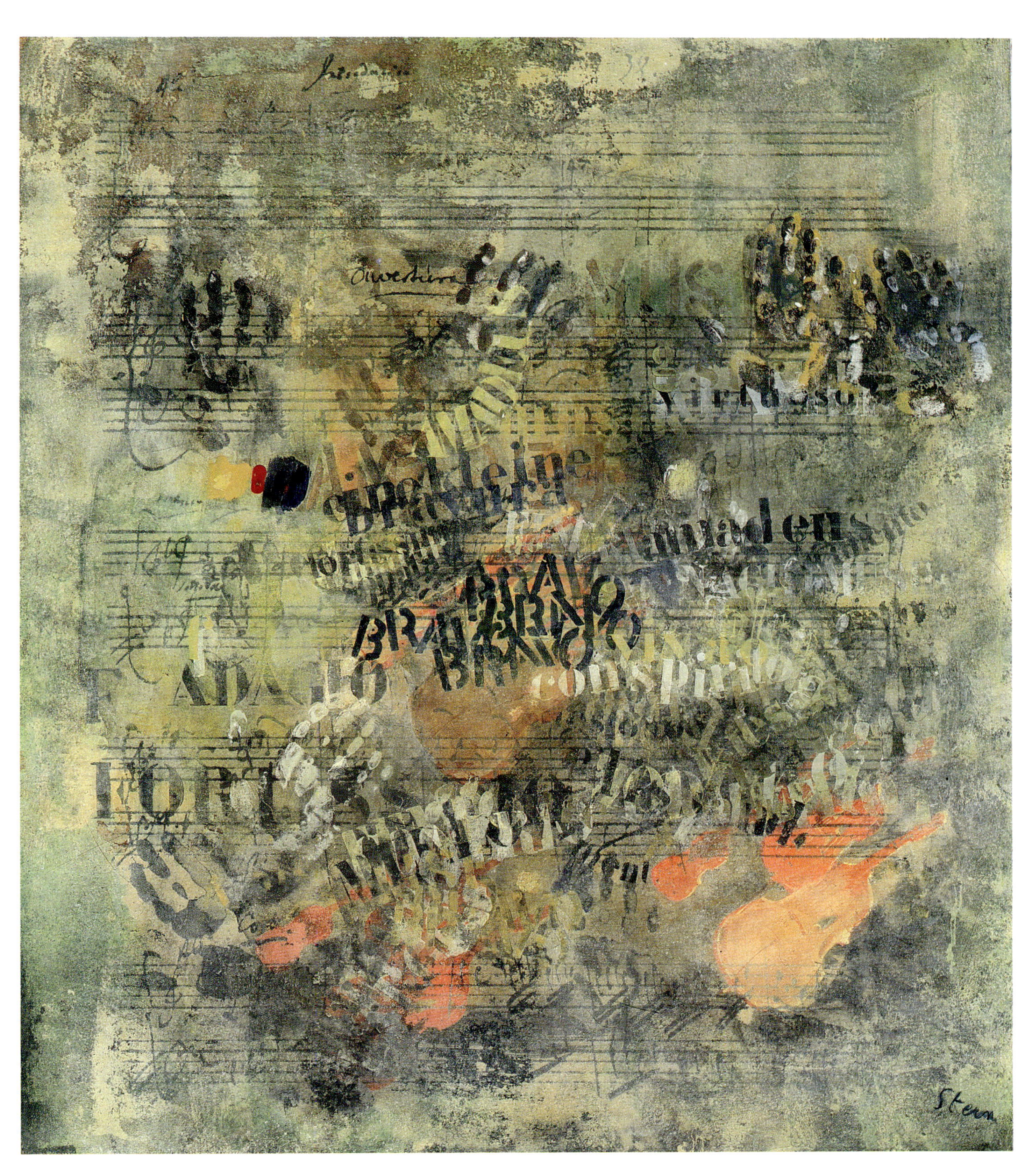

Applause, 1980, acrylic on canvas, 102x92cm, Private Collection, Florida

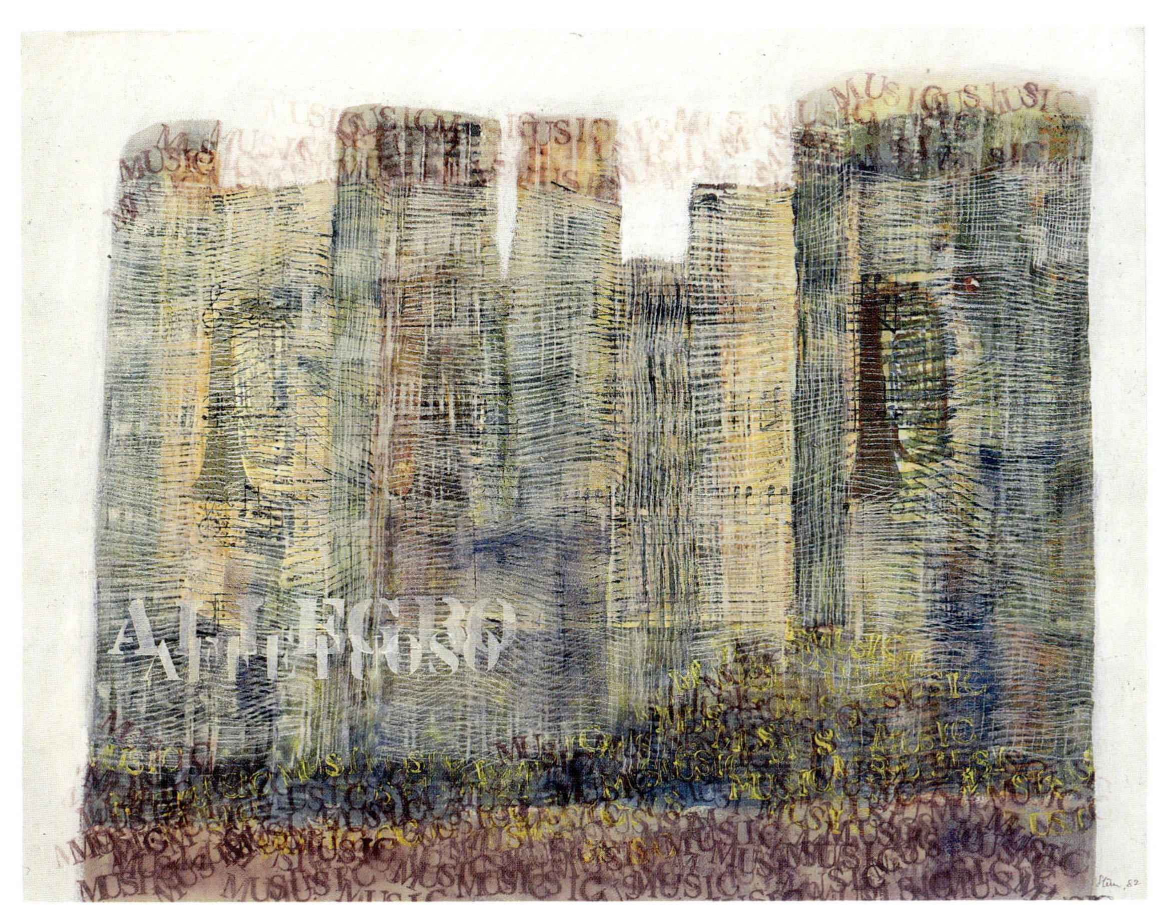

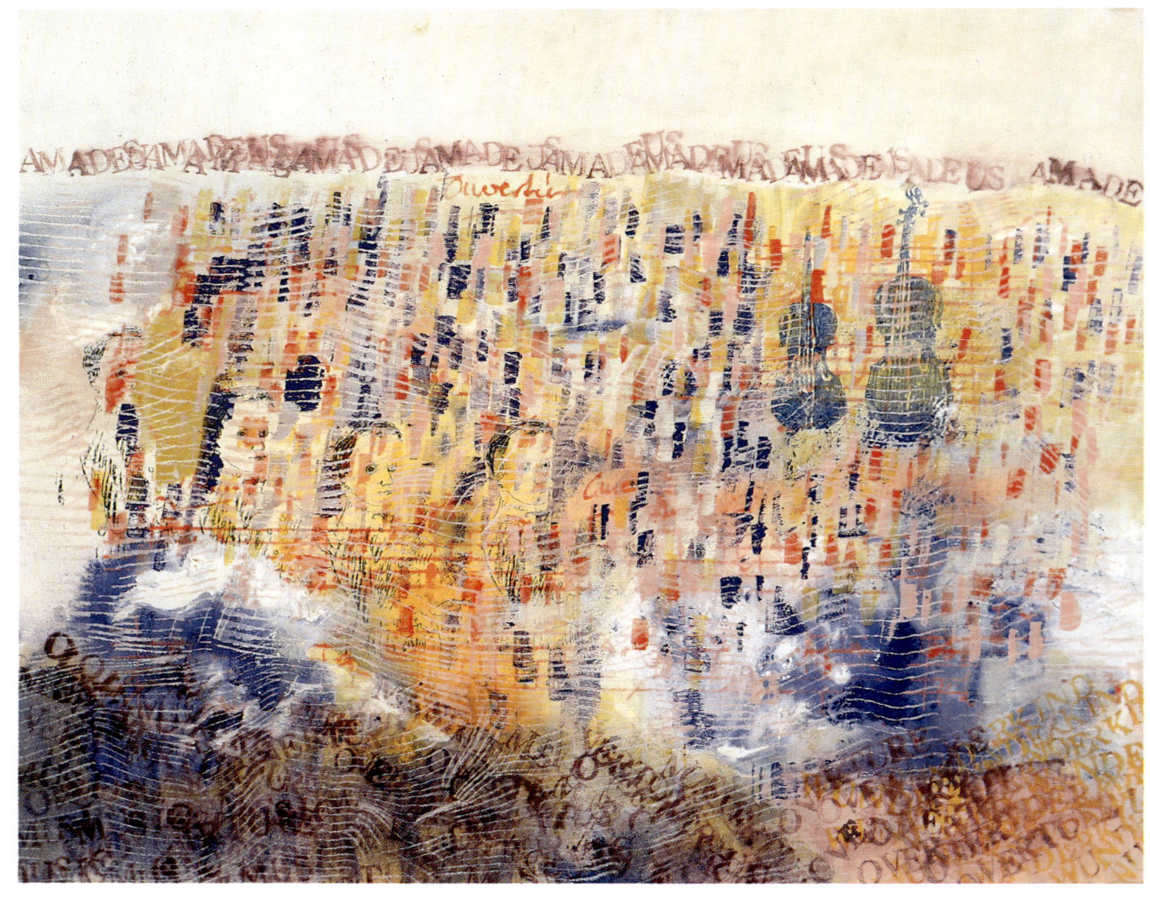

Music City, 1982, mixed media on paper, 61x80cm, Private Collection, Tokyo
L'ami Amadeus, 1982, mixed media on paper, 61x79cm, Private Collection, Tokyo

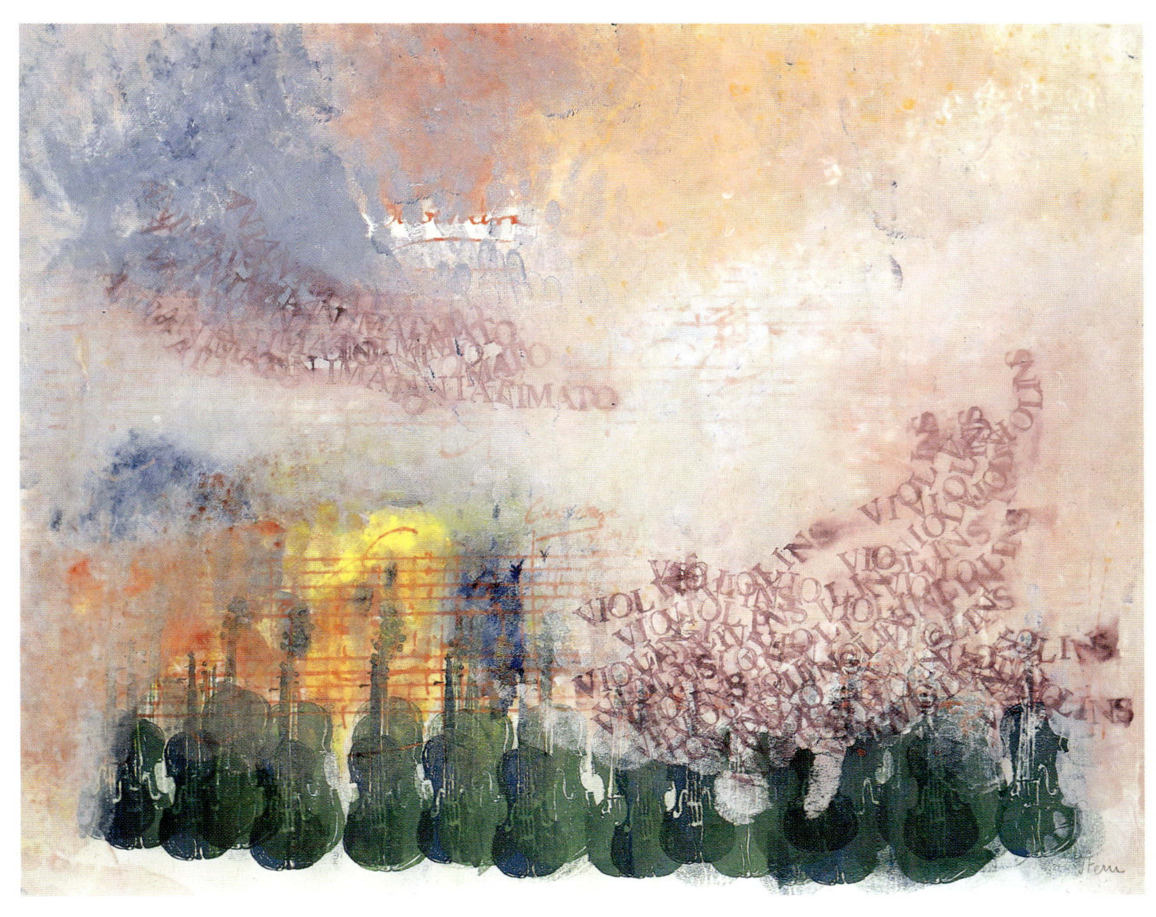

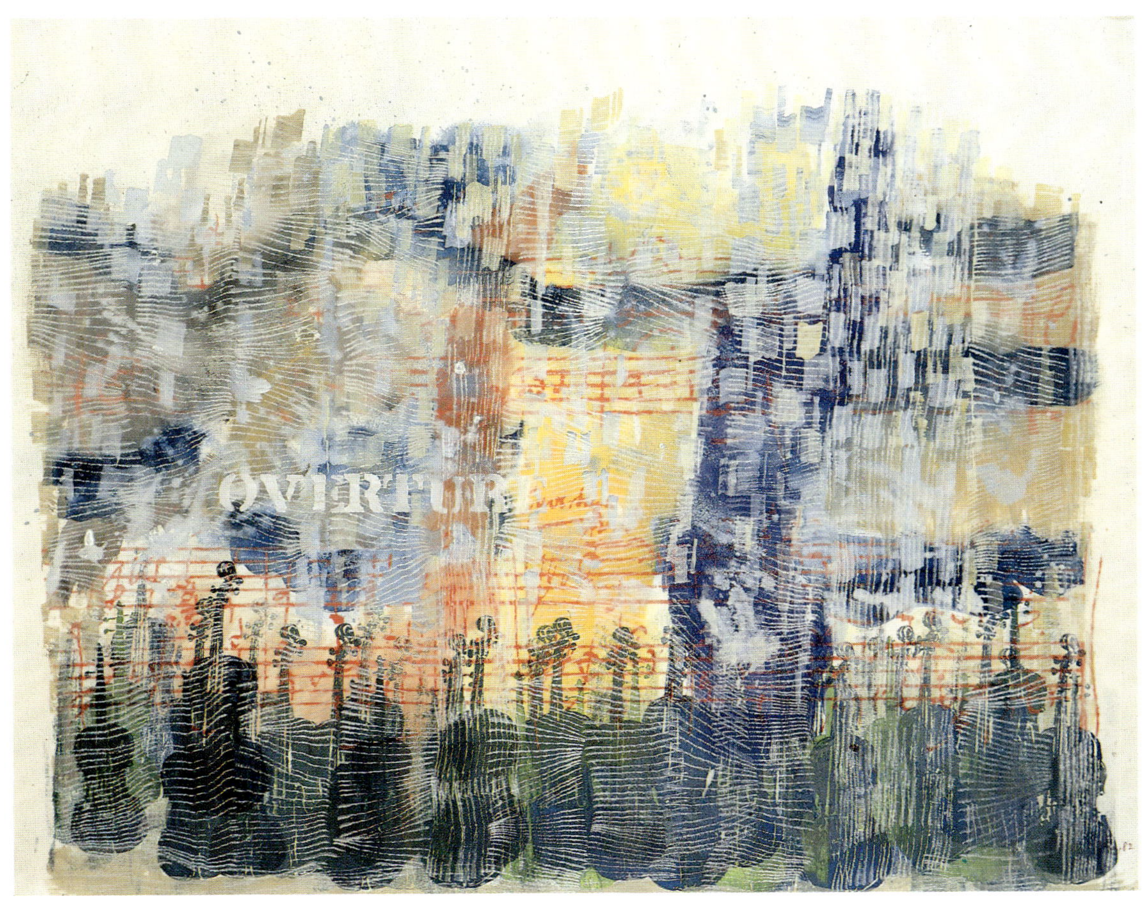

Animato, 1982, mixed media on paper, 61x80m, Private Collection, Tokyo
Overture, 1982, mixed media on paper, 61x80cm, Private Collection, Tokyo

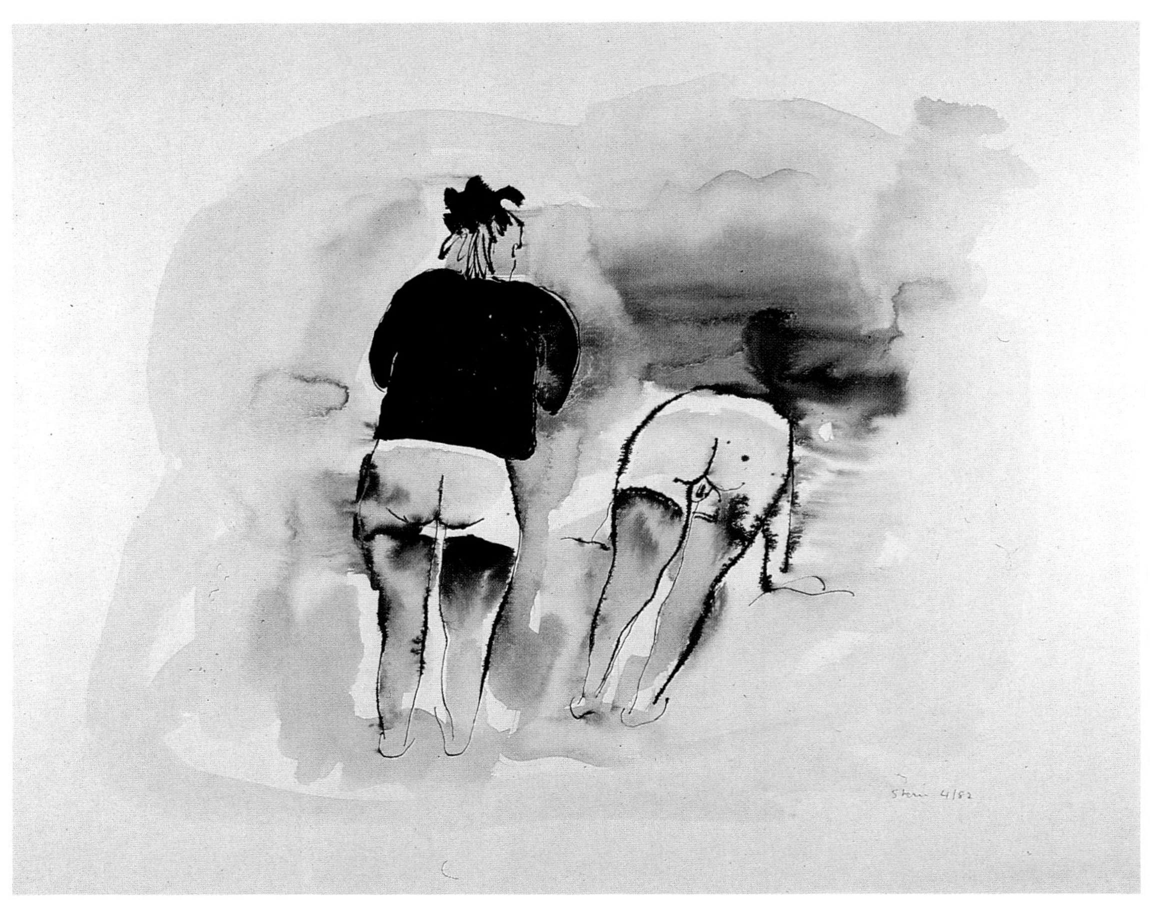

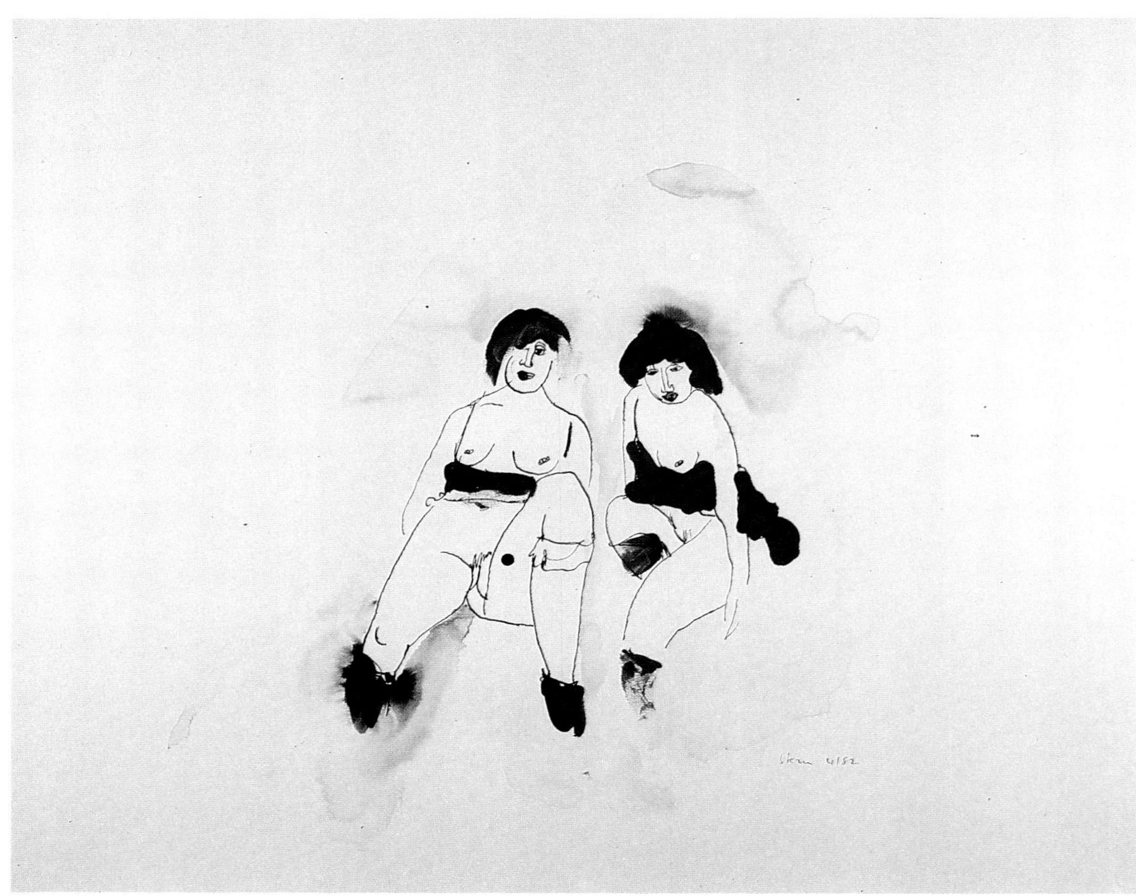

Untitled, 1982, ink on paper, 50x65cm, Artist's Collection
Untitled, 1982, ink on paper, 50x65cm, Artist's Collection

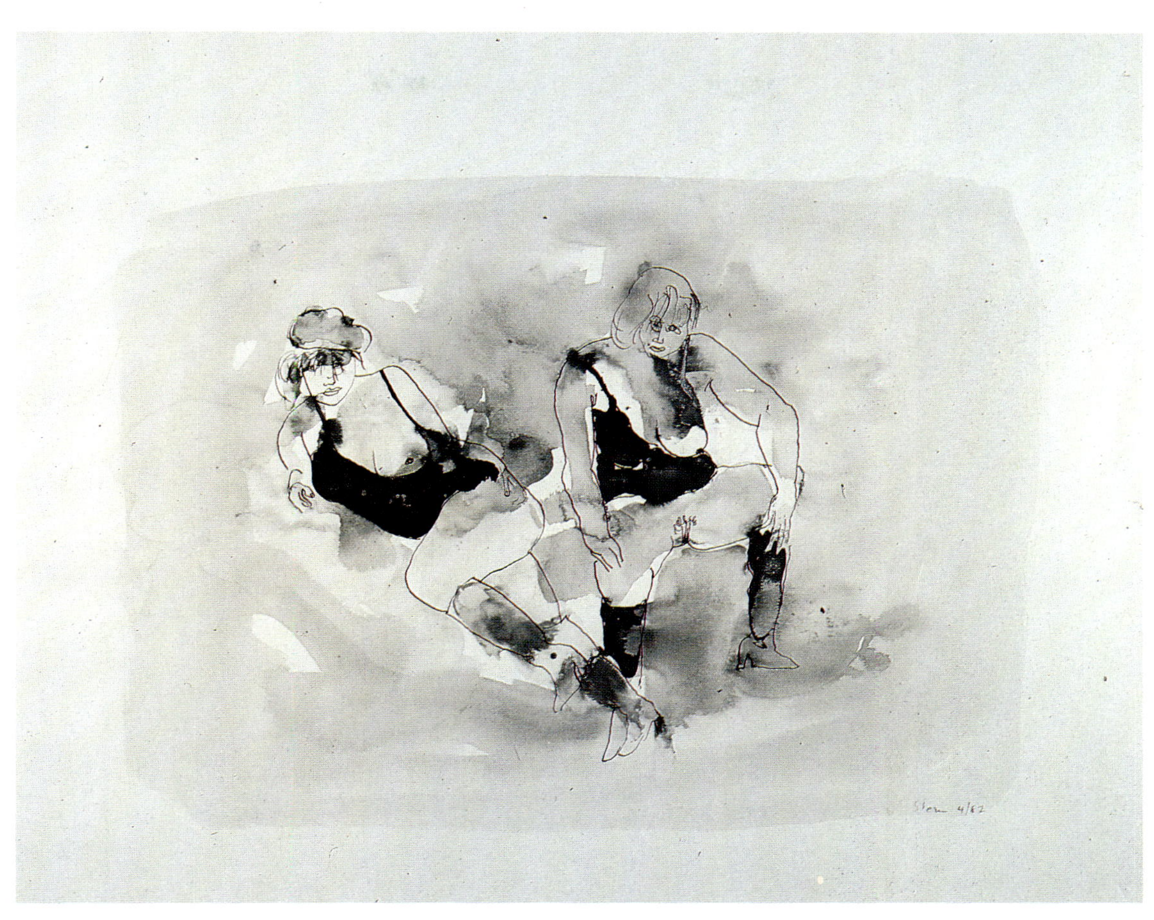

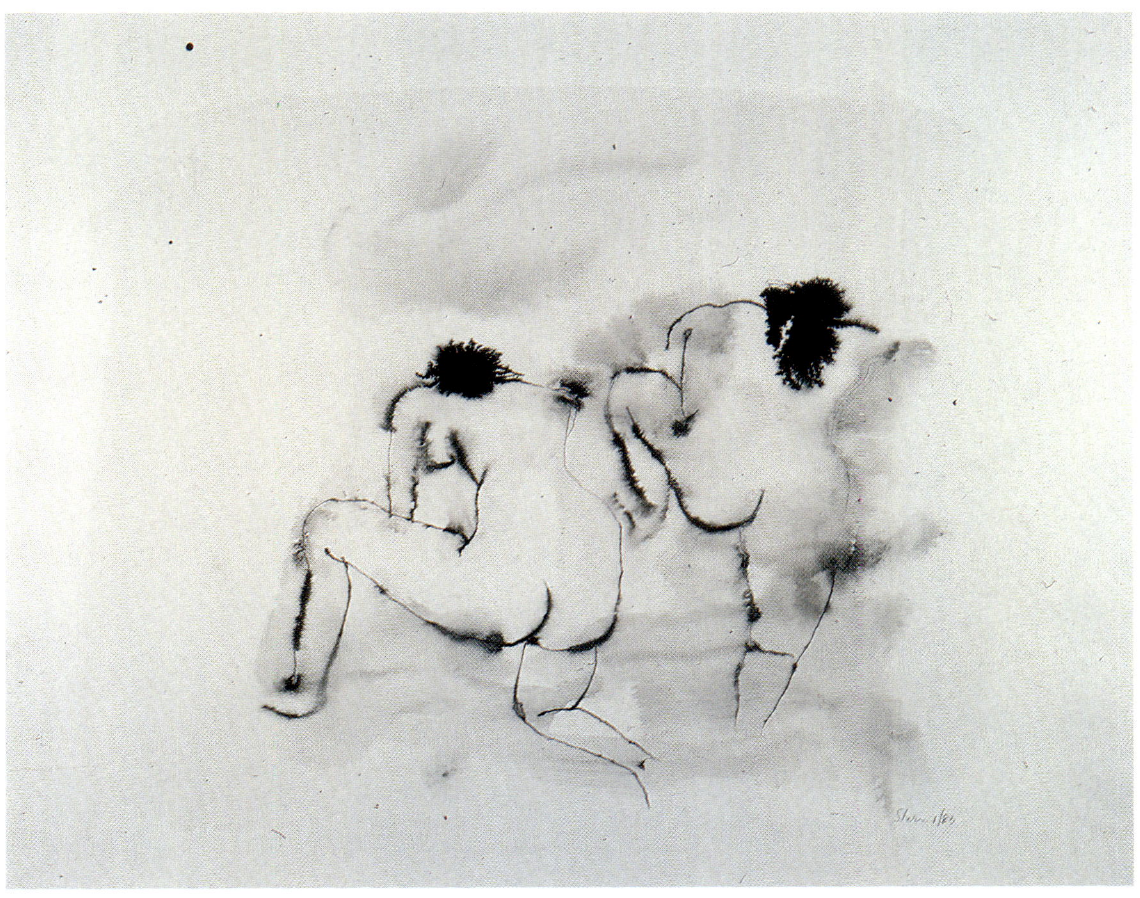

Untitled, 1982, ink on paper, 50x65cm, Artist's Collection
Untitled, 1982, ink on paper, 50x65cm, Artist's Collection

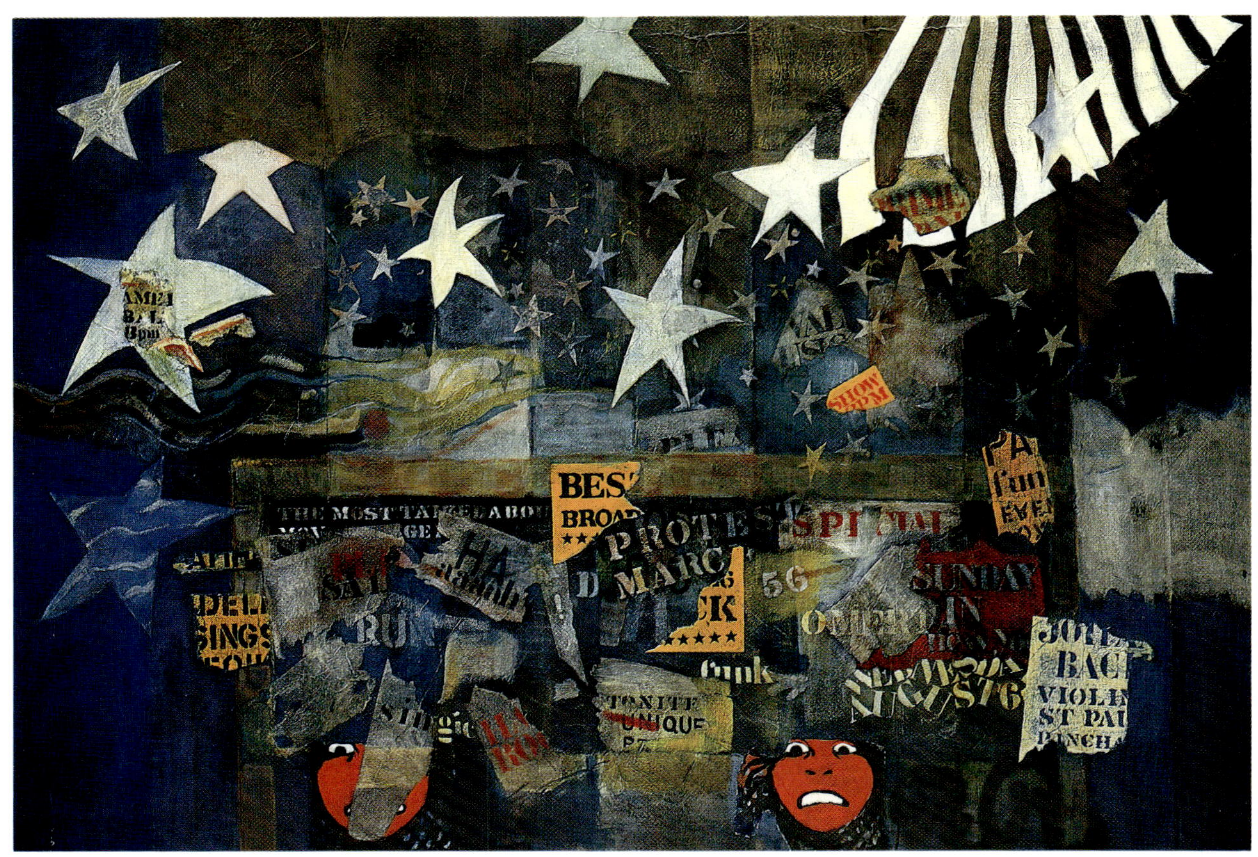

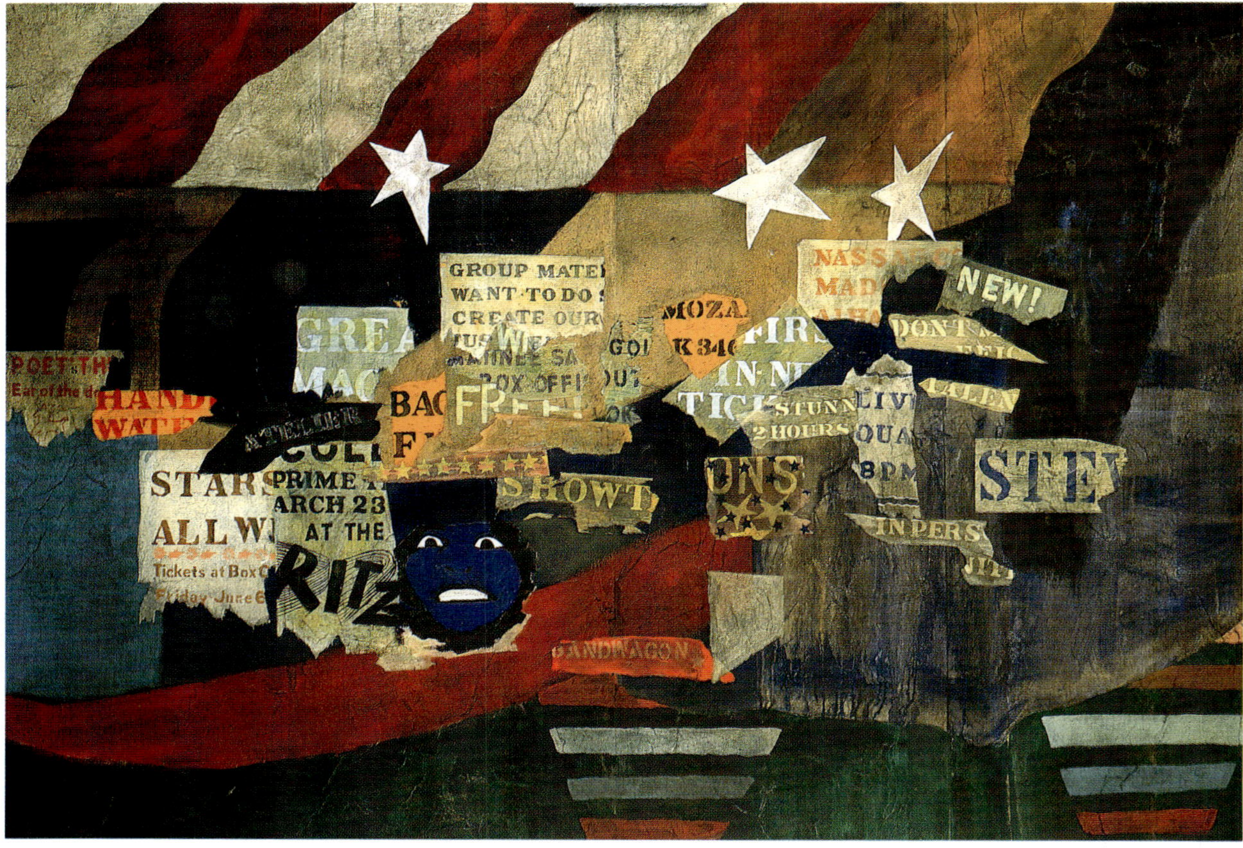

Union Square XIII, New York, 1982, oil on canvas, 130×95cm, Private Collection, West Germany
Union Square V, 1982, acrylic/oil/canvas, 143×196cm, Private Collection, West Germany

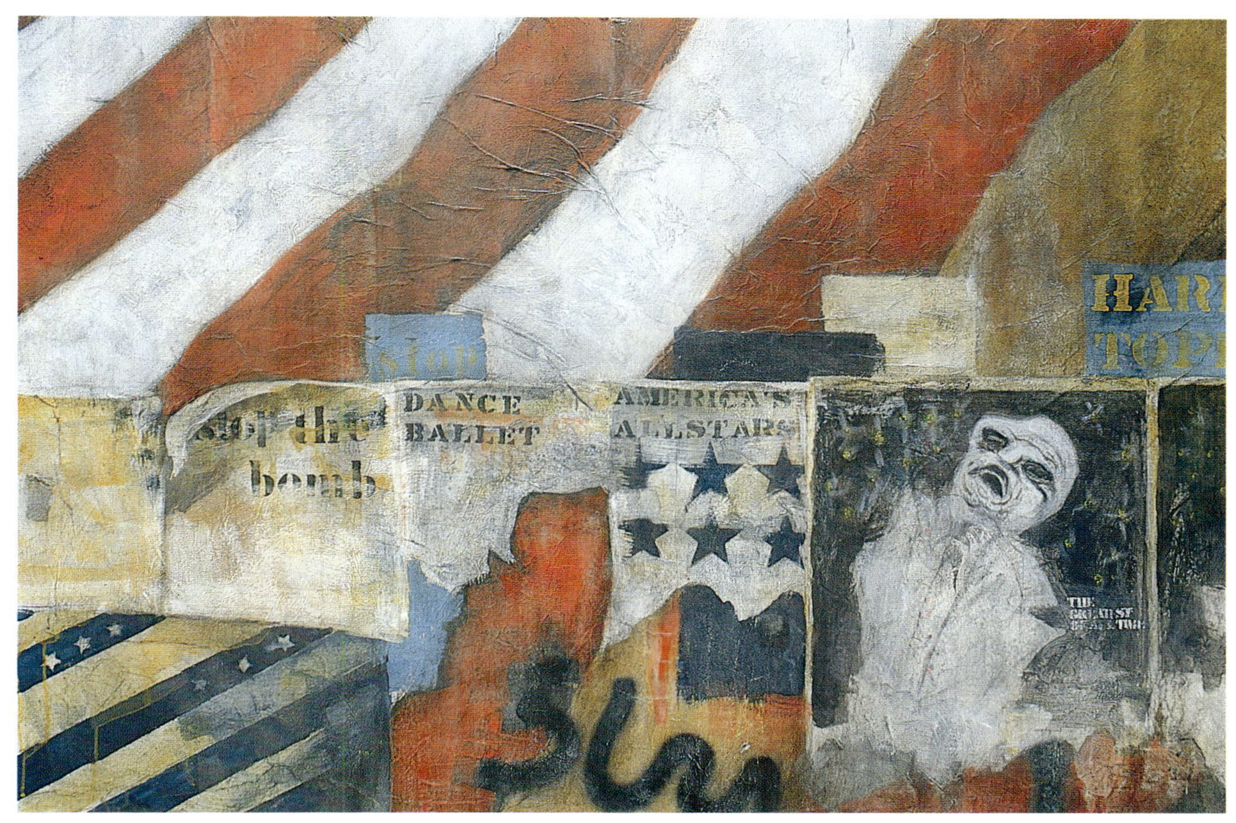

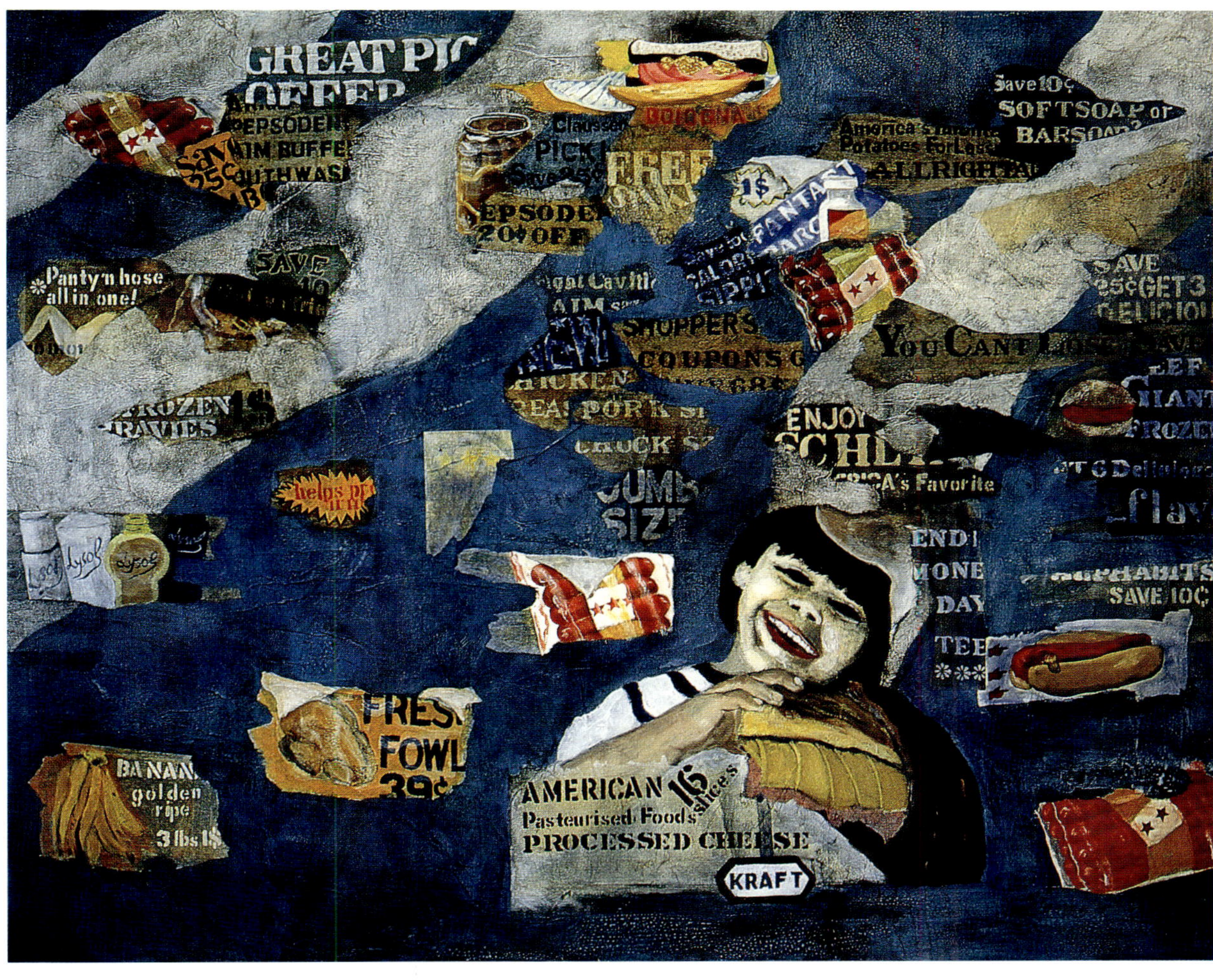

Union Square II, 1982, acrylic on canvas, 143x196cm, Artist's Collection
Union Square IV, 1982, acrylic on canvas, 114x146cm, Artist's Collection

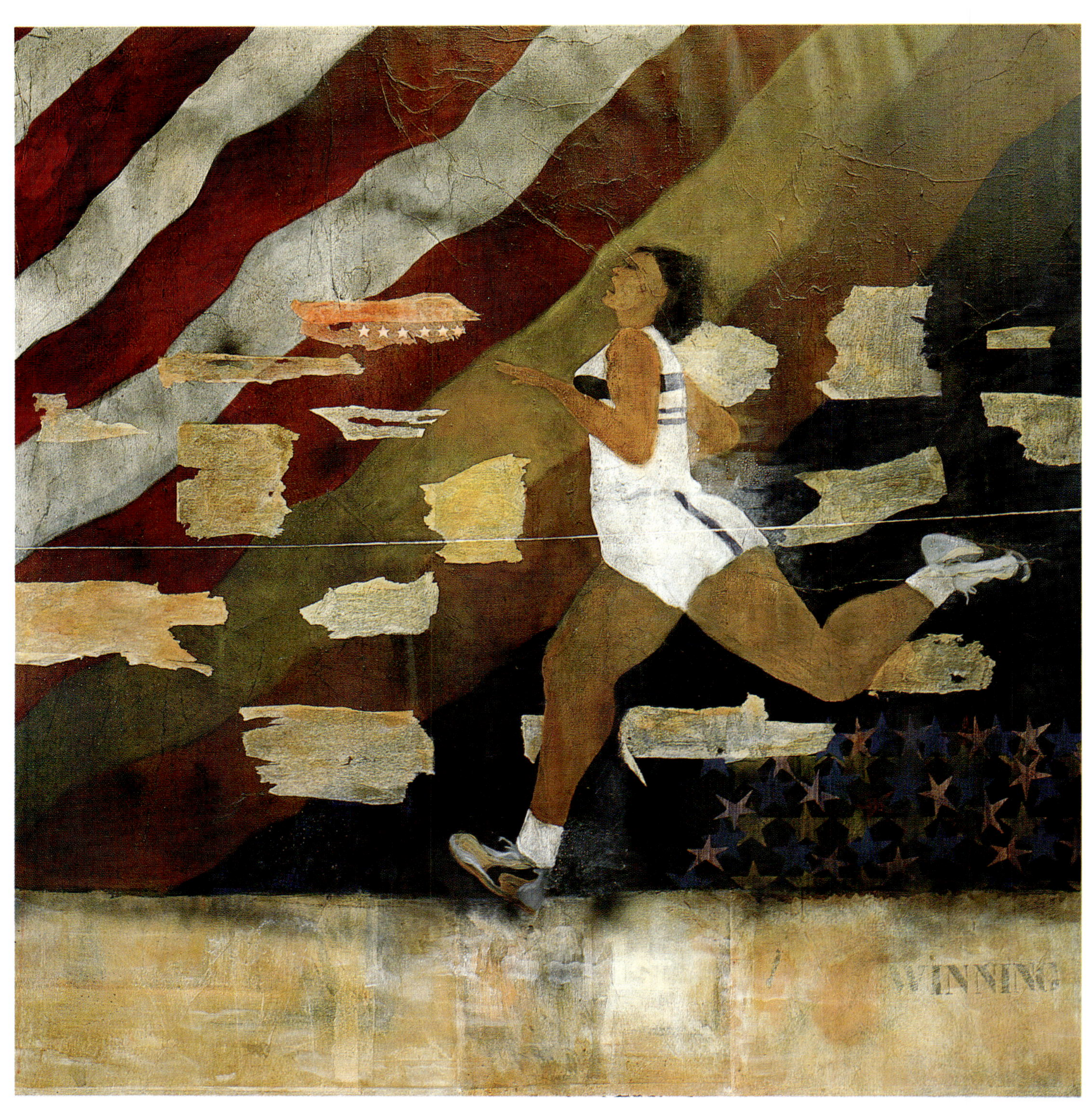

Runner, 1982, oil on canvas, 152x152cm, Della Turca Collection, Paris

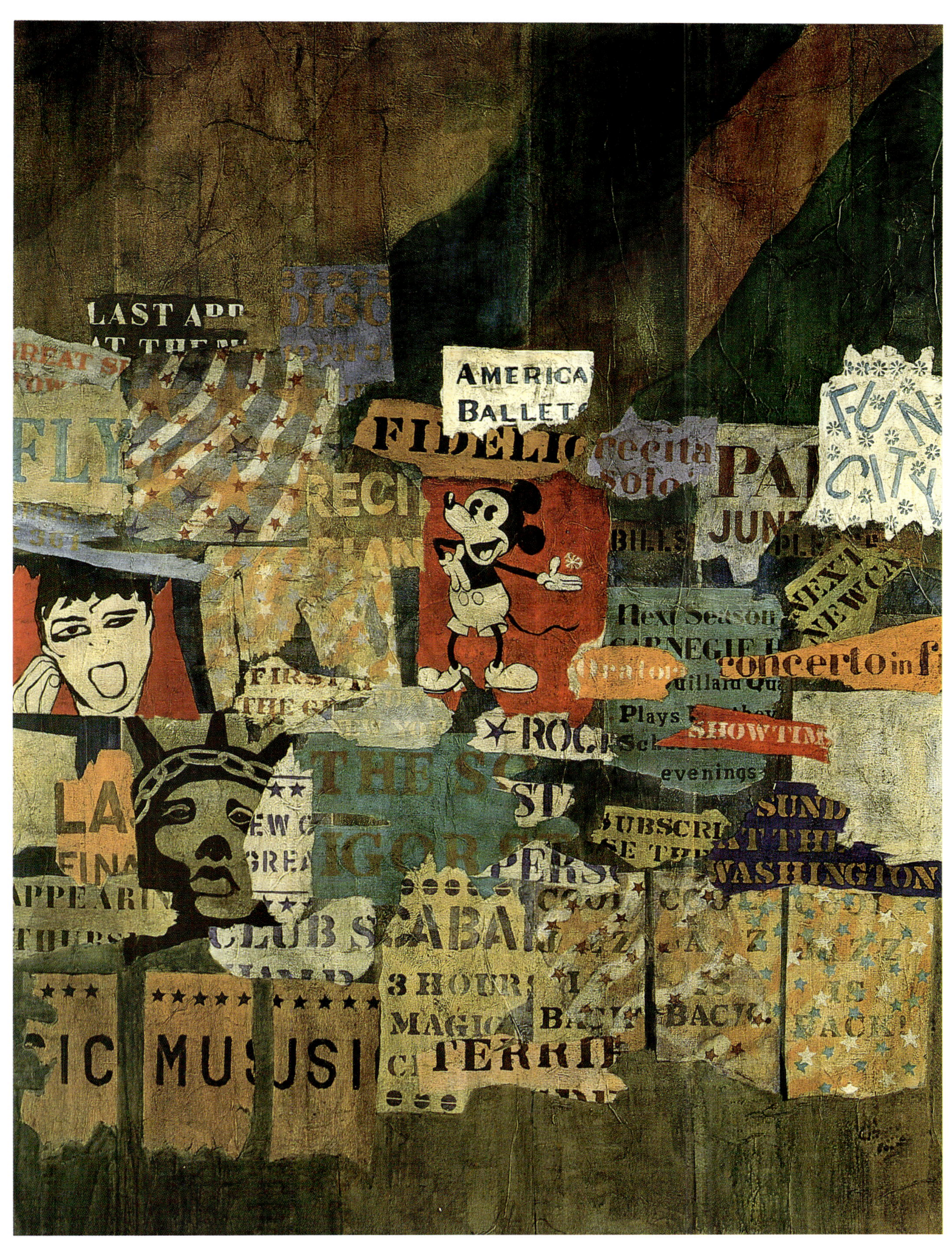

Union Square, New York, 1982, oil on canvas, 146x114cm, Private Collection, Paris

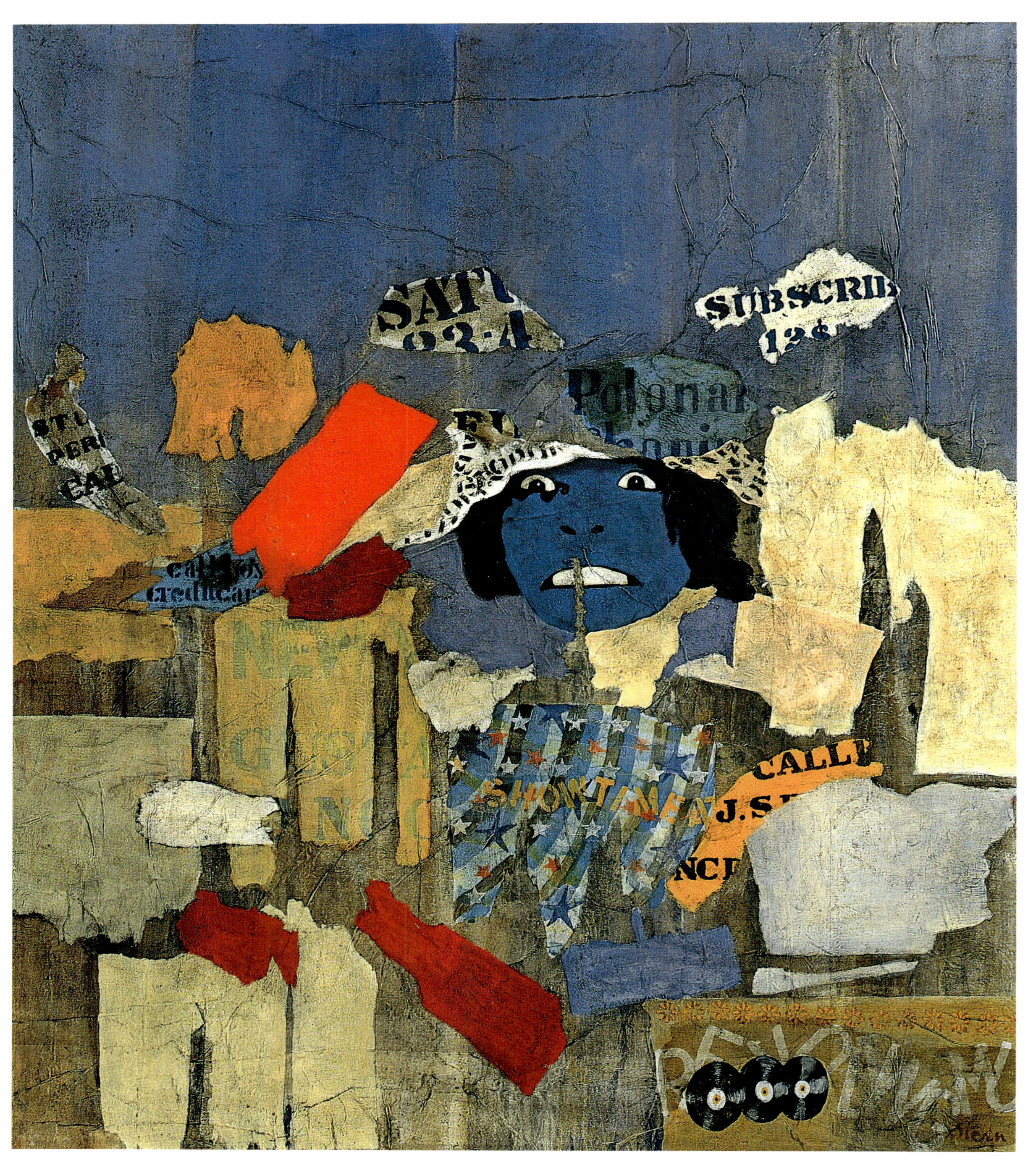

Union Square, 1982, acrylic on canvas, 102×92cm, Ashkenazy Collection, Los Angeles

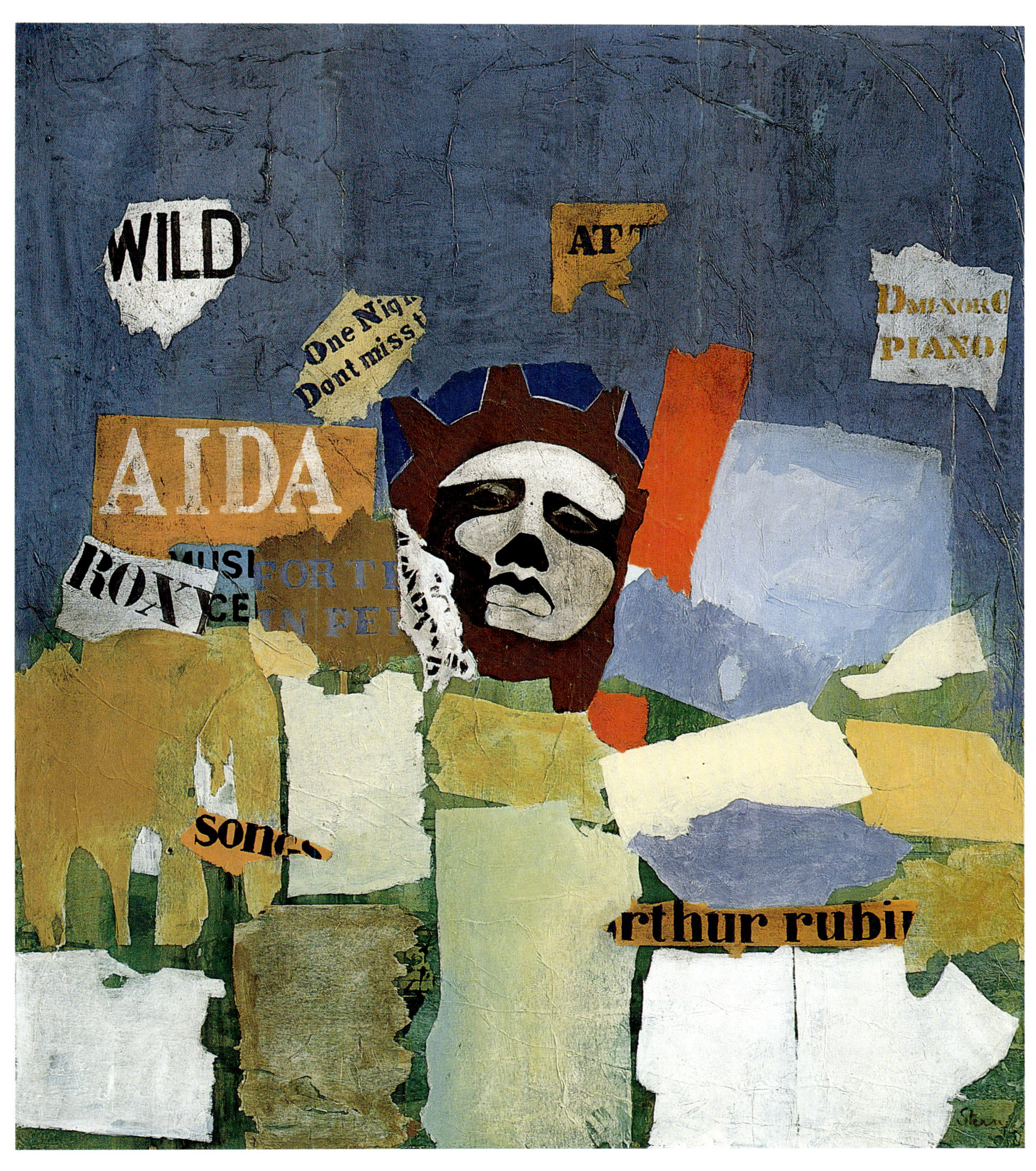

Union Square VII, 1982, acrylic on canvas, 102x92cm, Artist's Collection

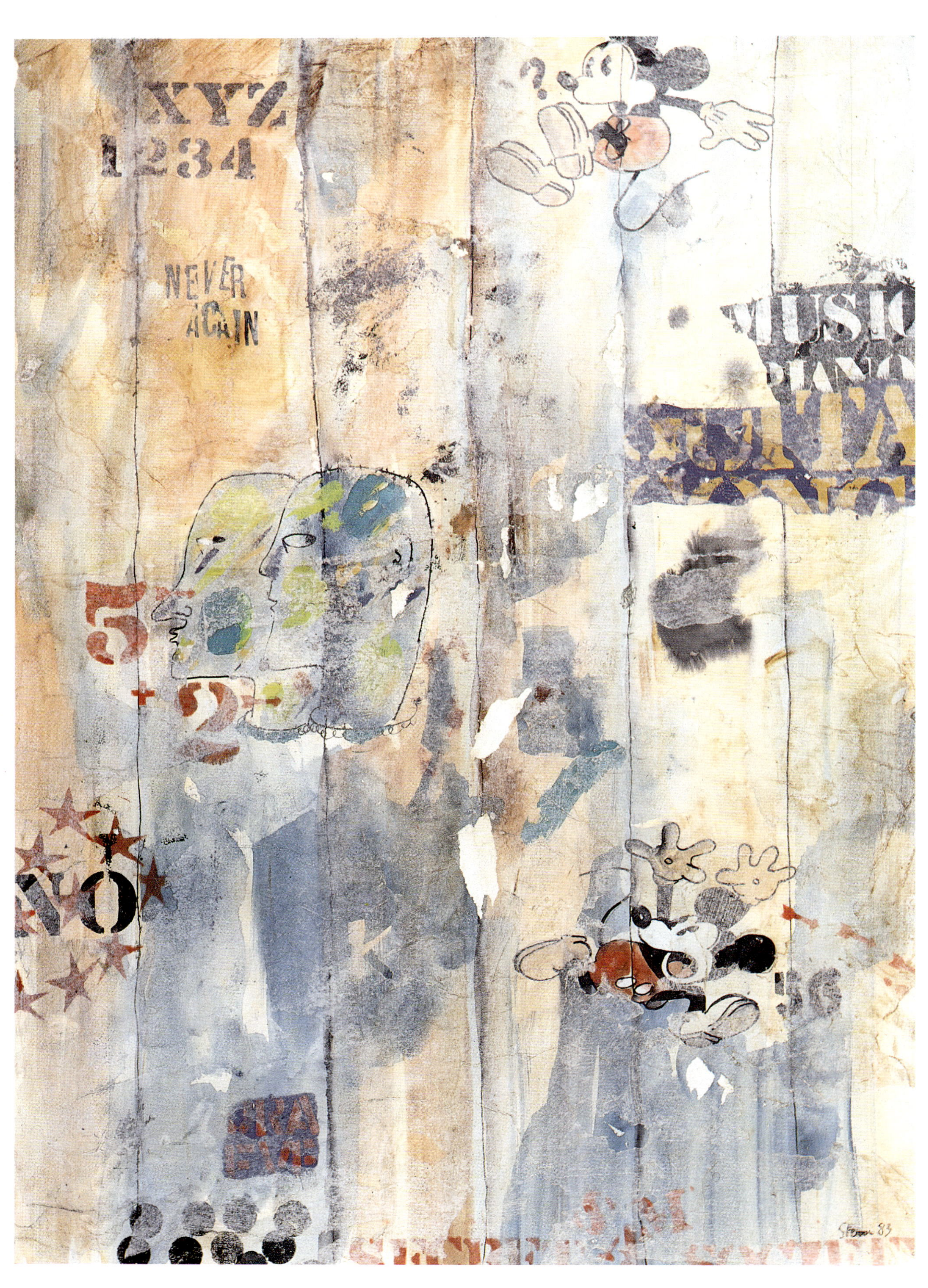

Méfiance, 1982, mixed media on paper, 75x56cm, Artist's Collection

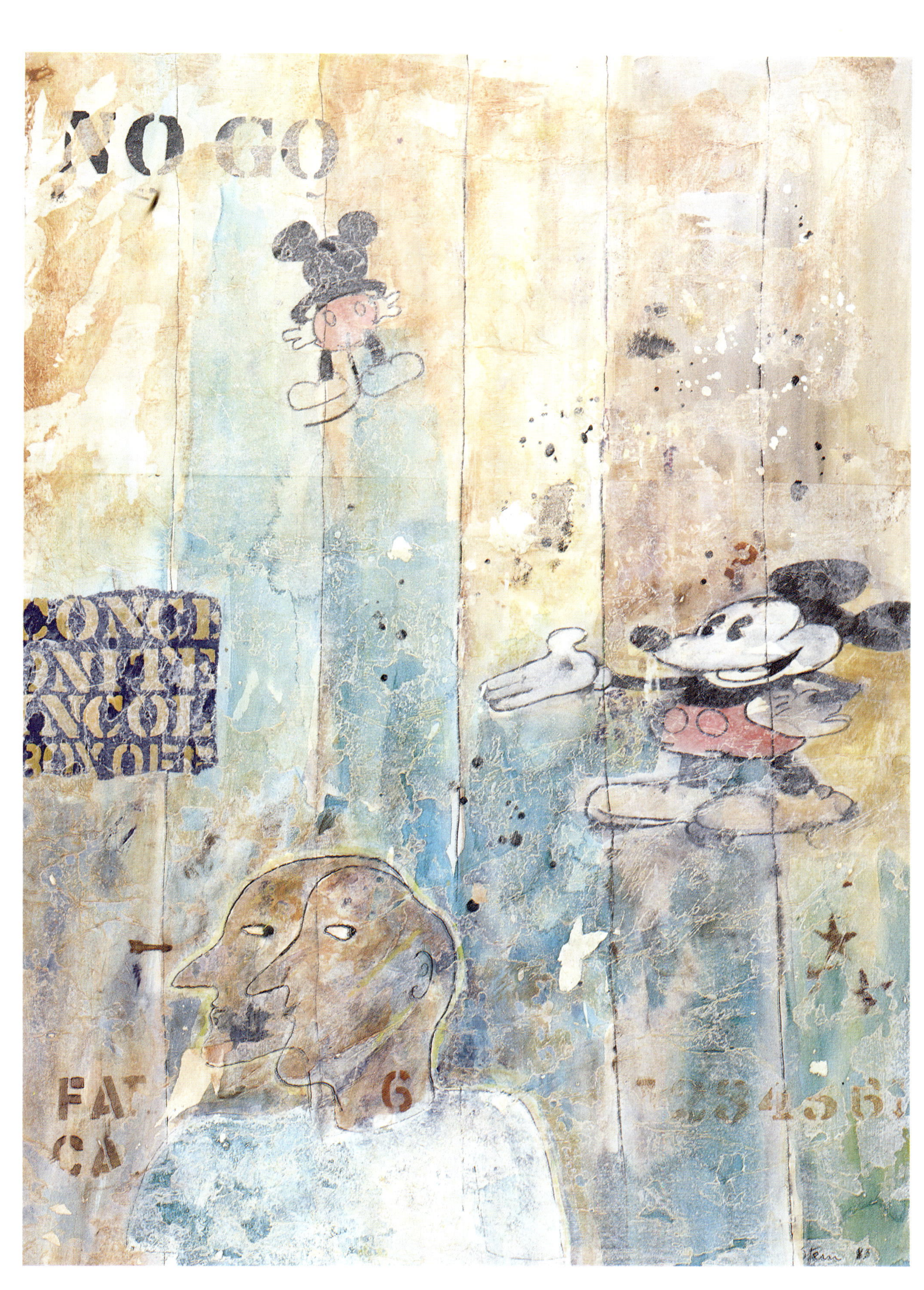

Mickey au Mur, 1982, mixed media on paper, 75x56cm, Artist's Collection

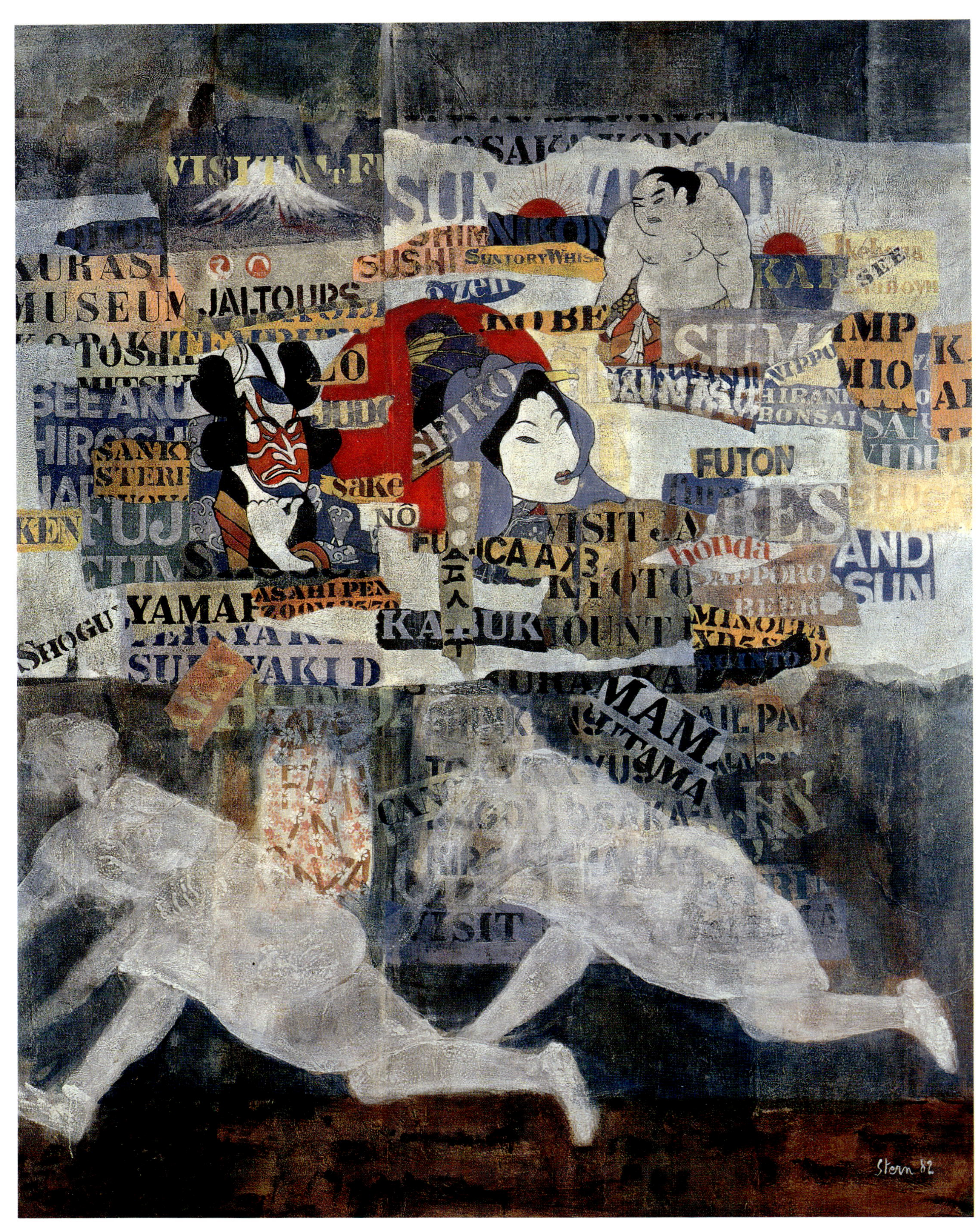

Tourism in Japan, 1983, oil on canvas, 162×130cm, Private Collection, New York

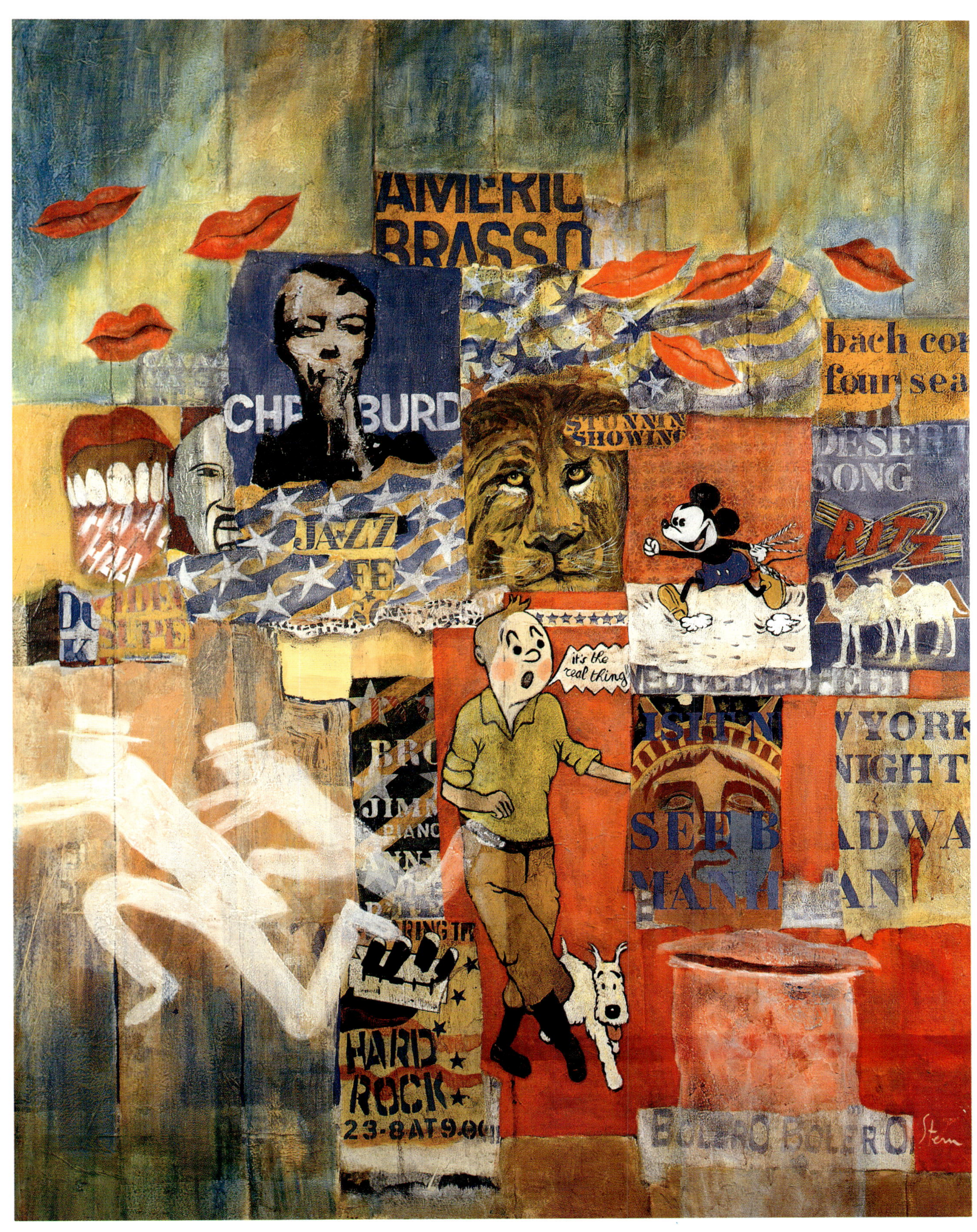

Tintin en Amérique, 1983, oil on canvas, 162x130cm, J. M. Muller Collection, Luxemburg

137

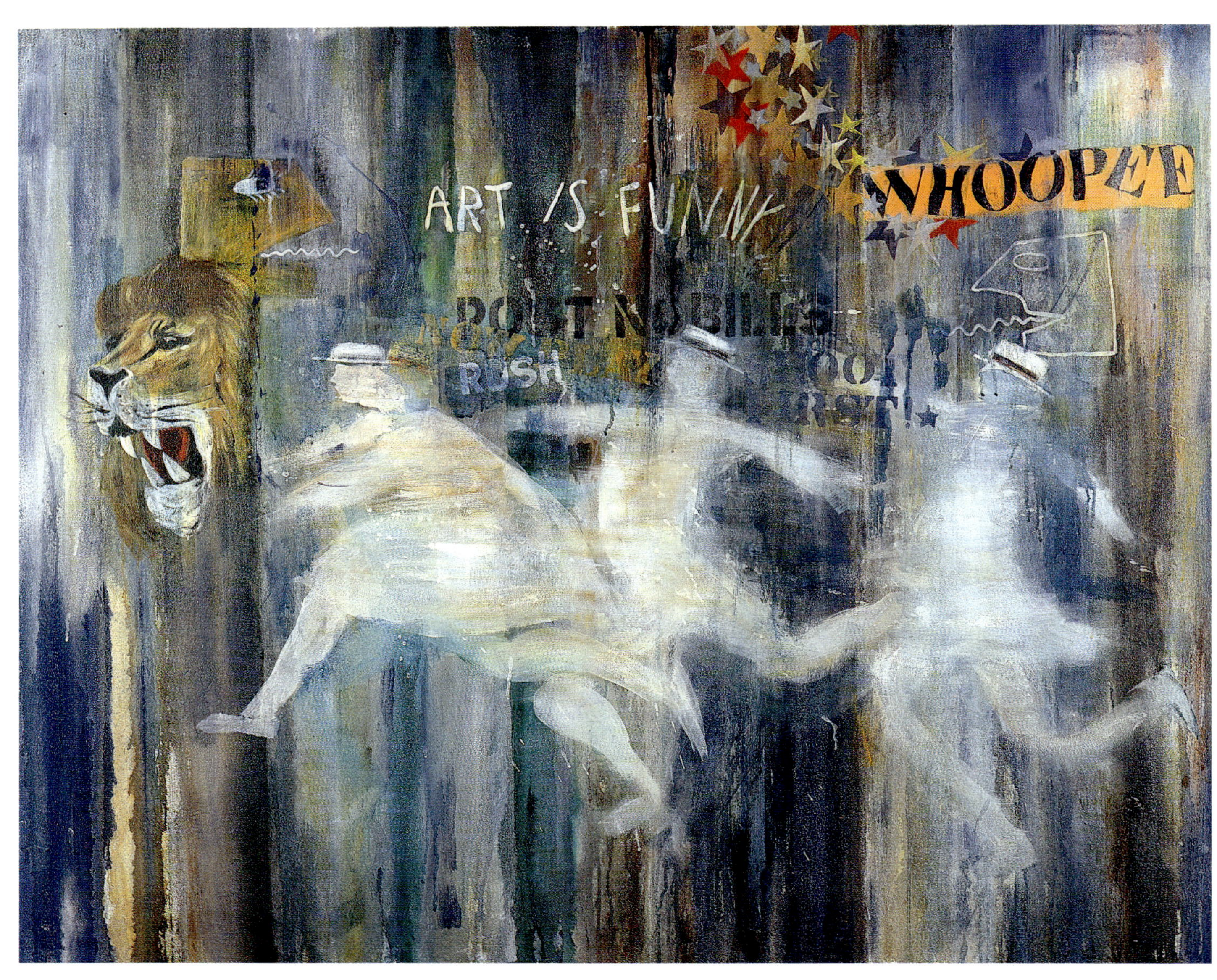

Whoopee!, 1983, oil on canvas, 114x146cm, Artist's Collection

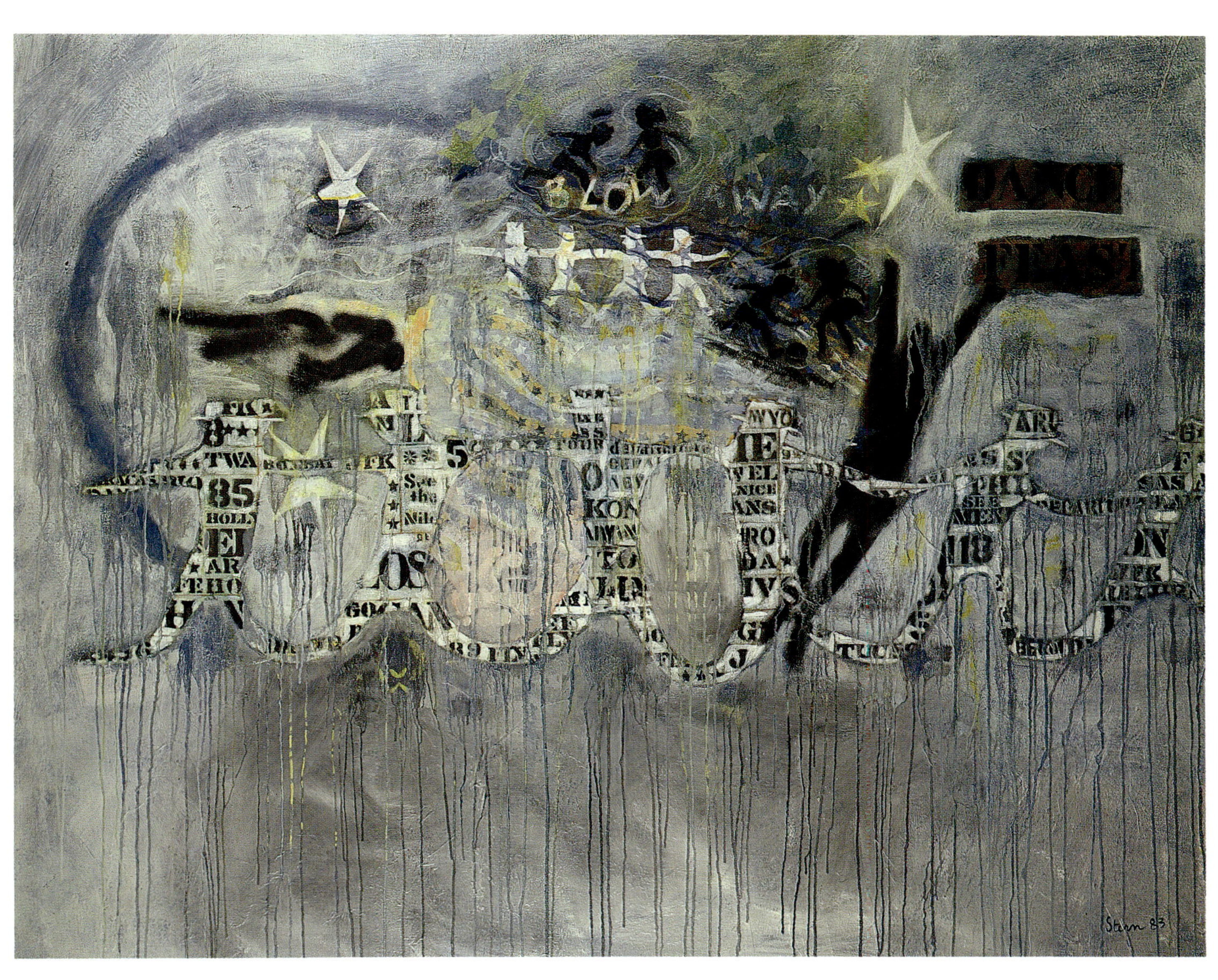

Le Mur des Voyages, 1983, oil on canvas, 130x162cm, C. Bragigand Collection, Reims

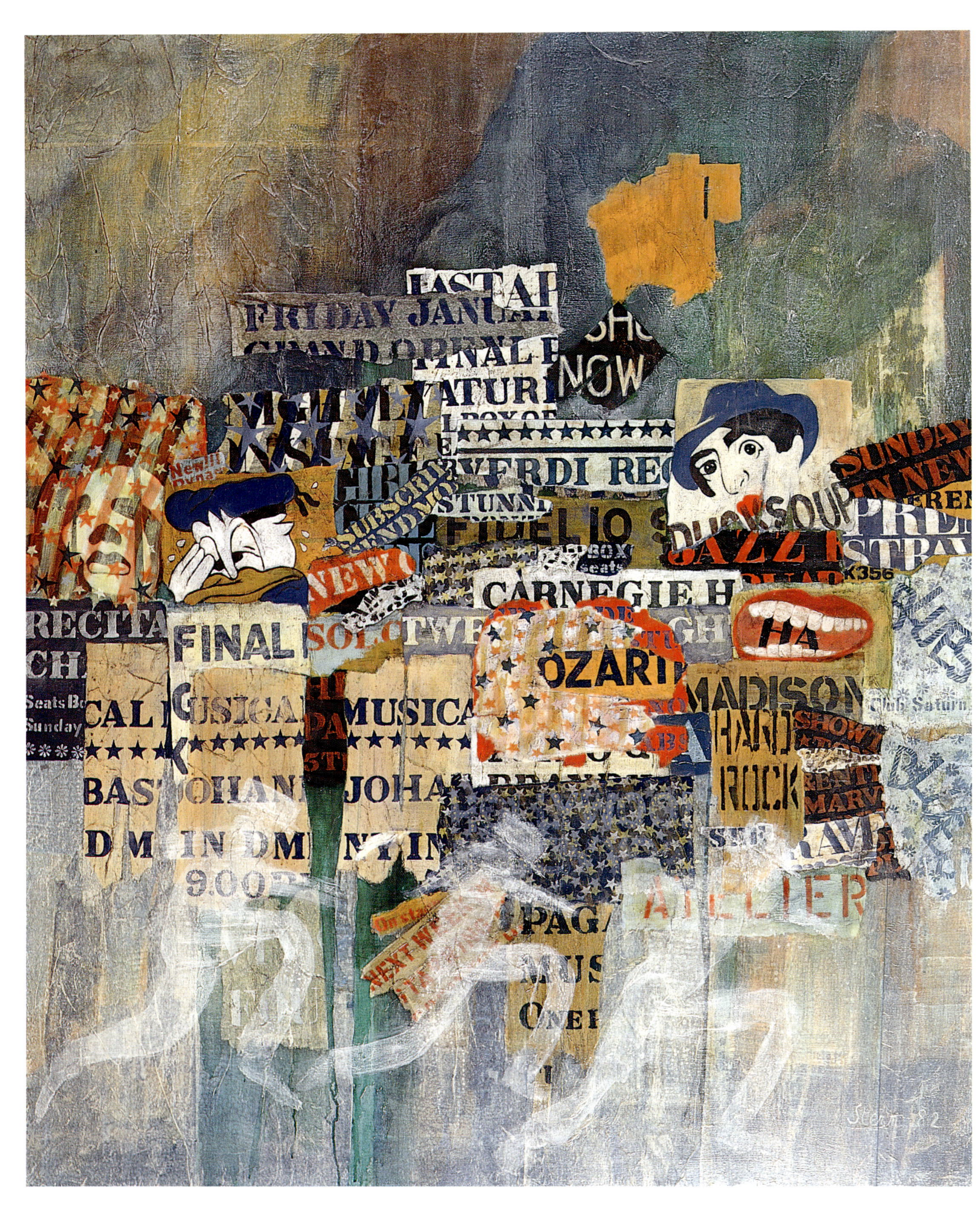

Billboard, 1983, oil on canvas, 168×137cm, Collection d'Art Moderne, Ville de Paris

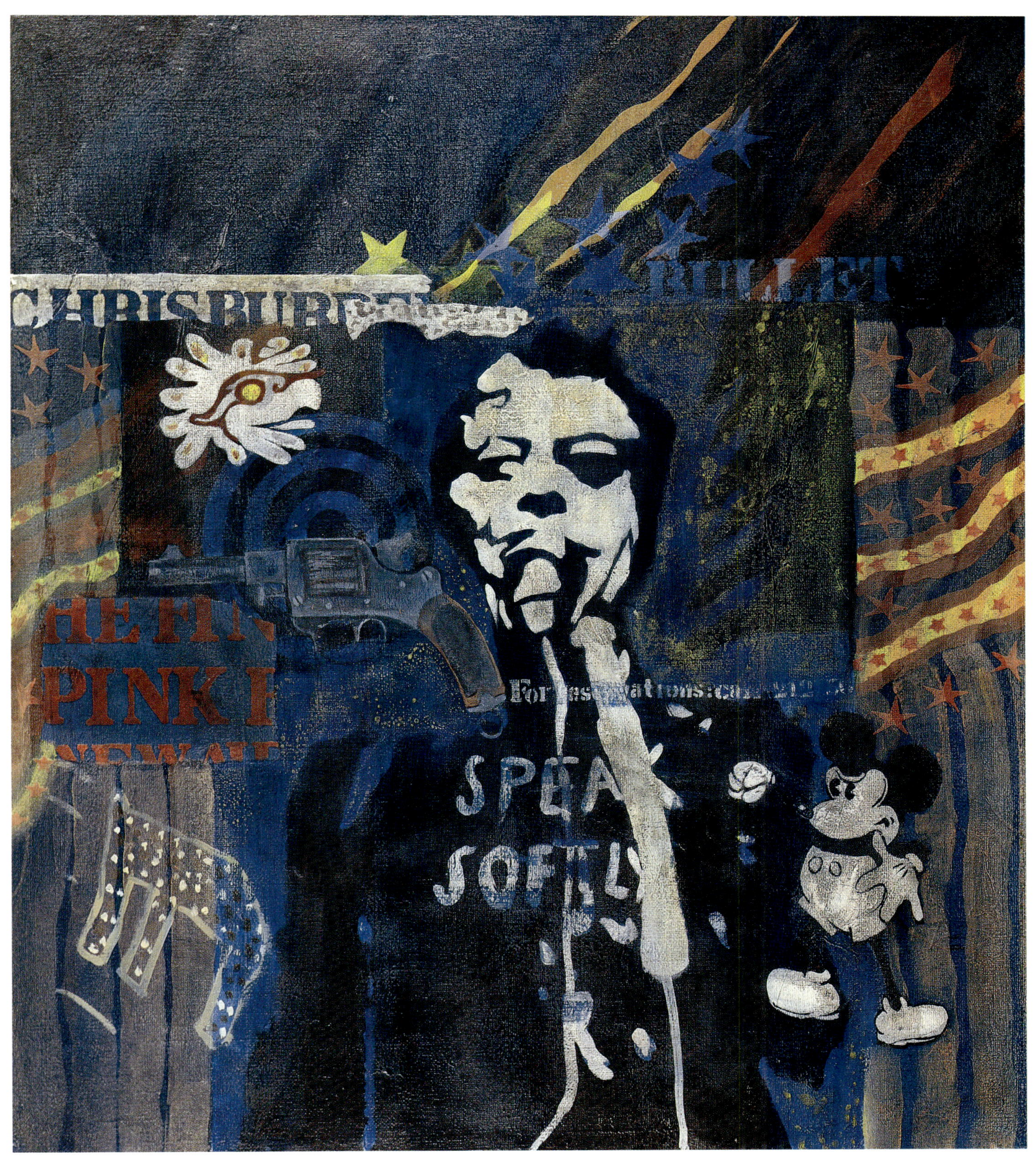

Chris Burden à l'Affiche, 1983, acrylic on canvas, 102x92cm, Private Collection, Paris

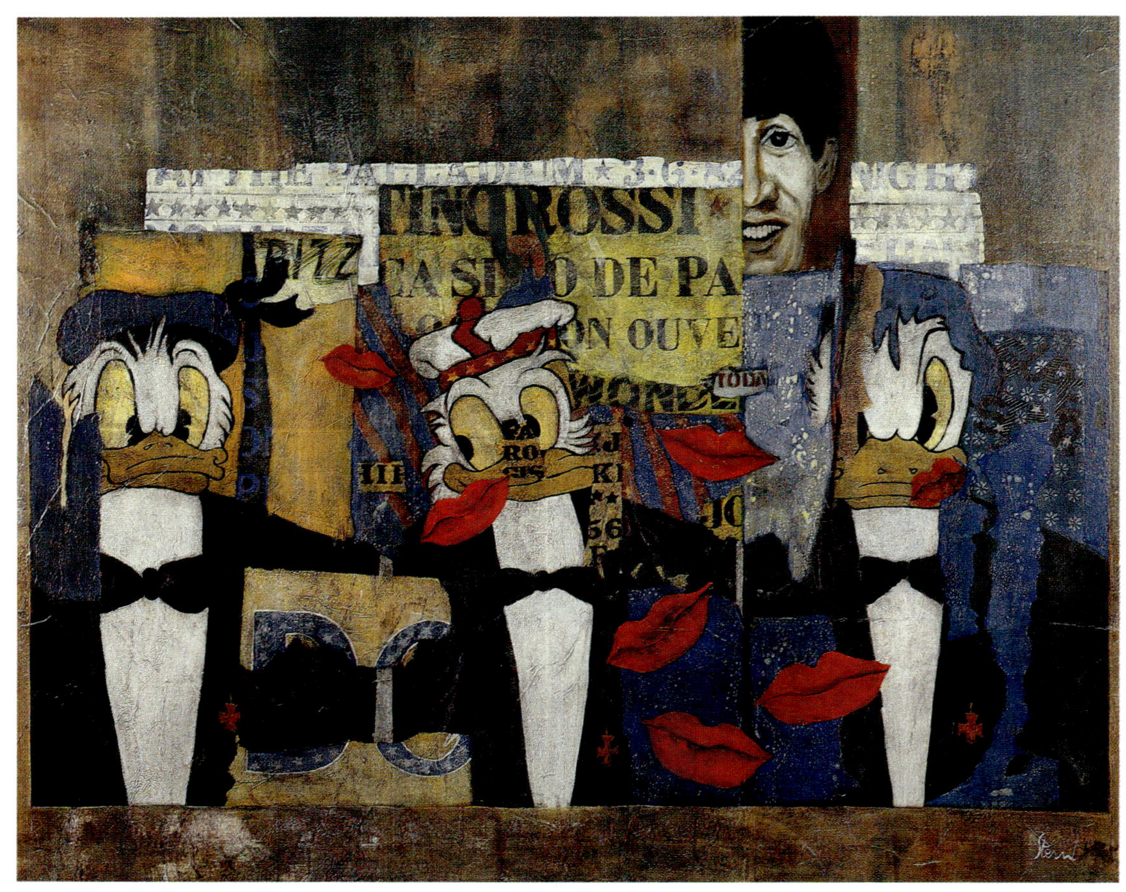

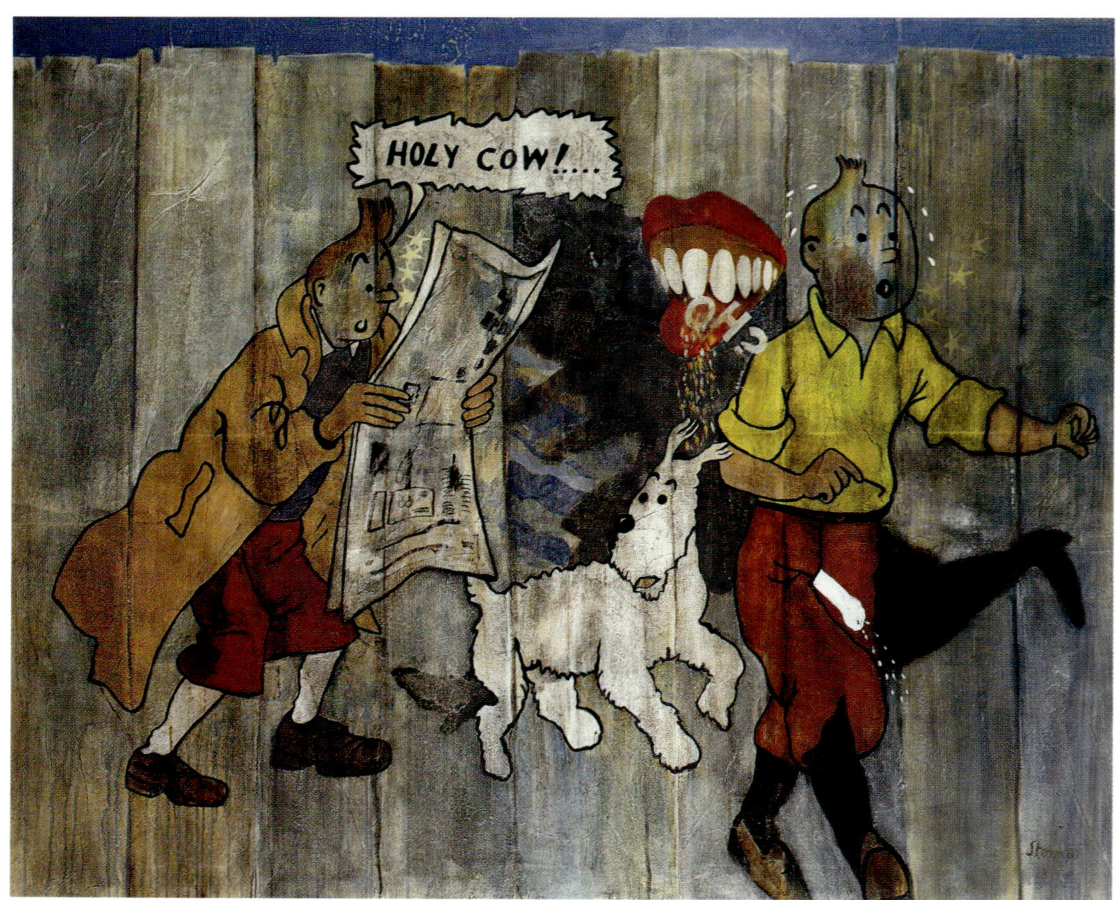

Des Baisers pour Tino, 1983, acrylic on canvas, 114x146cm, M. Henochsberg Collection, Paris
La Moustache de la Joconde, 1983, oil on canvas, 130x162cm, Artist's Collection

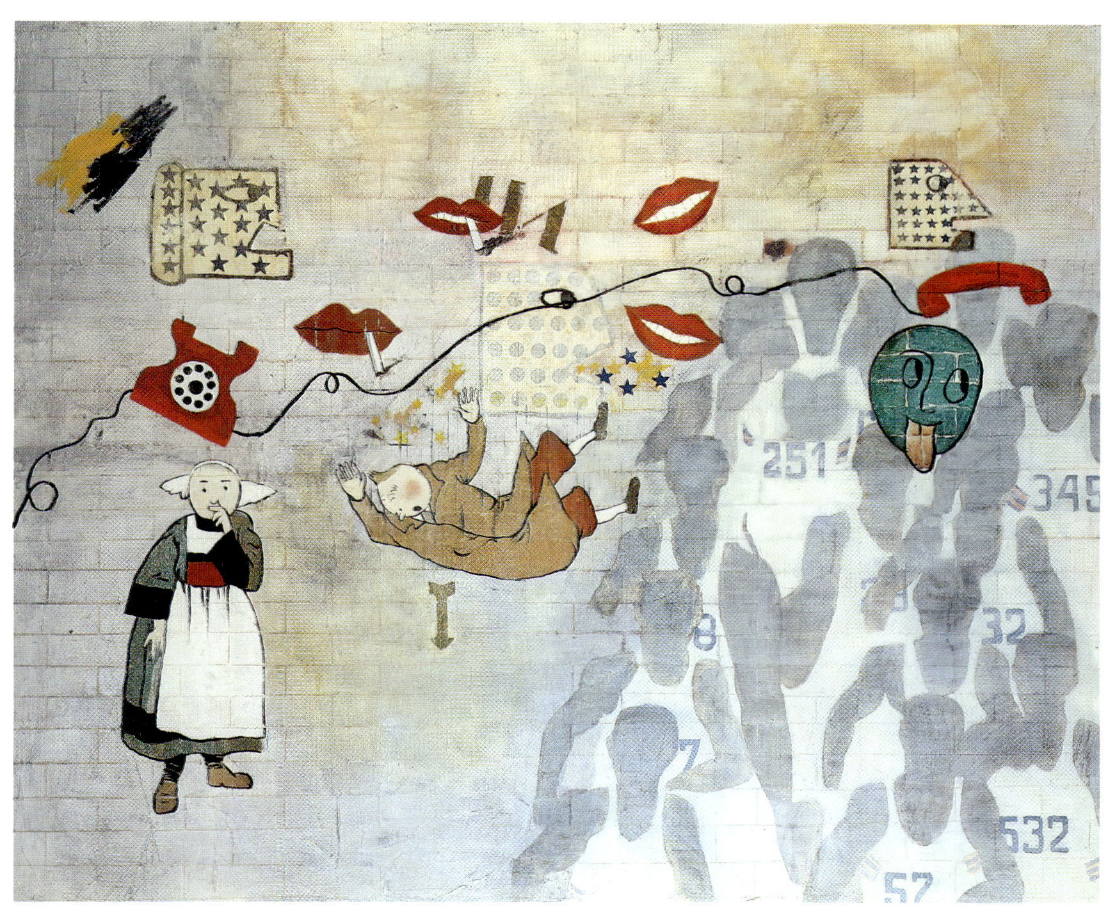

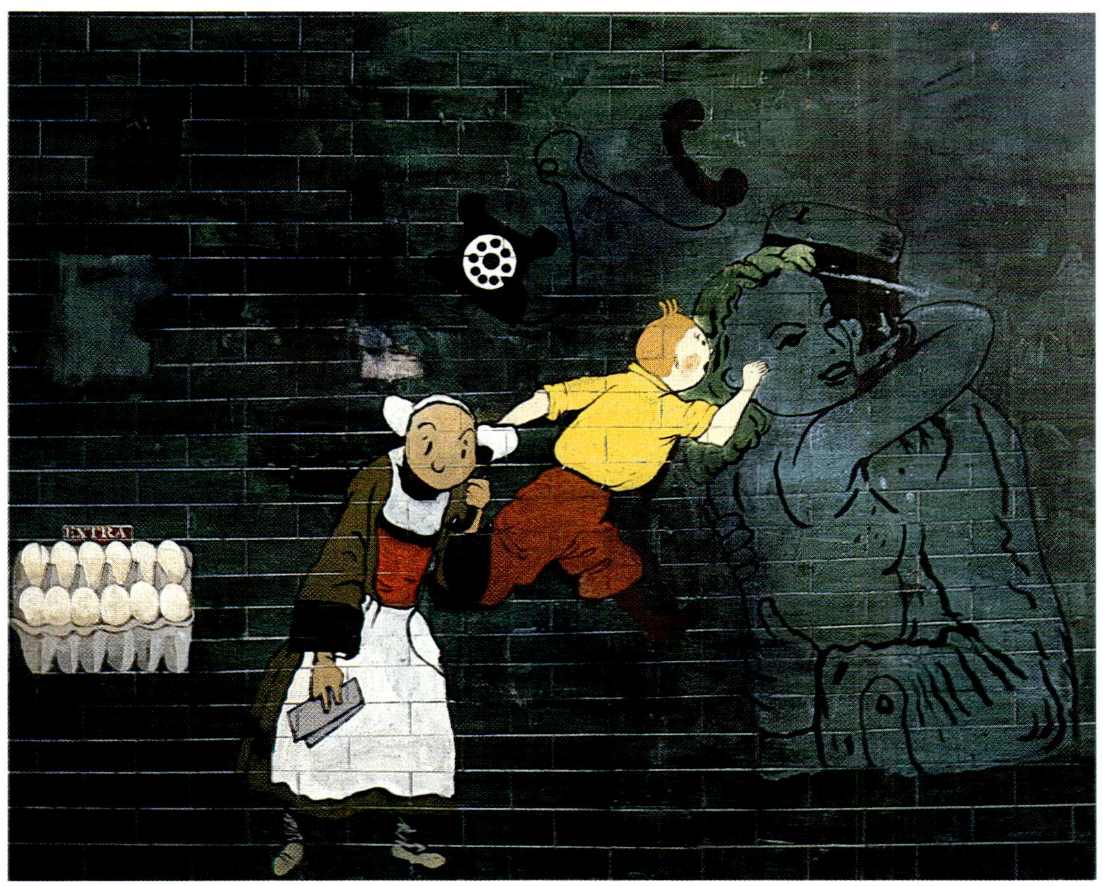

Marathon Wall, 1983, acrylic on canvas, 130x162cm, Eric Degove Collection, Paris
Calling the Wall, 1983, acrylic on canvas, 114x146cm, Artist's Collection

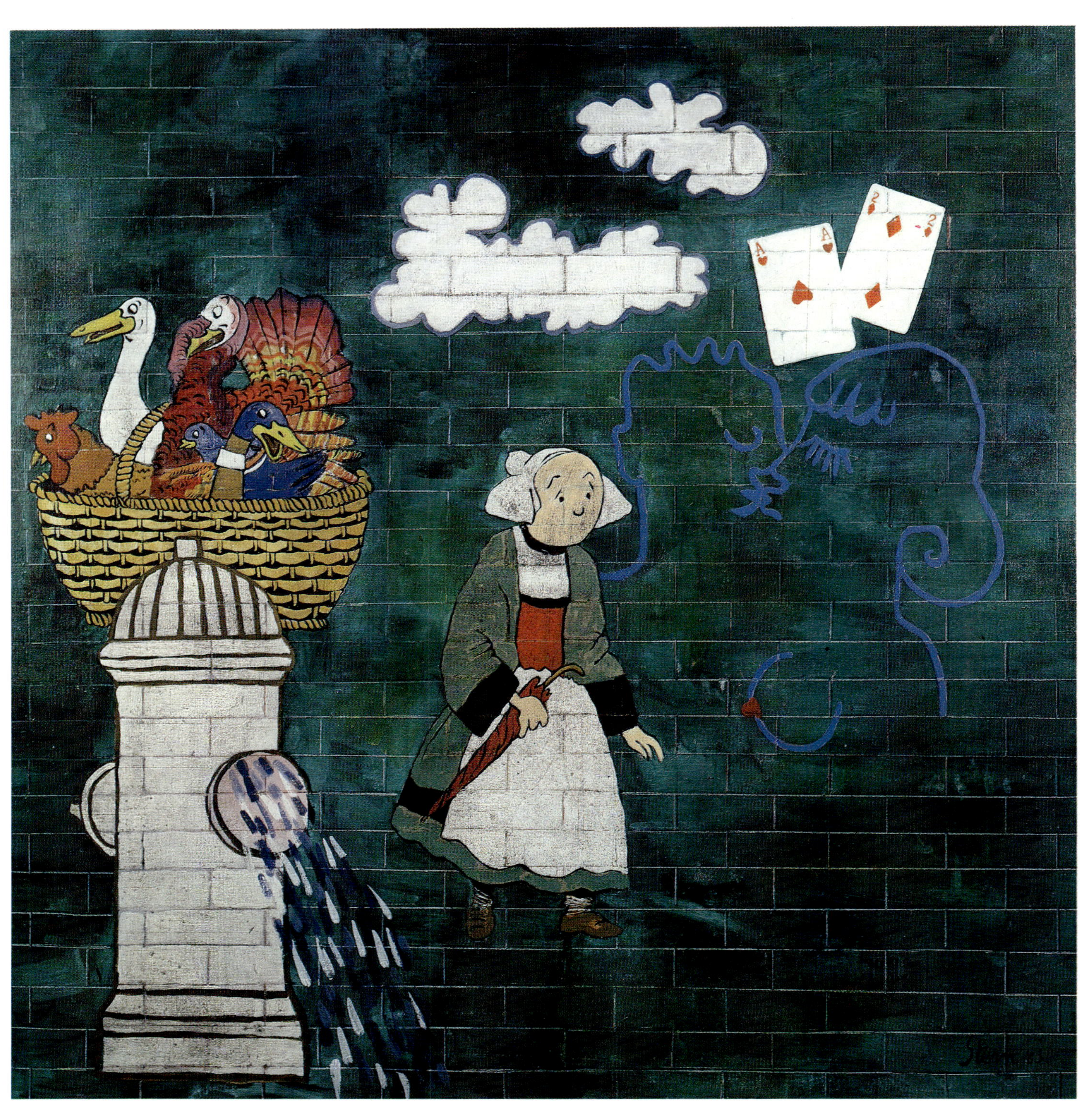

Le Mur au Panier, 1983, acrylic on canvas, 152x152cm, Daniel Hechter Collection, Paris

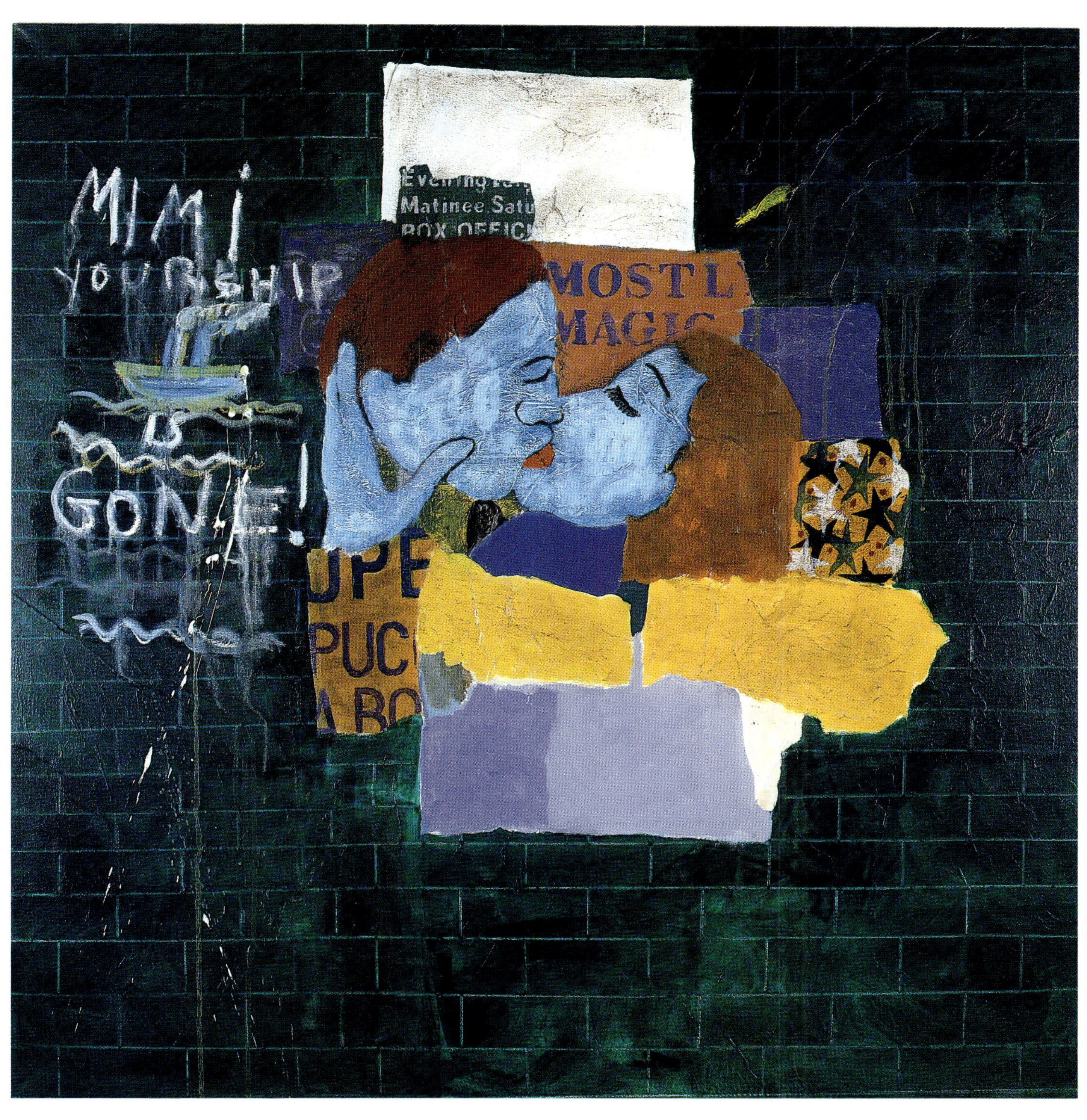

Mimi's Love, 1983, acrylic on canvas, 122x122cm, Private Collection, New York

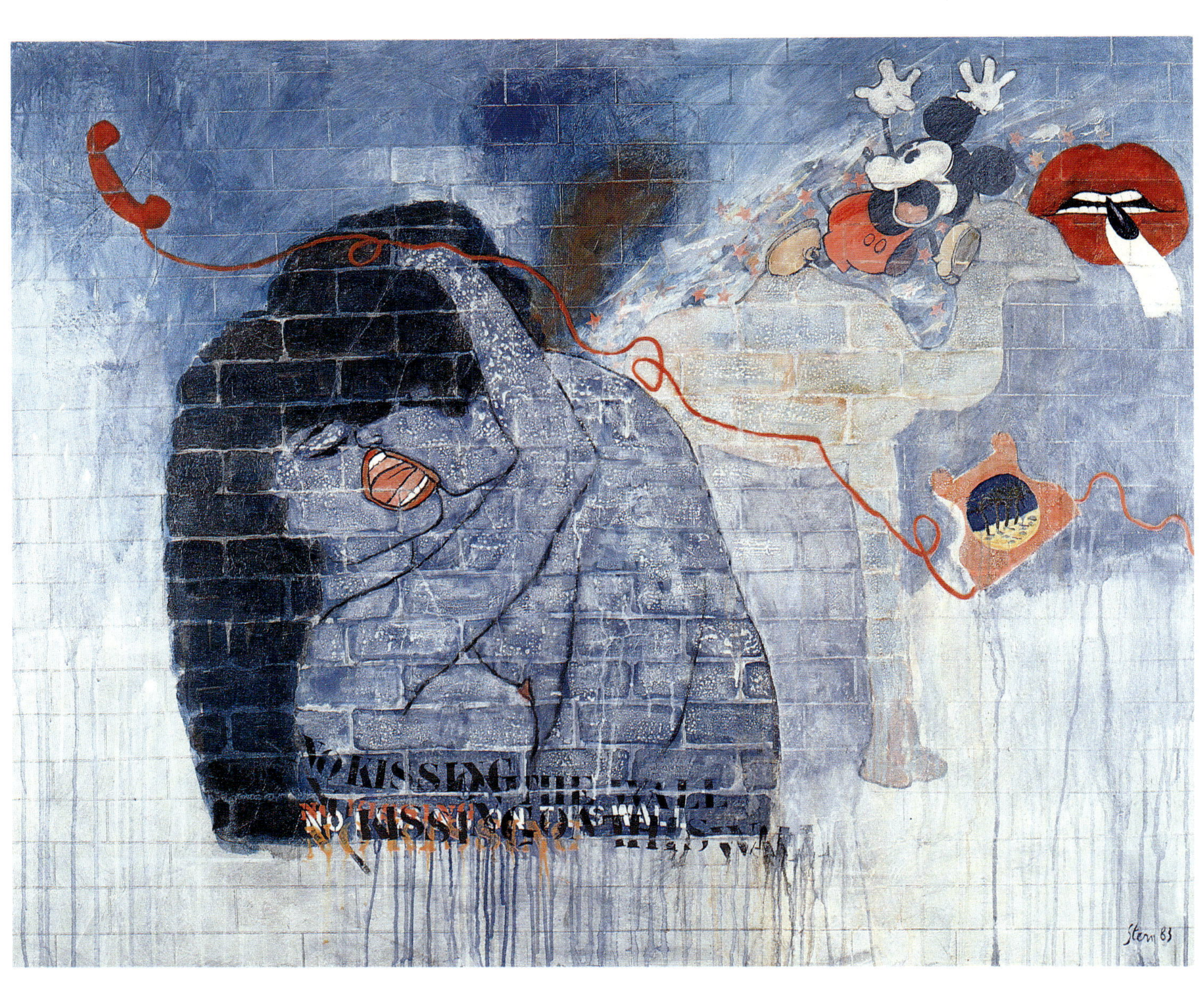

Lovers, 1983, oil on canvas, 119x146cm, J. L. Bachoud Collection, Paris

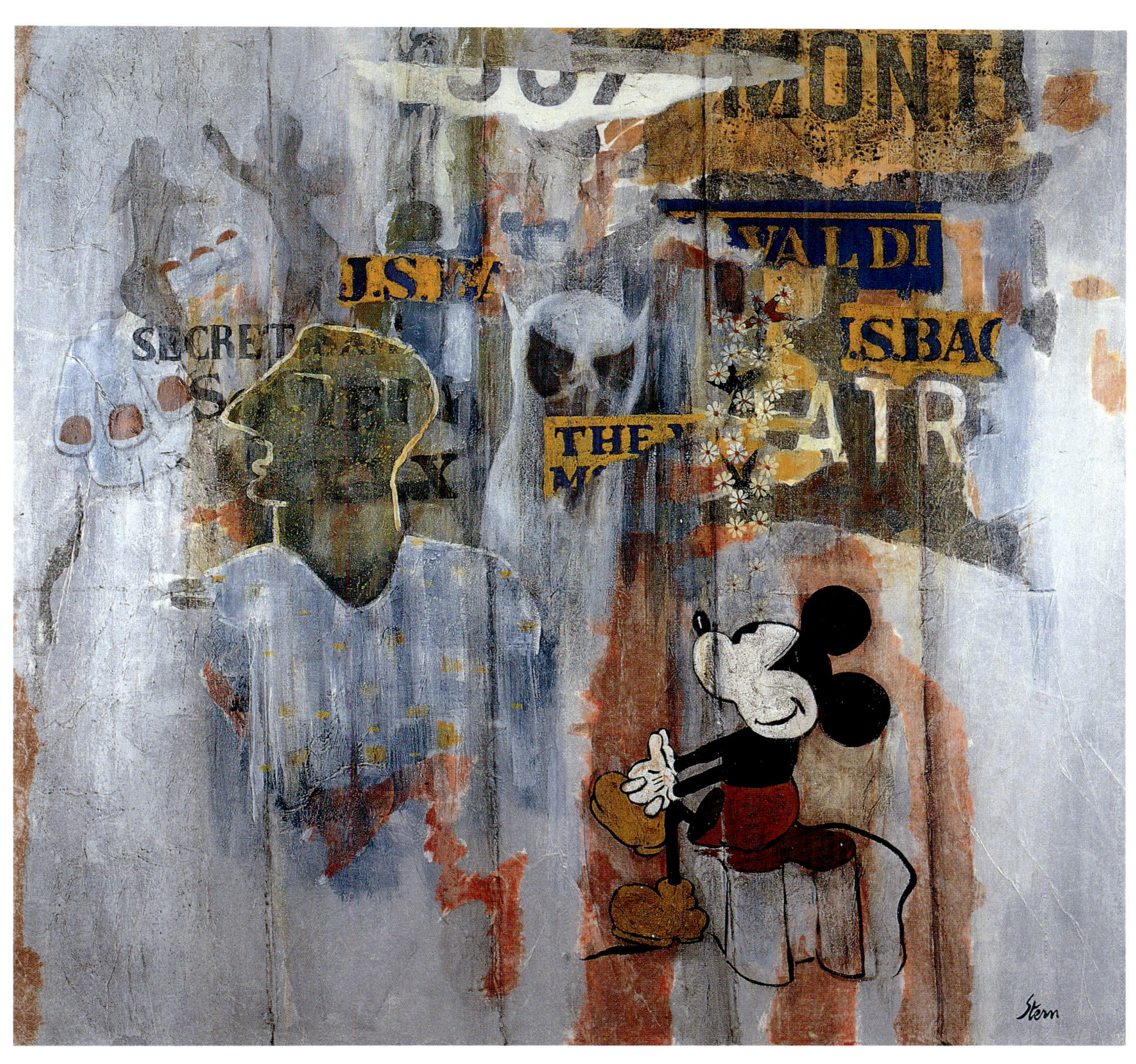

Watching the World Go By, 1983, acrylic on carvas, 102x92cm, Private Collection, New York

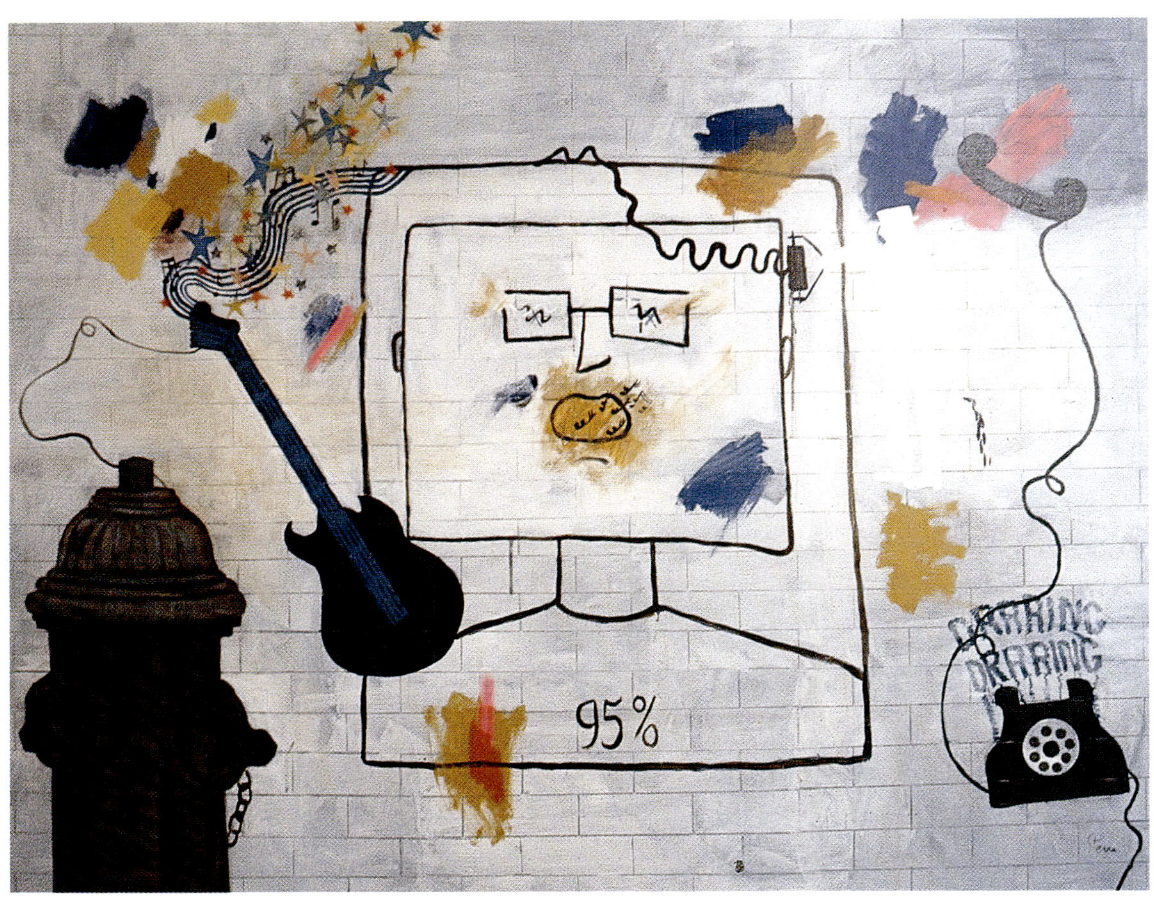

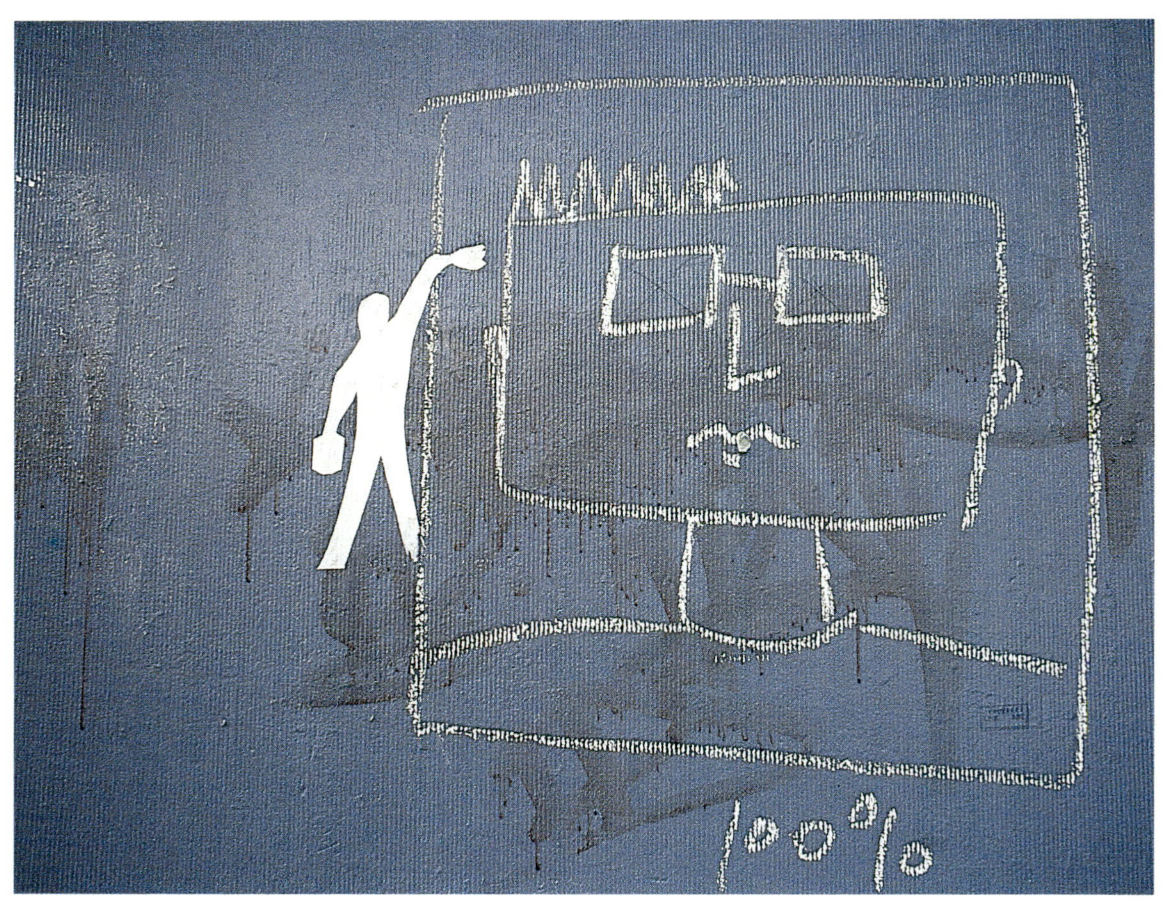

Man at 95%, 1983, acrylic on canvas, 114x146cm, Private Collection, Paris
Chauvinist Pig, 1983, acrylic on canvas, 114x146cm, C. Rosenblum Collection, Paris

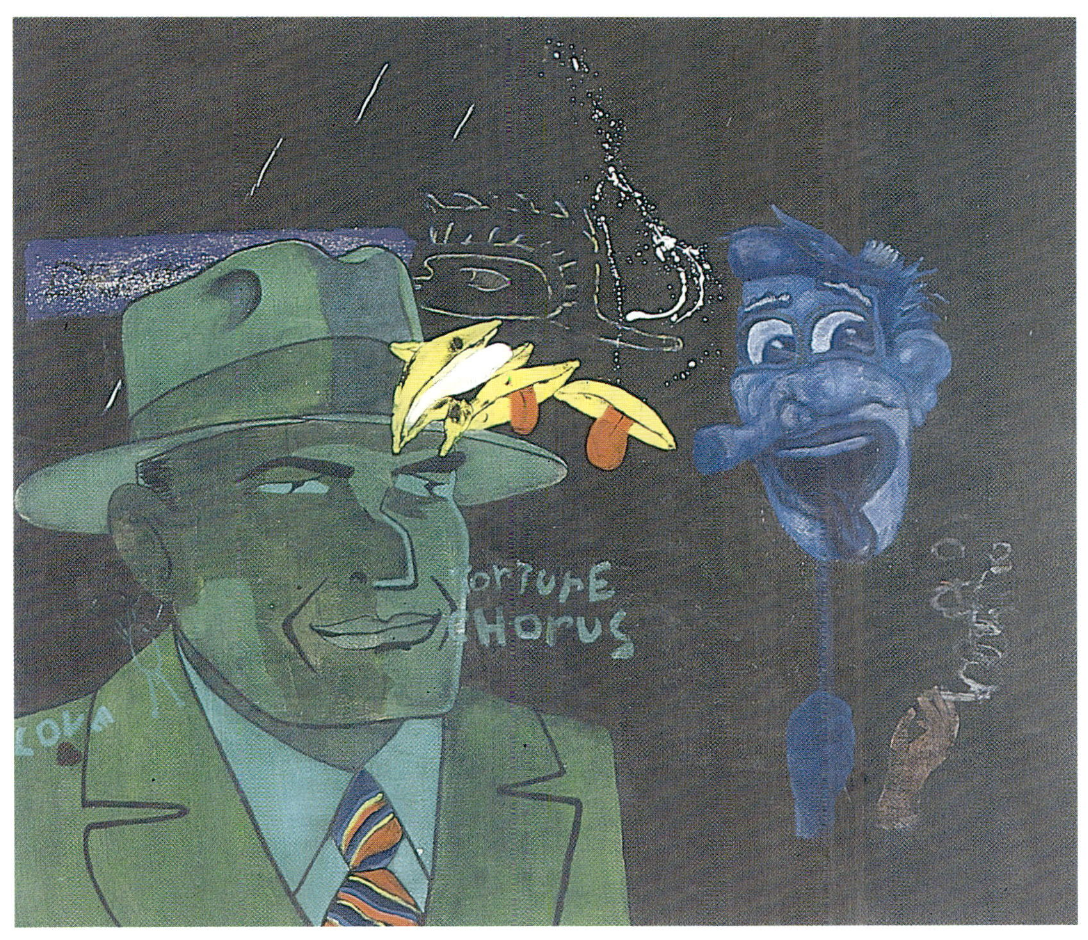
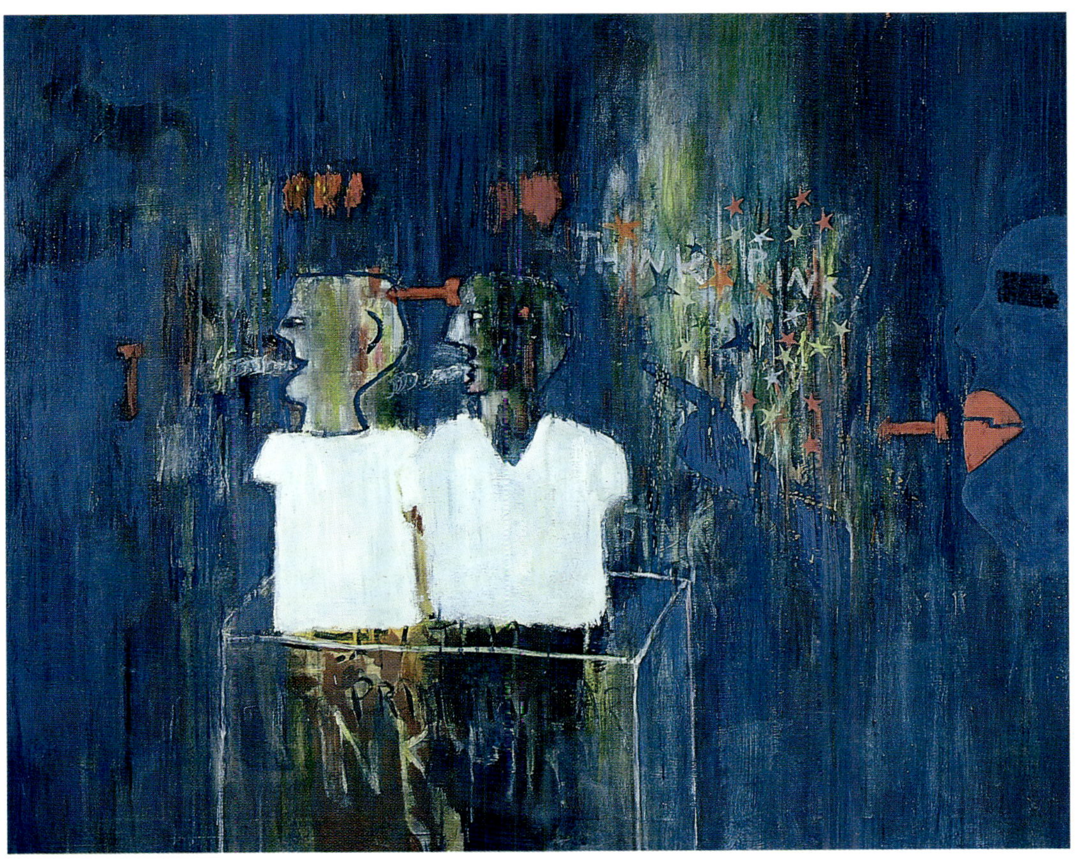

Halloween, 1984, acrylic/oil/canvas, 122×142cm, Artist's Collection
Love Eternal, 1984, acrylic on canvas, 114×146cm, Private Collection, Munich

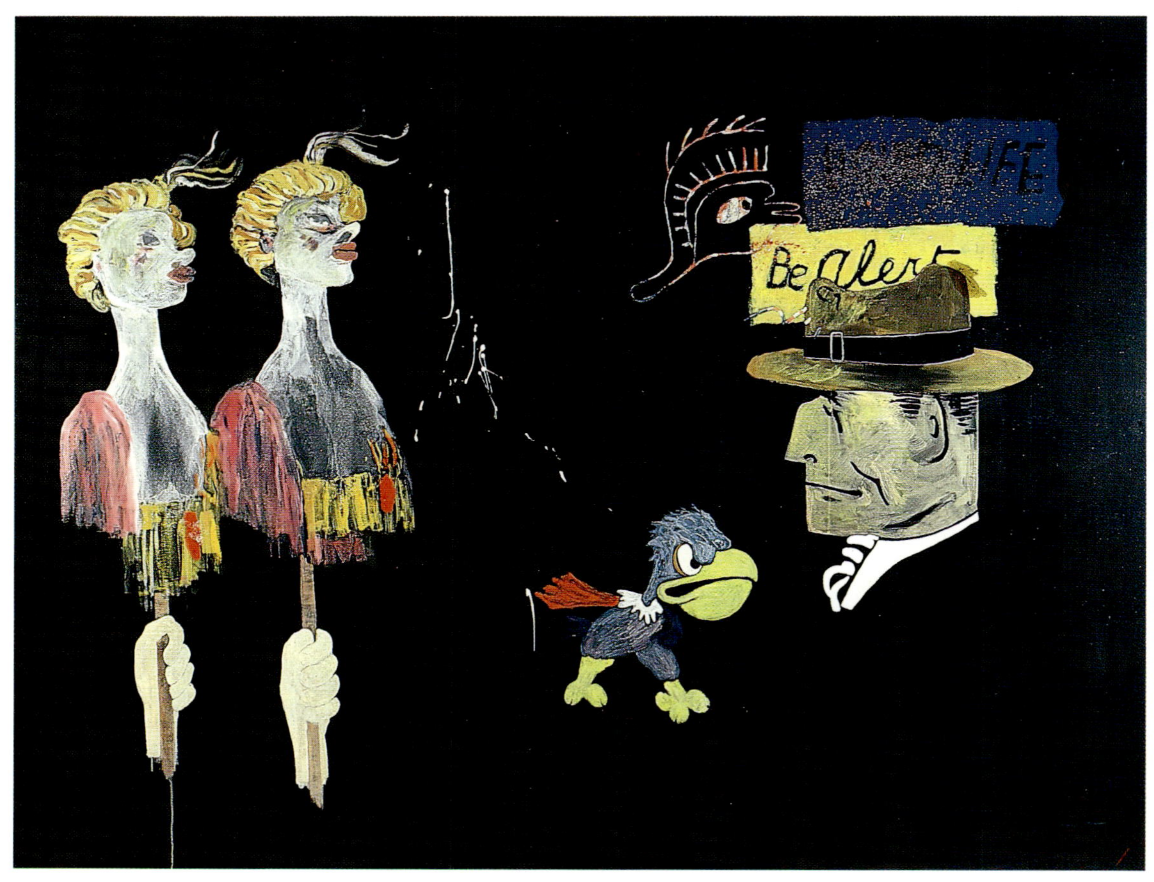

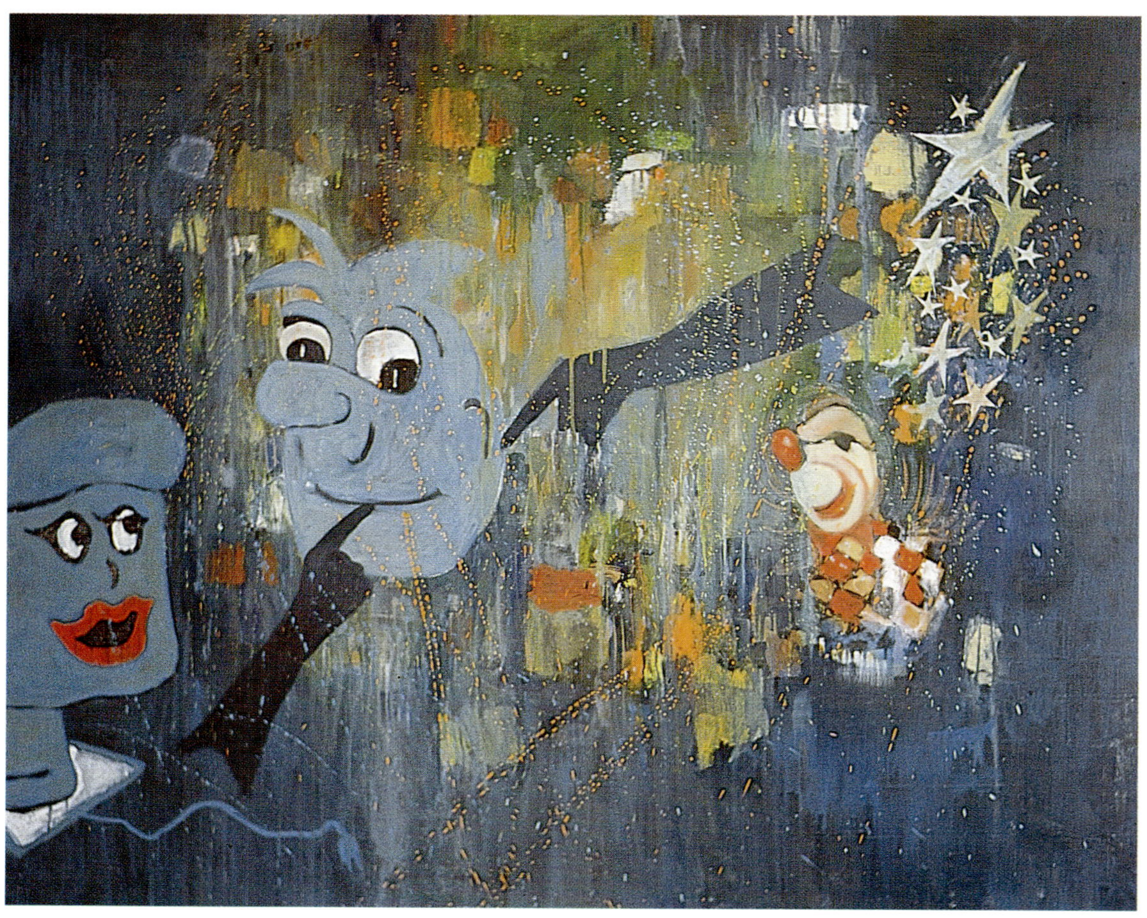

Halloween on the Wall, 1984, acrylic on canvas, 183x244cm, R. Livingston Collection, New York
Halloween, 1985, oil on canvas, 117x117cm, Private Collection, Paris

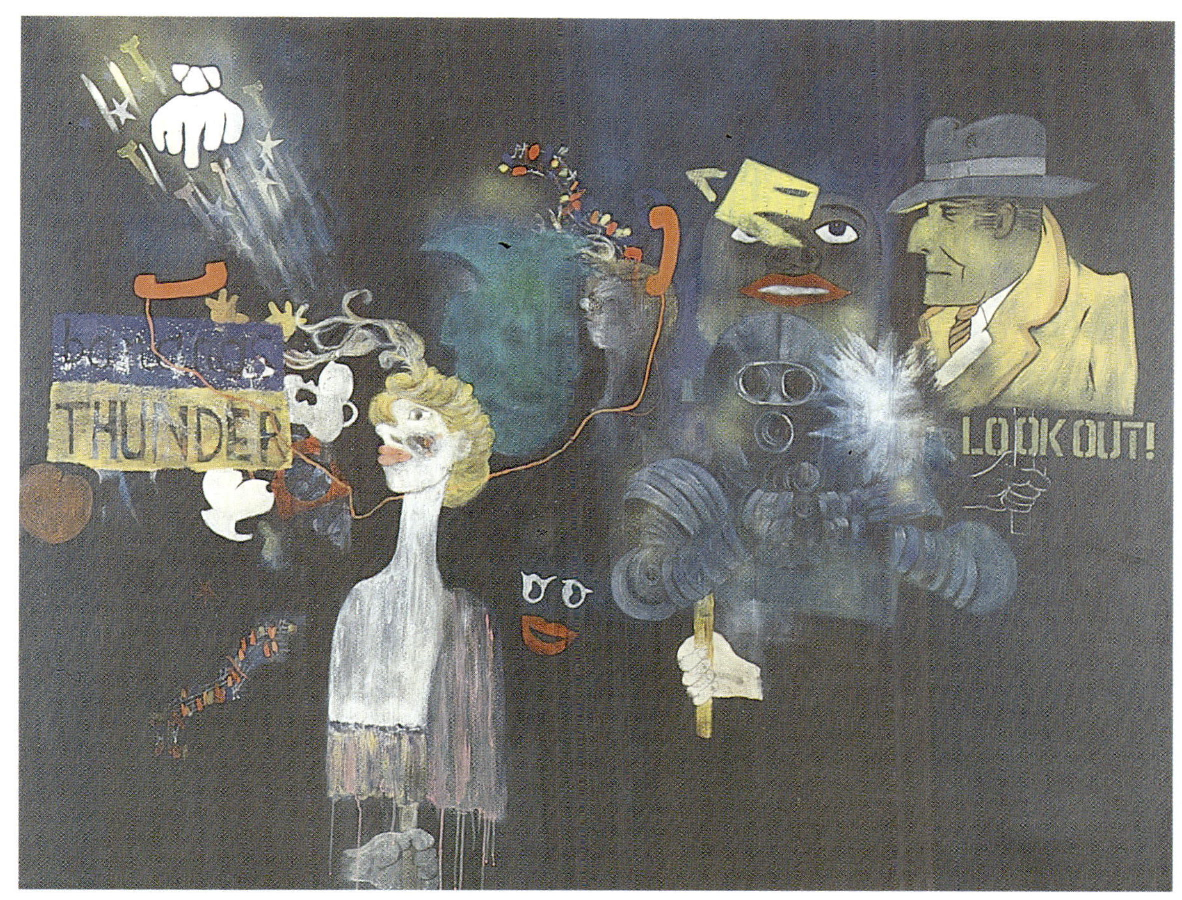

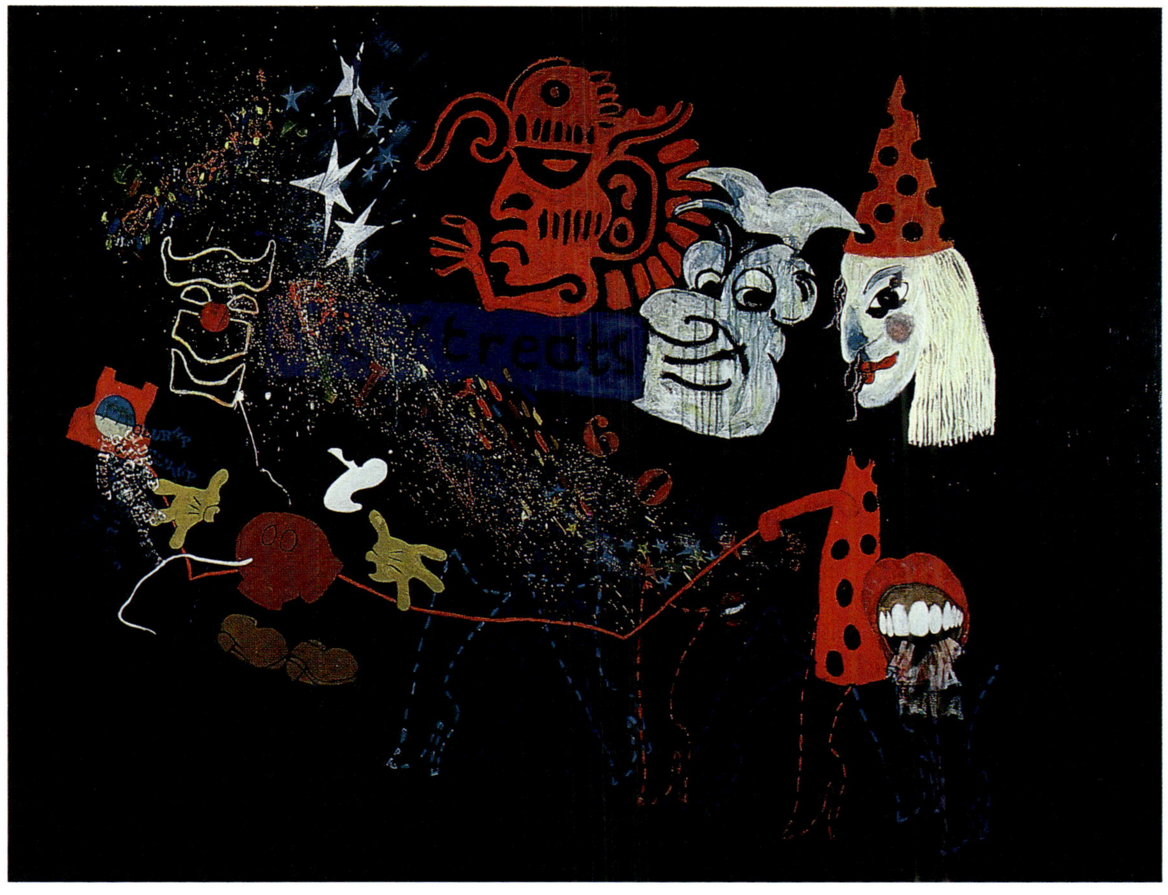

Halloween Parade I, 1984, acrylic on canvas, 183x244cm, Artist's Collection
Halloween Parade II, 1984, acrylic on canvas, 183x244cm, Artist's Collection

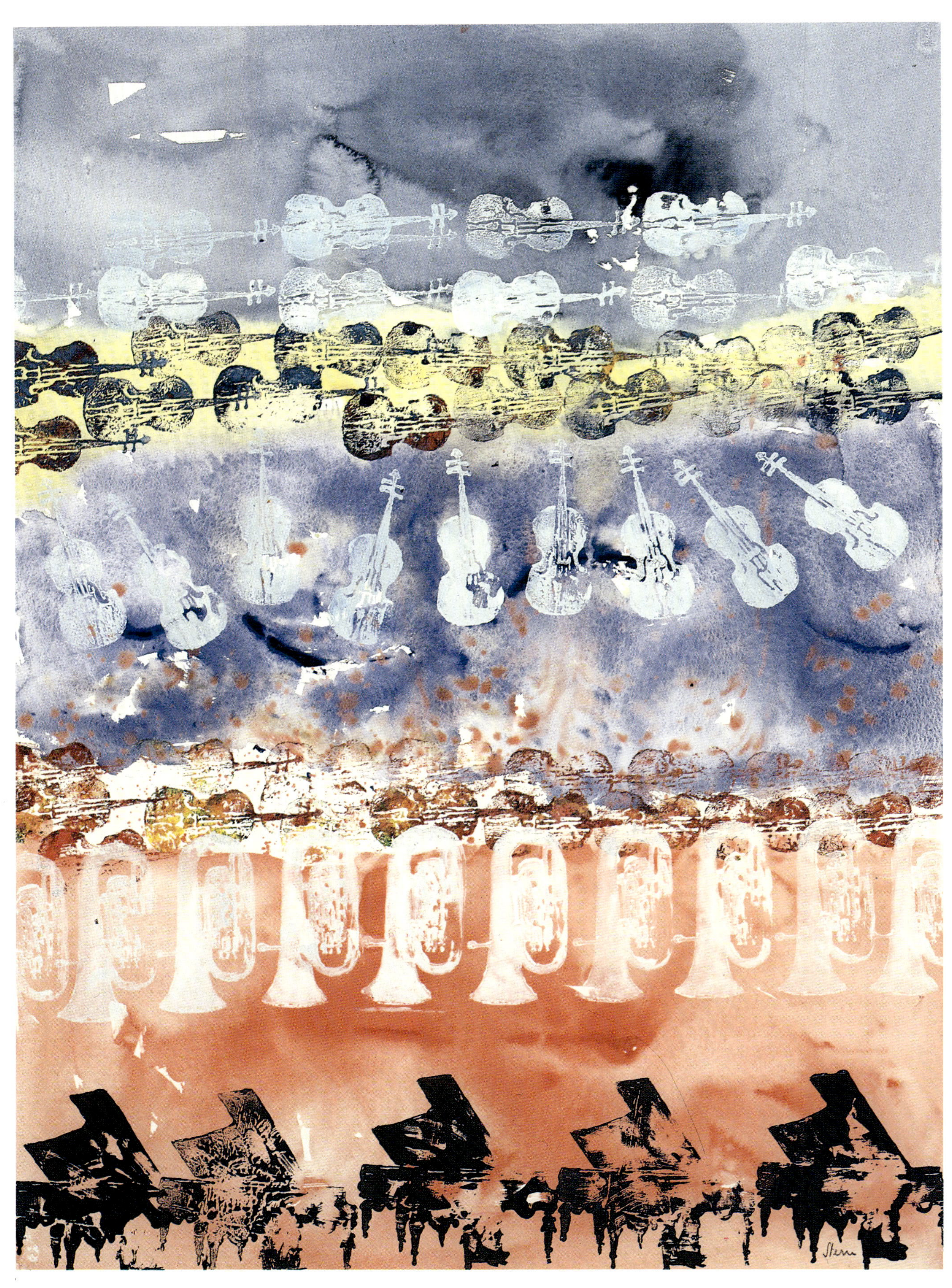

Music for Christmas, 1984, mixed media on paper, 102x76cm, Private Collection, Paris

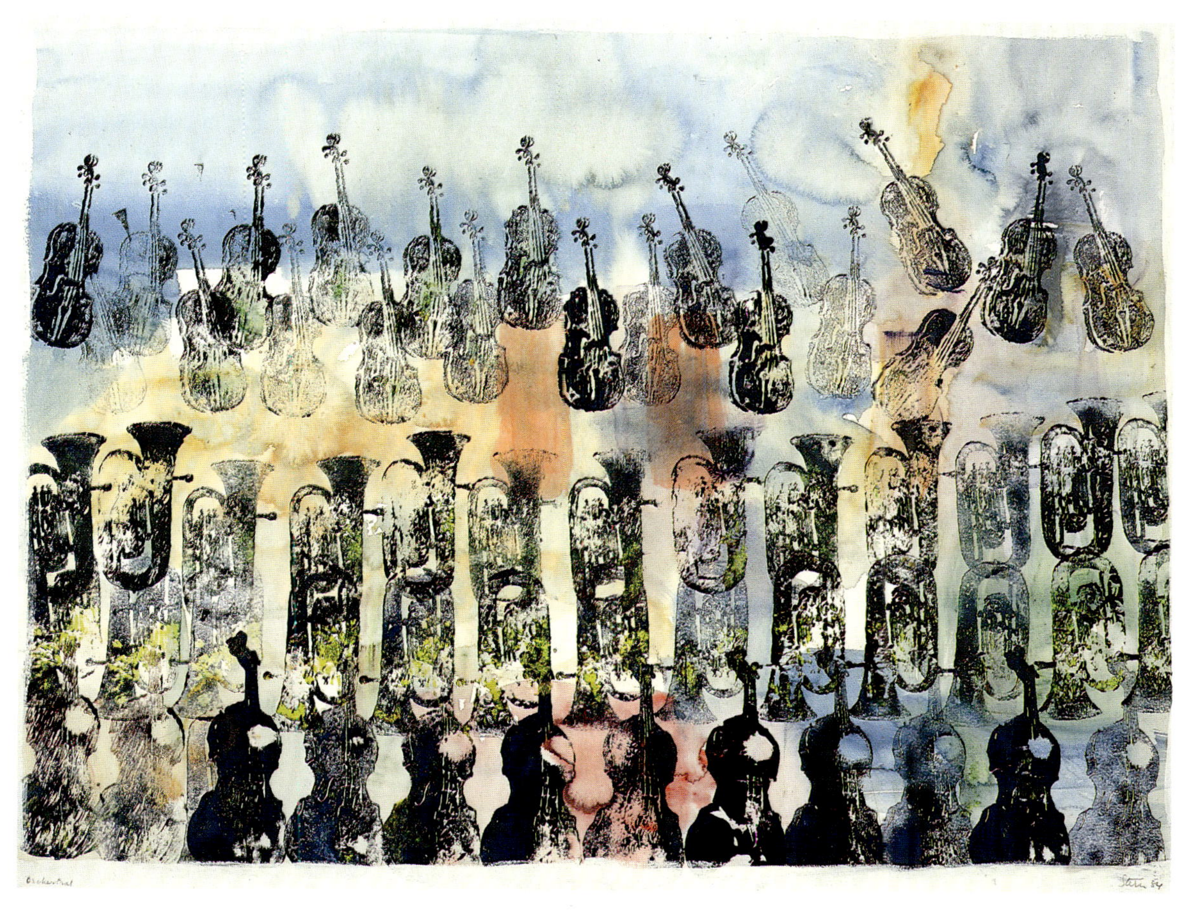

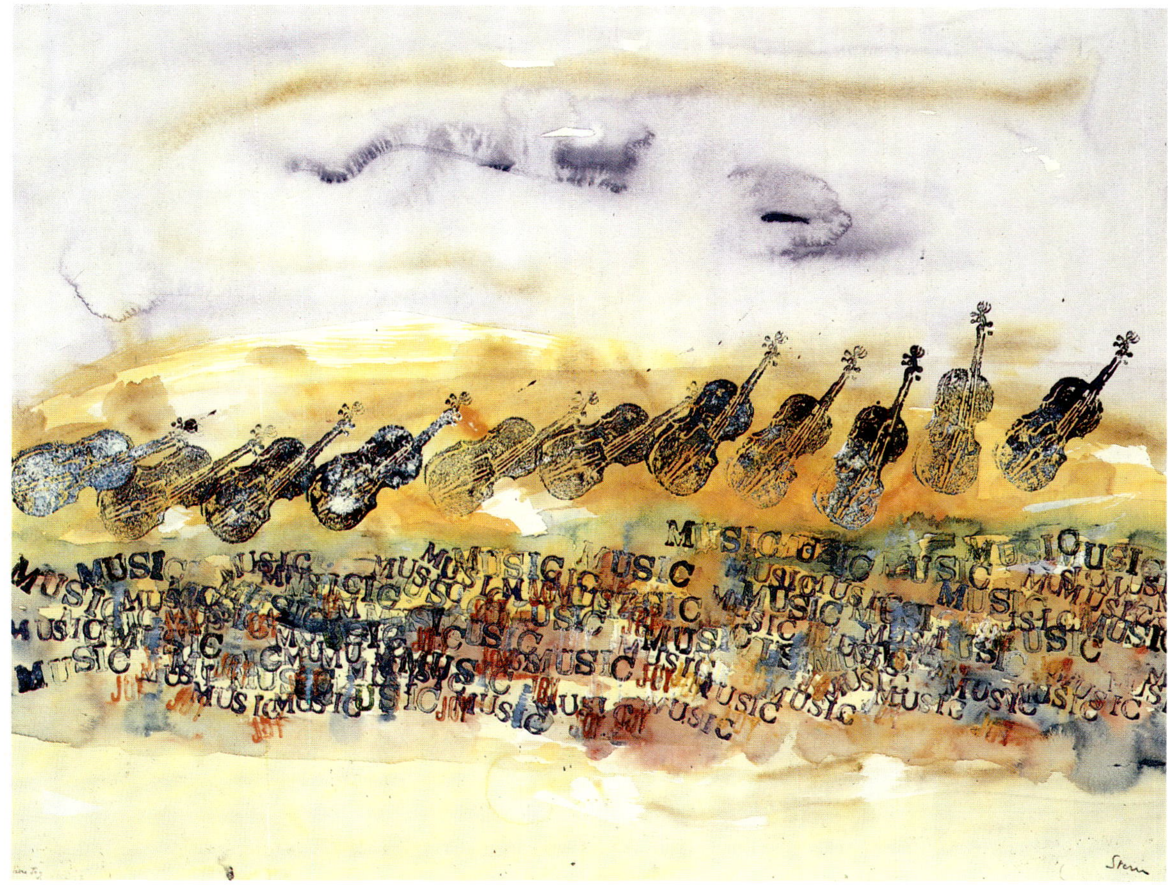

Symphonia, 1984, mixed media on paper, 75×100cm, Artist's Collection
Serenade, 1984, mixed media on paper, 75×100cm, Jean Antoine Collection, Paris

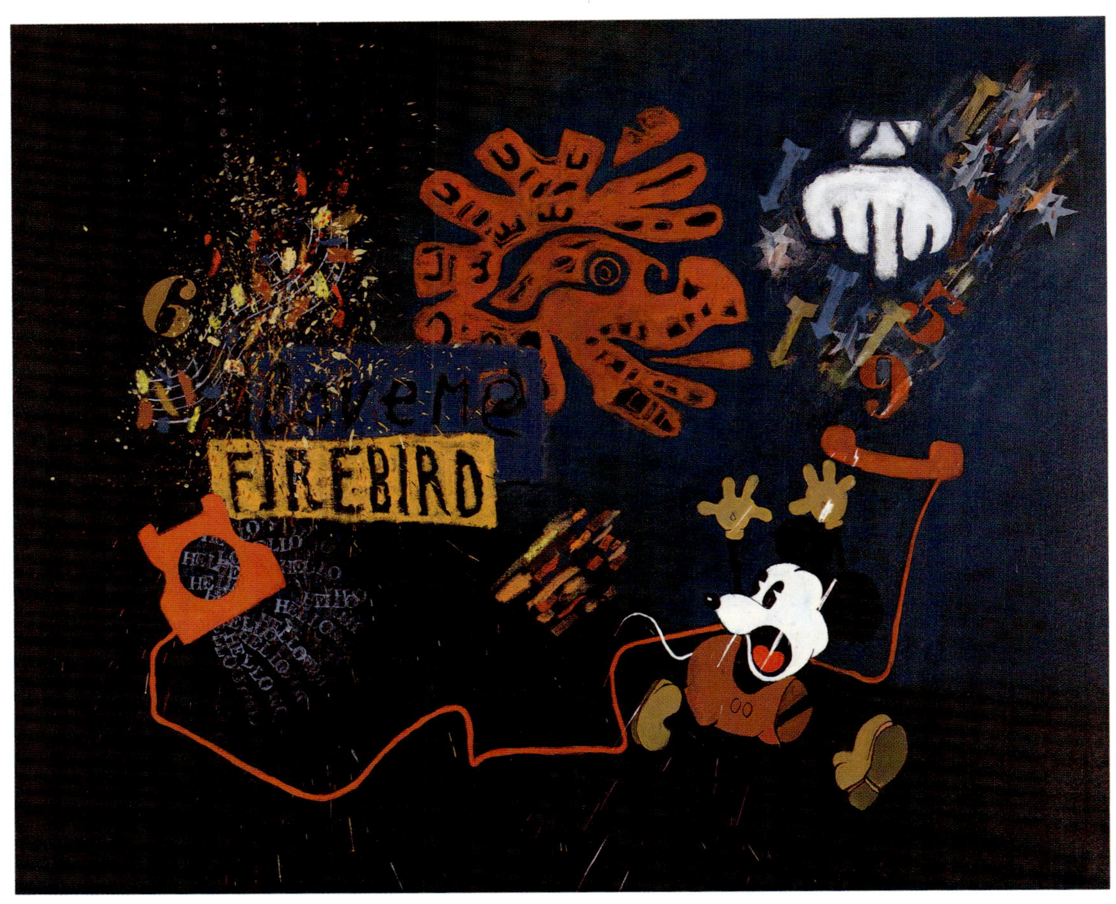

juventud
FIREBIRD

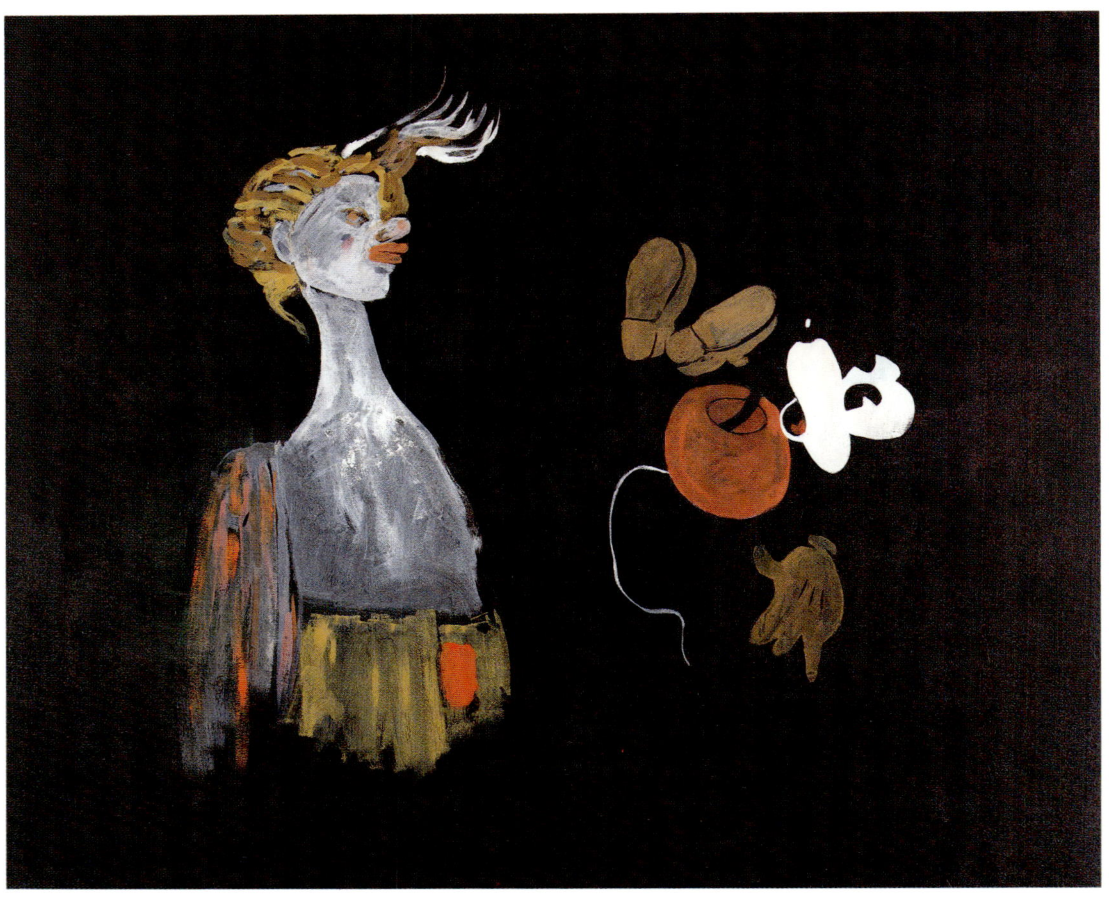

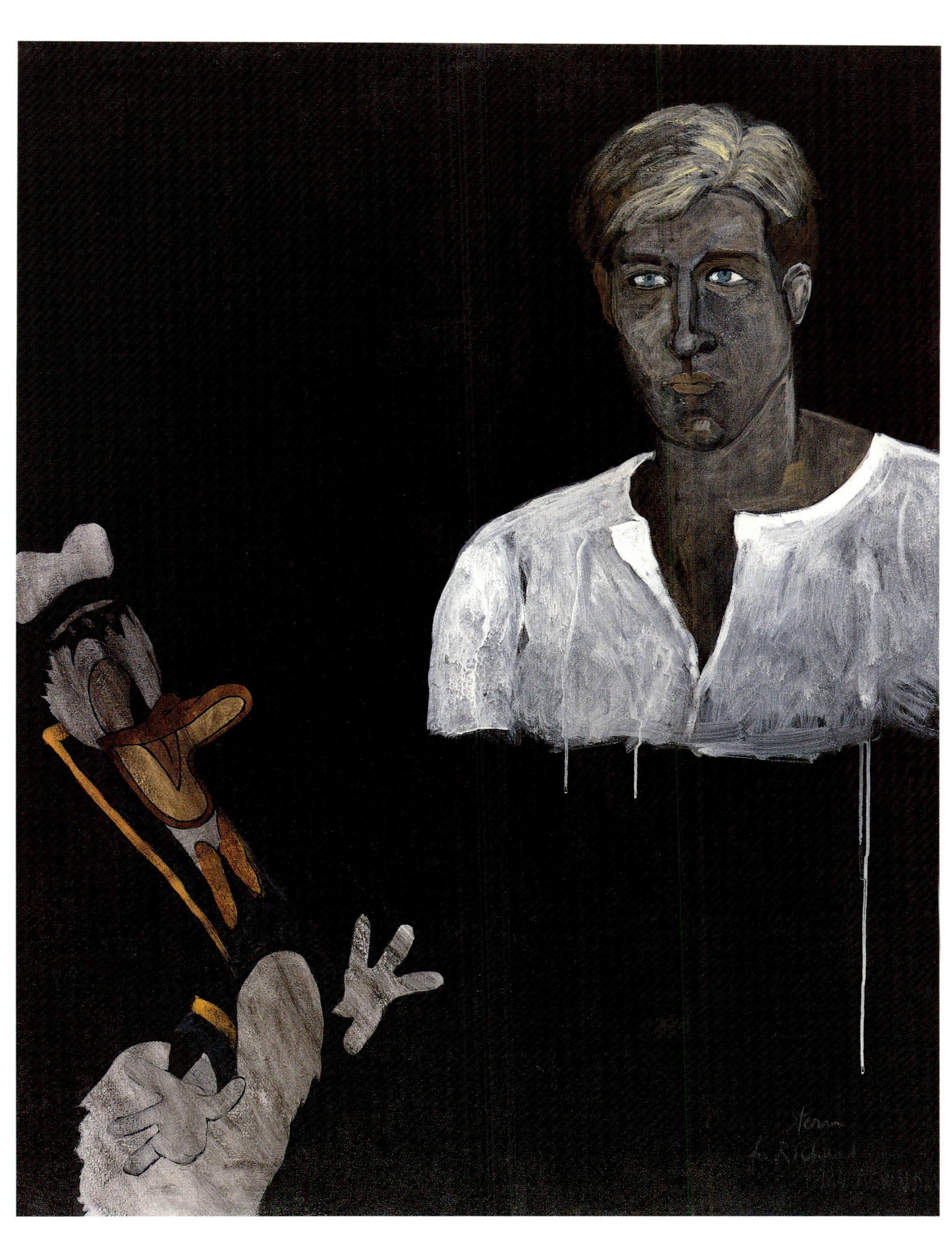

Portrait of Richard, 1984, acrylic on carvas, 147x117cm, Artist's Collection

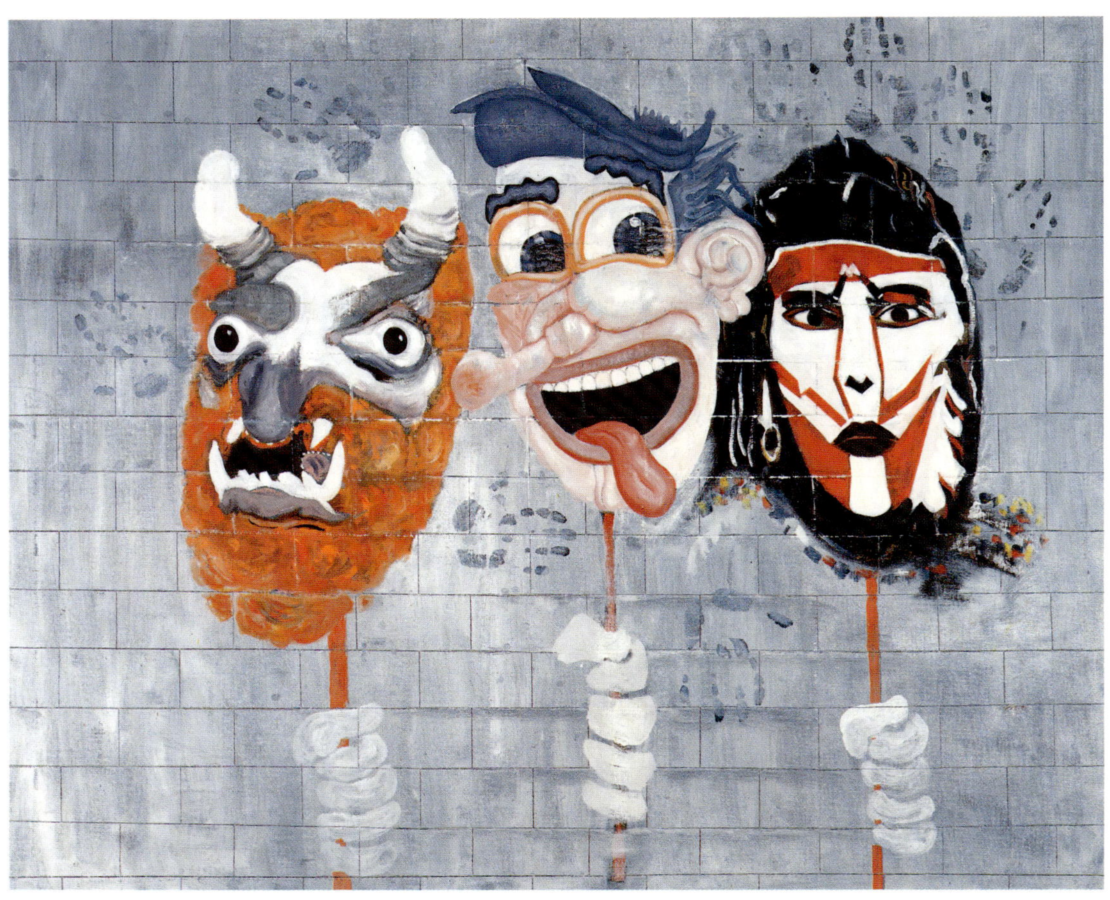

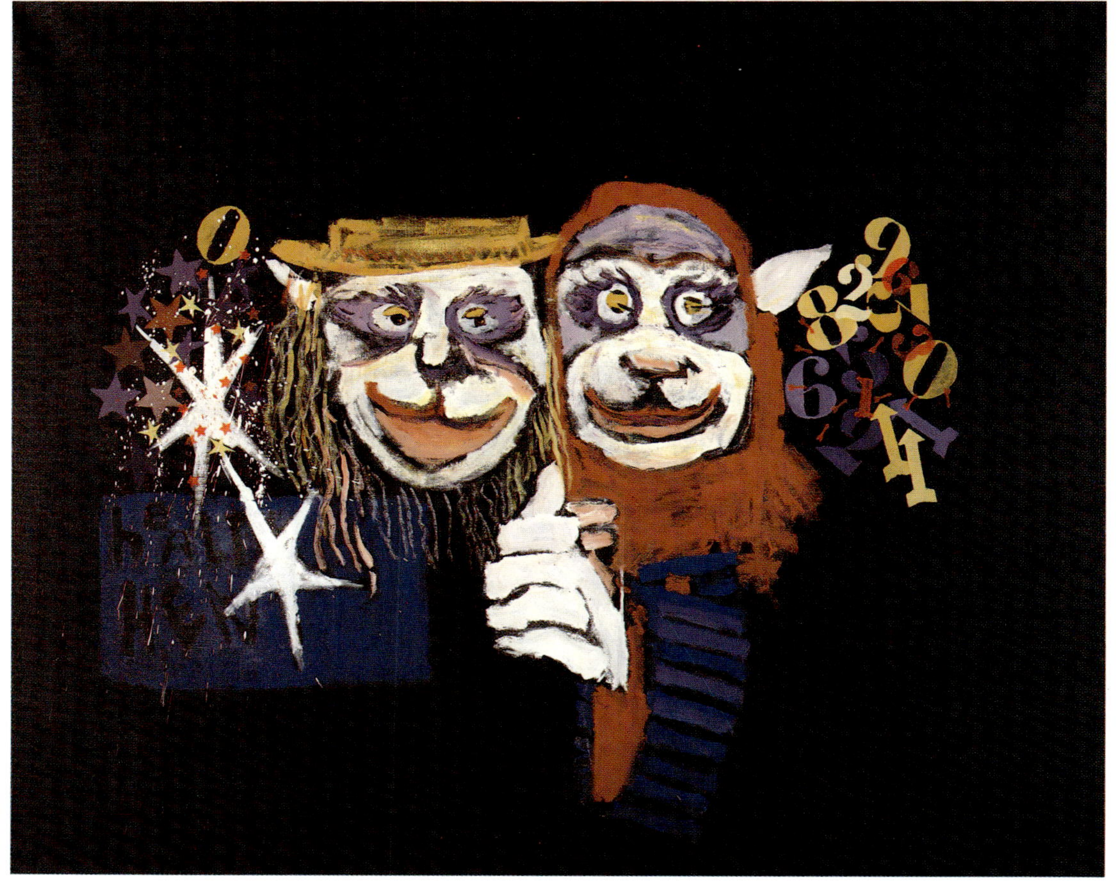

Halloween on the Wall, 1984, acrylic on canvas, 117x147cm, Ashkenazy Collection, Los Angeles
Halloween, 1984, acrylic on canvas, 117x147cm, Ashkenazy Collection, Los Angeles

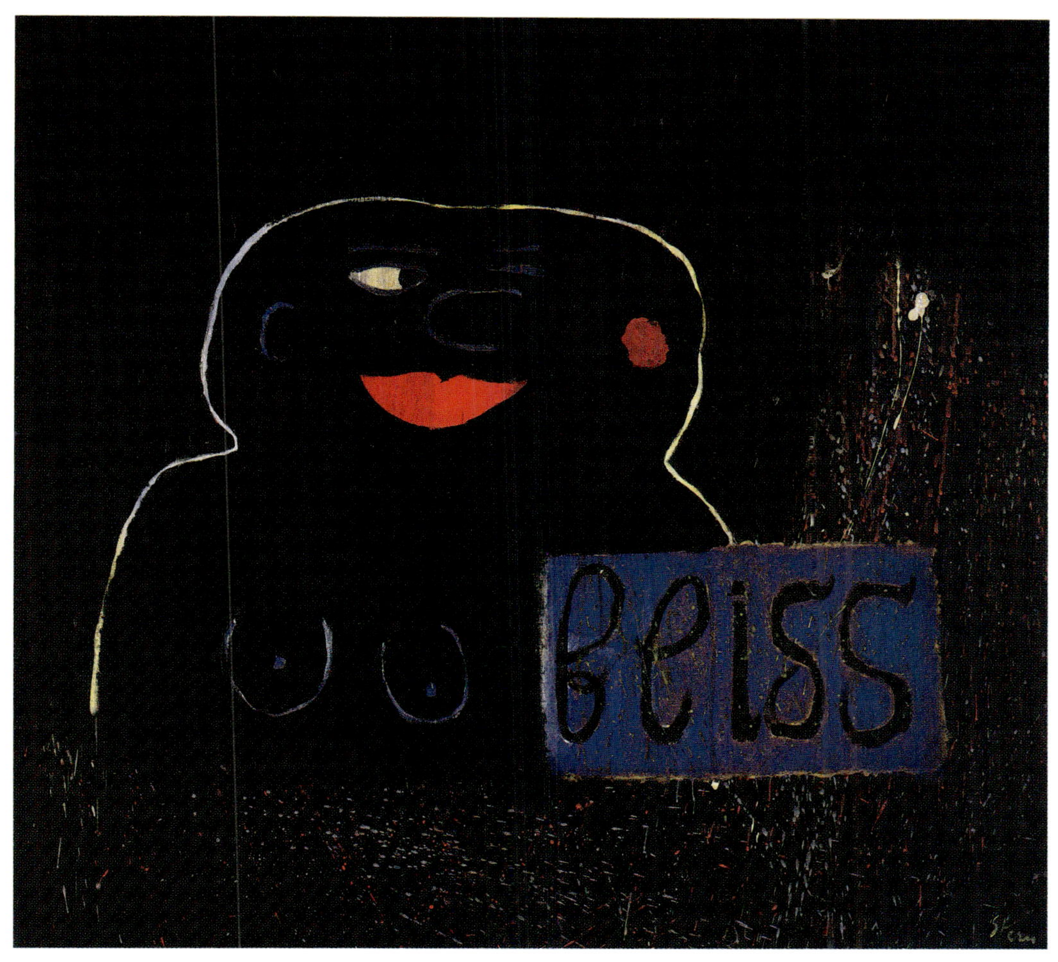

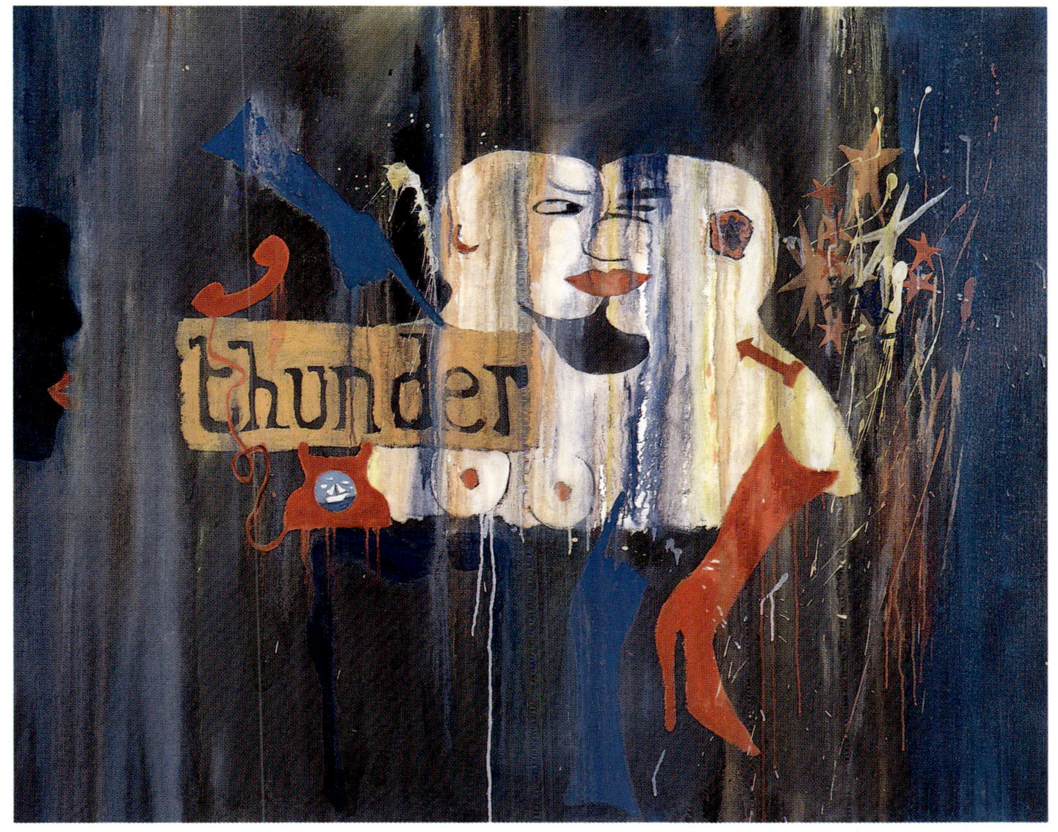

Bliss!, 1984, acrylic on canvas, 92x102cm, Artist's Collection
Eternal Love, 1984, acrylic on canvas, 117x147cm, Artist's Collection

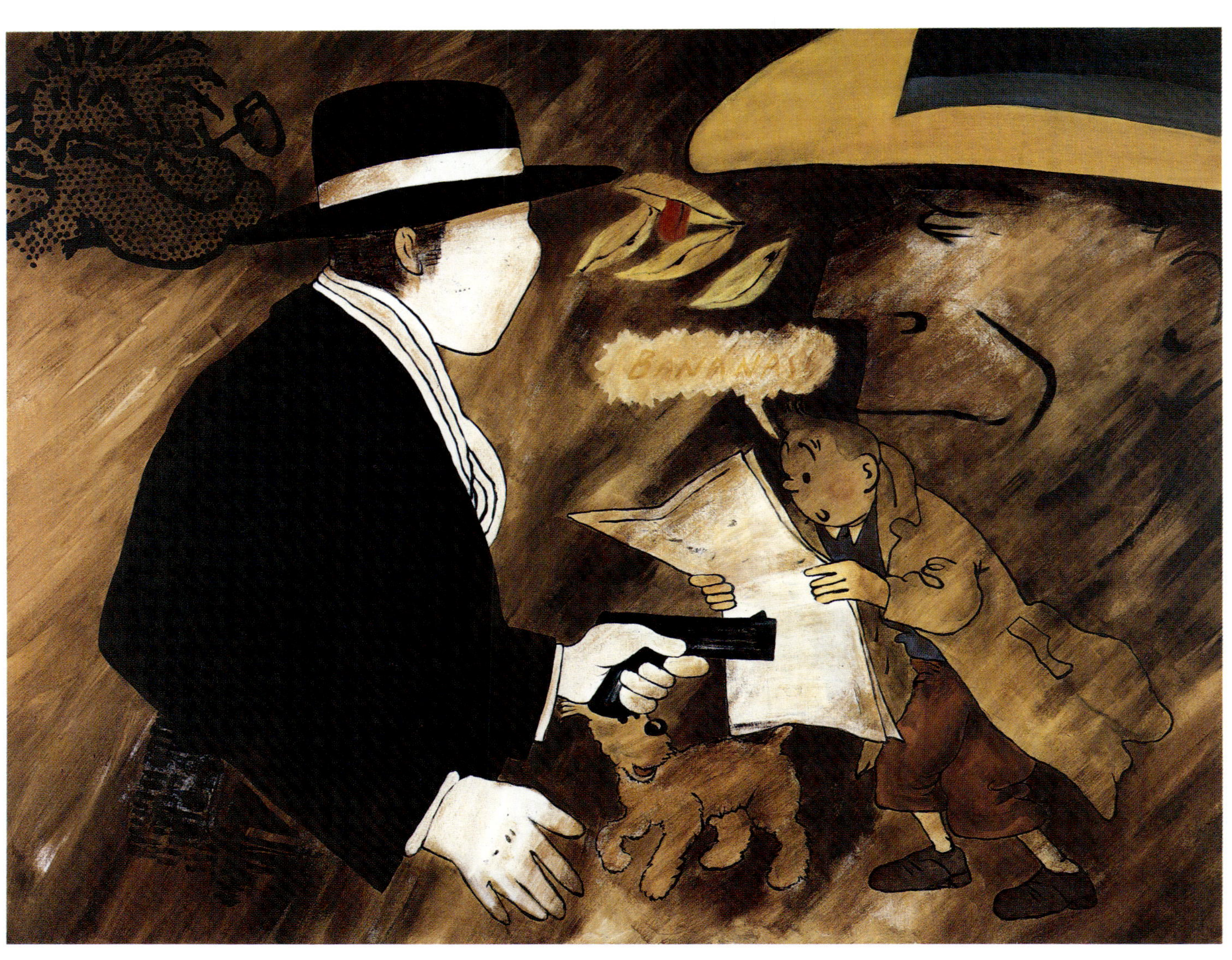

Bananas!, 1985, acrylic/oil/canvas, 137×183cm, Mark Straus Collection, New York

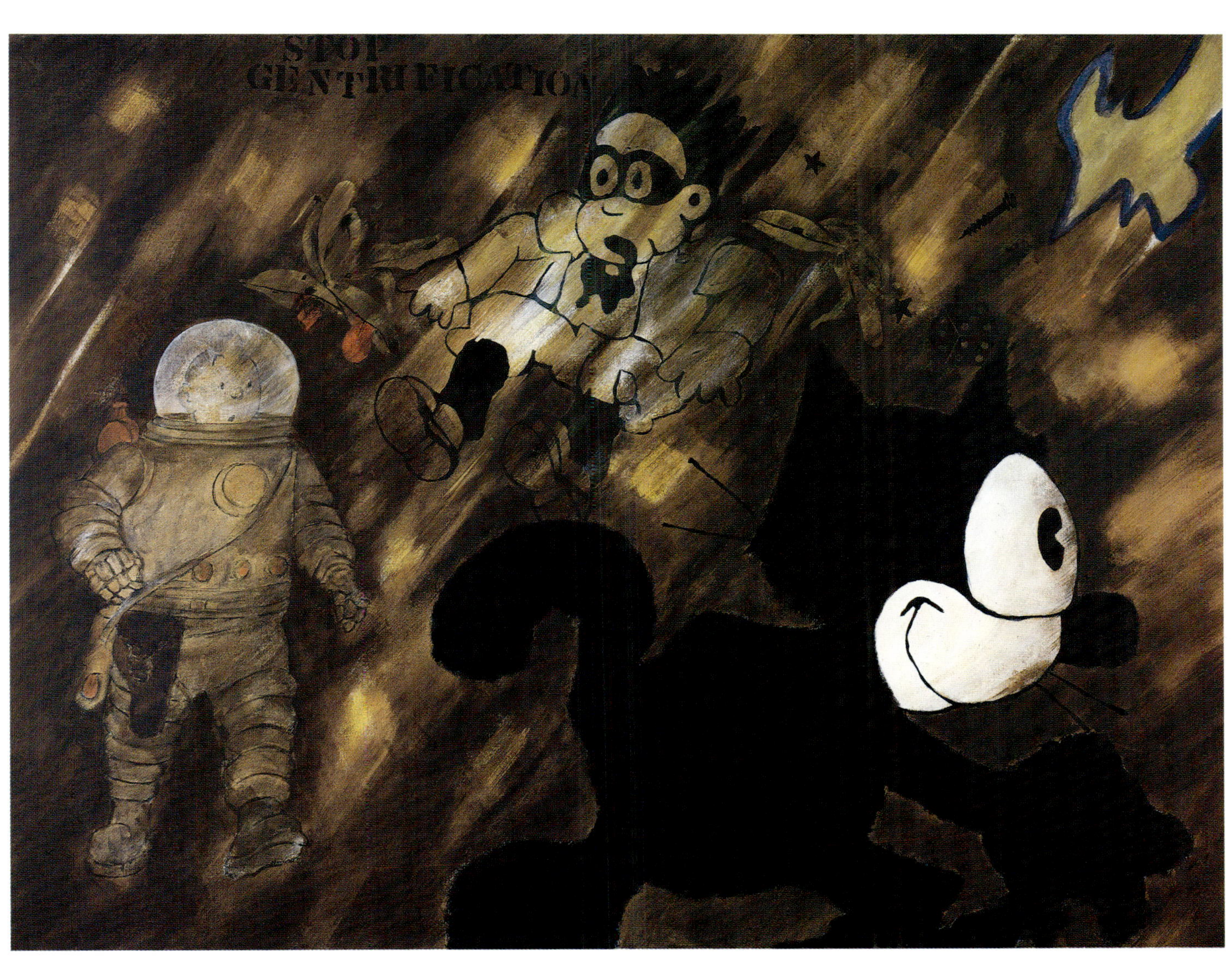

Space Cat, 1985, acrylic on canvas, 137x 83cm, Ashkenazy Collection, Los Angeles

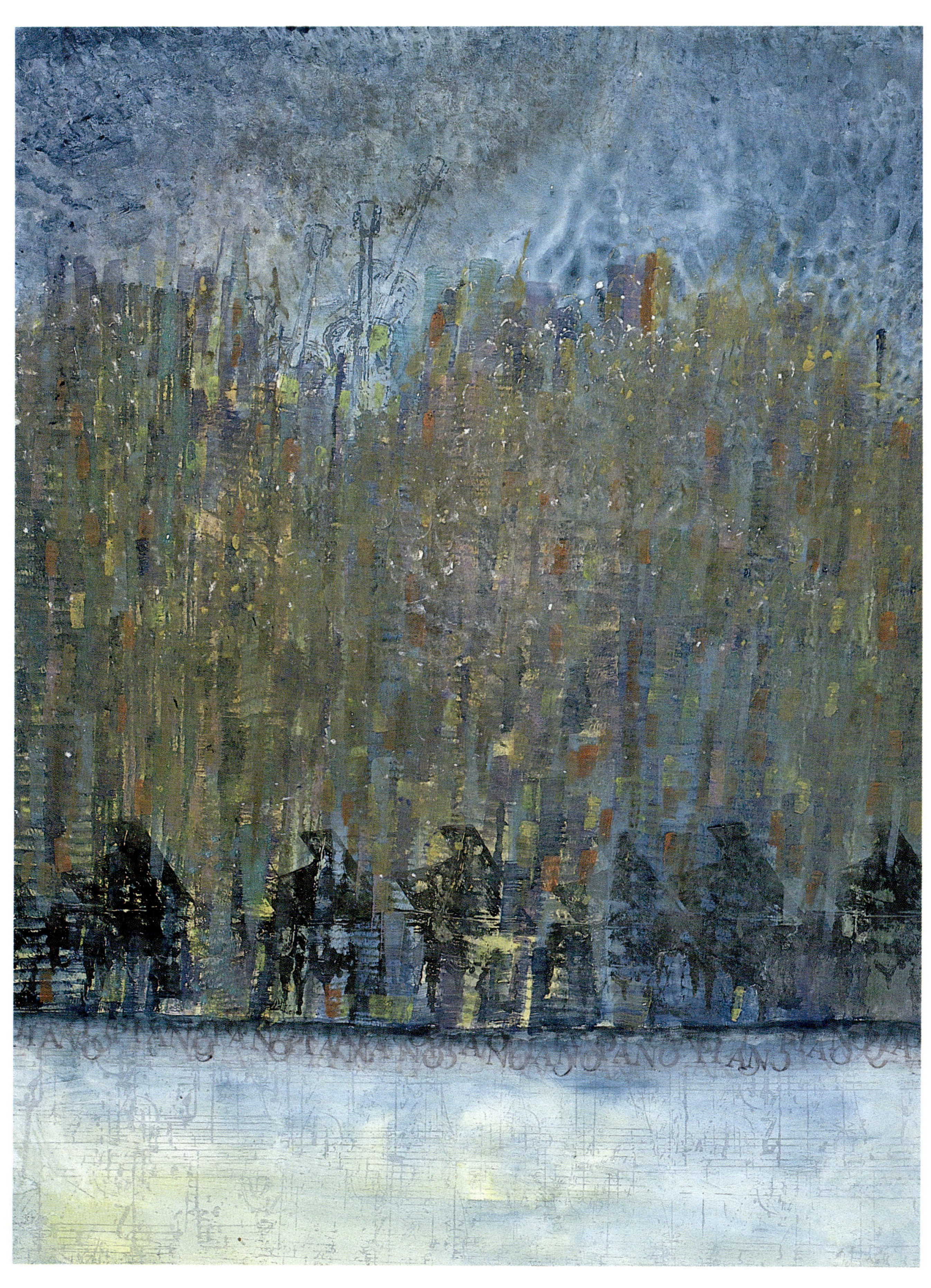

Piano, Piano!, 1986, mixed media on paper, 100x102cm, Private Collection, Tokyo

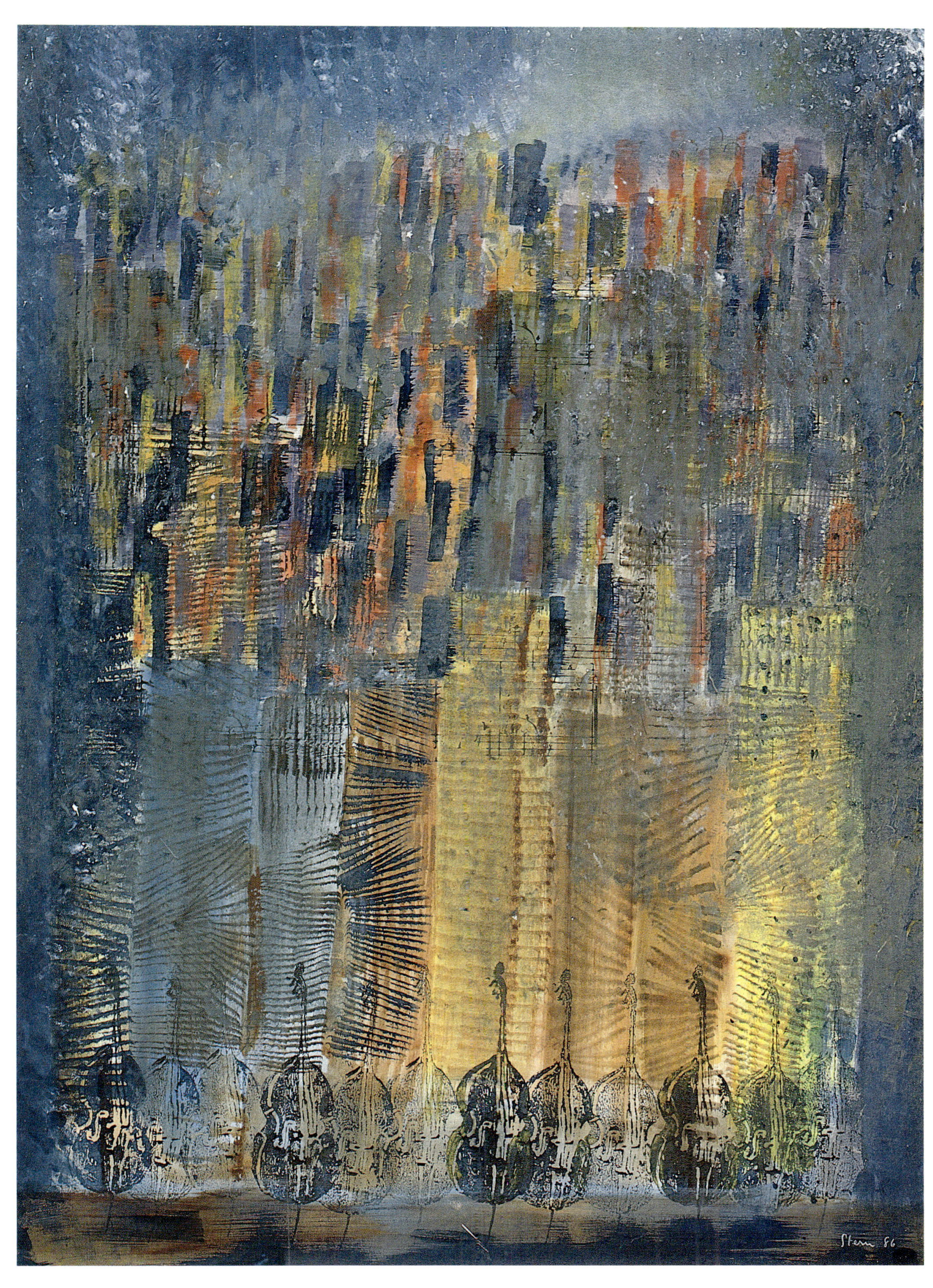

Musical City, 1986, mixed media on paper, 100x76cm, Private Collection, Tokyo

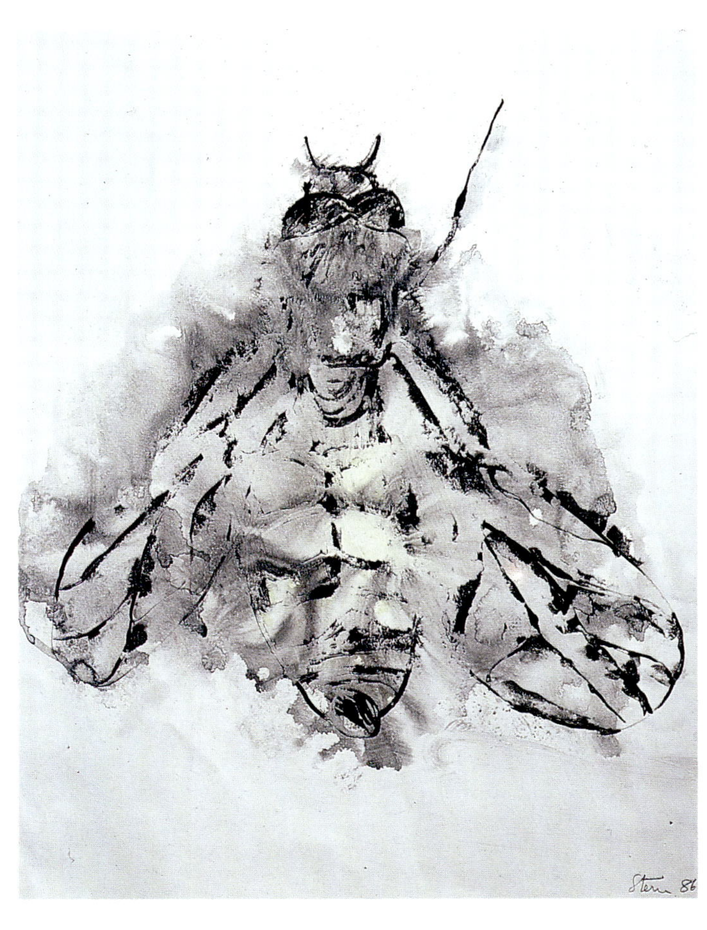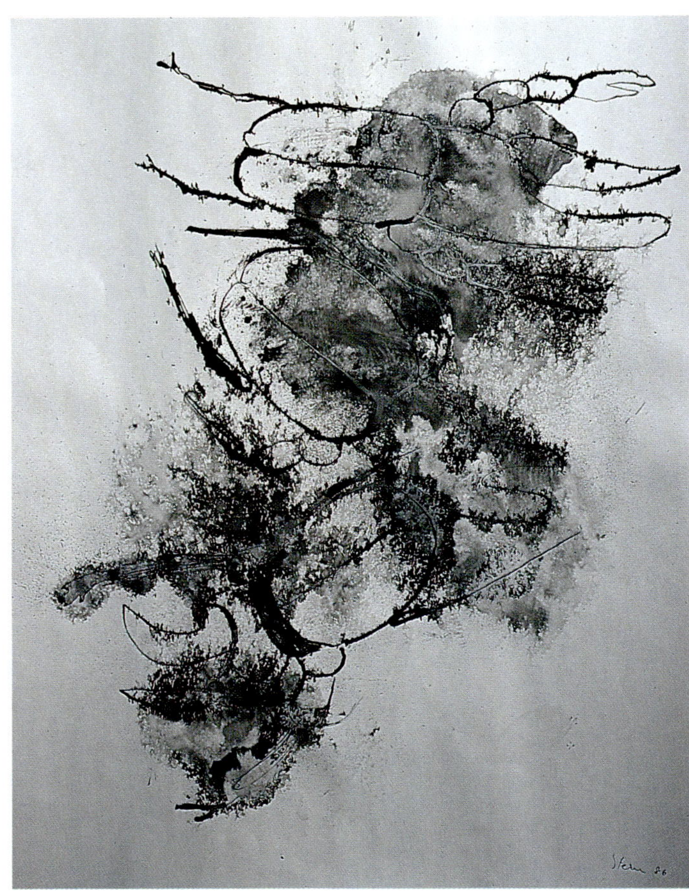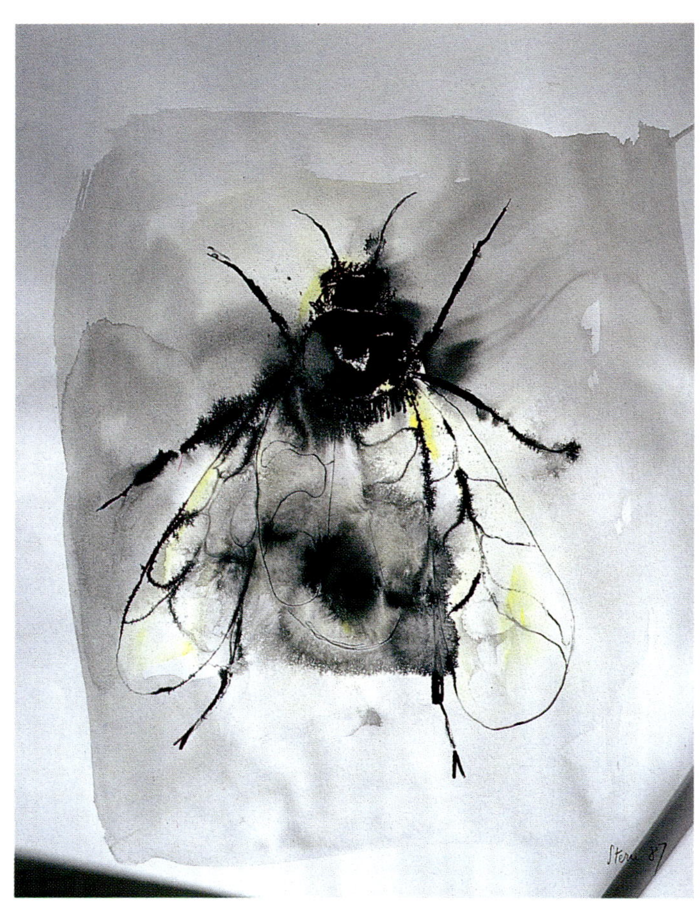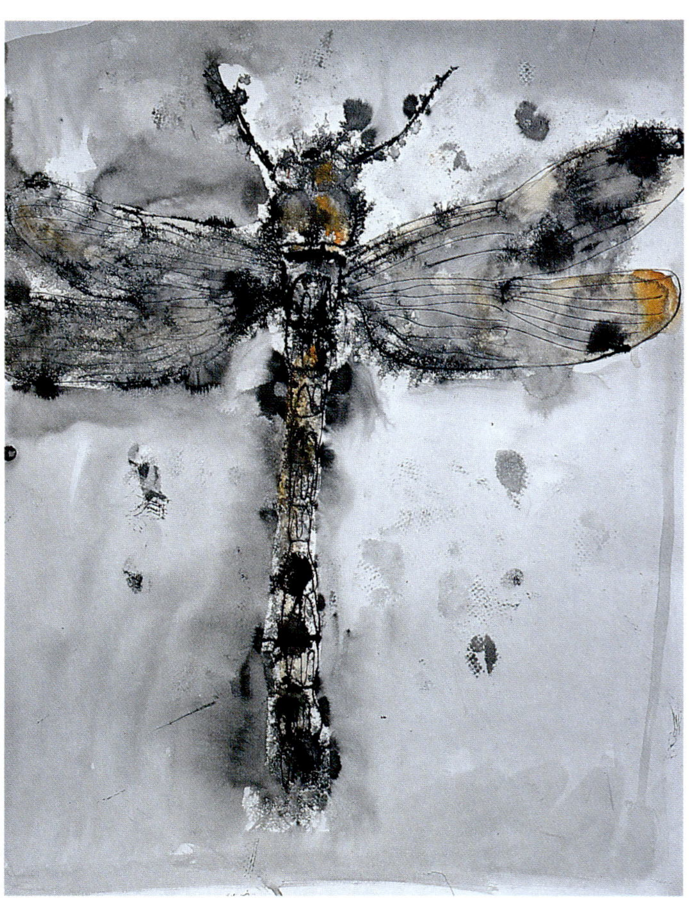

Untitled, 1987, watercolour/ink/paper, 102x76cm; *Untitled*, 1987, watercolour/ink/paper, 40x30cm;
Untitled, 1987, watercolour/ink/paper, 65x50cm, Private Collection, Paris; *Untitled*, 1987, watercolour/ink/paper, 65x50cm

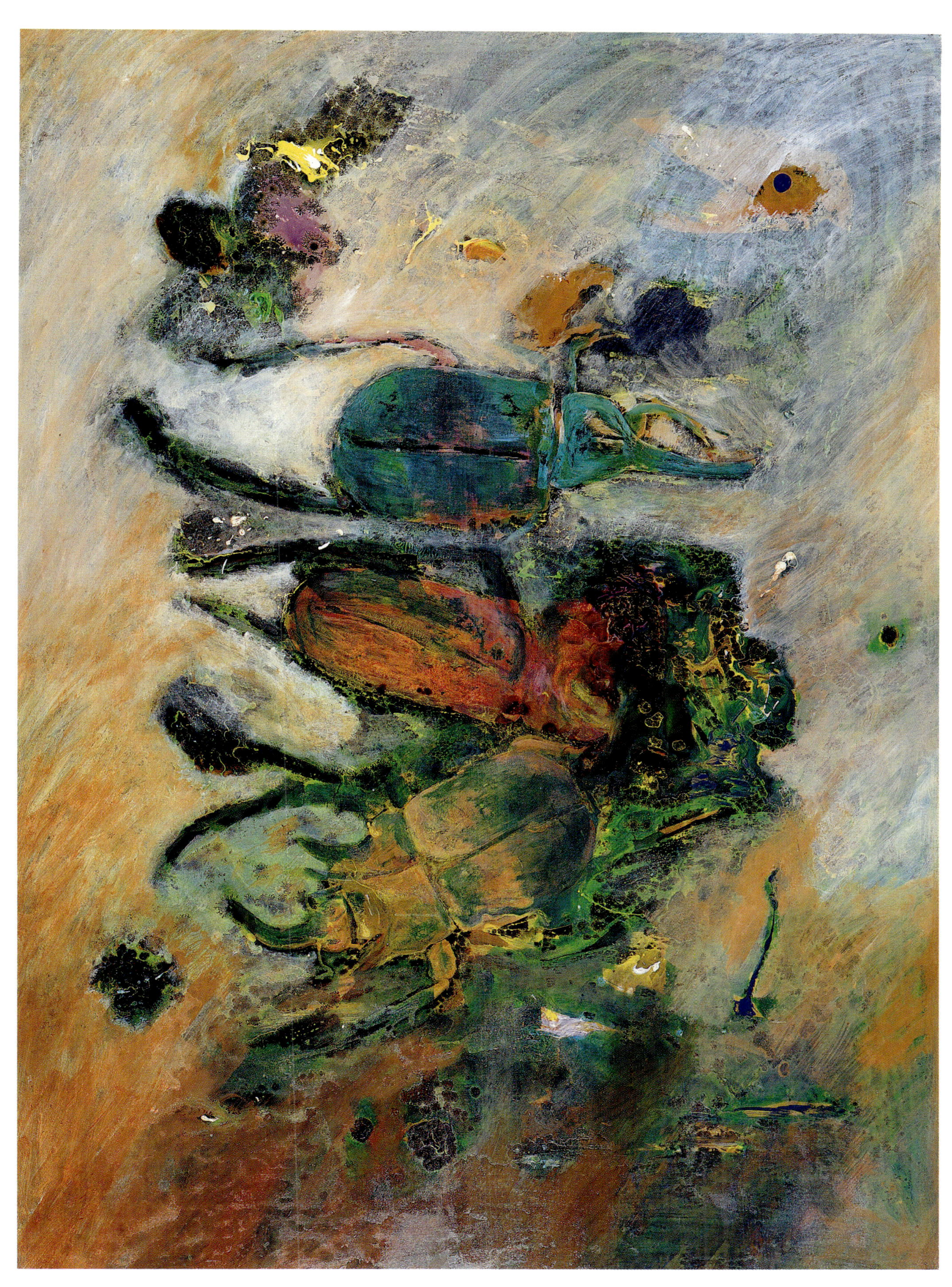

Live Graffiti, 1987, oil on canvas, 183×137cm, Private Collection, Hollywood

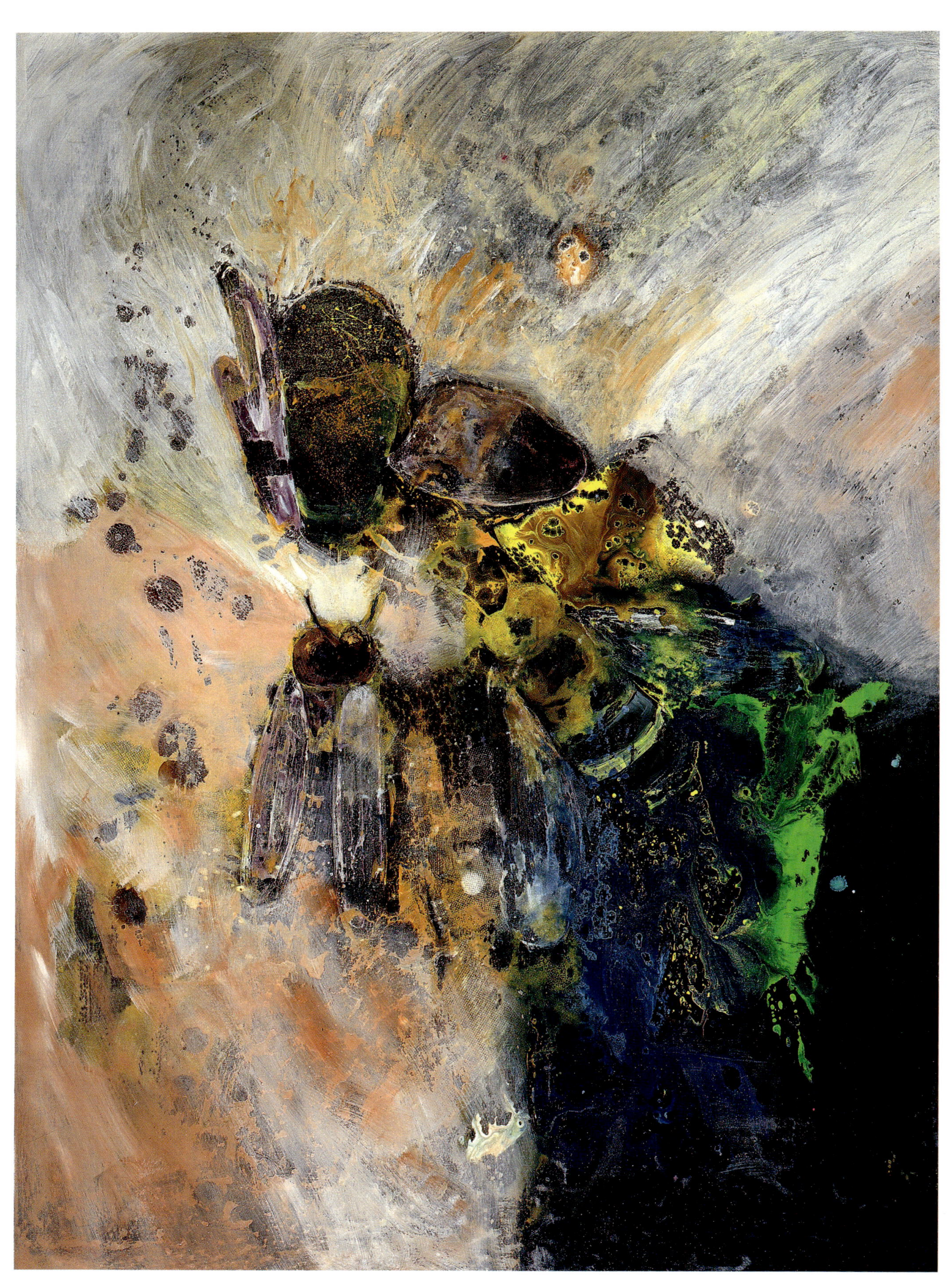

The Quest, 1987, oil on canvas, 183×137cm, A. Debbas Collection, Paris

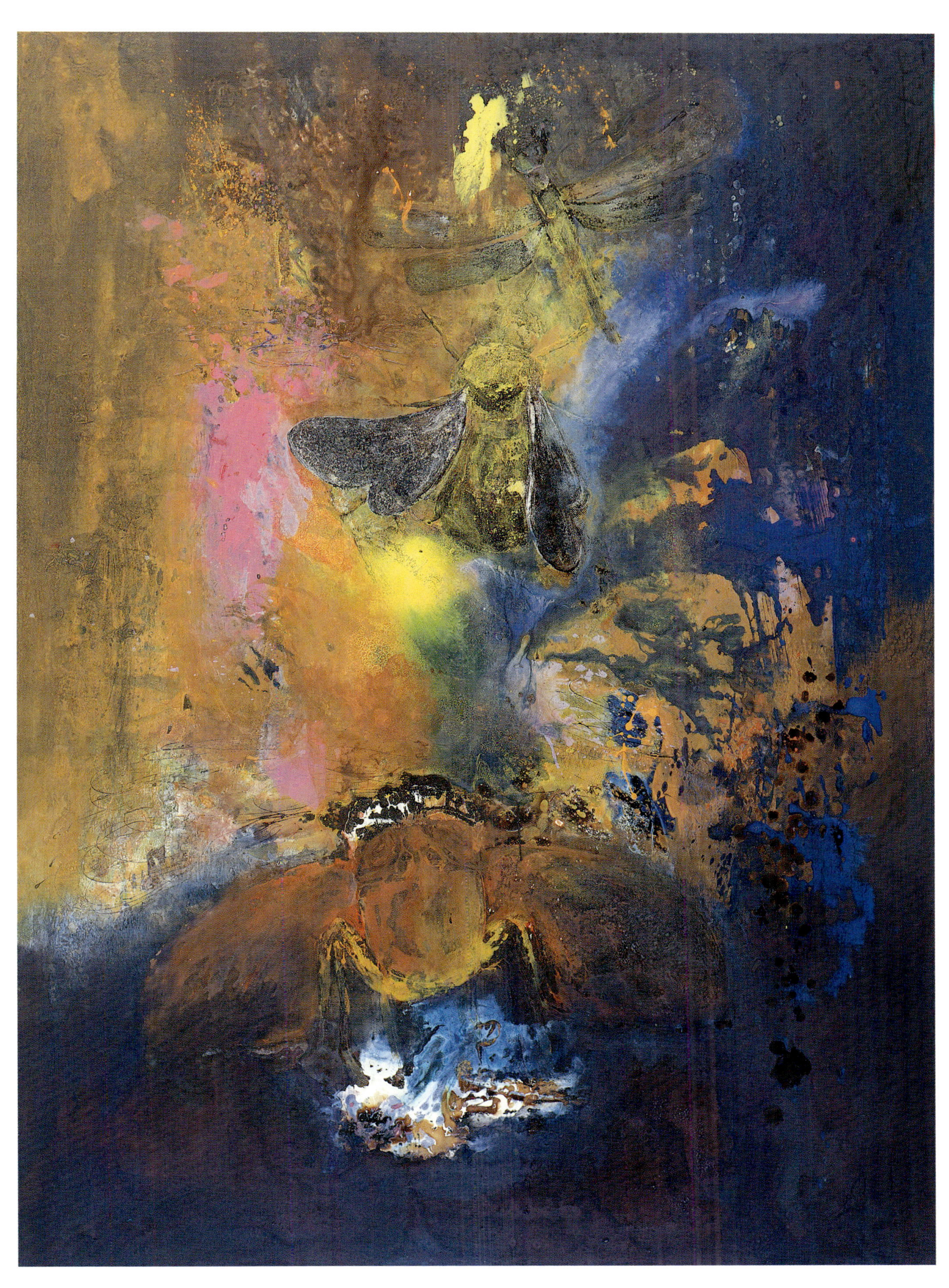

The Forgotten World, 1987, oil on canvas, 183x137cm, I. Hoffman Collection, New York

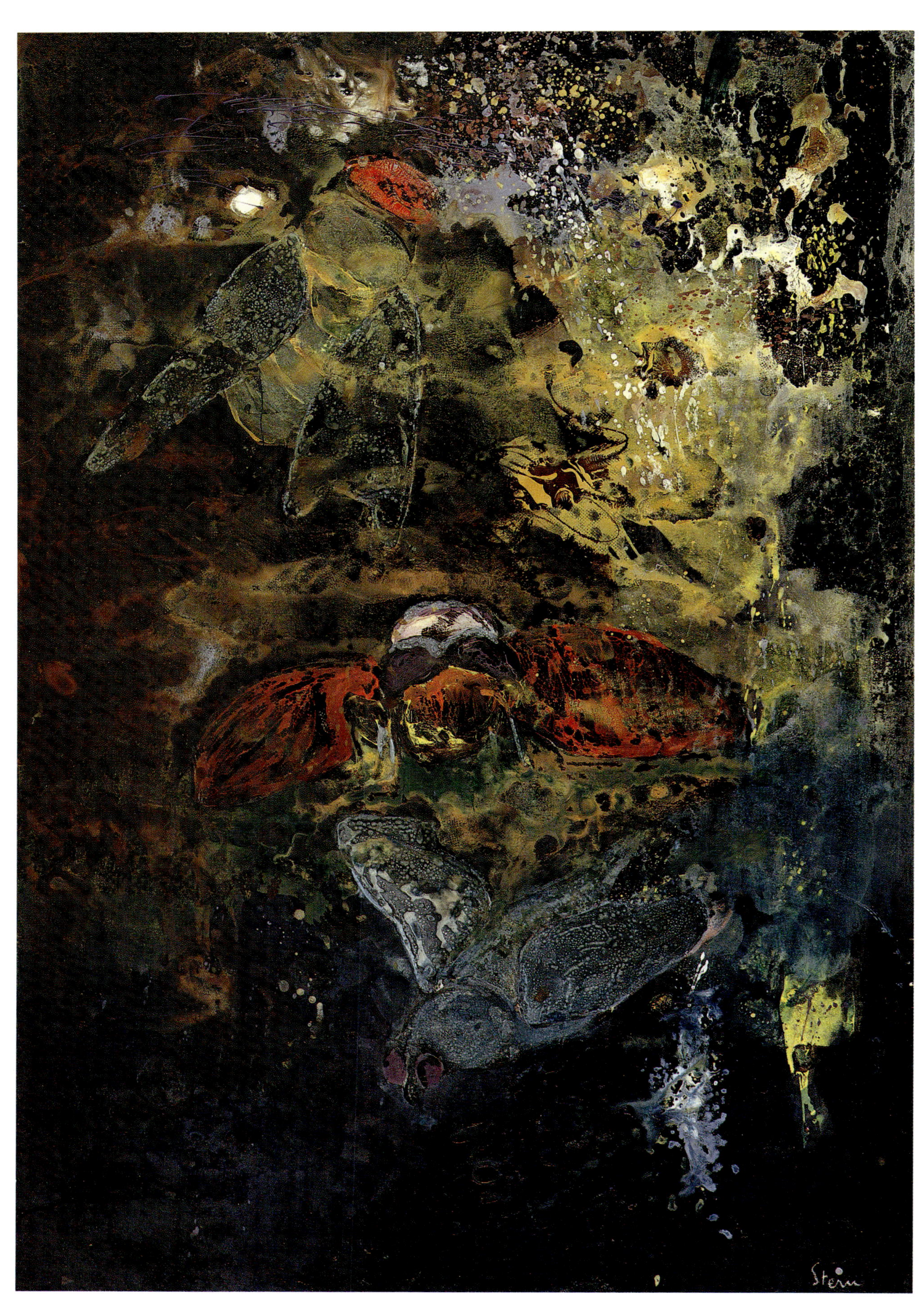

Summertime, 1987, oil on paper, 152x107cm, Mrs. Hedi Label Collection, Santa Cruz, California

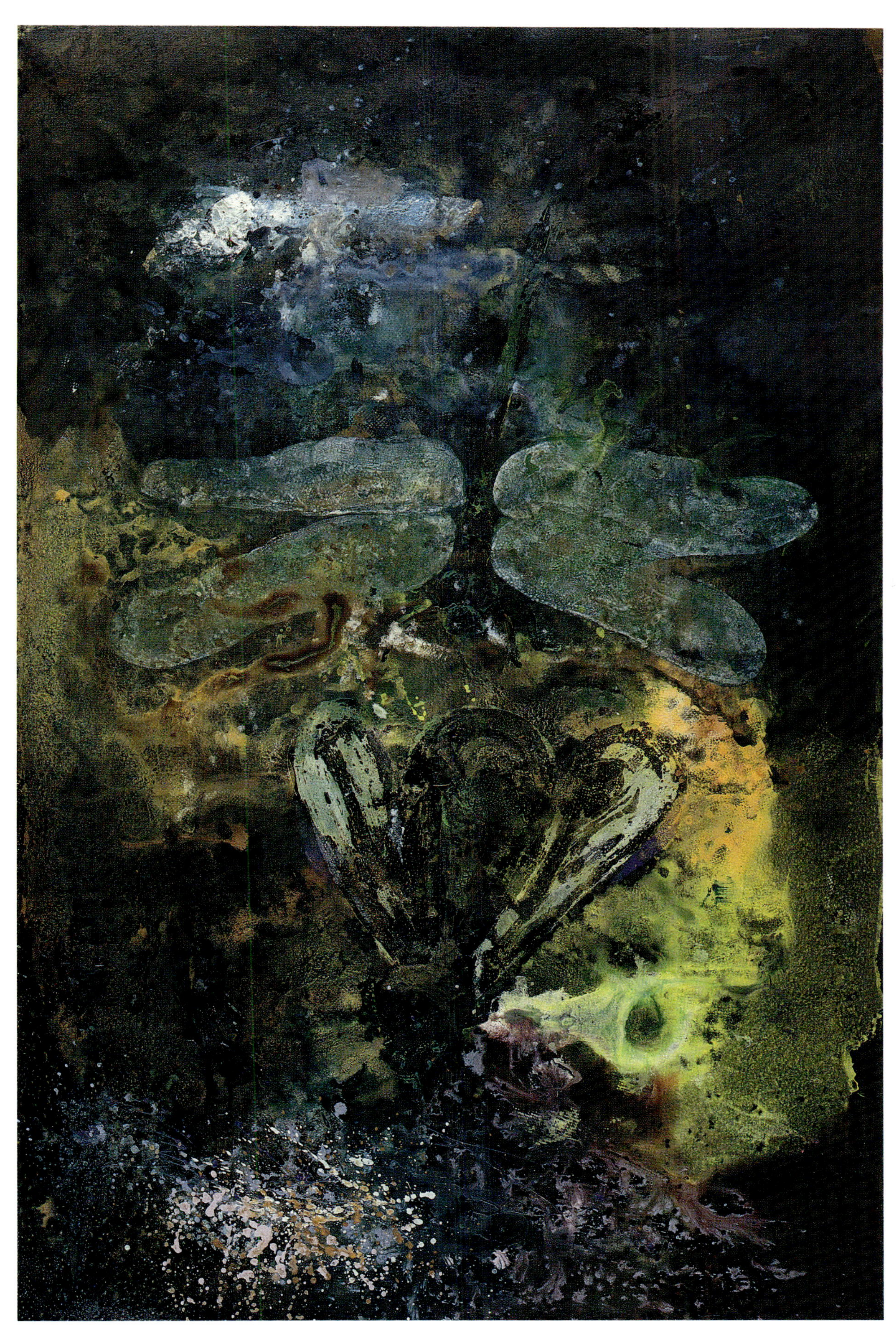

Rise and Fall, 1987, oil on paper, 129.5x86cm, I. Hoffman Collection, New York

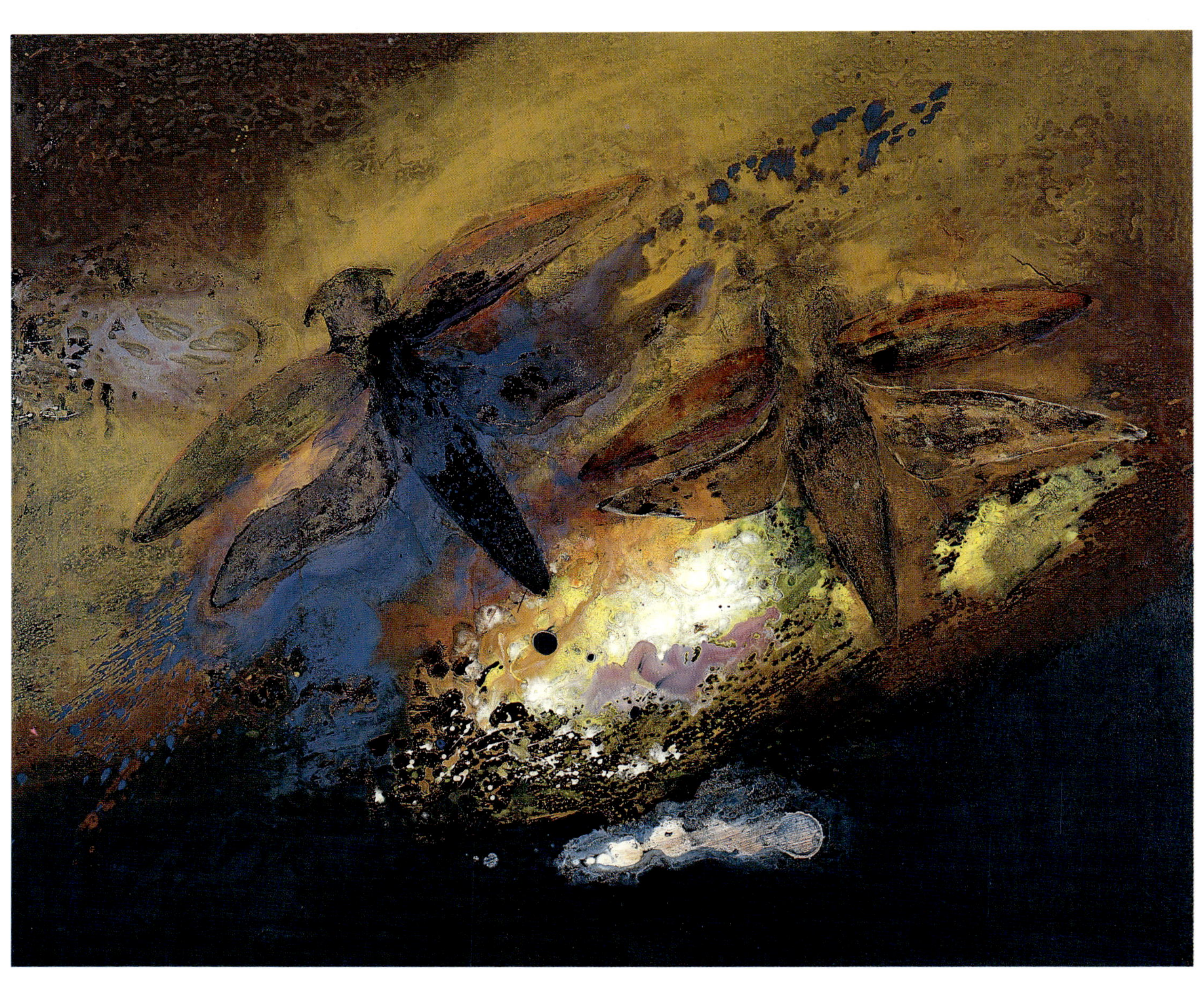

The Great Escape, 1987, oil on canvas, 117x147cm, W. Blitzer Collection, New York

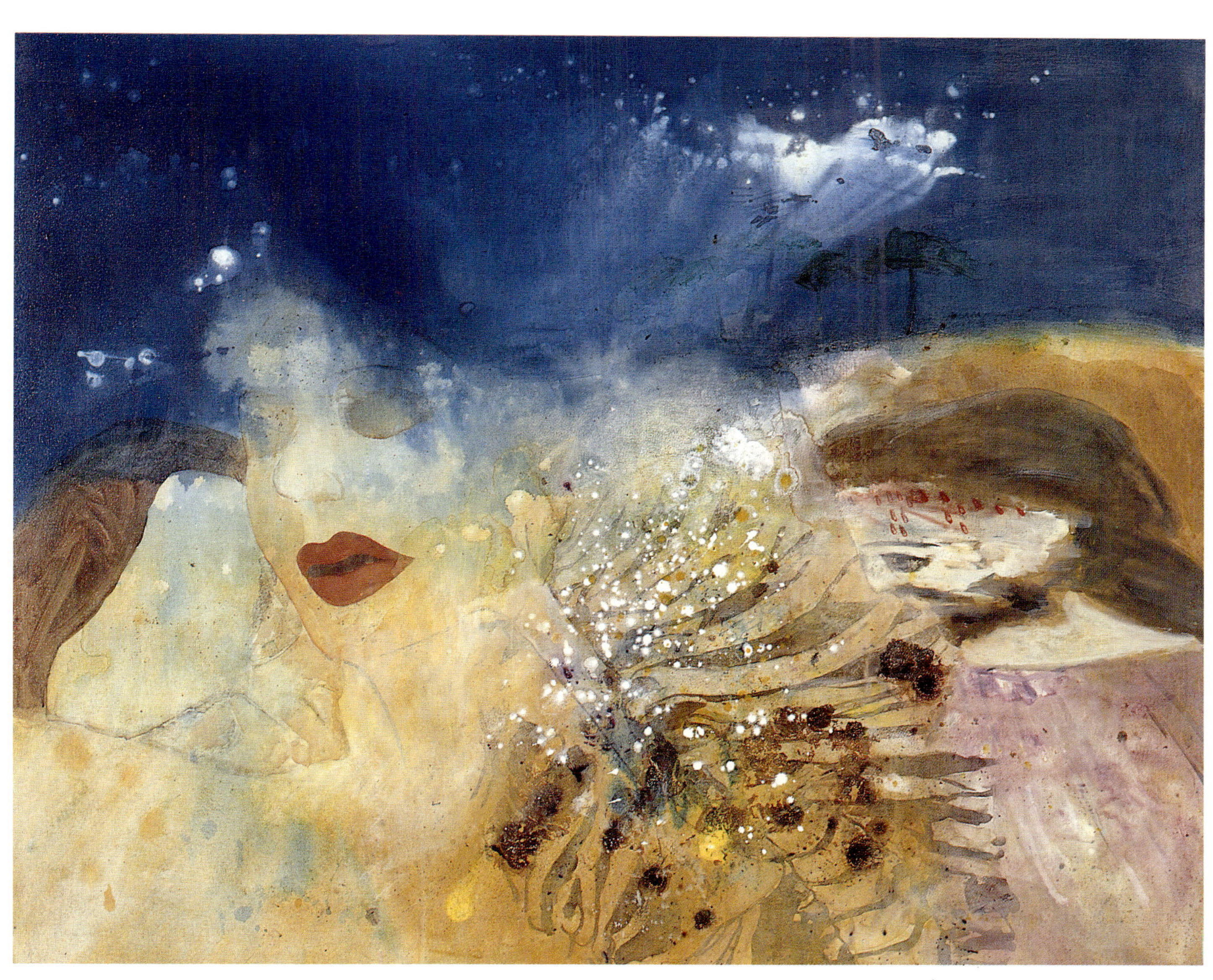

Jesus Inventing Love, 1988, oil on canvas, 117×142cm

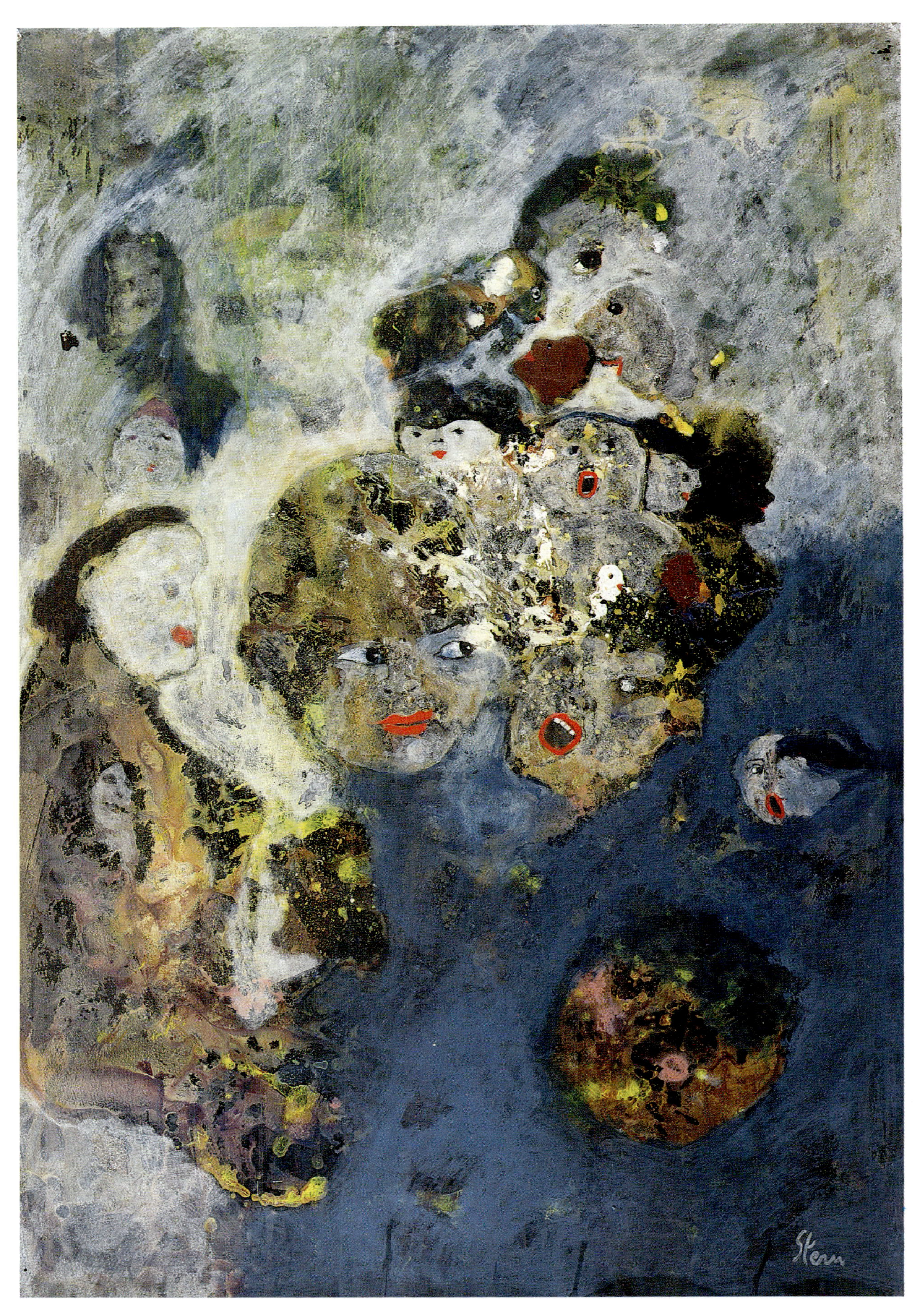

Transformation, 1988, oil on paper, 152x107cm, Artist's Collection

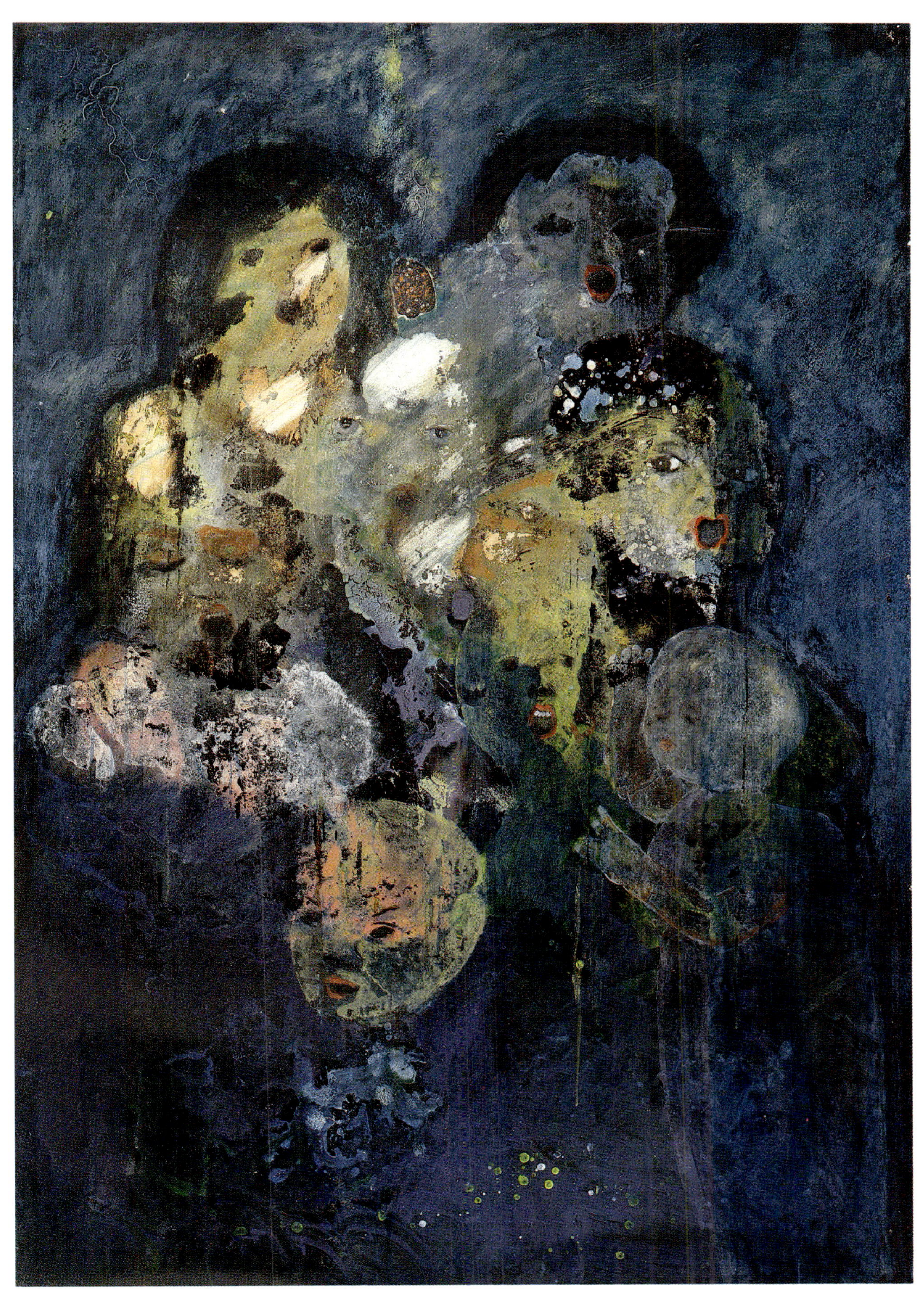

Dream I, 1988, oil on paper, 152×107cm

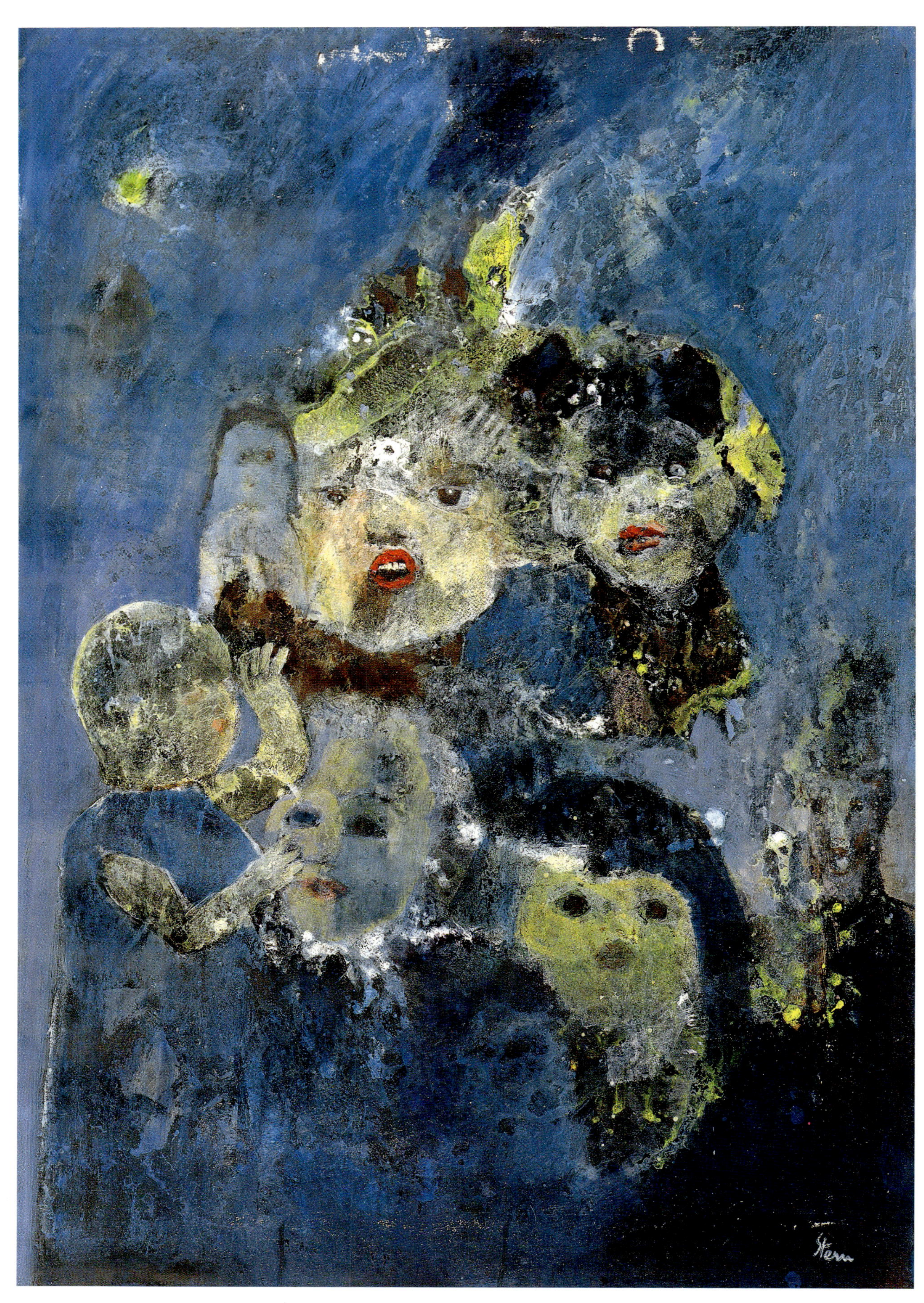

Metamorphosis III, 1988, oil on paper, 152×107cm

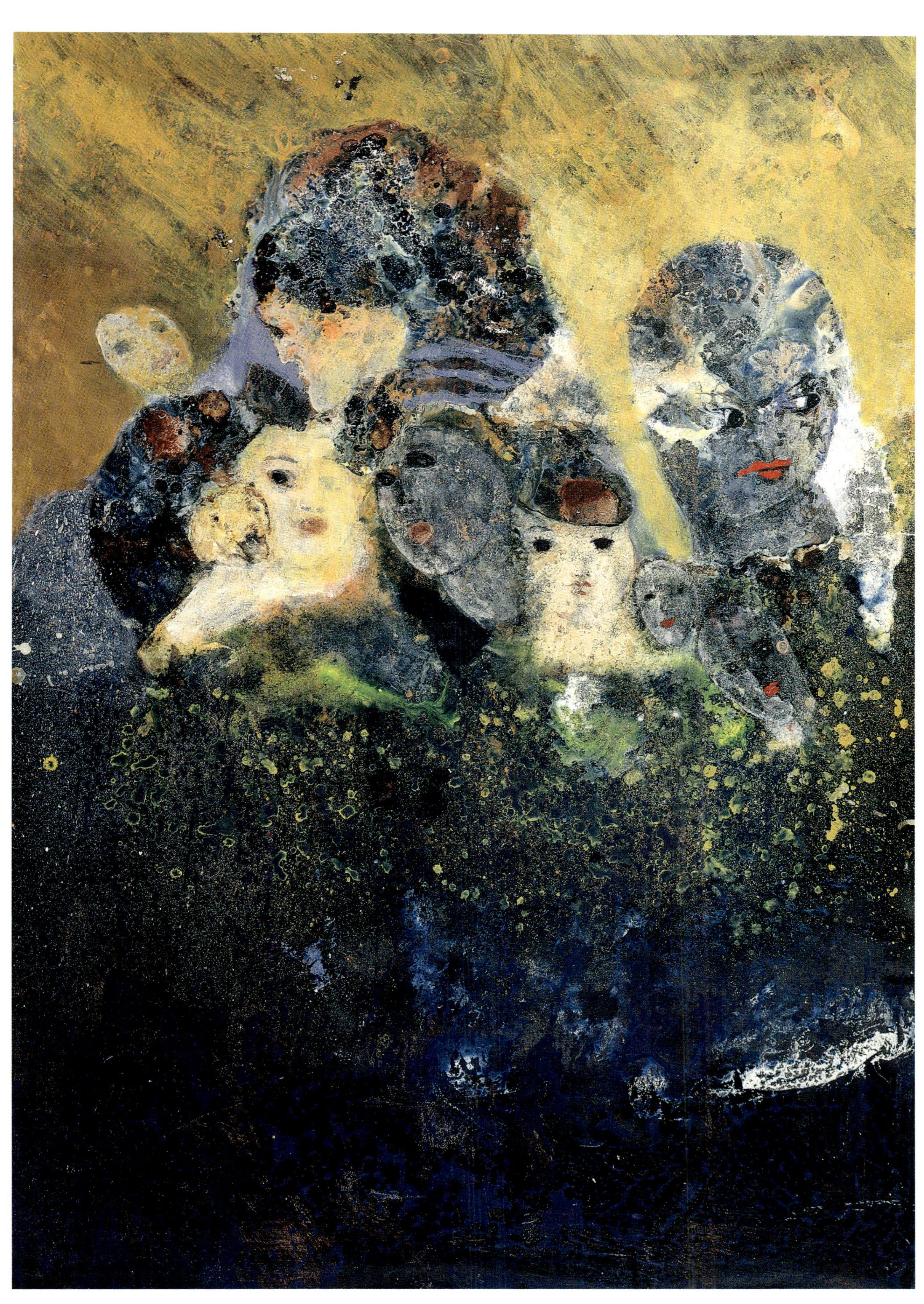

Cosmos III, 1988, oil on paper, 152x107cm, Private Collection, Frankfurt

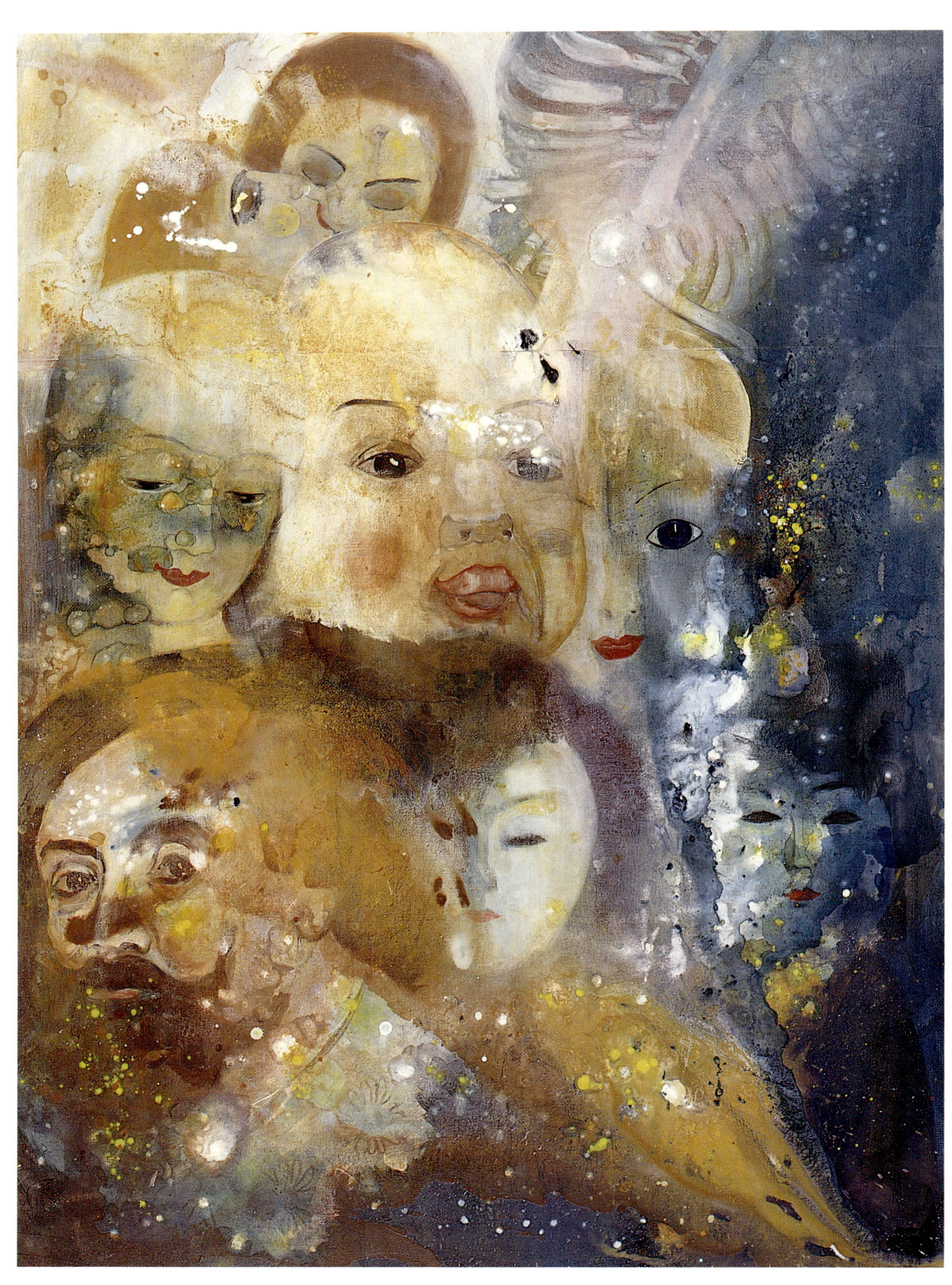

Dream of Rubens, 1988, oil on canvas, 152x177cm, Nelly Debbas Collection, Paris

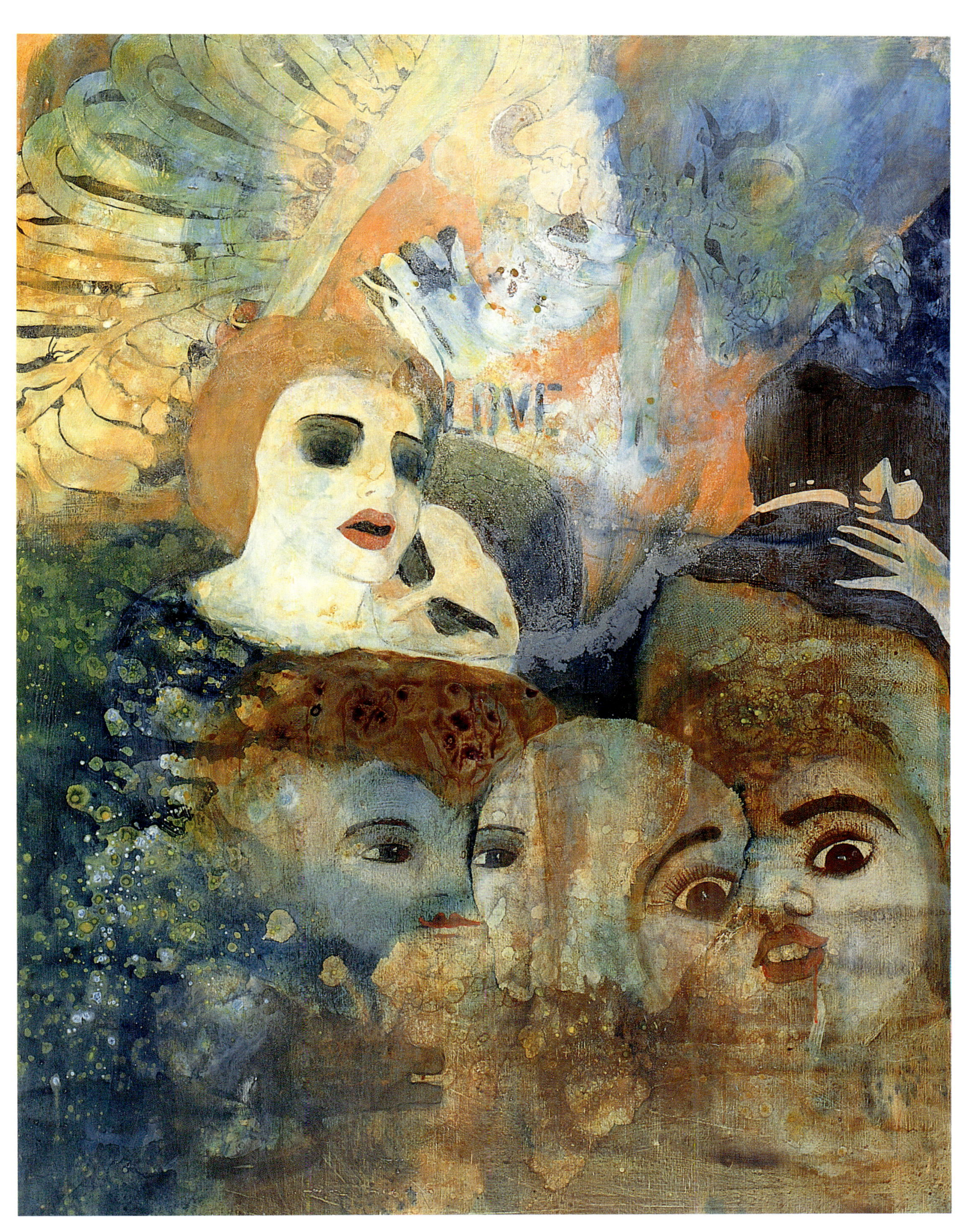

Dreams of the Perfumed Garden, 1988, oil on canvas, 147×117cm, Private Collection, Chicago

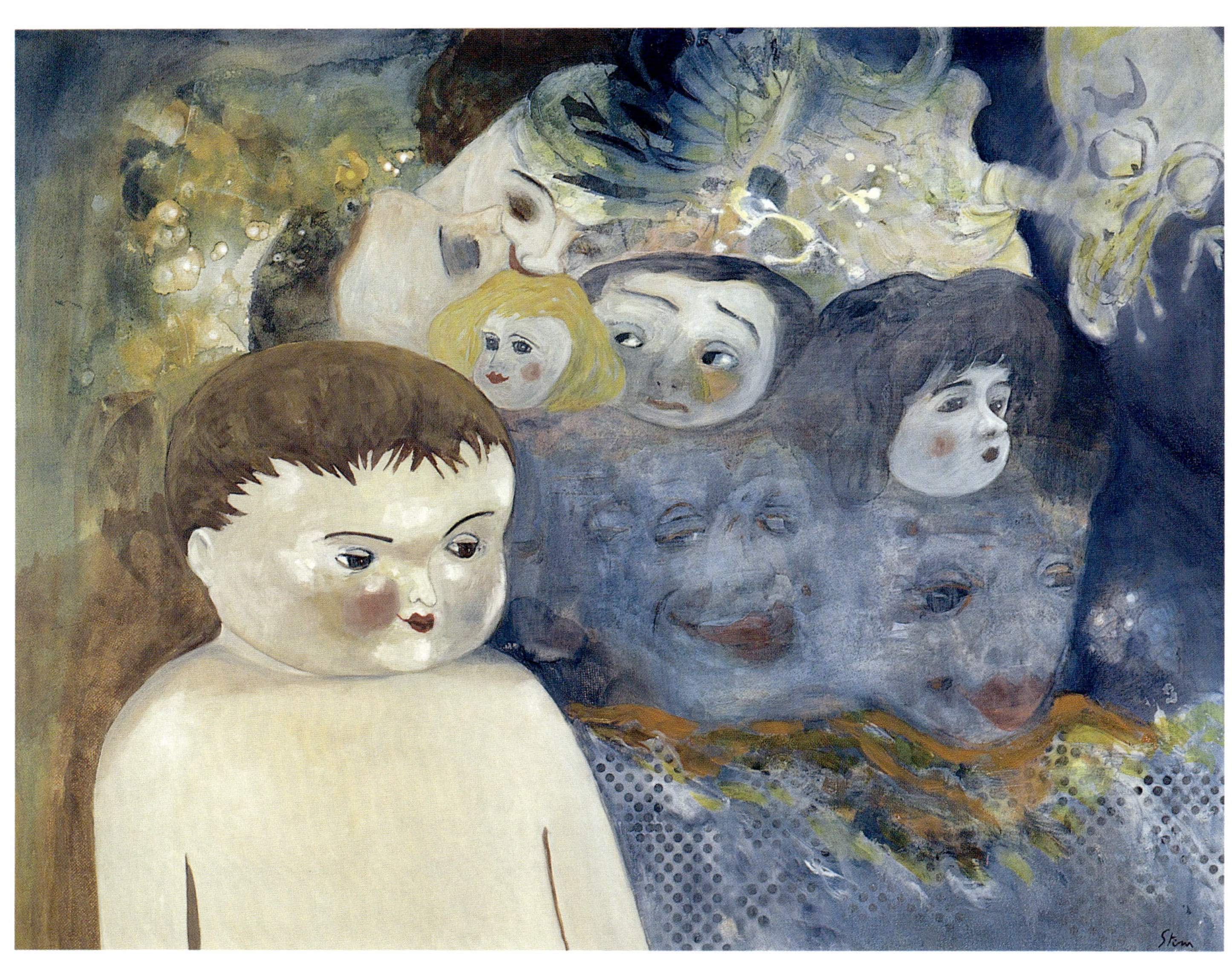

Childhood Memories, 1988, oil on canvas, 117x142cm

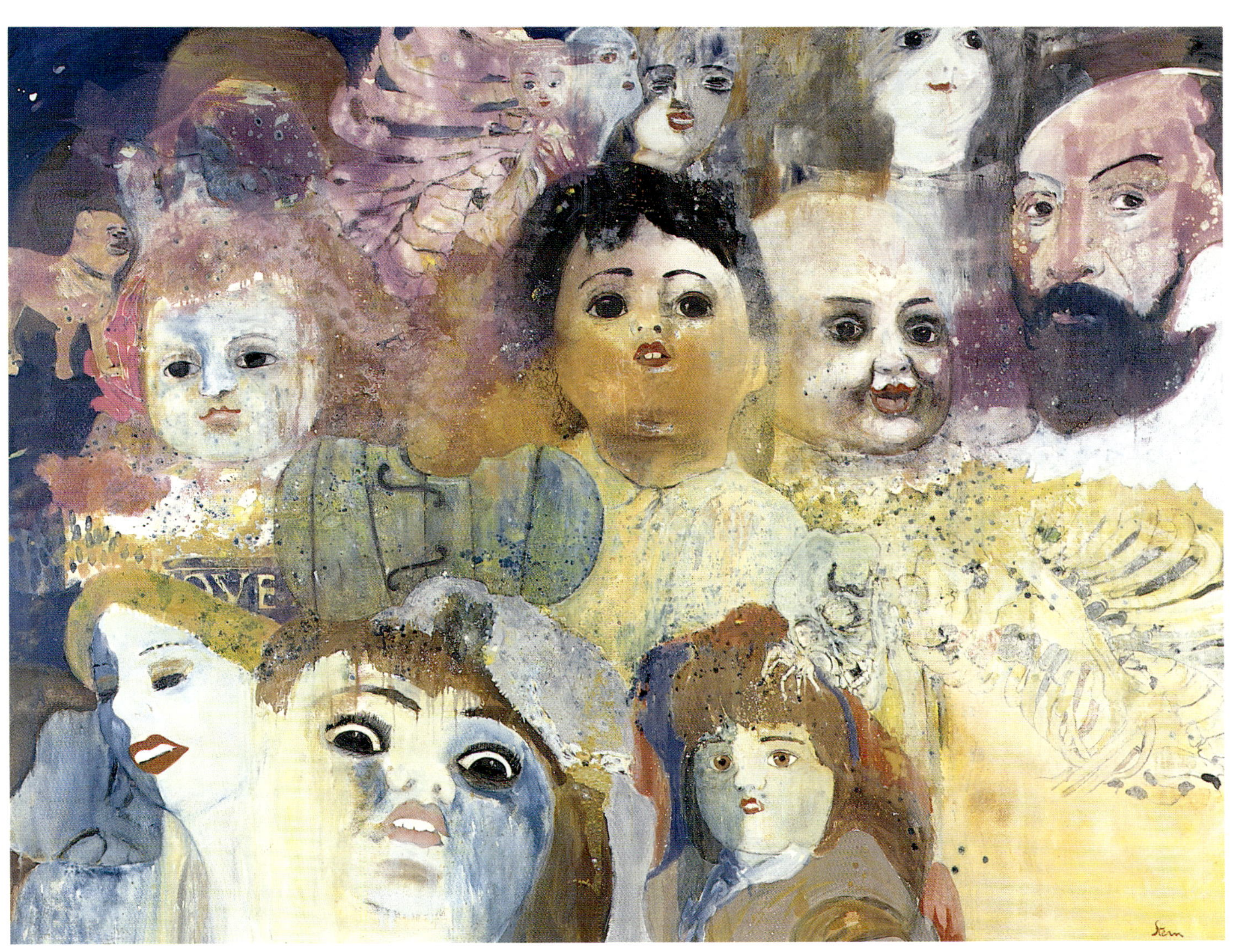

The Great Dream, 1988, oil on canvas, 152x203cm, Artist's Collection

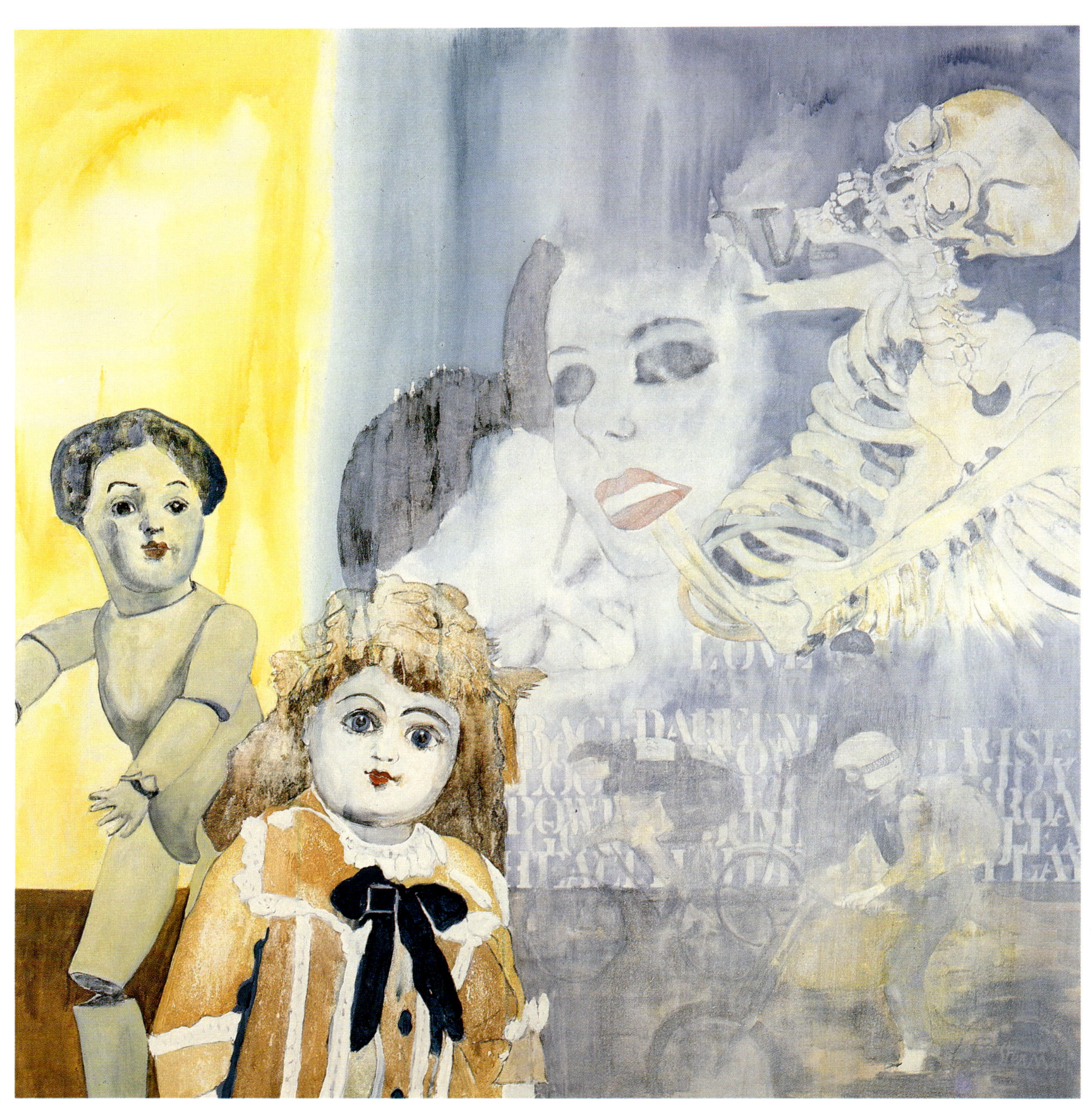

Witnesses to Love, 1988, acrylic on canvas, 183x183cm, Artist's Collection

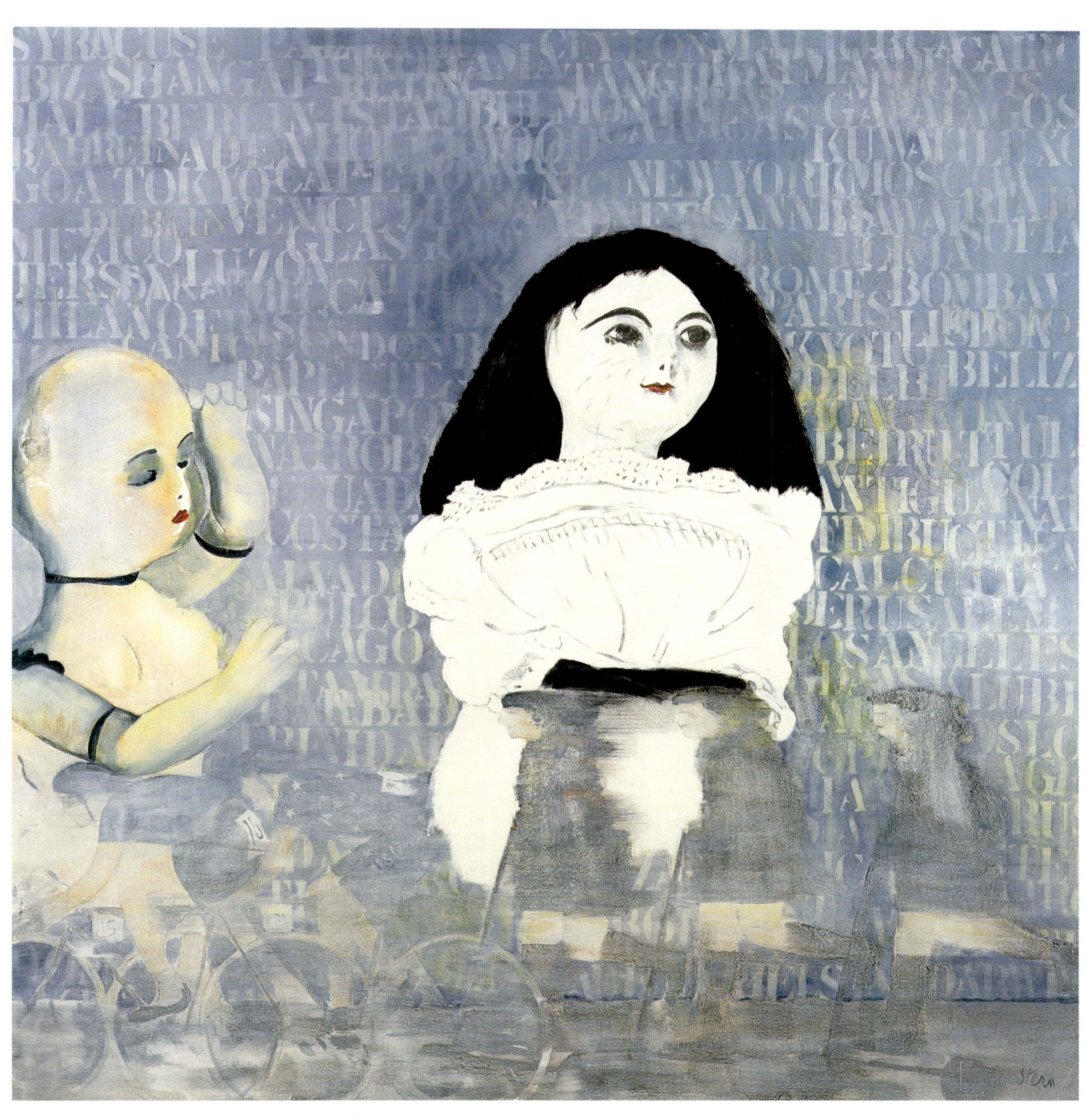

Wall of Great Departures, 1988, acrylic on canvas, 183×183cm, Artist's Collection

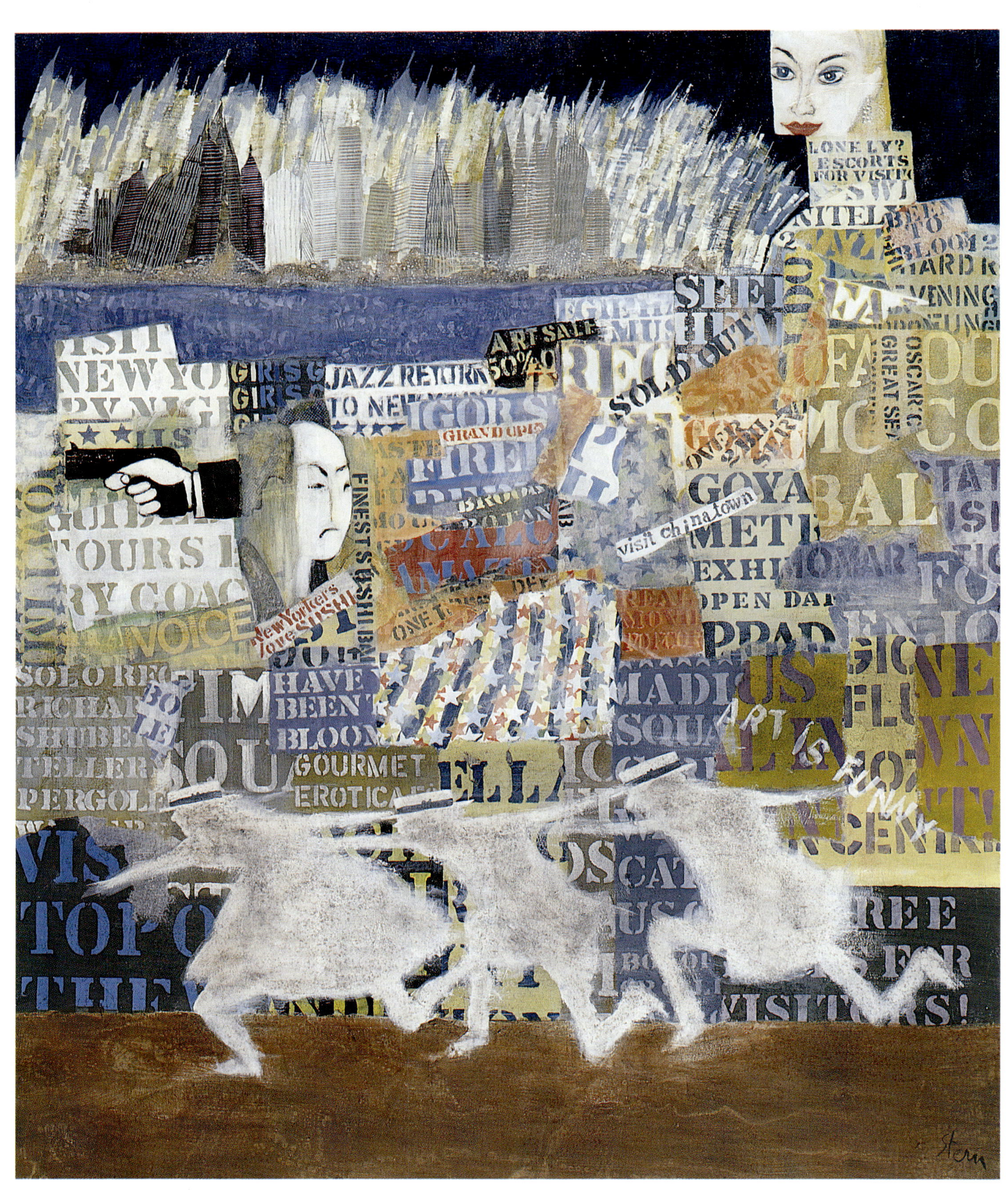

Tourists in Manhattan, 1989, acrylic on canvas, 152x122cm, Private Collection, Tokyo

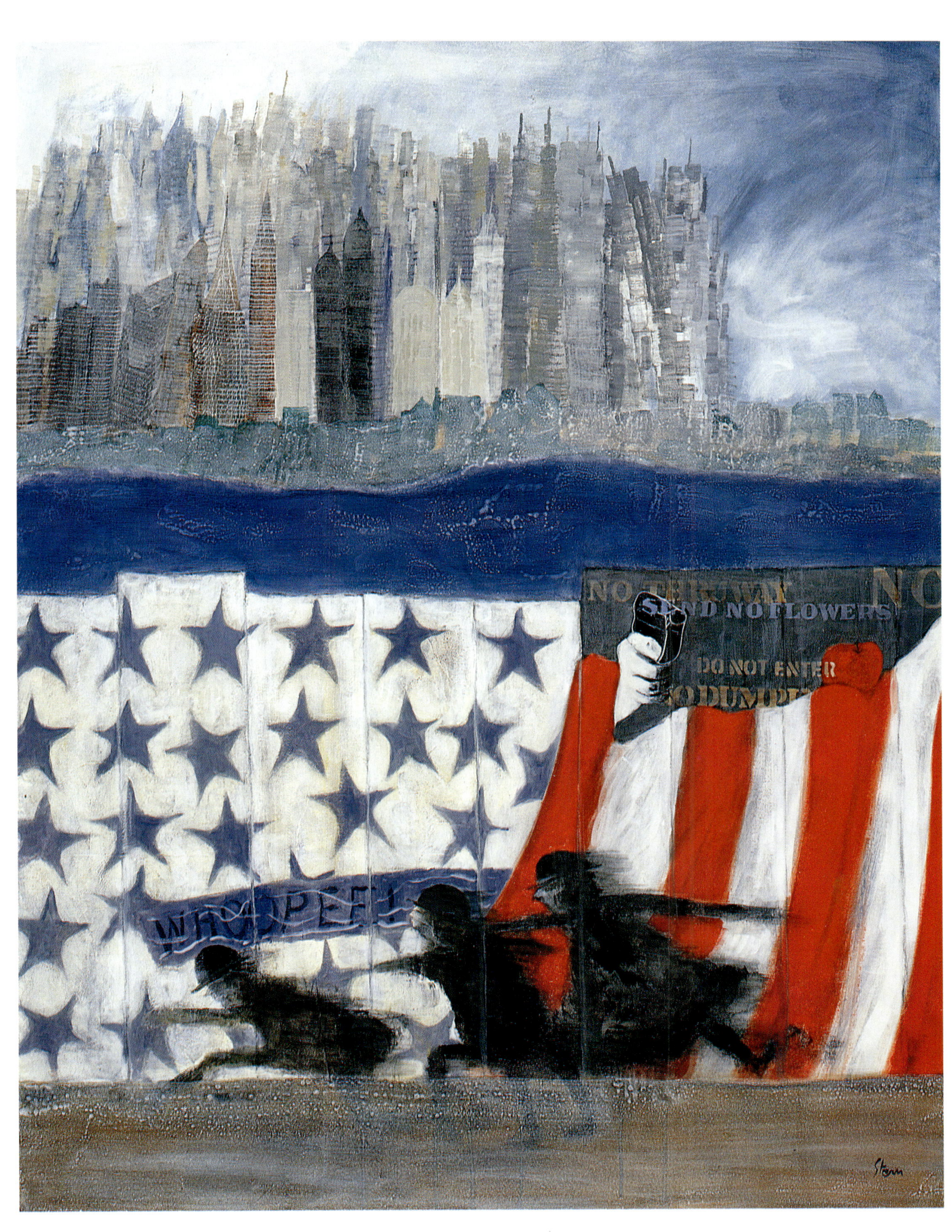

Send no Flowers!, 1989, acrylic on canvas, 147x117cm, Private Collection, Tokyo

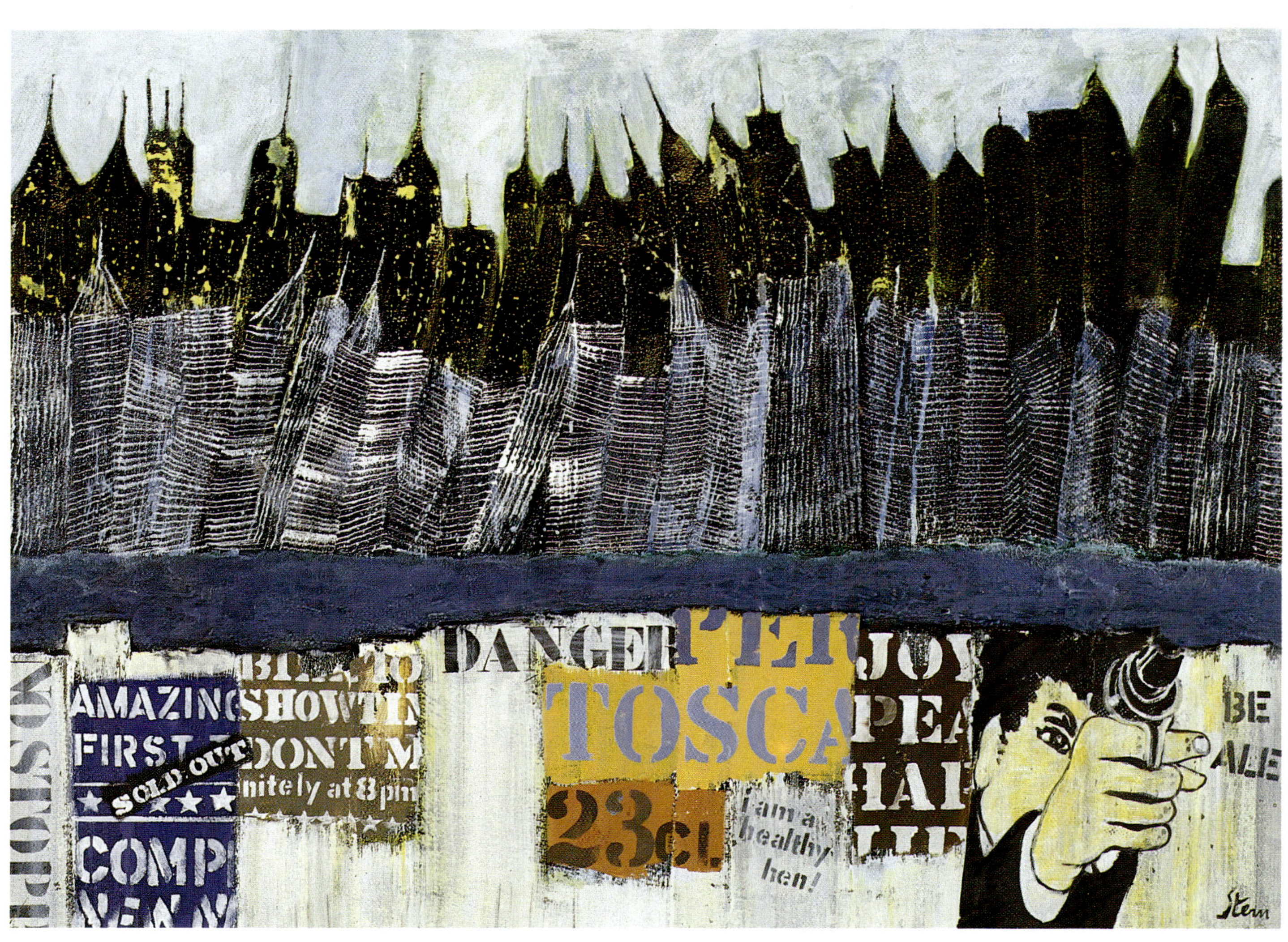

Manhattan, 1989, acrylic on paper, 81×102cm, Private Collection, Tokyo

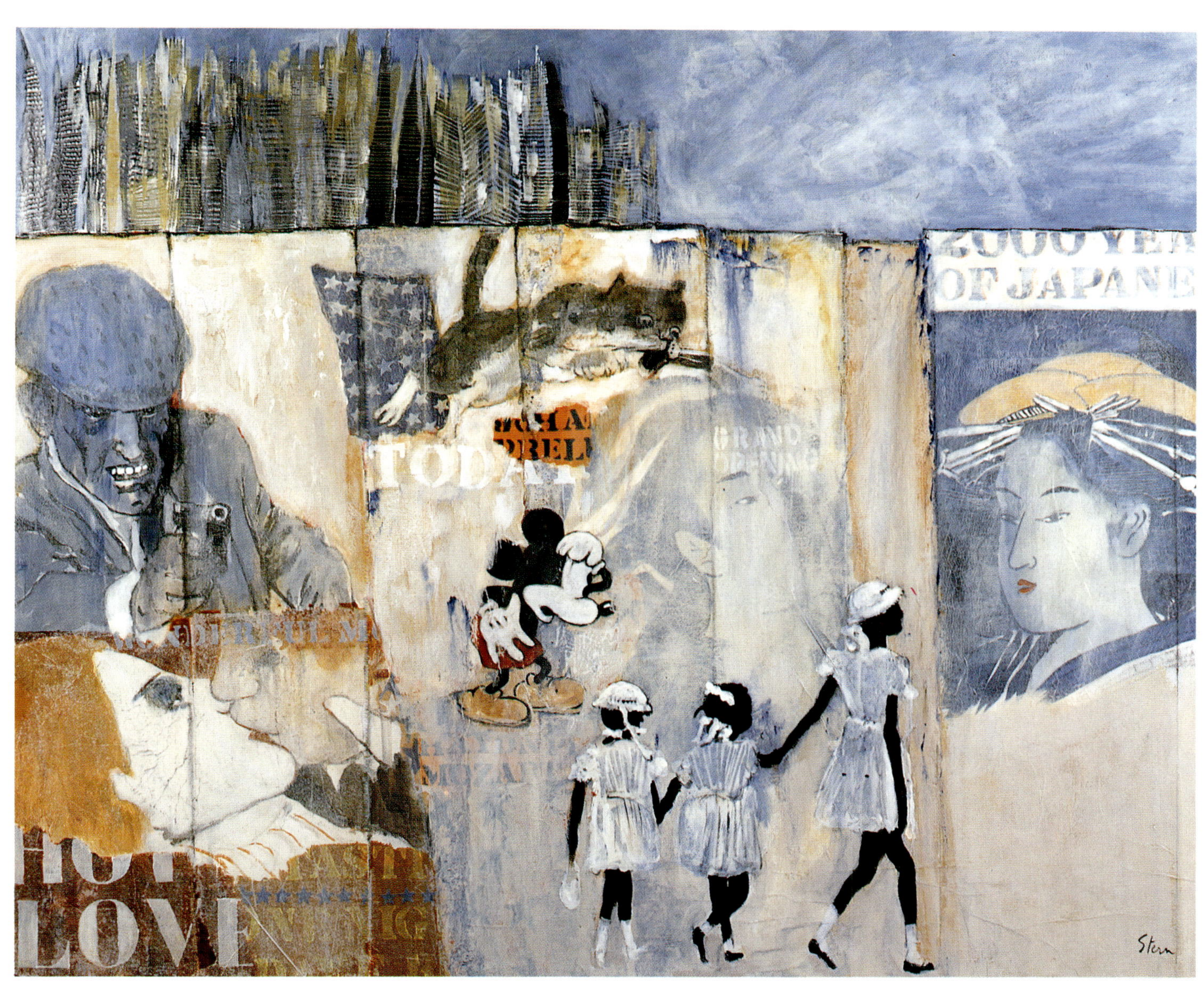

Oh! My Wall!!, 1989, acrylic on canvas, 114x146cm

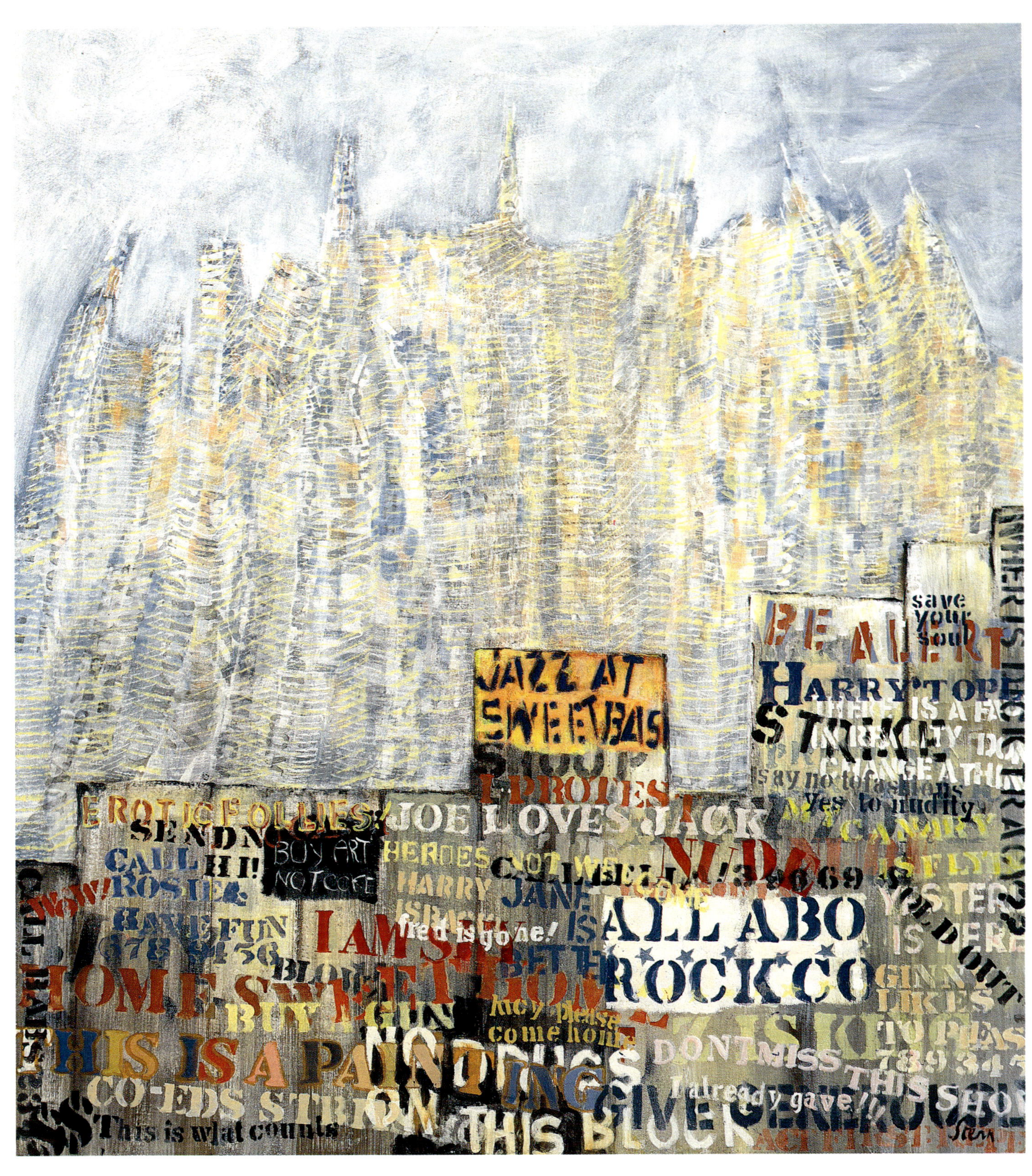

Man, That's Living!, 1989, acrylic on canvas, 102x92cm, Private Collection, Tokyo

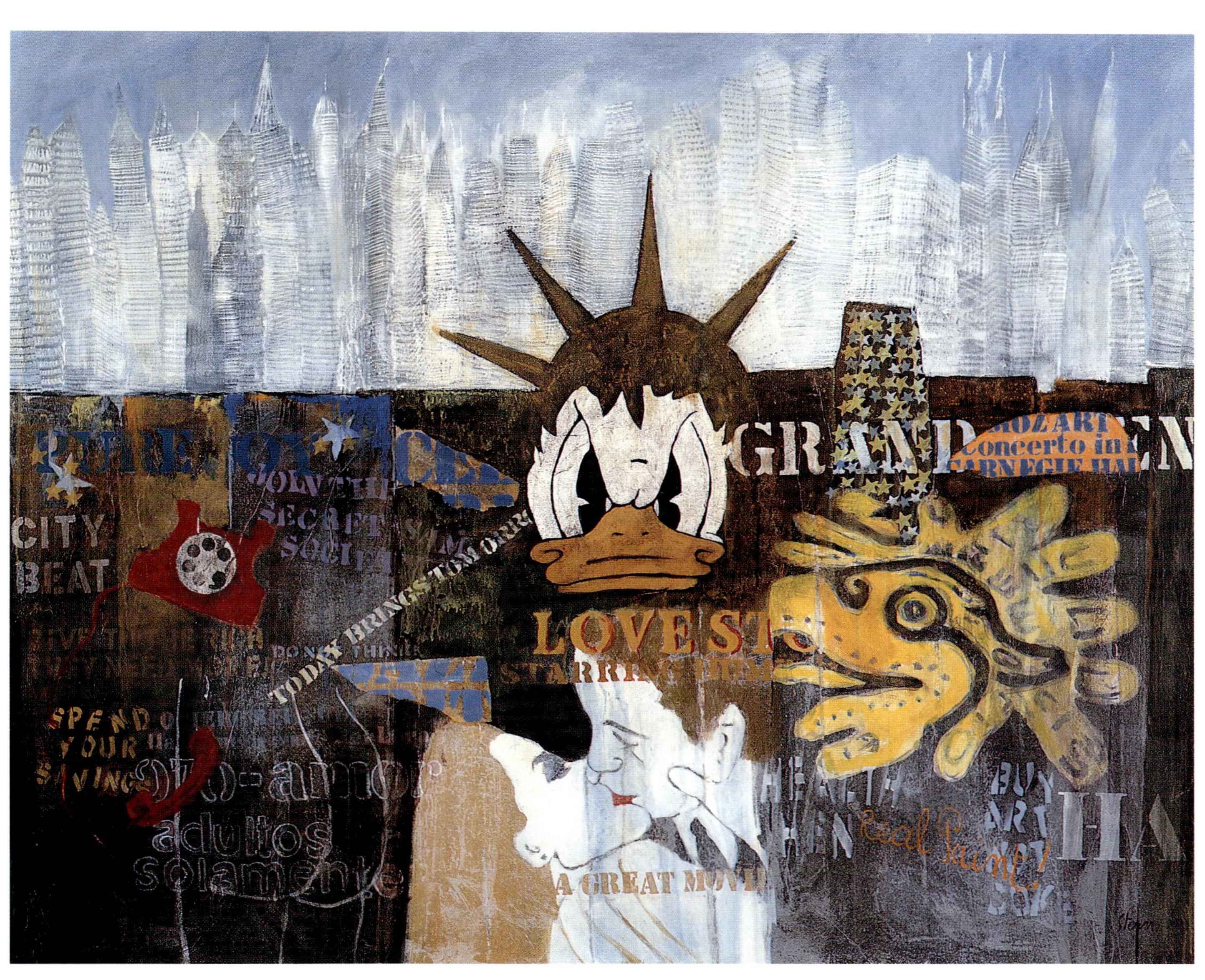

City Beat, 1989, acrylic on canvas, 117×146cm

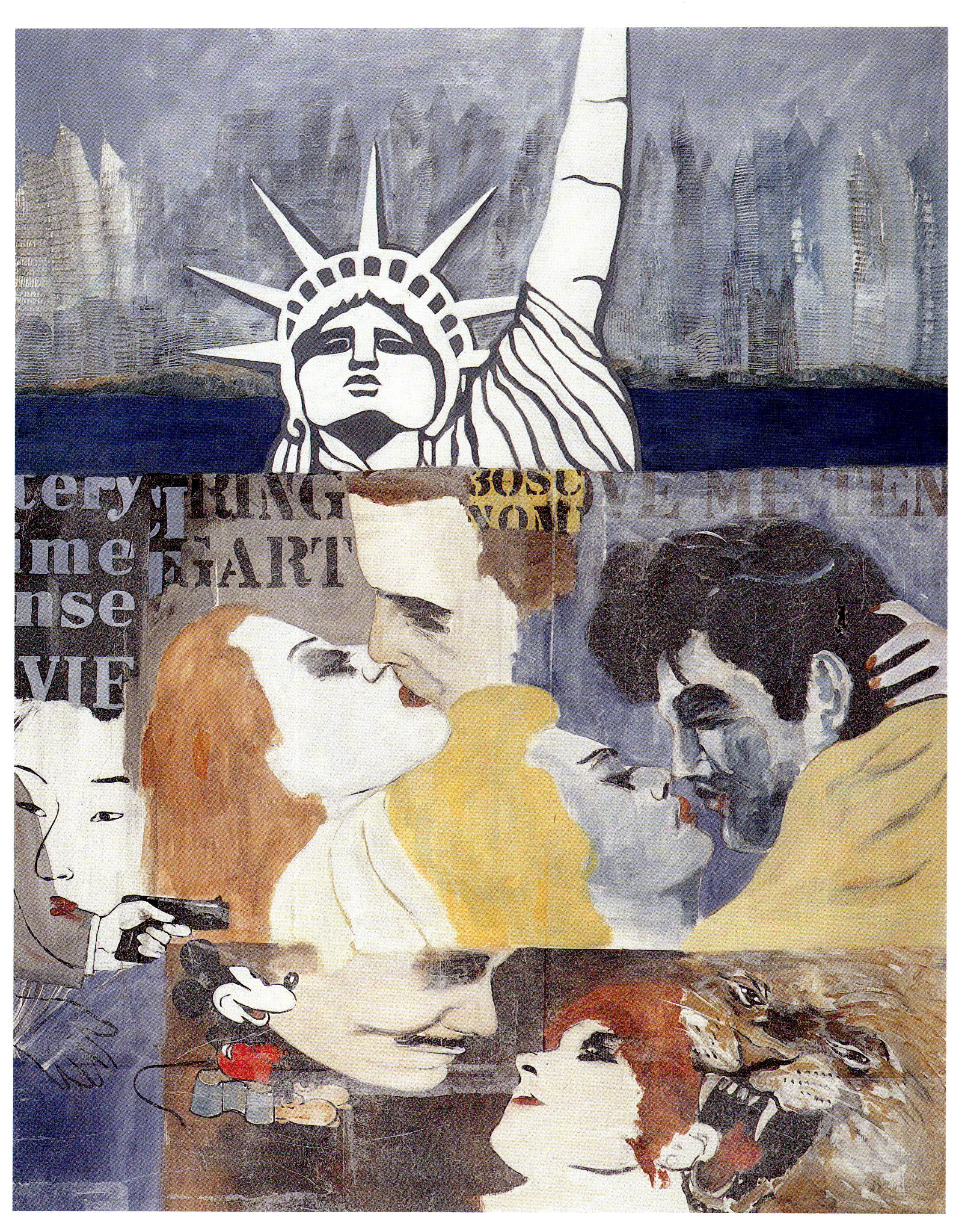

Wall of Fame, 1989, acrylic on canvas, 148x117cm

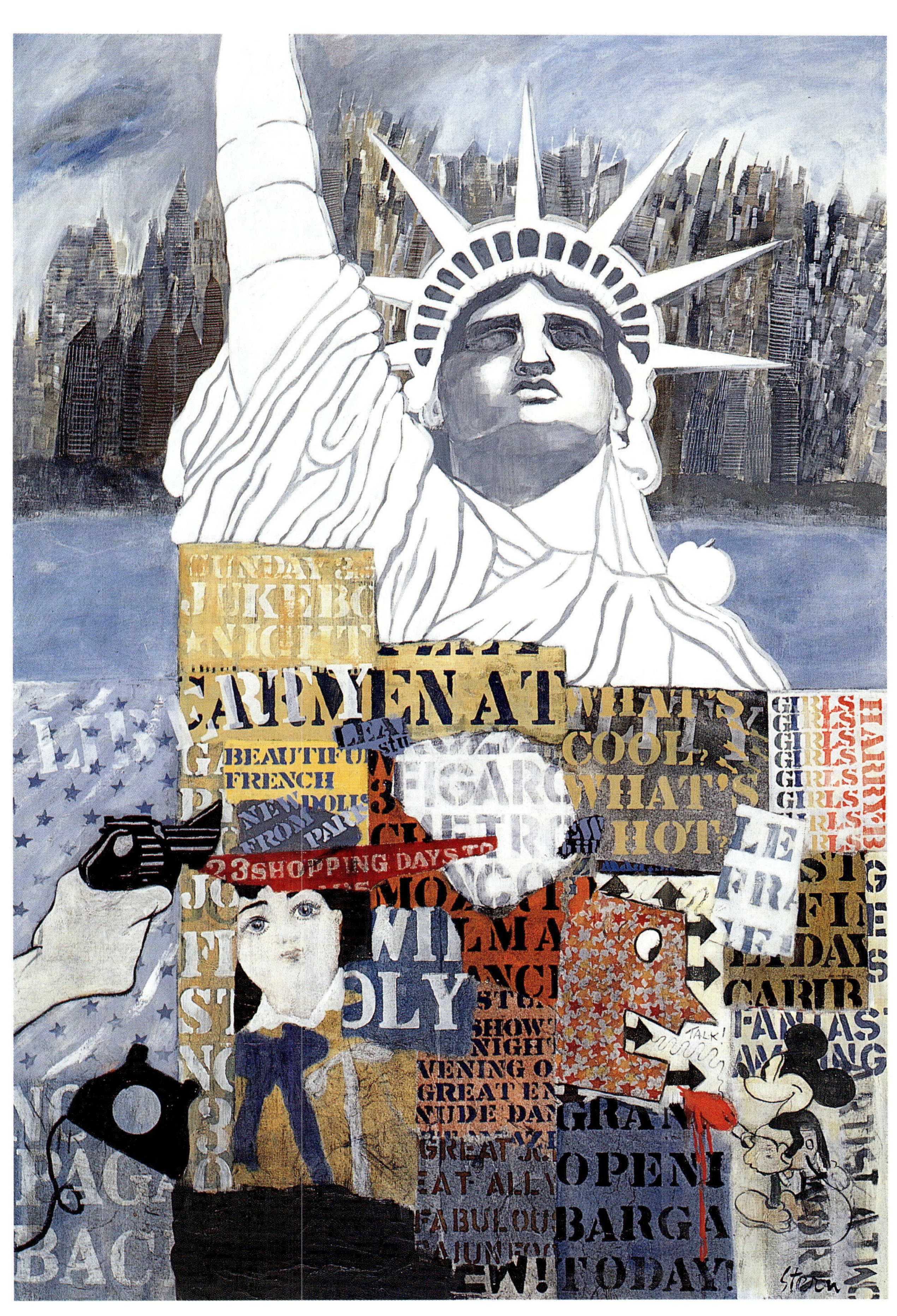

Our Beloved Cardboard Liberty, 1989, acrylic on canvas, 137x117cm, Private Collection, Tokyo

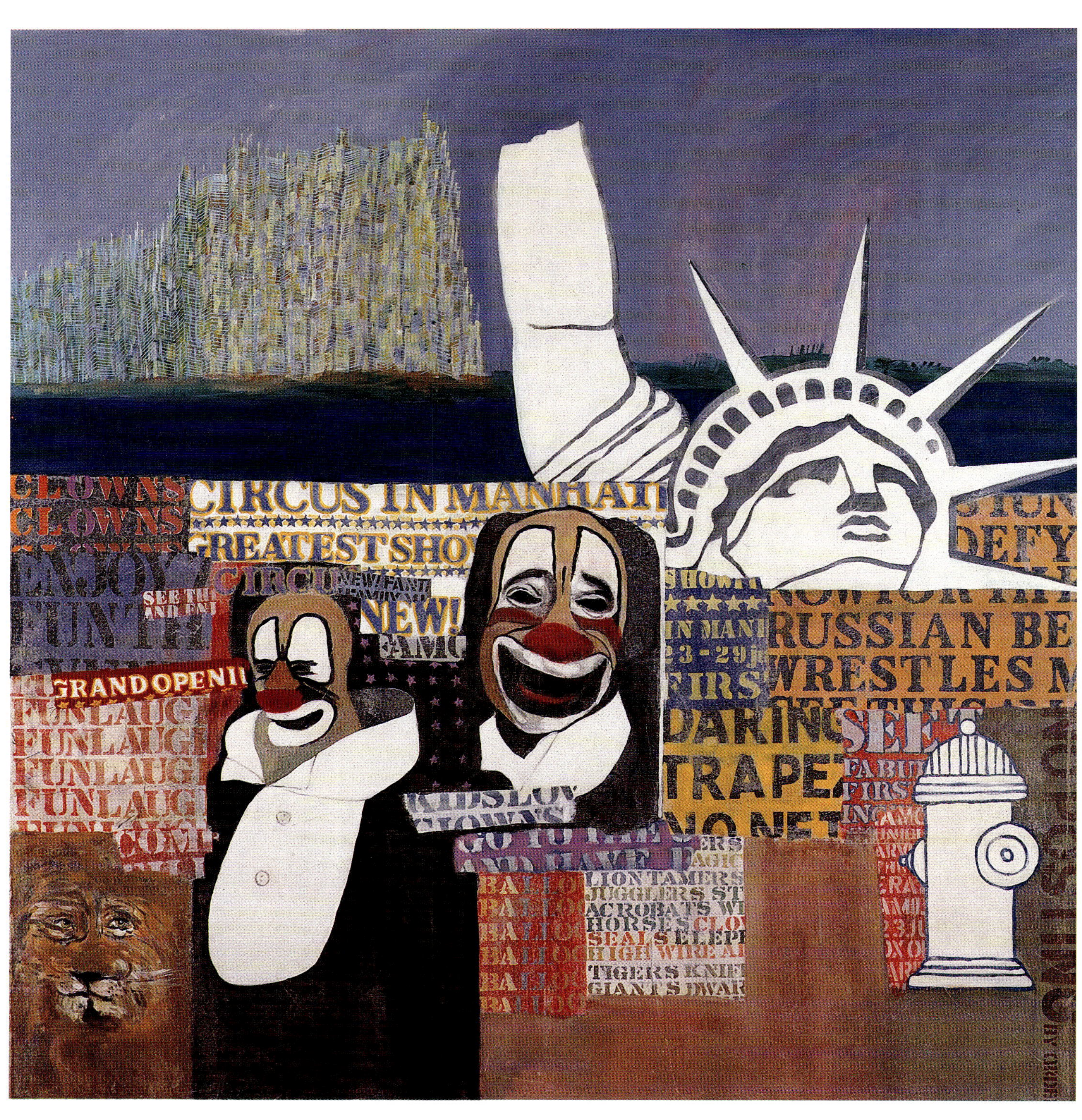

Circus in Manhattan, 1989, acrylic on canvas, 152x152cm

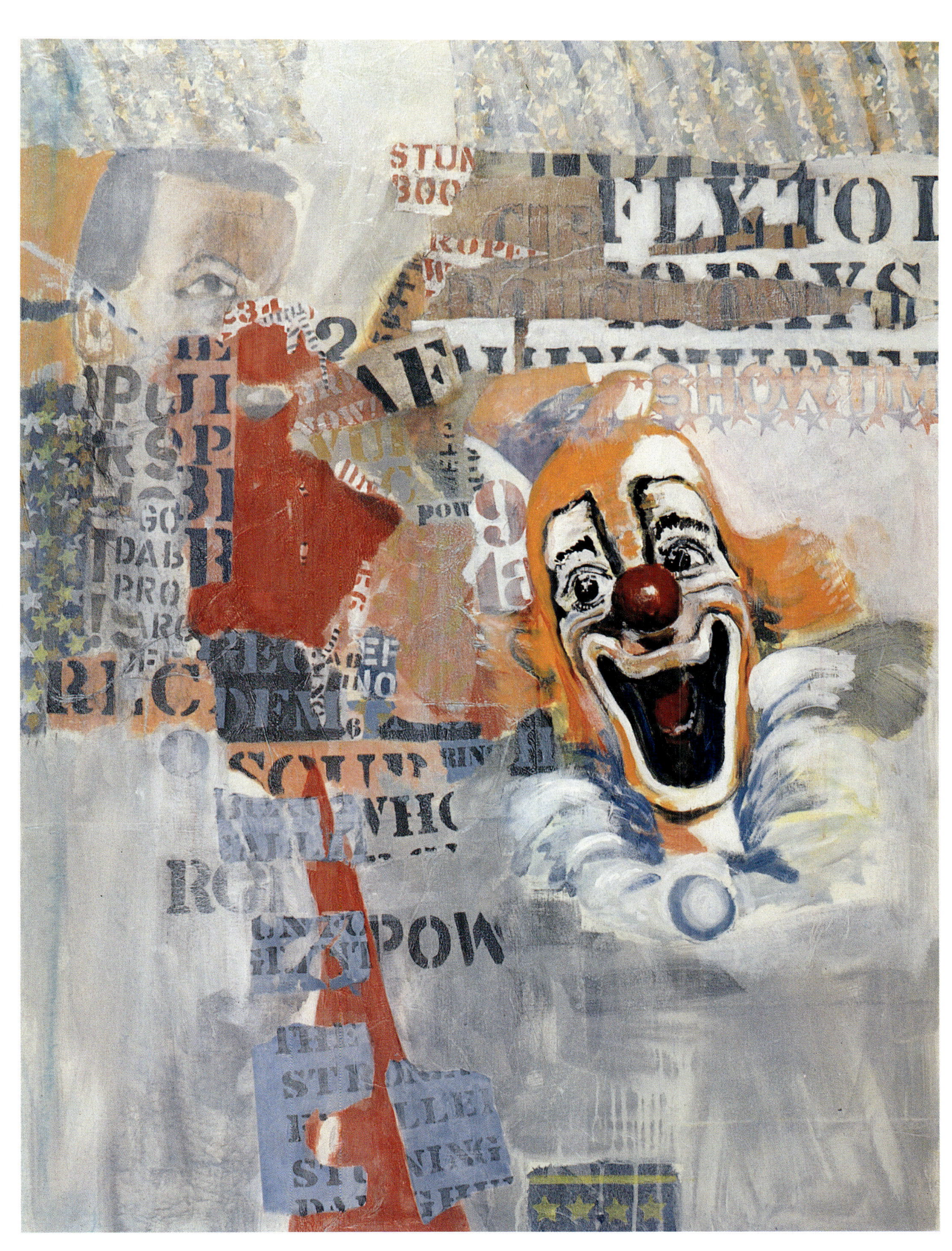

Billboard, 1989, acrylic on canvas, 117×89cm

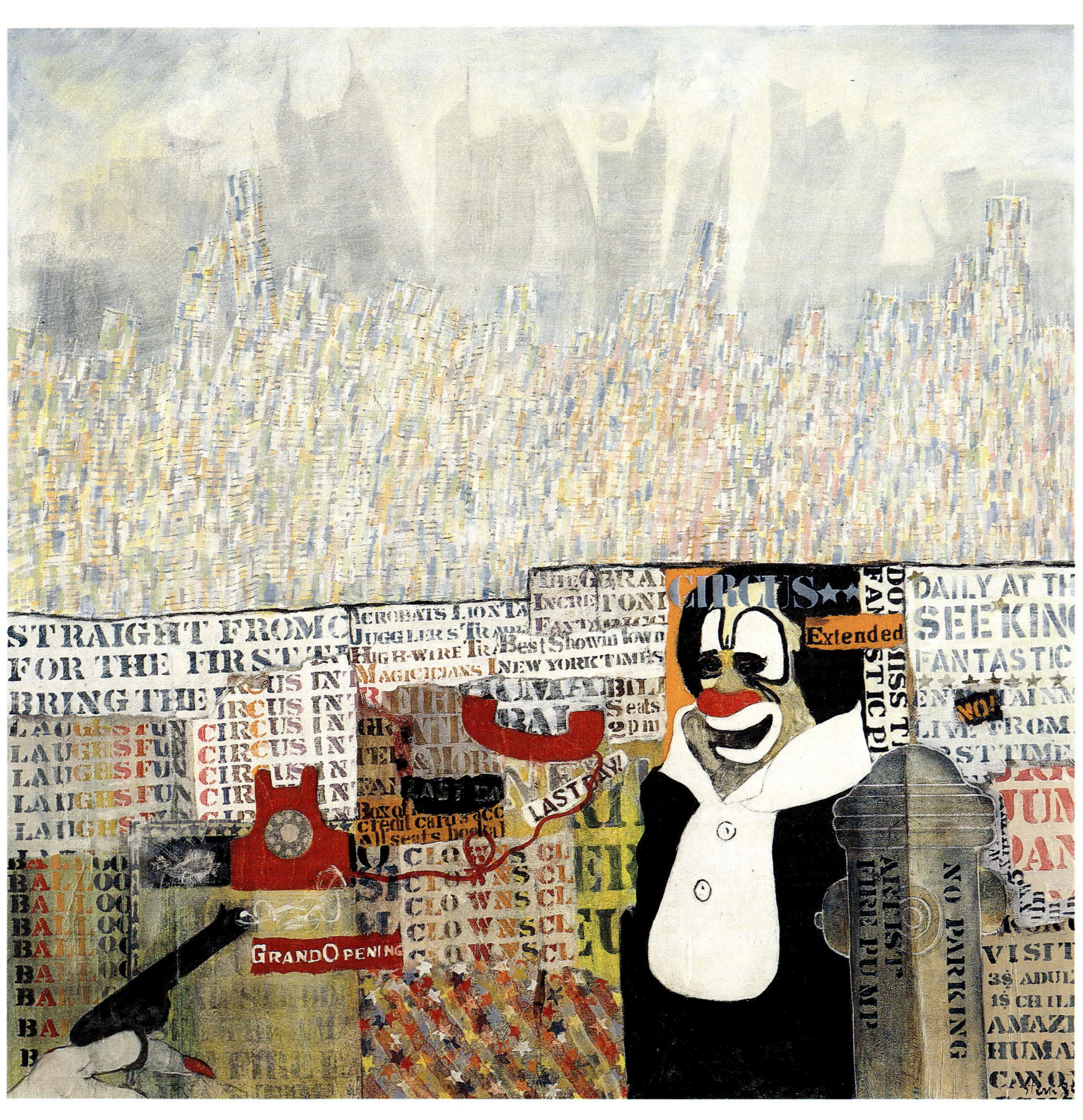

Circus on the Fence, 1989, acrylic on canvas, 122x122cm, Private Collection, Tokyo

LIST OF PLATES / *INDEX DES ŒUVRES*

Page:

52 *La Japonaise en jaune*, 1972
oil on canvas, 183x183cm
Private Collection, London

53 *The Star*, 1972
oil on canvas, 183x183cm
Artist's Collection

54 *Movie Maker*, 1972
oil on canvas, 183x244cm
Artist's Collection

55 *Making a Movie*, 1972
oil on canvas, 183x244cm
Artist's Collection

56 *The Performers*, 1972
oil on canvas, 183x244cm
Artist's Collection

57 *Cross Roads (Michael Kustow)*, 1972
oil on canvas, 183x244cm
Artist's Collection

58 *Flower Composition*, 1972
oil on canvas, 122x122cm
Private Collection, Zurich

59 *Fruit Crates III*, 1972
oil on canvas, 183x183cm
Private Collection, New York

60 *Fruit Crates in the Market*, 1972
oil on canvas, 183x183cm
Sir Joseph Lockwood Collection,
London

61 *Fruit Crates*, 1972
oil on canvas, 183x183cm
Mrs. Hedi Label Collection, Santa
Cruz, California

62 *Music Machine*, 1972
oil on canvas, 102x92cm
Manuel Solana Collection, Madrid

63 *Musical Notes*, 1973
oil on canvas, 102x91cm
Petit Palais Collection, Geneva

64 *Born a Harlequin*, 1973

oil on canvas, 102x91cm
Artist's Collection

65 *Fête des Rois*, 1973
oil on canvas, 122x122cm
Luciano Zucchi Collection, London

66 *Pierrot*, 1973
oil on canvas, 76x64cm
Private Collection, Israel

67 *Sad Harlequin*, 1973
oil on canvas, 76x64cm
Private Collection, Israel

68 *Double Exposure*, 1973
oil on canvas, 152x152cm
David Weisz Collection, Caracas

69 *Dames au Salon*, 1973
oil on canvas, 152x152cm
Private Collection, Munich

70 *Melon Crates*, 1973
oil on canvas, 183x183cm
Sir Joseph Lockwood Collection,
London

71 *Still Life With Crates*, 1973
oil on canvas, 152x152cm
Nicoline Pon Collection, Zurich

72 *Paysage Fruité*, 1973
oil on canvas, 64x76cm
H. Recanati Collection, Buenos
Aires

72 *Festival*, 1974
oil on canvas, 91x102cm
Petit Palais Collection, Geneva

74 *Country Walk*, 1973
oil on canvas, 91x102cm
Makoto Iida Collection, Tokyo

75 *Fruit Lovers 1st Picnic*, 1974
oil on canvas, 91x102cm
Mr. & Mrs. Cervellini Collection,
Paris

76 *Drum Beat*, 1974

oil on canvas, 102x91cm
Petit Palais Collection, Geneva

77 *Adagio*, 1974
oil on canvas, 102x91cm
Ashkenazy Collection, Los Angeles

78 *Crates*, 1974
oil on canvas, 152x152cm
Artist's Collection

79 *Day and Night*, 1974
oil on canvas, 152x152cm
Mrs. Hedi Label Collection, Santa
Cruz, California

80 *Wagnerian Poem*, 1974
oil on canvas, 64x76cm
Manuel Solana Collection, Madrid

81 *Noah's Ark Landing in Yucatan*, 1974
oil on canvas, 91x122cm
Musée d'Art Moderne Collection,
Ostend

82 *Le Conquérant*, 1975
acrylic on canvas, 102x91cm
Ashkenazy Collection, Los Angeles

83 *Les Promesses du Député*, 1975
oil on canvas, 122x97cm
Private Collection, Reims

84 *Le Général*, 1975
oil on canvas, 183x122cm
Mrs. Hedi Label Collection, Santa
Cruz, California

85 *L'Anarchiste Arrivé*, 1975
oil on canvas, 183x122cm
Mrs. Hedi Label Collection, Santa
Cruz, California

86 *Bananas in Yucatan*, 1976
oil on canvas, 183x183cm
Mrs. Hedi Label Collection, Santa
Cruz, California

87 *Summer*, 1976
oil on canvas, 152x152cm
Mrs. Hedi Label Collection, Santa

Cruz, California

88 *Hat Shop*, 1976
oil on canvas, 150x100cm
Private Collection, Paris

89 *Le Calme de la Bourgeoisie*, 1976
oil on canvas, 90x77cm
Private Collection, Basel

90 *Curtain on a View*, 1975
oil on canvas, 72x60cm

91 *Les Rideaux*, 1978
oil on canvas, 92x73cm

92 *Colleagues*, 1977
oil on canvas, 102x92cm
Giulio Castelli Collection, Milan

93 *Side Show*, 1977
oil on canvas, 96x21cm
Della Turca Collection, Paris

94 *Changing Partners*, 1978
mixed media on paper, 80x57cm
Artist's Collection

95 *Not Any More*, 1978
mixed media on paper, 80x57cm
Artist's Collection

96 *Love Story*, 1978
mixed media on paper, 60x45cm
Artist's Collection

97 *Mimi, Your Ship is Gone*, 1978
mixed media on paper, 80x57cm
Artist's Collection

98 *Love*, 1978
mixed media on paper, 79x58cm
Artist's Collection

99 *Self Portraits*, 1978
oil on canvas, 152x152cm
Artist's Collection

100 *Easy Rider II*, 1978
oil on canvas, 183x183cm
Makoto Iida Collection, Tokyo

101 *The Great Race I*, 1978
oil on canvas, 183x183cm
Artist's Collection

102 *The Great Race II*, 1978
oil on canvas, 183x183cm
Makoto Iida Collection, Tokyo

103 *Sunday in Central Park*, 1979
acrylic on canvas, 183x183cm
Private Collection, New York

104 *Portrait of Sarah Medway*, 1979
oil on canvas, 152x152cm
Medway Collection, London

105 *Starry Night*, 1980
mixed media on paper, 57x46cm
Artist's Collection

106 *Bolivar, etc*, 1979
mixed media on paper, 57x45cm
Artist's Collection

107 *Turismo*, 1979
mixed media on paper, 57x45cm

108 *Volamos*, 1979
mixed media on paper, 55x79cm
J.Woods Collection, London
Aladino II, 1979
mixed media on paper, 59x45cm
Alain Berrier Collection, Paris

109 *Battle Confusion*, 1979
mixed media on paper, 59x44cm
Artist's Collection

110 *The Leader*, 1979
mixed media on paper, 59x45cm
Artist's Collection

111 *Aladino I*, 1979
mixed media on paper, 57x80cm
Alain Berrier Collection, Paris

112 *Racing!*, 1980
mixed media on paper, 57x80cm
Lou Morgan Collection, Chicago
Speedster, 1980
mixed media on paper, 57x80cm

Hans Ulrich Collection, Frankfurt

113 *Teamwork*, 1980
mixed media on paper, 57x80cm
Lou Morgan Collection, Chicago
Race, 1980
mixed media on paper, 57x80cm
H. Braasch Collection, New York

114 *Vroom!*, 1980
oil on canvas, 102x92cm
Stephen Lazzaro Collection, New York

115 *Speed*, 1980
oil on canvas, 102x92cm
Private Collection, Frankfurt

116 *Washington Square*, 1980
acrylic on canvas, 183x183cm
Private Collection, New York

117 *Last Effort*, 1980
oil on canvas, 102x92cm
R. D'Ieteren Collection, Brussels

118 *Power and Noise*, 1980
oil on canvas, 146x114cm
Ashkenazy Collection, Los Angeles

119 *Crowd Noise IV*, 1980
oil on canvas, 146x114cm, M. Henochsberg Collection, Paris

120 *Crowd Noise I*, 1980
acrylic on canvas, 146x114cm
Ashkenazy Collection, Los Angeles

121 *Cheering*, 1980
oil on canvas, 146x114cm
Private Collection, Palm Beach, Florida

122 *Concerto*, 1981
acrylic on canvas, 102x92cm

123 *Applause*, 1980
acrylic on canvas, 102x92cm
Private Collection, Florida

124 *Music City*, 1982

mixed media on paper, 61x80cm
Private Collection, Tokyo
L'ami Amadeus, 1982
mixed media on paper, 61x79cm,
Private Collection, Tokyo

125 *Animato*, 1982
mixed media on paper, 61x80m
Private Collection, Tokyo
Overture, 1982
mixed media on paper, 61x80cm
Private Collection, Tokyo

126 *Untitled*, 1982
ink on paper, 50x65cm
Artist's Collection
Untitled, 1982
ink on paper, 50x65cm
Artist's Collection

127 *Untitled*, 1982
ink on paper, 50x65cm
Artist's Collection
Untitled, 1982
ink on paper, 50x65cm
Artist's Collection

128 *Union Square XIII, New York*, 1982
oil on canvas, 130x95cm
Private Collection, West Germany
Union Square V, 1982
acrylic/oil/canvas, 143x196cm
Private Collection, West Germany

129 *Union Square II*, 1982
acrylic on canvas, 143x196cm
Artist's Collection
Union Square IV, 1982
acrylic on canvas, 114x146cm
Artist's Collection

130 *Runner*, 1982
oil on canvas, 152x152cm
Della Turca Collection, Paris

131 *Union Square, New York*, 1982
oil on canvas, 146x114cm
Private Collection, Paris

132 *Union Square*, 1982
acrylic on canvas, 102x92cm

Ashkenazy Collection, Los Angeles

133 *Union Square VII*, 1982
acrylic on canvas, 102x92cm
Artist's Collection

134 *Méfiance*, 1982
mixed media on paper, 75x56cm
Artist's Collection

135 *Mickey au Mur*, 1982
mixed media on paper, 75x56cm
Artist's Collection

136 *Tourism in Japan*, 1983
oil on canvas, 162x130cm
Private Collection, New York

137 *Tintin en Amérique*, 1983
oil on canvas, 162x130cm
J.M. Muller Collection, Luxembourg

138 *Whoopee!*, 1983
oil on canvas, 114x146cm
Artist's Collection

139 *Le Mur des Voyages*, 1983
oil on canvas, 130x162cm
C. Bragigand Collection, Reims

140 *Billboard*, 1983
oil on canvas, 168x137cm
Collection d'Art Moderne, Ville de
Paris

141 *Chris Burden à l'Affiche*, 1983
acrylic on canvas, 102x92cm
Private Collection, Paris

142 *Des Baisers pour Tino*, 1983
acrylic on canvas, 114x146cm
M. Henochsberg Collection, Paris
La Moustache de la Joconde, 1983
oil on canvas, 130x162cm
Artist's Collection

143 *Marathon Wall*, 1983
acrylic on canvas, 130x162cm
Eric Degove Collection, Paris
Calling the Wall, 1983
acrylic on canvas, 114x146cm

Artist's Collection

144 *Le Mur au Panier*, 1983
acrylic on canvas, 152x152cm
Daniel Hechter Collection, Paris

145 *Mimi's Love*, 1983
acrylic on canvas, 122x122cm
Private Collection, New York

146 *Lovers*, 1983
oil on canvas, 119x146cm
J. L. Bachoud Collection, Paris

147 *Watching the World Go By*, 1983
acrylic on canvas, 102x92cm
Private Collection, New York

148 *Man at 95%*, 1983
acrylic on canvas, 114x146cm
Private Collection, Paris
Chauvinist Pig, 1983
acrylic on canvas, 114x146cm
C. Rosenblum Collection, Paris

149 *Halloween*, 1984
acrylic/oil/canvas, 122x142cm
Artist's Collection
Love Eternal, 1984
acrylic on canvas, 114x146cm
Private Collection, Munich

150 *Halloween on the Wall*, 1984
acrylic on canvas, 183x244cm
R. Livingston Collection, New York
Halloween, 1985
oil on canvas, 117x117cm
Private Collection, Paris

151 *Halloween Parade I*, 1984
acrylic on canvas, 183x244cm
Artist's Collection
Halloween Parade II, 1984
acrylic on canvas, 183x244cm
Artist's Collection

152 *Music for Christmas*, 1984
mixed media on paper, 102x76cm
Private Collection, Paris

153 *Symphonia*, 1984

mixed media on paper, 75x100cm
Artist's Collection
Serenade, 1984
mixed media on paper, 75x100cm
Jean Antoine Collection, Paris

154 *Firebird*, 1984
acrylic on canvas, 117x147cm
J.M. Muller Collection, Luxembourg
Comedia del Arte, 1984
acrylic on canvas, 117x147cm
Private Collection, New York

155 *Portrait of Richard*, 1984
acrylic on canvas, 147x117cm
Artist's Collection

156 *Halloween on the Wall*, 1984
acrylic on canvas, 117x147cm
Ashkenazy Collection, Los Angeles
Halloween, 1984
acrylic on canvas, 117x147cm
Ashkenazy Collection, Los Angeles

157 *Bliss!*, 1984
acrylic on canvas, 92x102cm
Artist's Collection
Eternal Love, 1984
acrylic on canvas, 117x147cm
Artist's Collection

158 *Bananas!*, 1985
acrylic/oil/canvas, 137x183cm
Mark Straus Collection, New York

159 *Space Cat*, 1985
acrylic on canvas, 137x183cm
Ashkenazy Collection, Los Angeles

160 *Piano, Piano!*, 1986
mixed media on paper, 100x102cm
Private Collection, Tokyo

161 *Musical City*, 1986
mixed media on paper, 100x76cm
Private Collection, Tokyo

162 *Untitled*, 1987
watercolour/ink/paper, 102x76cm
Untitled, 1987
watercolour/ink/paper, 40x30cm

Untitled, 1987
watercolour/ink/paper, 65x50cm
Private Collection, Paris
Untitled, 1987
watercolour/ink/paper, 65x50cm

163 *Live Graffiti*, 1987
oil on canvas, 183x137cm
Private Collection, Hollywood

164 *The Quest*, 1987
oil on canvas, 183x137cm
A. Debbas Collection, Paris

165 *The Forgotten World*, 1987
oil on canvas, 183x137cm
I. Hoffman Collection, New York

166 *Summertime*, 1987
oil on paper, 152x107cm
Mrs. Hedi Label Collection, Santa
Cruz, California

167 *Rise and Fall*, 1987
oil on paper, 129.5x86cm
I. Hoffman Collection, New York

168 *The Great Escape*, 1987
oil on canvas, 117x147cm
W. Blitzer Collection, New York

169 *Jesus Inventing Love*, 1988
oil on canvas, 117x142cm

170 *Transformation*, 1988
oil on paper, 152x107cm
Artist's Collection

171 *Dream I*, 1988
oil on paper, 152x107cm

172 *Metamorphosis III*, 1988
oil on paper, 152x107cm

173 *Cosmos III*, 1988
oil on paper, 152x107cm
Private Collection, Frankfurt

174 *Dream of Rubens*, 1988
oil on canvas, 152x117cm
Nelly Debbas Collection, Paris

175 *Dreams of the Perfumed Garden*,
1988
oil on canvas, 147x117cm
Private Collection, Chicago

176 *Childhood Memories*, 1988
oil on canvas, 117x142cm

177 *The Great Dream*, 1988
oil on canvas, 152x203cm
Artist's Collection

178 *Witnesses to Love*, 1988
acrylic on canvas, 183x183cm
Artist's Collection

179 *Wall of Great Departures*, 1988
acrylic on canvas, 183x183cm
Artist's Collection

180 *Tourists in Manhattan*, 1989
acrylic on canvas, 152x122cm
Private Collection, Tokyo

181 *Send no Flowers!*, 1989
acrylic on canvas, 147x117cm
Private Collection, Tokyo

182 *Manhattan*, 1989
acrylic on paper, 81x102cm
Private Collection, Tokyo

183 *Oh! My Wall!!*, 1989
acrylic on canvas 114x146cm

184 *Man, That's Living!*, 1989
acrylic on canvas, 102x92cm
Private Collection, Tokyo

185 *City Beat*, 1989
acrylic on canvas, 117x146cm

186 *Wall of Fame*, 1989
acrylic on canvas, 148x117cm

187 *Our Beloved Cardboard Liberty*, 1989
acrylic on canvas, 137x117cm
Private Collection, Tokyo

188 *Circus in Manhattan*, 1989
acrylic on canvas, 152x152cm

189 *Billboard*, 1989
   acrylic on canvas, 117x89cm

190 *Circus on the Fence*, 1989
   acrylic on canvas, 122x122cm

Private Collection, Tokyo

196 *Le Penseur*, 1935
   Conté crayon, 36x23cm
   Artist's Collection

199 *Boogie-Woogie*,1952
   pen and ink, 46x58cm
   Alain Amoreau Collection, Rochefort

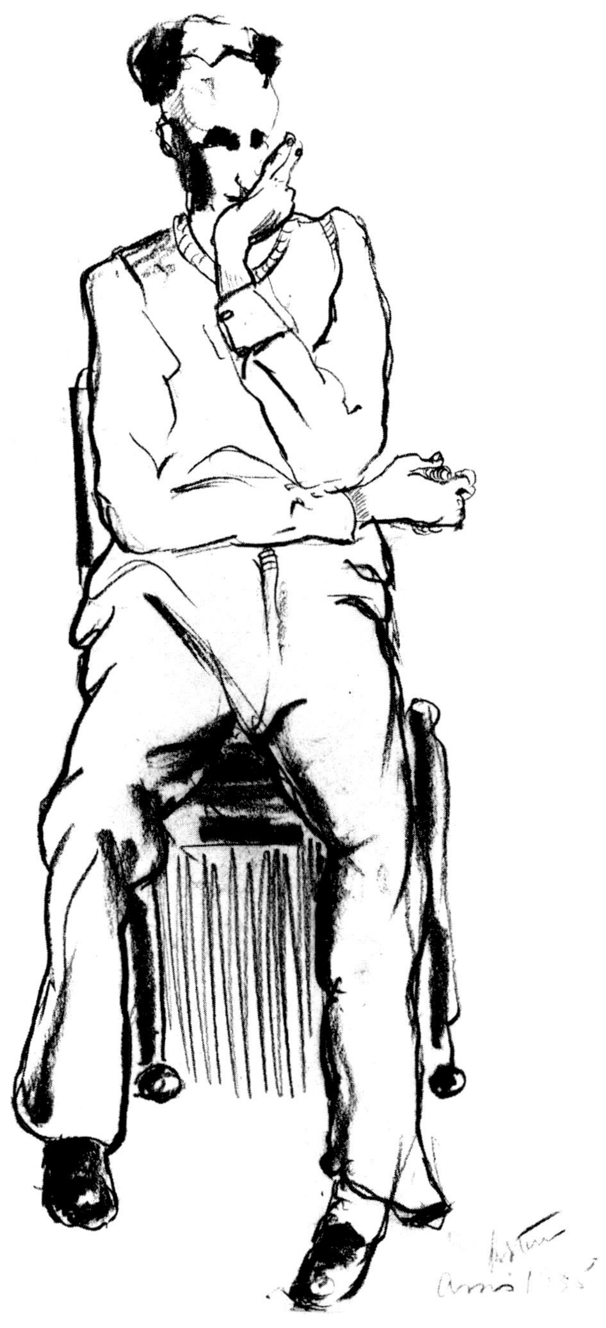

Le Penseur, 1935, Conté crayon, 36x23cm, Artist's Collection

EXHIBITIONS / *EXPOSITIONS*

ONE MAN SHOWS SINCE 1970
EXPOSITIONS PARTICULIERES DEPUIS 1970

1970 Archer Gallery, London

1972 Drian Gallery, London

1973 Galeria de Arte, Caracas, Venezuela
The Modern Art Gallery, Jaffa, Israel
John Whibley Gallery, London

1974 Studio Exhibition, London

1975 David Paul Gallery, Chichester, England
Gallery 24, Shaftesbury, England
Petit Palais, Musée d'Art Moderne, Genève, Schweiz

1976 Galerie Nicoline Pon, Zürich, Schweiz
Galerie Isy Brachot, Bruxelles

1977 Tampa Bay Art Center, Florida, U.S.A.
Carlton Gallery, New York
Galerie Isy Brachot, Knokke, Belgicue
Galerie Saint-Césaire, Nyons, France
Aberbach Fine Arts, London

1978 Galerie Isy Brachot, Bruxelles

1979 ART 10 '79', Basel, Schweiz
National Theatre, London

1980 Margaret Fischer, London
Galerie des Hayes, Brion, France

1981 Leinster Fine Art, London
Academy Editions, London
Camden Arts Centre, London
Patricia Judith Gallery, Florida

1982 F.I.A.C. Paris, Galerie Isy Brachot, Bruxelles

1983 Camden Arts Centre, London
Galerie Isy Brachot, Paris

1985 5th Avenue Studio Show, New York

1986 Chicago International Art Exhibition,
Leinster Fine Art, London
Galerie 20, Paris

Leinster Fine Art, London

1987 Sid Deutsch Gallery, New York
Espace Kiron, Paris
Galerie Michel Broomhead, Paris
(Retrospective of work on paper 1933-1987)
Leinster Fine Art, London

1988 Thomas Poller Kuntshandel, Frankfurt

1989 Sid Deutsch Gallery, New York
Thomas Poller Kunsthandel, Frankfurt
Forum des Arts, Reims
Fuji International Art, Tokyo

GROUP SHOWS SINCE 1970
EXPOSITIONS COLLECTIVES DEPUIS 1970

1973 John Whibley Gallery, London
Royal Academy of Arts Summer Exhibition, London

1974 John Whibley Gallery, London
Royal Academy of Arts Summer Exhibition, London
National Museum of Wales

1975 Roland, Browse and Delbanco Gallery, London
Royal Academy of Arts Summer Exhibition, London
'Arts Sans Frontières', Galerie Isy Brachot, Bruxelles
David Paul Gallery, Chichester, England
British Season, London
National Museum of Wales
Salon d'Automne, Paris
Musée de Troyes, France

1976 Salon de l'Enclave, Valréas, France

1977 F.I.A.C., Paris, Galerie Isy Brachot, Bruxelles
ART 8 '77', Basel, Schweiz

1978 Fischer Fine Arts, London
ART 9 '78', Basel, Schweiz
Galerie Isy Brachot, Bruxelles

1980 Leinster Fine Art, London

1981 Galerie Nina Dausset, Paris

1982 Camden Arts Centre, London

1983 'Arts Sans Frontières', Galerie Isy Brachot, Bruxelles
Arco, Madrid
Bath Festival, Bath
Edward Lucie-Smith 50th Birthday Choice, Leinster Fine Art, London
Art 14, '83', Basel, Galerie Isy Brachot, Bruxelles
Works by Modern Masters, Leinster Fine Art, London
Richard Wills Gallery, New York
Patricia Judith Gallery, Florida
F.I.A.C., Paris, Galerie Isy Brachot, Bruxelles

1987 San Antonio Museum, Texas (Sculptures)
Sid Deutsch Gallery, New York
Forum des Arts, Reims
Galerie Michel Broomhead, Paris
Prestige et Beauté, Paris

1988 Sid Deutsch Gallery, New York
Chicago International Fine Art Fair, Leinster Fine Art, London
Forum des Arts, Reims
Galerie Rambert, Paris
Prestige et Beauté, Paris
Galerie 20, Paris

BIBLIOGRAPHY / *BIBLIOGRAPHIE*

BOOKS/*LIVRES*

Hodin, J.P., *Bernard Stern Paintings and Drawings*, Three Eagles Press, London, 1972

Antoine, Jean, Bernard Stern, (with essay by Bernard Stern), Academy Editions, London and St. Martin's Press, New York, 1981

Bernard Stern, *Pas de Réponse, et autres contes*, Editions la Bruyère, Paris, 1987

Gerard Xuriguera, *Les Figurations*, Editions Mayer

Gerard Schurr, *Le Guidargus de la Peinture*, Editions de l'amateur, 1988

Halima Nalecz, *3 Decades of Private Views*, Drian Galleries, London, 1986

CATALOGUES/*CATALOGUES*

Archer Gallery, London 6.1970 (introduction by Michael Kustow, 'Bernard Stern's Circus')

The Modern Art Gallery, Jaffa, Israel 10.1973 (foreword by J.P. Hodin)

Studio Exhibition, London 1974 (introduction by J.P. Hodin, 'Recent Works')

Petit Palais, Musée d'Art Moderne, Genève, Schweiz 1975 (essai de J.P. Hodin, 'A Master of Transfiguration/Un Maître de la Transfiguration')

Galerie Isy Brachot, Bruxelles 11.1976 (introduction de Jean Antoine)

Tampa Bay Art Center, Florida, U.S.A. 3.1977 (introduction by the curator)

The New York Gallery Guide 5.1977 (illustration of *The Beaching of Noah's Ark*)

Galerie Isy Brachot, Bruxelles 8.1978 (essai de Jean Antoine)

National Theatre, London 9.1979 (introduction by Michael Kustow)

Isy Brachot, F.I.A.C. catalogue Paris, 1982 ('The Walls are looking at us', introduction by Jean Antoine)

Isy Brachot, catalogue of exhibition in 1983, Paris (essay by Edward Lucie-Smith, 'The Contemporary Artist'; essay by Alain Trez, 'Stern')

Studio Show New York, 1985 (introduction by Edward Lucie-Smith)

Chicago International Art Exhibition, 1986 (essay by Edward Lucie-Smith)

Sid Deutsch Gallery, New York, 1987 (introduction by Edward Lucie-Smith)

Galerie Michel Broomhead, 1987 (introduction by Jean Antoine, 'Parcours Sur Papier 1935-1987')

PERIODICALS/*REVUES*

Blakeston, Oswald 'Bernard Stern' *Arts Review* 11.1973

Collis, Louise *Art and Artists* 11.1979

Drweska, Alicja *Tydzein Polski* 5.1972

Glander-Bandyk, Janice 'Bernard Stern' *Arts Magazine* 9.1977

Kara, K. 'Bernard Stern' *Revue de l'Art* 12.1976

Neuburg, Hans 'Bernard Stern' *Die Tat* 6.1976

Otlet, Suzanne 'Le monde de Bernard Stern' *Jalons et Actualités des Arts* 12.1976

Rouve, Pierre 'Ascetic Explorer' *Arts Review* 4.1972

Rouve, Pierre 'A Matter of Dignity' *Arts Review* 11

Rouve, Pierre 'Bernard Stern in Europe and at Home' *Arts Review* 9.1977

Rovera, Marina 'Vivere in una Chiesa' *Vogue Italia* 6.1976

Vaizey, Marina 'Bernard Stern' *Arts Review* 6.1970

Whittet, G.S. 'To Recover the Innocence of our Childhood Dreams' *Art and Artists* 4.1972

Wykes-Joyce, Max *Arts Review* 9.1979

NEWSPAPERS/*JOURNAUX*

Sunday Express (England) 1.1966: 'The Artist who Found Success'

International Herald Tribune 6.1970: Max Wykes-Joyce, 'Bernard Stern Paints as a Bird Flies'

El Universal (Venezuela) 9.1973: 'Bernard Stern, el Ingles!'

El National (Venezuela) 9.1973: 'Bernard Stern, Gran Valor de la Pintura'

El Universal (Venezuela) 10.1973: 'Notable Pintor Ingles en Caracas'

Jewish Chronicle (England) 11.1973: Peter Stone, 'A Fresh Approach'

International Herald Tribune 12.1974: review by Max Wykes-Joyce

La Dernière Heure (Bruxelles) 2.1975: 'STYLE'

La Suisse 11.1975: 'Un Peintre Merveilleusement Libre'

Libération-Champagne (France) 11.1975: Dr. Doan, 'L'Art de Bernard Stern'

L'Est Eclair (France) 11.1975: 'Un Evènement Exceptionel'

L'Est Eclair (France) 11.1975: André Beury,

'Le Sympathique Bernard Stern'

Berner Zeitung (Schweiz) 5.1976: 'Bernard Stern, Maler der Seele'

L'Echo de la Bourse (Bruxelles) 12.1976: critique de Stephane Rey

La Dernière Heure (Bruxelles) 12.1976: Alain Viray, 'Les Natures Vivantes de Bernard Stern'

La Libre Belgique (Belgique) 12.1976: Stephane Rey, 'Bernard Stern'

Tampa Times (Florida, U.S.A.) 3.1977: Robert Martin, 'Bernard Stern Brushes Poetry Across his Paintings'

L'Echo de la Bourse (Bruxelles) 10.1978: critique de Stephane Rey

Le Soir Illustré (Bruxelles) 10.1978

La Dernière Heure (Bruxelles) 10.1978: Alain Viray, 'Bernard Stern . . . et Solitude'

Le Soir (Bruxelles) 10.1978: Paul Caso, 'Les Animaux de Bernard Stern'

International Herald Tribune 9.1979: Max Wykes-Joyce, 'Bernard Stern at the National Theatre'

Daily Telegraph (England) 9.1979: Terence Mullaly, 'Exhibition by Artist Bernard Stern'

Courier de l'Ouest (France) 2.1980: Joseph Fumet, 'L'Univers Capricieux de l'Imaginaire'

Ouest France (France) 2.1980: Daniel Tirot, 'Un grand Peintre aux Multi-visages'

The Times, (London) 1983, John Russell Taylor, 'Powerful Peak of a Deeper Representation'

L'Oeil, (France) 4.1987: 'Wunderkind'

Art & Antique Auctions (New York) 1987: Review of Espace Kiron Exhibition in Paris

Art Press, (Paris) 1987: Review of Espace Kiron Exhibition in Paris, by Nora Taylor

FILMS/*FILMS*

Film (Colin Hart, BBC 2 England 5.1972)

Bernard Stern, Peintre Anglais (Jean Antoine, Radio Télévision Belge 2.1975 & Radio Télévision Suisse Romande 10.1975)

L'Imagination au Galop (Radio Télévision Suisse Romande 8.1976)

Nouvelles Peintures (Jean Antoine, Radio Télévision Belge 1980)

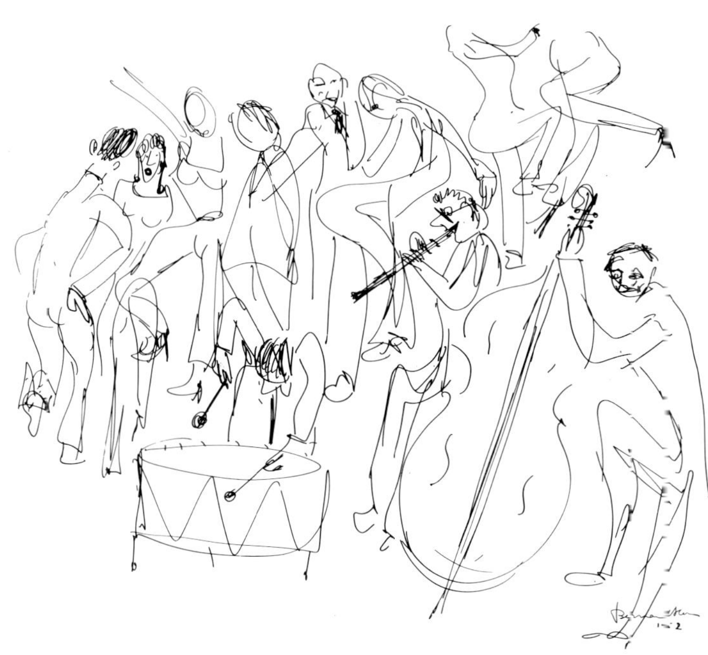

Boogie-Woogie, 1952, pen and ink, 46x58cm, Alain Amoreau Collection, Rochefort, France

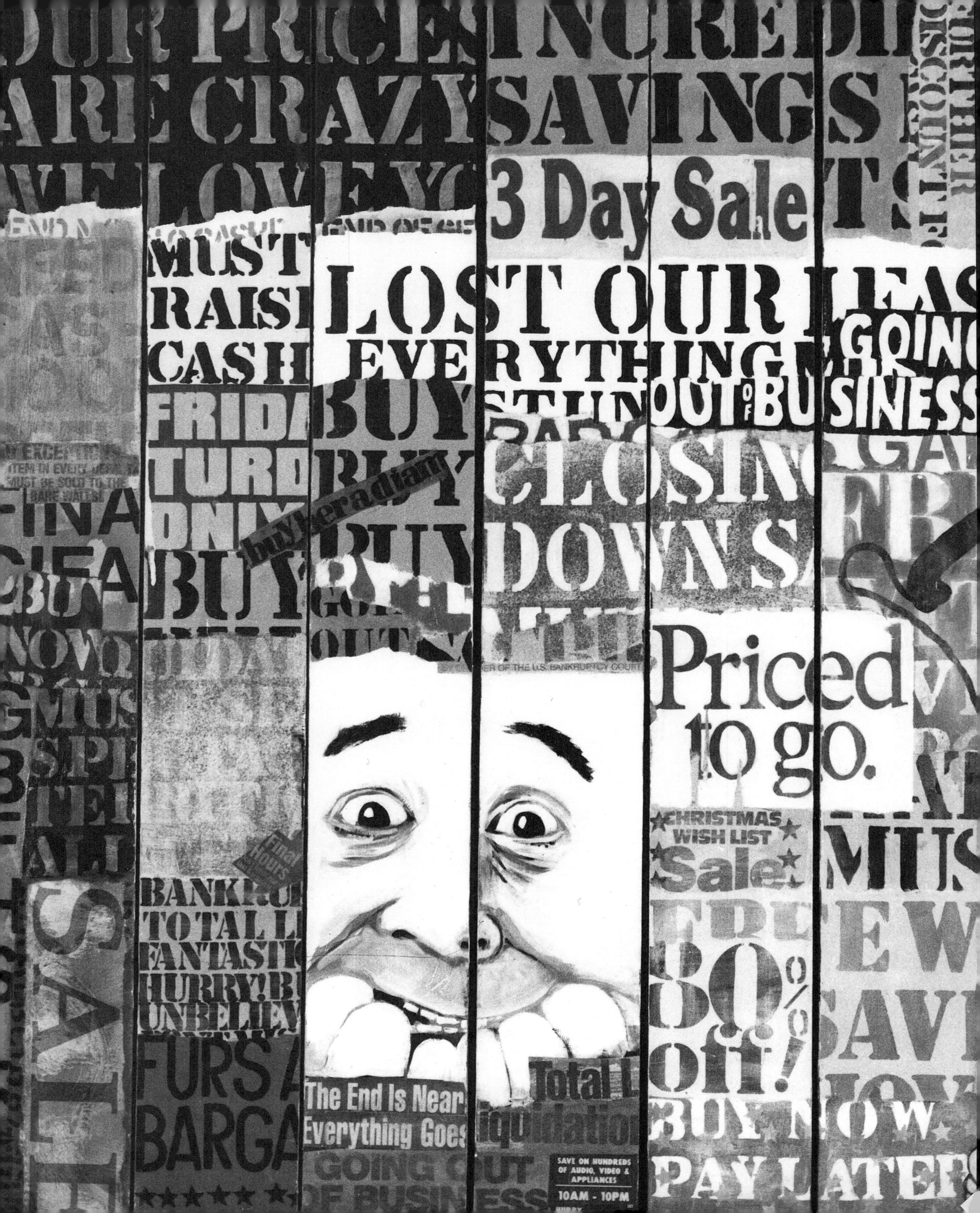

OUR PRICES
ARE CRAZY
WE LOVE YOU
3 Day Sale
MUST
RAISE
CASH
FRIDAY
SATURDAY
ONLY
BUY
LOST OUR LEASE
EVERYTHING
BUY
CLOSING
DOWN SALE
Priced to go.
GOING
OUT OF BUSINESS
INCREDIBLE
SAVINGS
CHRISTMAS
WISH LIST
Sale
BANKRUPT
TOTAL
FANTASTIC
HURRY
UNBELIEVABLE
FURS
BARGAIN
The End Is Near
Everything Goes
Total
Liquidation
GOING OUT
OF BUSINESS
SAVE ON HUNDREDS
OF AUDIO, VIDEO &
APPLIANCES
10AM - 10PM
BUY NOW
PAY LATER